# Who Will Provide the Next Financial Model?

Sahoko Kaji · Eiji Ogawa
Editors

# Who Will Provide the Next Financial Model?

## Asia's Financial Muscle and Europe's Financial Maturity

Springer

*Editors*
Sahoko Kaji
Professor
Keio University
2-15-45 Mita, Minato-ku
Tokyo 108-8345, Japan

Eiji Ogawa
Professor
Hitotsubashi University
2-1 Naka, Kunitachi
Tokyo 186-8601, Japan

ISBN 978-4-431-54281-0 ISBN 978-4-431-54282-7 (eBook)
DOI 10.1007/978-4-431-54282-7
Springer Tokyo Heidelberg New York Dordrecht London

Library of Congress Control Number: 2013932550



Printed on acid-free paper

Springer is part of Springer Science+Business Media (www.springer.com)

# Preface

In the past 4 years, our faith in the present financial model has been shaken in terms of monetary, regulatory and exchange rate policies, as well as the business model of the financial sector itself. Past and present policies of the world's most respected central banks have come under fire. Regulations that defined the system underwent major reviews. Fancy financial instruments that provided new ways of financial intermediation and wealth creation were exposed as the culprits behind the near financial meltdown. And after ten successful years, Europe's single currency came under threat. In short, the established financial model was not only unable to prevent the crises but also arguably a cause.

Inasmuch as there are business cycles, economies recover at some point. However, economic recovery is one thing, finding a financial model conducive to stability is quite another. To avoid the repetition of the near collapse of the global economy, we cannot just aim for a simple recovery. Important questions are staring us in the face; the broadest is whether the West is ceding its position as leader to the East. Without agreeing on an answer to this broad question, we can ask who will provide the new financial model conducive to stability and prosperity. Clearly, we cannot go back to business as usual. But if that is the case, what do we do now? As the crisis deepens, the temptation is to change as little as possible, out of fear of the unknown. But no change now means further trouble down the road. The world is in search of a new financial model.

Japan knows this search all too well. Back in the 1980s, Japan's economy was rapidly approaching the status of "number one". In the middle of this fateful decade, a bubble emerged in the Japanese financial and real estate markets and while it lasted gave the false impression of success and prosperity. Japan's method of financial intermediation and financial regulation changed in the eyes of the West from obscure to commendable. The visibility and status of Japan's banks, insurance companies and securities houses soared in the global arena. Purportedly, Japan's unique method of financial intermediation was superior in enabling long-term planning by borrowers, supporting low unemployment and economic stability. Many thought that Japan's financial model represented an alternative to the Anglo-American model and that it should be adopted by fellow Asians and even eventually by those in the West.

Then we learnt that this was only an illusion. Japan's bubble burst and was followed by two "lost decades". Japan's financial model not only did support long-term business ties, but it also preserved cosy, unproductive relationships among regulatory authorities, financial institutions and firms.

After Japan's financial model lost its shine, life actually became simpler for the Japanese. They just had to say "mea culpa", abandon the Japanese way of finance and adopt Western finance methods. This became a national goal. Many were the meetings held, reports written, and papers and books published to press this point. Under the banner of "from saving to investment", households were encouraged to move money out of savings accounts and into mutual funds, and schools were encouraged to teach young children the principles of investing. Japanese financial authorities, as well as Japanese private financiers, believed that all that was needed to avoid another bubble was to adopt more Western methods of finance and policy-making. The goal was clear, even if it was not being achieved soon enough.

However, this also proved to be an illusion. Unfortunately (or fortunately), before Japan completely adopted Western methods of finance, the subprime crisis and Lehman shock hit. This was followed by the euro crisis. The situation in Japan today is not dissimilar to the early 1990s where some said "give us back the (Berlin) wall". Life was simpler when systems were classified as either Capitalist or Communist. In the same way, life was simpler for the Japanese when financial systems were divided into Western and Japanese. Now things are more complicated. One of the two contrasting models was discredited, but blind faith in the remaining one does not assure stability and prosperity. There is no longer a model, at least not an obvious one, to work towards. Every country is looking for a new financial model. How do Asia and Europe compare in the quest for this model?

We need to seriously rethink how we conduct monetary policy and regulate the financial sector. How should central banks conduct monetary policy in crises? How should financial regulation be coordinated, and what kind of incentive should they create to avoid a crisis, to recover from a crisis and to sustain growth? Another important aspect of finance is exchange rate systems. What does the crisis in the euro area tell us about exchange rate regimes in Asia and in general? These questions are even more pertinent with the increased, if not exploding, fiscal deficits and debts in Japan and the West.

This conference volume records the cumulative result of three EUSI conferences on these topics. The first, held in December of 2009, was entitled "Financial Crises, learning from Europe, learning from Asia". The second and third, held in December 2010 and 2011, respectively, both shared the title of this volume; the agendas of these two conferences essentially carry over into the content of this book.

First on the agenda is financial regulation. Iain Begg and Atsushi Mimura discuss the efforts to improve financial regulation in the EU and in Asia, respectively. Their analyses show that even as the EU takes steps in the context of integration, the "premium forum" for cooperation is moving to the G20 and the FSB (Financial Stability Board), which include emerging economies and international authorities. Europe is facing the triple task of getting its own house in order, leading the way in financial integration, while maintaining consistency with and seeking funds from the diverse world outside the EU. In Asia, where the level of diversity is much greater than in the EU, no concrete model of unique financial regulation is emerging. This is not necessarily a weakness because it shows that diversity is the norm in Asia.

The second topic is monetary policy. Francesco Drudi, Alain Durree and Francesco Paolo Mongelli explain why central banks must have a clear policy objective and appropriate risk management. They also describe the European Central Bank's policies during the different phases of the crisis since August 2007. This is followed by an assessment of unconventional monetary policy by Shigenori Shiratsuka. The Bank of Japan's policies in the late 1990s "demonstrate more similarities than differences" with those taken by major central banks in the current crisis. The asset sides of the central banks' balance sheets reflect their choice between emphasis on macroeconomic stability and financial system stability. The last paper on this topic is by Akira Ariyoshi, who states that Europe learnt very little from the Asian financial crisis and lists some lessons for Asia from Europe. A common underlying theme of all three papers is that monetary authorities in both Asia and Europe face the same economic logic (the impossible trinity, moral hazard, information asymmetry, importance of market expectations, the blurred line between monetary and fiscal policy during crises). Every policy choice has a trade-off and all policy authorities must choose the combination (including eclectic mid-points) of costs and benefits that is best under the circumstances.

The third topic is developments in the financial sector. Carlo Altomonte and Lorenzo Saggiorato point to another law of economics, i.e., the policy tools must be at least as numerous as the policy goals. More specifically, they stress the need to complement short-term reactions to the crisis with regulatory changes that aim at prosperity in the longer term. Such changes must enable the financial sector to allocate credit to high productivity firms in an environment characterised by firm heterogeneity. Mitsuhiro Fukao discusses the similarities (excessive monetary easing, financial deregulation and regulatory distortions) between Japan's post-bubble crisis and the present situation in the USA and Europe. Finally, Alicia Garcia-Herrero and Daniel Santabarbara assess China's banking reforms since 1998 and evaluate the risk that the 2008 fiscal package may pose for Chinese banks in terms of asset quality. One important weakness is the fact that "(b)ank lending continues to be dependent on the interests of the public sector", a clear case being the "bank financing of the fiscal stimulus package". In terms of balance sheets, this exhibits a curious and dismal coincidence with post-crisis Europe, USA and Japan, where banks and governments are sustaining each other, as one unintended consequence of fiscal expansion to avoid a financial meltdown. This means that even after China successfully reforms itself out of this interdependence, it may easily slip back into the same structure in a crisis. The dissolution of such interdependence is one of the goals of the European Banking Union (EBU) under construction. The EBU itself is novel, and if in the process of forming the EBU Europe becomes the first to emphasise the allocation of funds to competitive firms, it will be a refreshingly positive silver lining of the crisis.

The final topic is the exchange rate regime. Helmut Wagner starts out by confirming that "(r)eal convergence is an original goal of the European integration process" and shows that there "was no uniform institutional and structural convergence within the E(M)U". He also warns against hastily constructing such a union without incentive mechanisms that lead to structural convergence. Thus, Wagner presents an expanded version of the "economist" argument, in that structural and economic convergence must come before monetary convergence. In contrast, Eiji Ogawa's discussions are "monetarist" in giving priority to regional monetary cooperation to reduce misalignments of Asian currencies, which in turn adversely affect international trade and investment, while stressing the importance of holding "a sound fiscal position". Then, Paola Subacchi and Stephen Pickford take us back to the "economist" (expanded to include structural) view and warn that policymakers who fail to address the longer-term structural problems do so at their peril, risking a euro break-up. Sahoko Kaji discusses the possibility of using the exchange rate regime (single currency) as a tool to advance such reforms, in the final chapter.

All our commentators provided additional information, new angles and directions for further research.

The chapters of this book show that "the new financial model" has not yet emerged out of the crises. But they provide useful clues, contrasts and comparisons, by explaining the different approaches taken by Europe and Asia, even as both come under the same economic logic. If Europe provides a financial model in an "ever closer union", Asia would seem to do so under diversity, not just in terms of stages of economic development and economic systems but also in policy choices between the two corner solutions. Europe is becoming the first in the world to cede such a degree of sovereignty. Asia shows that some diversity and an eclectic approach (such as capital controls) may actually be beneficial.

The real test is whether either, or both, can achieve sustainable prosperity.

We would like to thank the European Commission for making EUSI possible and all participants of the three EUSI conferences for their high-level intellectual input and camaraderie. The Japan Society of Monetary Economics, Mizuho Financial Group and the Hitotsubashi-Keio Support Project for Strategic University Collaborations provided generous financial support for the conferences. We are also grateful to Springer Japan for their patience and cooperation. Last but not least, our thanks go to all the EUSI staff, in particular Ms Tomoko Fujino who played an important part in making this publication possible.

Tokyo, Japan

Sahoko Kaji
September 2012

# Contents

# List of Contributors

## Editors

**Sahoko Kaji** is a professor of economics and coordinator of the Professional Career Programme at Keio University and deputy director at EUSI. She has a B.A. and an M.A. from Keio and a Ph.D. in economics from the Johns Hopkins University. Her major field of research is European economies. Details are at http://k-ris.keio.ac.jp/Profiles/0030/0005959/prof_e.html.

**Eiji Ogawa** is a professor at the Graduate School of Commerce and Management, Hitotsubashi University and chairman of the Governing Board, EU Studies Institute in Tokyo. He has a B.A., M.A., and Ph.D. in commerce from Hitotsubashi University. His major field of research is international finance and currencies. Details are at https://hri.ad.hit-u.ac.jp/html/217_profile_en.html.

## Authors

**Iain Begg** is a professorial research fellow at the European Institute, London School of Economics and Political Science. His main research work is on the political economy of European integration and EU economic governance. He has directed and participated in a series of research projects on different facets of EU policy, and his current projects include studies on future employment prospects in the EU, the impact of cohesion policy, the governance of economic and monetary union in Europe, the EU's "Europe 2020" strategy and reform of the EU budget. Other recent research projects include work on policy coordination and the social impact of globalisation.

**Atsushi Mimura** currently is the director of the Securities Business Division, Financial Services Agency of Japan (FSA). From July 2010 to September 2012 he was the director of the Office of International Affairs, FSA. Prior to that, from August 2007 to July 2010, he was a member of the secretariat of the Financial Stability Board (FSB) in Basel. At FSA, he has also served as director in charge of overall policy coordination and also of human resource management in the Planning and Coordination Bureau. He was the administrative secretary to the Minister of State for Financial Services from 2005 to 2006. Before joining the FSA, he had been in the Ministry of Finance of Japan, beginning in 1989. Mr. Mimura received his LL.B. from the University of Tokyo in 1989 and the Diploma of International Public Administration from the École nationale d'administration (ENA) of France in 1993.

**Francesco Drudi** is head of the Monetary Policy Stance Division in Directorate Monetary Policy at the European Central Bank. He holds a B.A. in economics from Bocconi University in Milan and a master of philosophy and a Ph.D. in finance from the Stern School of Business of New York University. He has worked at the ECB since 1998 holding various positions, including head of section and senior adviser in the Monetary Policy Stance Division and head of division in the Capital Markets/ Financial Structure Division. Prior to that he worked at the World Bank and in the Research Department of the Bank of Italy. He has published numerous working papers as well as articles in books and in refereed journals.

**Alain Durré** is currently principal economist in the Financial Research Division of the Directorate General Research of the European Central Bank and associate professor of finance at IÉSEG-School of Management of Lille Catholic University (France). He is also a member of the Centre National de la Recherche Scientifique in France (LEM-CNRS). On occasion he also acts as monetary policy adviser for the International Monetary Fund on topics related to the money market and the conduct of monetary policy (strategy and implementation) and teaches at the Economics School of Louvain from the Université catholique de Louvain. He was educated at Facultés universitaires Saint-Louis (Belgium), the University of Mannheim (Germany) and at the Université catholique de Louvain (Belgium) from which he holds a Ph.D. in financial economics. He then moved to the National Bank of Belgium as a member of the Research Department before joining the Monetary Policy Stance Division in the Directorate Monetary Policy at the European Central Bank in 2004. He also spent some time as research analyst at Deutsche Bank and as visiting scholar at the London School of Economics during his Ph.D. programme. He has published various papers on monetary and financial economics in many leading academic journals. His main research areas focus on the microstructure of money markets, interaction between monetary and fiscal policy and economic impact of the central bank balance sheet. In 2005 he was awarded the Joseph de la Vega Prize for his work on the microstructure analysis of the Euronext Stock Exchange focusing on volatility regimes and the provision of liquidity in order book markets. He is also co-editor with Jagjit Chadha, Mike Joyce and Lucio Sarno of the second volume of the series Modern Macroeconomic Modelling on

*New Developments in Macro Finance Yield Curve Modelling*, which will be published by Cambridge University Press in the second half of 2013.

**Francesco Paolo Mongelli** is a senior adviser in Directorate Monetary Policy at the ECB and honorary professor at the Johann Wolfgang Goethe University of Frankfurt. He holds a B.A. in economics from the Free University for Social Studies (LUISS) in Rome and a master's degree and a Ph.D. in economics from the Johns Hopkins University in Baltimore. He has worked at the ECB since 1998 holding various positions, including those of organiser of the analytical agenda of DG Economics and editor of the *ECB Occasional Paper Series*. Prior to that he spent several years as an economist at the International Monetary Fund in Washington. His main area of research pertains to the effects of the euro on the functioning of EMU, the links between monetary policy and heterogeneity in the euro area, the links between economic integration and institutional integration, and comparing monetary policy preparation and decision making in the main central banks. He also teaches Economics of Monetary Unions at the Johann Wolfgang Goethe University of Frankfurt. His papers have been published in various scientific and policy-oriented journals such as the *Open Economies Review*, the *Journal of Money Credit and Banking*, the *Journal of Common Market Studies*, *Integration and Trade*, *Economie Internationale*, *Bancaria* and the *Journal of Economic Integration*.

**Shigenori Shiratsuka** is the general manager of the Matsuyama branch of the Bank of Japan, a position he has held since 2011. Prior to his current position, he served the Bank as an associate director-general in charge of the Economic and Financial Studies Division at the Institute for Monetary and Economic Studies. He has written a number of articles on issues related to monetary policy, such as inflation measurement, asset price bubble and monetary policy under zero interest rates. He received a B.A. and a Ph.D. in economics from Keio University. He has served as a senior economist of the Institute for Monetary and Economic Studies of the Bank of Japan since 1999 and a staff economist of the Financial Markets Department, Research and Statistics Department. In 1998–1999 he was a visiting economist at the Federal Reserve Bank of Chicago.

**Akira Ariyoshi** is a professor in the School of International and Public Policy, Hitotsubashi University. He has extensive experience in international financial policies, having worked in senior positions in the Japanese Ministry of Finance and the International Monetary Fund. He is a graduate of Tokyo University and holds a doctorate in economics from Oxford University.

**Carlo Altomonte** is associate professor of the economics of European integration at Bocconi University in Milan. At the SDA Bocconi School of Management, he teaches international business environment within the executive MBA programmes. His main areas of research and publication are European economic policy, industrial economics and economic geography, theory of multinational corporations and foreign direct investment.

**Lorenzo Saggiorato** graduated in economics and social sciences from Bocconi University. He currently works as research assistant at ISLA—Bocconi University. His main research interests are internationalization patterns, credit constraints, foreign direct investment and micro-level firm analysis.

**Mitsuhiro Fukao** has been a professor of economics in the Faculty of Business and Commerce of Keio University since 1997. His primary fields of expertise are financial regulations, international finance and monetary economics and policy. He has numerous publications in Japanese and in English on international finance, exchange rate policy, corporate governance and, recently, on the financial system and its crisis. Prior to joining Keio University, he was head of the Strategic Research Division of the Research and Statistics Department of the Bank of Japan. During 1991–1993, he was a senior economist of the OECD in Paris and a G-10 secretary. In 1989 and 1990, he was a senior economist of the International Department of the Bank of Japan and a member of the Danielsson subgroup of the Basel Committee on Banking Supervision. During 1983–1985, he served as a senior economist of the Economic Planning Agency of Japan and participated in drafting the official White Paper on the Japanese Economy. He received his bachelor's degree on engineering from Kyoto University in 1974 and was awarded a Ph.D. in economics from the University of Michigan in 1981.

**Alicia Garcia-Herrero** is the chief economist for emerging markets at the Banco Bilbao Vizcaya Argentaria (BBVA). She is also a member of the advisory board of the Hong Kong Institute of Monetary Research and an advisor to the European Commission on Chinese Issues. Prior to her work with the BBVA, she was part of the Asian Research Programme of the Bank for International Settlements in Hong Kong. From 2001 to 2006, she was the head of the International Economy Division of the Bank of Spain as well as a visiting professor at the Johns Hopkins University.

**Daniel Santabárbara** is an economist at the Bank of Spain. His work is mainly focused on global issues and EMEs financial markets. Previously, he was the economist responsible for China at the European Central Bank. He was also an adjunct professor at the Universidad Complutense de Madrid. Before joining the public sector, he worked as a consultant in the private sector. He has written papers on EMEs financial issues published in the *Journal of Banking and Finance*, *CESifo Economic Studies* and the *China Economic Review*.

**Helmut Wagner** is currently chair and professor of economics at the University of Hagen and director at the Hagen Institute for Management Studies. Before that, he was full professor of economics and Jean Monnet chair at HWP University of Hamburg. He has also held visiting positions at the Massachusetts Institute of Technology, Princeton University, the University of California, the John Hopkins University (AICGS), Harvard University, International Monetary Fund (IMF), as well as at the Institute for Monetary and Economic Studies, Bank of Japan (IMES) and Hitotsubashi University. His main current research areas are financial crisis and the appropriate role of central banks, European integration and economic growth and development. He has published numerous articles and books (see details on his web-page "www.fernuni-hagen.de/hwagner)".

**Paola Subacchi** is the director of International Economics Research at Chatham House in London. Her main research interest is in the functioning and governance of the international financial and monetary system, with a particular focus on post-crisis policy and institutional change. She is a contributor to peer-reviewed journals and current affairs publications. She is a regular media commentator with the BBC, CNN, Bloomberg, CNBC, *Newsweek*, the *Financial Times*, the *Wall Street Journal*, the *International Herald Tribune* and *European Voice*. Paola Subacchi's recent publications include "The Connecting Dots of China's Renmenbi Strategy: London and Hong Kong"; *Shifting Capital: The Rise of Financial Centres in Greater China*; and *Grappling with Global Imbalances* (with Paul van den Noord). An Italian national, she studied at Bocconi University in Milan and at the University of Oxford.

**Stephen Pickford** is an associate fellow at Chatham House working on international economic issues. From July 2007 to January 2010 he was managing director, International and Finance, at HM Treasury in London. Prior to this, Stephen served as both director for Europe and director for International Finance in HM Treasury, with responsibility for the UK's interests in a wide range of international issues. From 1998 to 2001 Stephen was the UK's executive director at the IMF and World Bank, in Washington DC. Prior to that, his previous treasury roles included responsibility for monetary policy and the introduction of the Bank of England Act 1998, which gave the bank monetary policy independence, and he worked in the New Zealand Treasury between 1989 and 1993 on macroeconomic policy and forecasting.

# EU Studies Institute

The EU Studies Institute in Tokyo (EUSI) was launched on 1 April 2009 as a consortium comprising Hitotsubashi University, Tsuda College, and Keio University. The Institute is sponsored by the European Commission for a four-and-a-half-year period. As a centre for academic education, research and outreach, it aims to strengthen EU–Japan relations. Details are at http://eusi.jp/content_en/

# Part I
# Financial Regulation

# The EU's Approach to Improving Financial Regulation

**Iain Begg**

**Abstract** The financial, economic and debt crises in Europe have prompted a flurry of governance reforms, as part of which substantial changes in financial regulation and supervision have been undertaken. This chapter describes the evolution of the crises and discusses the constraints on EU action, including the difficult political context and the constitutional limits on what the European Central Bank is able to do, as well as the complications of having only 17 out of 27 EU Members States inside the euro area. It summarises and appraises the governance changes made since 2009 and highlights "unfinished business" that still requires the attention of policy-makers. The paper concludes that although the governance changes are extensive and generally well-conceived, the fact that there is no European tax-payer, only national ones, will continue to limit what the EU can do.

**Keywords** EU sovereign debt crisis • European financial integration • Financial regulation and supervision • Governance reform in Europe

Although the initial sentiment in continental Europe was that the financial crisis that started in 2007 was "Made in America", possibly with the connivance of those perfidious "anglo-saxons" on both sides of the Irish Sea, it did not take long before the depth of the threats to all the economies in the European Union became clear. Since then, the EU has sought, collectively and at the level of individual Member States, to put in place a new approach not just to financial regulation, but to economic governance more generally. In a context of crisis management, these governance reforms have been difficult to agree.

I. Begg (✉)
European Institute, London School of Economics and Political Science, Houghton Street, London WC2A 2AE, United Kingdom, London, UK
e-mail: iain.begg@lse.ac.uk

S. Kaji and E. Ogawa (eds.), *Who Will Provide the Next Financial Model?: Asia's Financial Muscle and Europe's Financial Maturity*,
DOI 10.1007/978-4-431-54282-7_1, 

Along the way, the breadth and intensity of the problems have multiplied as the indebtedness of sovereign states in the EU interacted with continuing weaknesses in the banking sector, accentuating the systemic threats and bringing the continuing viability of the euro itself into question. Yet in finding ways to contain the problems, institutional responsibilities have been blurred and the rest of the world has often looked on in dismay at the procrastination and prevarication exhibited by Europe' leaders. Part of the problem is, as former European Central Bank (ECB) President Trichet noted,[1] that "central banks often have an explicit mandate in the area of financial stability. But typically this mandate is formulated in very general terms, and it would have been written before growing recognition of the key role of macro-prudential oversight".

The governance reforms are still a work in progress and have revealed differences of philosophies, preferences and interests that are proving hard to reconcile. Progress has been hampered by the complexities of the EU institutional structure and, especially, by the fact that ten out of twenty-seven Member States remain outside the euro area. One result is that the ECB, among the most significant actors in dealing with the crisis and developing a new approach, always has to take care not to intrude in areas of policy that national central banks or supervisory authorities of (to use the EU jargon) "non-participating" Member States jealously guard as "mine".

The financial crisis has forced policy-makers to distinguish more clearly between macro- and micro-prudential risks and, as a consequence, to look afresh at the balance of prudential supervision. A concise definition of the two forms of supervision is provided in a House of Lords report[2]:

> Macro-prudential supervision is the analysis of trends and imbalances in the financial system and the detection of systemic risks that these trends may pose to financial institutions and the economy. The focus of macroprudential supervision is the safety of the financial and economic system as a whole, the prevention of systemic risk.
>
> Micro-prudential supervision is the day-to-day supervision of individual financial institutions. The focus of micro-prudential supervision is the safety and soundness of individual institutions as well as consumer protection. The same or a separate supervisor can carry out these two functions.

The de Larosière report (2009), based on the deliberations of a high-level group appointed by the European Commission, offered a persuasive analysis of the origins of the financial crisis and the flaws in the regulatory framework that warranted attention. An equally trenchant analysis was provided by the Turner Review (FSA 2009) and these and other contributions point to the following factors that lay behind the financial crisis:

- An extended period of loose monetary policy and rapid financial innovation
- A misplaced belief in the ability of markets to self-regulate in a way that would forestall overly risky behaviour

[1] Speech on "Macro-prudential oversight and the future European Systemic Risk Board", delivered to the European banking Congress, Frankfurt, 19th November 2010.

[2] House of Lords (2009).

- Inadequate recognition of growing macroeconomic imbalances, despite the evidence of unsustainable trends in, for example, current account imbalances and asset prices
- Failings in corporate governance and oversight of senior management
- Misjudgements by ratings agencies and too great a reliance on their verdicts, at the expense of due diligence
- Failures by regulators to recognise the immediacy and intensity of problems.

This chapter first reviews the different phases of financial and economic crisis in Europe since 2007. It then presents an overview of the regulatory and governance responses and how they are building into a new approach. Section 3 explores the extent to which the new approach addresses the challenges, and concluding comments complete the paper.

## 1 Phases of the Crisis

The perception that the regulatory system was partly to blame for the crises led to a search for both an accurate diagnosis of what had gone wrong and an approach that would avoid a recurrence. Although, in Europe, there were different viewpoints among the Member States on where the faults lay, there was a degree of consensus on the remedies and on the need to ensure that a recurrence be prevented. Yet what has also emerged is that too far too little attention has been paid to the determinants and causes of systemic risk. According to a definition put forward by the Institute for International Finance (2010):

> **Systemic risk is different** from other risks, being defined by its effects rather than its cause. It is **multiform, mutating, rapidly developing, and unpredictable**. It has to do with **interconnectedness** as well as with individual entities, with **smaller entities as well as larger**, and with financial firms of many different types and scope of activities. **Systemic risk is not national in nature** and whether an event has systemic consequences will often depend crucially on circumstances and context. [emphasis in original]

If there were any doubts about whether systemic risk could emerge, the events of the autumn of 2008 proved they were only too real. Following the collapse of Lehman Brothers in September 2008, four main phases of the crisis (crises in the plural is probably a more accurate term) can be identified, all of which affected the interactions between the state and the financial sector. These phases partly overlapped and the political urgency around them has fluctuated. Indeed, even before then, there had been a pre-crisis phase in which the ECB led the way by pumping large amounts of liquidity into the system from August 2007 onwards. Over the next year, the fallout from the US sub-prime crisis appeared to have been contained and the inflationary threat from a surge in oil and other commodity prices even led the ECB to decide in July 2008 on a small increase in its policy interest rate.[3]

[3] This increase has since been strongly criticised, but did not seem unduly cavalier at the time.

Following Lehman, the extent of the systemic perils became increasingly clear and urgent over the next 3–6 months and gave rise to a phase of response that can best be described as fire-fighting. Ireland was quick to offer a blanket guarantee to depositors in a very over-extended Irish banking system, a decision which the current government no doubt now regrets. In the UK, equity injections, guarantees and central bank liquidity were all used to prop up several of the largest banking groups, and a shotgun marriage was arranged between the relatively sound Lloyds TSB and the hugely over-lent HBOS. A number of smaller former building societies were either nationalised or absorbed (for example, by the Spanish bank Santander).

Elsewhere, the picture was more mixed. In France, Italy and Spain, few problems arose, partly because bank regulation had been more robust and, in several cases, banks were less international in their outlook. However, the Benelux bank, Fortis, had to be rescued and was broken up and sold. In Germany, Hypo Bank had to be rescued and there were fears for some of the Austrian and Nordic banks that had been especially active in central Europe and the Baltics, respectively. In much of central and eastern Europe, the high degree of foreign ownership, almost paradoxically, limited exposure with the result that most of the countries were only mildly affected (Latvia being an extreme exception). During the fire-fighting phase more than 40 financial intermediaries had to be recapitalised, requiring permission from the European Commission to overlook standard competition rules governing state aids to competitive companies.

A second phase of the crisis can be dated from late in 2008 to roughly the London G20 meeting at the beginning of April 2009, in which the focus was on measures aimed at macroeconomic stabilisation, but with a strong emphasis on shoring-up the solvency of the financial sector (especially the banks). There was a coordinated fiscal recovery package, accompanied by further measures to underpin the financial sector through various guarantees and extensive provision of liquidity by the ECB and other central banks. On the whole, these macroeconomic measures succeeded in stabilising output and saw many Member States edge back towards growth in the second half of 2009.

With the publication of the de Larosière report, the Turner report in the UK and other analyses of the causes of the crises and how to ensure "never again", a third phase that can be dated from early spring 2009 was about how to consolidate recovery, to recast financial regulation and to rein in banks. This phase exposed a number of differences of emphasis among EU actors. For example, Germany and France sought to include hedge funds, private equity and tax havens among the targets of regulatory reform, and have been highly critical of the role of what they see as US dominated ratings agencies. Others were much more concerned about the capital adequacy of the largest banks. Control of remuneration, especially the incentives around bonuses, was prominent in the discourse of many protagonists and a number of countries imposed ad hoc taxes on bonuses.

From the autumn of 2009 onwards, a fourth, initially slow-burning phase of the crisis can be identified. Following the change of government in Greece in October, it was revealed that the indebtedness of the Greek state had been substantially understated, leading to a steady rise in the premium Greece had to pay to sell sovereign bonds.

In the end, the Greeks had to throw in the towel and accept a complex rescue package to which the IMF, the EU as a whole and the euro area subscribed separate pools of funding. Subsequently, fears about the sustainability of sovereign debt mounted, leading to the creation of the European Financial Stability Facility (funded by the euro area members), backed up by further commitments from the IMF and from the EU as a whole through the European Financial Stabilisation Mechanism.

The sovereign debt phase continued to bubble away during the rest of 2010 and saw further rescue packages for Ireland in November 2010 and Portugal in February 2011, amid continuing fears about Italy and Spain. Although Europe's leaders continued to resist calls for default or euro exit, markets intensified the pressures on the euro area and the gravity of the Greek position led to a further rescue package initially agreed in July 2011. Market doubts dogged the package as it underwent ratification across the EU and led to a more extensive package agreed at the end of October 2011. For the first time, an explicit resort to default was part of the package, with banks eventually being asked to take a haircut of 74%, after difficult and protracted negotiations, on their holdings of Greek debt.

By the autumn of 2011, the turmoil in the markets for bonds of euro sovereigns was being seen as a source of systemic threat to the stability of the EU banking system. German and (especially) French banks had sizeable amounts of Italian sovereign debt. British banks have high exposures to the Irish banking system which is at the root of the Irish meltdown, with the debts of the banks having been taken over by the state, while the sheer size and interconnectedness of the Spanish system puts creditors from several other Member States at risk.

## 2 A Rapidly-Evolving Governance Agenda

As the crisis has unfolded, so too has the governance agenda, with a number of themes especially prominent as different phases have been assimilated. Some of the emphasis has been on reform of financial regulation, but there has also been a search for wider recasting of the governance arrangements at EU level and, especially, within the euro area. Europe's financial system had been developed around a number of core principles (especially the doctrine of home country control) that inevitably came under scrutiny in the aftermath of the crisis, but as events have shown, the thrust of governance reforms could not be limited to financial regulation and has widened significantly.

In the EU, an additional level of complexity arises because of the tensions between the national and the EU level, and the conflicts that they engender. Europe is much more than a loose grouping of countries of the sort seen in many parts of the world, where trade is the principal motivation for integration. But it does not have the coherence and common purpose of a large federation: it is not the United States of Europe. The distinctive character of the EU always has to be borne in mind as an explanation for seemingly strange compromises, incomplete frameworks and some of the delays or apparently eccentric objections to policy proposals that might appear persuasive to an outsider.

## 2.1 The Supervisory Framework

The de Larosière group produced a series of proposals which effectively provided the template for the new European approach to supervision of financial services. Its core recommendations were for a new European Systemic Risk Board (ESRB—initially labelled as Council) and a European System of Financial Supervisors (ESFS). After rather difficult negotiations between the Council of Ministers and the European Parliament over a number of aspects, agreement was reached in November 2010 on the details of these new bodies and a new system became operational in January 2011. It is portrayed in Fig. 1, which shows that the ESRB is made up of a mix of central bankers, representatives of the three sectoral European supervisory authorities and the European Commission. Its primary role is to assess macro-prudential risk and will include monitoring of Member States budgetary positions as well as developments in the financial sector as such.

The ESFS consists of the three EU level supervisory authorities and their respective national counterparts. The focus of the ESFS will be on micro-prudential supervision of individual financial entities. As the chart shows, there will be close concertation between the two new bodies in assessing systemic risk.

Although the sectoral European Supervisory Authorities (ESAs) will not, in general, directly supervise financial companies, on the grounds that the national authorities will be closer to their respective regulates, there are special provisions for credit ratings agencies. Early in December 2010, the legislation setting up a new pan-European supervisory authority was agreed. It included provisions for directly supervising credit rating agencies by the ESMA, and there is scope

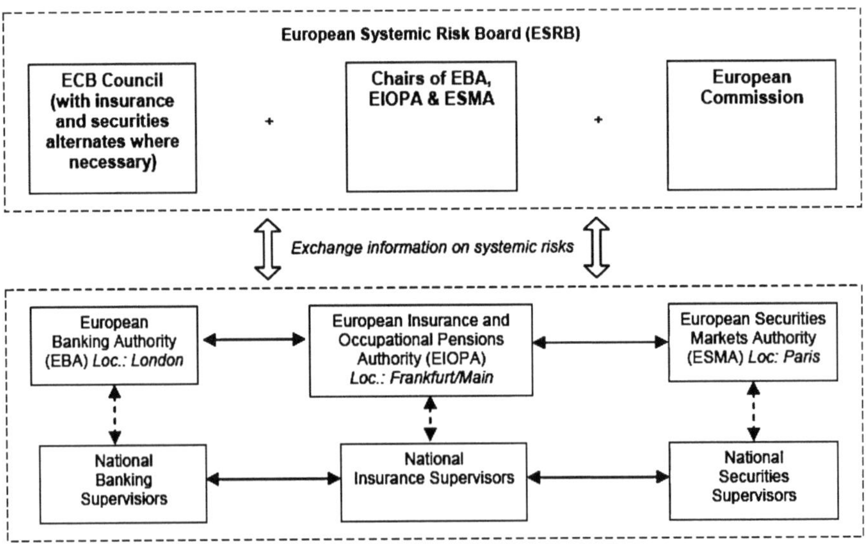


**Fig. 1** The new supervisory architecture in Europe

for fining agencies which breach rules within prescribed limits and subject to specific procedures.

One outcome of the legislative process that followed the initial proposals was an agreement to empower the new ESAs to impose temporary bans or restrictions on activities that might imperil financial stability, for example on uncovered short selling. A reason for this power is to avoid piecemeal action by individual Member States, although the EU authorities are at pains to suggest that they anticipate a cooperative model of coordination and, indeed, will be pleased if their preventative role means that emergency measures can be avoided. An implication is that it is going to be much more a reserve power than something that will be used routinely. A much more technical orientation of the new approach will be a drive to establish common rules across the EU and, in so doing, to reduce some of the differences that currently both add to costs of compliance where companies operate in multiple markets and constitute conditions that reduce transparency in a way that can also lead to less stability.

The limits of European integration always have to be borne in mind in assessing the EU approach. Tensions between the national and EU levels are a feature of much that goes on in the European Union and one of the more delicate issues that had to be resolved for the ESAs was establishing the circumstances in which they could intervene in national decisions. These are:

- Where arbitration is needed between Member States that cannot agree
- Where a national authority is applying EU regulations incorrectly
- In an emergency, subject to the Council agreeing that the course of action is justified

Any such intervention on a decision applicable to financial entities will only arise if the national authority concerned does not comply with a recommendation addressed to it by the ESA. In addition, the scope of intervention is limited to areas directly covered by EU regulations. The ESAs will not have the power to order a bank rescue or recapitalisation on the grounds that this is a competence reserved for Member States. The reason for this is, quite simply, that the risk would be borne by tax-payers and there is no EU-level tax-payer. This is recognised in a fiscal safeguard clause in the legislation which prevents the ESAs from taking decisions that have budgetary ramifications for the Member States, a clause which includes an adjudication procedure with Member States able to decide.

## 2.2 *Stress Tests and Other Measures*

One of the most high profile policy interventions since the formal start of the new system has been the carrying-out of stress tests on the banks. A first round of tests, completed in the summer of 2010, had found little cause for concern, identifying only five banks that needed to recapitalise their balance sheets. These results were widely derided and shown by the time of the Irish rescue package to have been far too soft.

A second round, published in the summer of 2011 under the responsibility of the newly constituted European Banking Authority (EBA), was tougher and resulted in a much larger number of banks being asked to seek additional capital (European Banking Authority 2011). The purpose of the 2011 tests was to appraise the resilience of the banks against what is described as an "adverse but plausible scenario" of a four percentage point drop in GDP compared with a baseline scenario. Although 20 banks had tier 1 capital below a 5% threshold at the start of the year, many had since raised new funds. The exercise identified eight banks (out of 90 tested in 21 countries) that needed to boost their tier 1 capital ratios above the 5% threshold, and a further 16 that are vulnerable because their capital ratio is between 5% and 6%.

However, as the sovereign debt crisis deepened, the methodology of the stress tests was, once more, subjected to criticism, notably that they had not made enough allowance for possible default by sovereigns, especially Greece. Although the EBA methodology included some allowance for direct exposure to Greek sovereign debt, it was criticised for neglecting second-order effects stemming from the problems that might arise if a bank holding substantial amounts of Greek debt were itself a risk for counterparties in other banks.

At both EU and national levels, diverse measures have been taken to lessen the stresses in the financial system. Spain, for example, has responded robustly to the threats hovering over its "cajas"—the savings banks, many of which are local and also subject to control by local politicians—from the bursting of the property bubble. The measures have included forced mergers to reduce the number of such banks, intensified reporting obligations and the creation of a special fund to assure liquidity. These measures are still evolving, like so many others, but initially appeared to have dealt with the most immediate dangers, but the position deteriorated during 2012 and led to a need to bail out Bankia—the new bank that had been created out of several cajas. However, there can be little doubt that the financial system in much of continental Europe (in contrast to the UK where a major effort went into recapitalising the banks) remains fragile. It might be able to withstand default by a small country like Greece, but would be in deep trouble if it had to cope with much more.

A further strand of governance reform is to hold the financial sector to account through a variety of interventions affecting the taxation of the sector and its conduct of business, as well as more direct supervisory action. Elements under consideration include:

- Curbs on bonuses
- Seeking new revenue sources that rely on finance as a tax base, whether through changes in how the activity of the sector is assessed (finding ways of taxing its value added) or possible financial transaction taxes (FTT)
- Restrictions on recruitment, especially of senior and key workers.

## 2.3 *Resolution Procedures*

The Commission stated in a communication on resolution of failing financial firms, its third on the subject in the space of 12 months, that new procedures are needed to ensure that a tax-payer bailout of major financial intermediaries does not happen again,

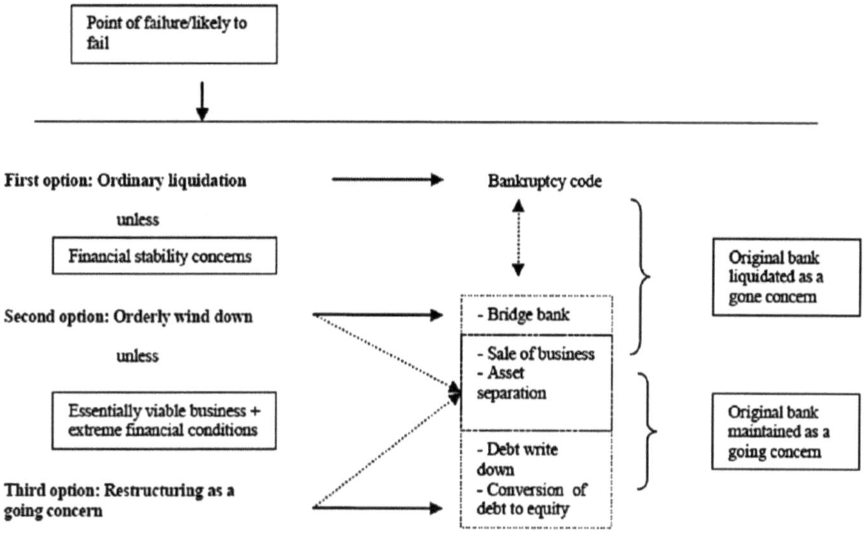


**Fig. 2** Resolution and insolvency

arguing that "a credible regime is needed to re-instil market discipline associated with the threat of failure and to reduce moral hazard—the implicit protection from failure that those in the banking sector currently enjoy". The Commission is working closely with the Financial Stability Board and in the context of the G20, with other leading governments. A proposal for new legislation on crisis resolution in the financial sector was promised for spring 2011, following a consultation exercise that was launched at the beginning of that year and ran until March 2011, with a summary of results published two months later. The initial focus was to be on credit institutions and certain investment firms, but extension to the rest of the financial sector is envisaged subsequently. The core aim is to allow intermediaries to fail without triggering systemic problems. This will involve three governance orientations:

- Preparatory and preventative measures designed to avoid the emergence of problems
- Early supervisory intervention to ensure corrective action is taken expeditiously
- Tools and powers to facilitate orderly resolution of problems

The communication stresses the importance of adaptation to national systems, where they currently exist, but also of clarity about what the system is. Under each heading, the communication sets out the components of the anticipated policy responses, including (under the first) what the trigger for action should be. Its approach to resolution is set out in Fig. 2.

The proposed approach also stresses the need for powers to arrange the sale of the business (or parts of it) as a going concern, and highlights the rights of shareholders—if appropriate—to compensation. In common with other governance reforms, the communication argues that because systems already exist in many

Member States, the EU approach should not be overly prescriptive. Instead, the emphasis should be on the outcomes, hence a single model is not proposed.

A particular concern that the communication addresses is how to resolve crises where more than one Member State is involved, recognising that there is no single EU level supervisor. The proposed answer is to have a coordinated system akin to that which is being established for supervision; specifically:

- The creation of resolution colleges is proposed, to be chaired by the home supervisor of the intermediary in question.
- A group level resolution authority would determine whether resolution at the level of the group or on a national basis should be undertaken.

### 2.4 Complementary Macroeconomic Coordination Changes

The shockwaves from the Greek crisis have impelled the EU towards comprehensive reforms of policy coordination aimed at assuring macroeconomic stability, which will fundamentally change the governance of the EU economy. These have been through their main legislative procedures and are now being put into operation. The main elements of these reforms include

- Improving surveillance of Member State fiscal positions (including a somewhat beefed-up Stability and Growth Pact which will add a debt criterion as well as the current deficit one)
- The introduction of a process for assessing excessive imbalances that could result in instability, such as asset bubbles, risky developments in competitiveness or rigidities on the supply-side
- Greater oversight by the EU level, through a two-semester system, in which the first semester in national budgets is "European", allowing scrutiny and coherence, then the second is national
- A requirement to introduce national fiscal frameworks that assure better disciplined fiscal policy
- More effective sanctions.

There has also been agreement to put in place a permanent crisis management mechanism to replace the ad hoc responses that were cobbled together in dealing with the Greek and Irish bailouts, enacted via a limited treaty reform.

## 3 The Challenges and Next Stages

The regulatory and governance frameworks affecting the financial sector, financial stability and macroeconomic management are all shifting rapidly in Europe and there is an evident sense of urgency about completing the reforms. Indeed, in its February 2011 progress report on *Regulating Financial Services for Sustainable*

*Growth*, the European Commission stresses the importance of rapid adoption of its extensive legislative package and states that it expects all the proposals in the package to enter into force early in 2013. The latest major proposal is for a reform of the EU Directive (MIFID) covering securities markets and products, with a draft having been published in October 2011. According to the European Commission, adoption of this legislation will mean that the EU will be quite closely aligned with the US system following the Dodd Frank Act. More fundamentally, proposals made during 2012 for a 'banking union' are now making progress, and plans are now on the table for a significant EU level role, led by the ECB, in prudential supervision.

The new supervisory system introduced from the beginning of 2011 has to contend both with a volatile (and still risky) environment, and with the fact that Europe's institutional complexity and political constraints restrict the scope for radical change. It is also arguable that after the bank rescues of 2008/9, EU governments have far less room for manoeuvre: the European Commission (2010a) asserts that public aid committed to financial rescues was 30% of EU GDP, of which 13 percentage points were used.

Nevertheless, the new architecture for governance is being gradually put in place and an assessment of its prospects can be attempted. It undoubtedly addresses many of the shortcomings of the previous system, notably by acknowledging the imperative of more effective and disciplined coordination, both between Member States and across policy domains. There is also growing evidence that inadequate compliance with agreed rules and a cavalier attitude to commitments can no longer be tolerated if future trouble is to be avoided.

## 3.1 Accommodating Different Interests

Even so, the outcome is, as is so often the case in Europe, a delicate compromise between competing interests and preferences. Members States generally agree on many of the broad aims, such as enhancing financial stability or having a system of macroeconomic surveillance that is better at preventing the emergence of imbalances, but will disagree on details. These disagreements stem, on the one hand, from genuine differences in philosophies of regulation, such as how much reliance to place on the market in disciplining financial intermediaries or, indeed, governments. A prominent German politician, for example, characterised private equity as "locusts" and there is an enduring suspicion of free-wheeling finance in France.

On the other, there are long-standing rivalries and competitive considerations to take into account. Thus, London's pre-eminence as a financial centre in Europe is a prize that Paris and Frankfurt would like to wrest away. For the City of London, heavier regulation of some segments of the financial sector (hedge funds or private equity, for instance) would be counter-productive not only because it would be potentially damaging to an important source of activity, but also because it would leave a gap in the market that might be filled by competitors outside Europe.

The debate around a FTT is a good example of an issue that has shown an ability to polarise opinion, with strong positions being adopted in favour of an EU level FTT (France and Germany) and opposition from the UK. Such a tax has also been proposed by the European Commission (2011a) as a solution to the perennial problem of identifying a genuine "own resource" to fund the EU budget. Protagonists of FTT see it as a desirable rebalancing of taxation that will extract revenue from a sector which is under-taxed, and may also help to curb excessive speculation. Opponents worry that it is not a well-conceived tax, as it would be easily avoided unless imposed at global level and would risk a fall in yield if it succeeded in deterring speculation. It could, therefore be seen, in effect, as a form of political grandstanding, though clearly one capable of generating considerable acrimony, despite it being of relatively minor economic significance (its yield might be around one quarter to one half of a percentage point of EU GDP). A minority of EU countries agreed early in 2013 to proceed with an FTT.

## *3.2 The Role of the ECB*

A sensitive issue for financial regulation is what the precise role of the European Central Bank should be. The House of Lords (2009, p 38) reports that most of the witnesses it heard from "agreed that the ECB should play a role in macro-prudential supervision, although there was much disagreement over its precise role. Mr Trichet, President of the ECB, argued that the ECB should play a strong role in EU macro-prudential supervision. He argued that macro-prudential supervision would be a 'natural extension' of the ECB's mandate, given that the ECB already undertakes monitoring and analysis of financial stability. He went on to argue that central banks had the best access to supervisory information that is necessary for financial stability assessments. He concluded that the ECB 'stands ready' to perform additional macroprudential supervisory tasks".

Latterly, there have been disputes about the role the ECB should play in both crisis management and in the longer term economic and financial governance or the euro area, amid reports of divisions on the ECB's Governing Council. The resignations of two German members,[4] in particular, was widely interpreted as a sign of dissent inside the ECB, and chimed with wider German unease. France, by contrast, has pushed for the ECB to act decisively as the lender of last resort to banks and (even if still indirectly, to respect constitutional niceties) to sovereigns, an orientation that has at least partly been satisfied by the announcement in September 2012 of plans for outright monetary transactions.

[4] First, in February 2011, Axel Weber resigned his post, following a number of episodes of public disagreement with the ECB approach. He had appeared to be a favoured candidate to succeed Jean-Claude Trichet, but support for him from the German government had appeared to be insufficiently strong. Hence it is a moot point whether his resignation was one of principled objection to ECB policies or not. Jürgen Stark's resignation as a member of the ECB Executive Board was reported to have been more directly triggered by opposition to the ECB's bond purchases.

Objections to a more extensive regulatory role for the ECB range from whether it has sufficient capabilities in the area to whether it should concentrate on its core mandate of assuring price stability. Buiter (2006), for example believes that the supervisor function and the lender of last resort function require different forms of accountability and greater political oversight. He is also adamant that there is no case for the ECB being assigned the leading role in euro area-level prudential supervision that it wanted to acquire, yet is sympathetic to the idea that there should be an EU-wide (as opposed to just euro area) supervisor. In the proposals for banking union, it has nevertheless been accepted that the ECB should have a core role in supervision, staring with the largest banks. Whether this should then extend to all 6,000 banks in the EU is an issue that divides the member States.

In addition, there is an evident political problem around the ECB, which stems form the difference in membership between the euro area and the ECB. Countries to which the ECB is not so directly accountable (certainly the UK) would be uncomfortable with assigning it greater powers, although it is worth noting that there is an enabling clause in the Treaty (Art. 127.6, TFEU) which states:

> The Council, acting by means of regulations in accordance with a special legislative procedure, may unanimously, and after consulting the European Parliament and the European Central Bank, confer specific tasks upon the European Central Bank concerning policies relating to the prudential supervision of credit institutions and other financial institutions with the exception of insurance undertakings.

What is intriguing about this article, which has not changed substantively from its predecessor version in the Maastricht Treaty (and thus from 20 years ago) is that only the ECB is mentioned in this context, but also the exclusion of insurance. With many member states having moved towards integrated supervision of the different segments of the financial sector (see Begg 2009), there is a prospect of institutional confusion. One possible solution, for example in relation to resolution of failing banks and the oversight of the ESRB is to exploit the fact that the ECB has two separate governance bodies: the 23 member (six Executive Board members and the 17 euro area central Bank Governors) Governing Council which is the main decision-taking body and which decides on monetary policy, and the General Council which comprises the governors of all 27 EU Member States. The latter can provide a way round some of the objections.

## 3.3 *Unfinished Business*

On of the more pressing concerns at present is how best to structure crisis management and resolution procedures. The "Greek" crisis was a costly wake-up call for Europe's leaders and the fact that it was still rumbling on, with ever more costly packages under discussion, well into 2012, with Cyprus and (to a lesser degree) Spain also seeking financial support, emphasised how severe it had become. As noted above, it showed that financial stability and fiscal policy were far more intimately linked than had been presumed, A disorderly default on its sovereign debt by

Greece would immediately have triggered systemic threats to Europe's banking system. Exhibiting the opposite chain of causality, Ireland's banking crisis very rapidly metamorphosed into a sovereign debt problem, and the position in other Member States such as Portugal has elements of both phenomena. But as the tensions of 2011 and 2012 showed, Europe has struggled to find timely and effective answers.

Having finally conceded the principle that private holders of Greek bonds should take a large haircut on existing debt, a major dilemma in Europe today is the extent to which the financial sector should share in any future crisis resolution mechanism. Following an agreement concocted at Deauville in October 2010, the French and German governments made clear that future bailouts could not rely on the state alone, and must entail some loss for bond-holders. In a medium- to longer-term perspective, this is undoubtedly the correct answer, but there is also little doubt that the announcement rapidly triggered bond market volatility that was only calmed down when Ireland was pushed to accept a bailout.

Euro-bonds of some description also elicit divergent views. There is an attractive interpretation in which, by pooling risk, a bond backed by the entire euro area will be much sounder than the average of the bonds of individual Member States. Just as a US Treasury bond is regarded as sounder than individual state bonds, this would appear to offer an alluring solution for funding debt in euro area countries. However, there are two major obstacles. First, the coupon on a euro bond is likely to be higher than has to be paid by the most credit-worthy governments—traditionally Germany—and would thus penalise the most disciplined Member States while giving a free (or freer) ride to the least disciplined. Leading German politicians have, so far, opposed the creation of such a bond precisely on the grounds that it would remove one of the incentives for the more reckless governments to adopt sound budgetary policies. This can be viewed as a moral hazard problem.

Second, the fact that there is no European (or even euro area) tax-payer means that there is an uncertainty about where ultimate responsibility for redeeming a euro bond would lie in bad times. The answer lies in mutualising the debt obligations through joint and several guarantees which, if called, would mean that any Member State would be liable not only for its own share, but potentially the total liability. Only Germany, in practice, could pay. It is not particularly hard to imagine a differentiated burden depending on the extent to which a Member State draws on the funding pool.[5] But the challenge is how to design a euro bond that will be sufficiently resilient to crisis, as opposed to normal times, yet have sufficiently robust conditions attached to it to deter unsafe borrowing by weaker sovereigns.

The European Commission (2011b) has now published a discussion paper about options, and makes a rather crass attempt to forestall German antagonism by eschewing the term Eurobonds in favour of "Stability bonds". While the label is unlikely to fool

[5] An option is presented by Delpa and von Weizsäcker (2010) in which they postulate blue bonds which would be pooled and allowed for debt up to 60% of GDP and red bonds that would be specific to the country and subject to orderly default.

anyone, the paper has the merit of putting the issue firmly on the table, forcing Germany, the Netherlands and other net creditor Member States to explain why it will not work.

## 4 Conclusions

The pace of financial reform in Europe at present is both frenetic and wide-ranging. It can reasonably be expected to result in extensive changes in how the financial sector is regulated, as well as in the nature of the connections between the sector and the real economy and the sector and the state. There is a strong sense in Europe that finance owes everyone else "reparations" for the damage it has inflicted and that "never again" should be a watchword to guide policy. It is also clear that enduring solutions must be found to problems such as: "too big to fail"; the excessive, ostentatious rent-seeking exemplified by the bonus culture; and the cavalier attitudes to risk that have been exposed.

The lack of a European tax-payer severely constrains what might be envisaged as a European approach, with the consequence that optimal solutions—especially if they involve assignment of powers to the EU level—are often out of reach, irrespective of constitutional or political objections. A statement by the UK FSA to the House of Lords inquiry underlines the point: "until the EU has fiscal powers which permit it to raise the funds needed to rescue distressed banks, or until there is a system of mandatory burden sharing between Member States for fiscal support, supervision will and should remain the responsibility of Member States".

The elaboration of a new approach to financial regulation is not, however, occurring in isolation, and much of the reform effort in the last year has been devoted to recasting the broader governance architecture within which finance functions. This is partly complete and promises to constitute a more effective means of preventing future problems by reducing the risk and likely extent of financial instability. But before then Europe has to navigate its way out of the present crisis and, although the latest initiatives to put in place a banking union and to deepen political integration offer promise, the challenges remain formidable. For the EU and the euro area these are undoubtedly tricky times.

## Appendix: The EU Legislative Programme on Financial Regulation

| Initiatives | Commission adoption | Political agreement |
|---|---|---|
| Measures proposed, under negotiation: | | |
| Alternative Investment Fund Managers Directive | April 2009 | Summer 2010 |
| 3rd Revision of the Capital Requirements Directive (CRD3) | July 2009 | Summer 2010 |
| Supervision package (European Systemic Risk Board and European Supervisory Authorities) | September 2009 | Summer 2010 |

(continued)

(continued)

| Initiatives | Commission adoption | Political agreement |
|---|---|---|
| Communication on options for bank resolution funds | May 2010 | n/a |
| Forthcoming proposals: | | |
| UCITS—implementing measures | June 2010 | June 2010 |
| Revision of Credit Rating Agencies Regulation (EU-level supervision of CRAs) | June 2010 | By end 2011 |
| Green Paper on Corporate Governance in Financial Institutions | June 2010 | By end 2011 |
| Creation of a Financial Services Users Group | Summer 2010 | n/a |
| Revision of the Deposit Guarantee Schemes Directive | July 2010 | By end 2011 |
| White Paper on Insurance Guarantee Schemes | July 2010 | n/a |
| Revision of the Investor Compensation Schemes Directive | July 2010 | By end 2011 |
| Derivatives-legislation on market infrastructure | Summer 2010 | By end 2011 |
| Revision of the Financial Conglomerate Directive | Summer 2010 | By end 2011 |
| Second "Omnibus" Directive of changes to sectoral legislation to align it with the proposals on supervision | Summer 2010 | By end 2010 |
| Directive on legal certainty of securities holding & transactions | September 2010 | By end 2011 |
| Regulation on SEPA (Single European Payments Area), setting a deadline for transition to SEPA | September 2010 | By end 2011 |
| Communication on a framework for crisis management | October 2010 | n/a |
| Measures on short selling/credit default swaps | October 2010 | By end 2011 |
| Initiative on access to minimum banking services | October/November 2010 | By end 2011 |
| Communication on sanctions in the financial services sector | December 2010 | n/a |
| Revision of the Capital Requirements Directive (CRD4) | December 2010 | By end 2011 |
| Revision of the Market Abuse Directive (securities) | December 2010 | By end 2011 |
| Review of the Markets in Financial Instruments Directive | Spring 2011 | By end 2011 |
| UCITS—depositories function | Spring 2011 | By end 2011 |
| Implementing measures for Solvency II Directive on capital requirements for insurance undertakings | Spring 2011 | By end 2011 |
| Packaged Retail Investment Products legislative proposals | Spring 2011 | By end 2011 |
| Crisis management legislative proposal (including bank resolution funds) | Spring 2011 | By end 2011 |
| Insurance mediation Directive revision | Spring 2011 | By end 2011 |
| Further amendments to the Credit Rating Agencies Regulation | Spring 2011 | By end 2011 |
| Legislation on corporate governance | Spring 2011 | By end 2011 |

Source: European Commission (2010b)

## References

Begg I (2009) Regulation and supervision of financial intermediaries in the EU: the aftermath of the financial crisis. J Common Mark Stud 47(5):1107–1128

Buiter WH (2006) Rethinking inflation targeting and central bank independence. Inaugural Lecture, LSE, October 26. www.lse.ac.uk/collections/LSEPublicLecturesAndEvents/pdf/20061026_Buiter.pdf

de Larosière J (chairman) (2009) The High-Level Group on Financial Supervision in the EU: Report. Brussels, 25 Feb 2009)

Delpa J, von Weizsäcker J (2010) 'The blue bond proposal' Bruegel Policy Brief 2010/03. Bruegel, Brussels

European Banking Authority (2011) European Banking Authority 2011 EU-wide stress test: aggregate report. EBA, London

European Commission (2010a) An EU framework for crisis management in the financial sector. Communication, Brussels, 20 Oct 2010

European Commission (2010b) Communication, Regulating financial services for sustainable growth, COM(2010) 301, Brussels, 2 June 2010

European Commission (2011a) A budget for Europe 2020. Communication, Brussels, 29 June 2010

European Commission (2011b) Green paper on the feasibility of introducing stability bonds. COM(2011) 818 Brussels, 23 Nov 2010)

FSA (2009) The Turner review: a regulatory response to the global banking crisis. Financial Services Authority, London

House of Lords (2009) The future of EU financial regulation and supervision. European Union Committee, 14th Report of 2008/9 session. The Stationery Office, London

# Asia's Approach to Improve Financial Regulation

**Atsushi Mimura**

**Abstract** The global financial crisis, beginning with the collapse of Lehman Brothers, resulted in fundamental changes in the structure of international forums for the discussion of financial regulatory and supervisory reforms. The most important forums that have emerged from the crisis are the G20 and the Financial Stability Board (FSB). Asian countries occupy an important weight in these forums; so the question is, how can Japan (and other Asian countries) take the best advantage of a larger Asian presence in the G20 and FSB to play a leading role in financial regulatory and supervisory reforms. The divergence among Asian countries poses a challenge in the formation of a single voice for Asia. However, this diversity also means that Asia can lead discussions in international forums to well-balanced conclusions. Regional dialogues within Asia should be enhanced to bring Asia's voices together as one. Japan is actively taking part in various multilateral and bilateral dialogues and forums from this perspective, and will continue to do so.

**Keywords** Financial Services Agency • FSB • G20

---

The views expressed in this paper are those of the author, and not the official views of the JFSA.

A. Mimura (✉)
Financial Services Agency, The Japanese Government,
Tokyo, Japan
e-mail: atsushi.mimura@fsa.go.jp

S. Kaji and E. Ogawa (eds.), *Who Will Provide the Next Financial Model?: Asia's Financial Muscle and Europe's Financial Maturity*,
DOI 10.1007/978-4-431-54282-7_2, © Springer Japan 2013

# 1 The G20 and FSB as New International Forums for Financial Regulation and Supervision

The global financial crisis, beginning with the collapse of Lehman Brothers in the fall of 2008, has revealed various weaknesses in the global financial system, including financial regulation and supervision. The crisis not only pushed authorities to embark on a wide range of financial regulatory and supervisory reforms, but also resulted in fundamental changes in the structure of international forums for the discussion of those reforms. The most important forums to have emerged from the crisis are the G20 and the Financial Stability Board (FSB) (Fig. 1).

## *1.1 G20*

The G20 existed and met at a finance minister and governor level even before the crisis, but the recent crisis has resulted in a fundamental enhancement to its role as "the premium forum for our economic cooperation" (G20 Leaders' Statement, Pittsburgh Summit, September 2009). Unlike past crises that mainly occurred and hit emerging economies (e.g., the Asian Crisis in the 1990s), the Lehman crisis

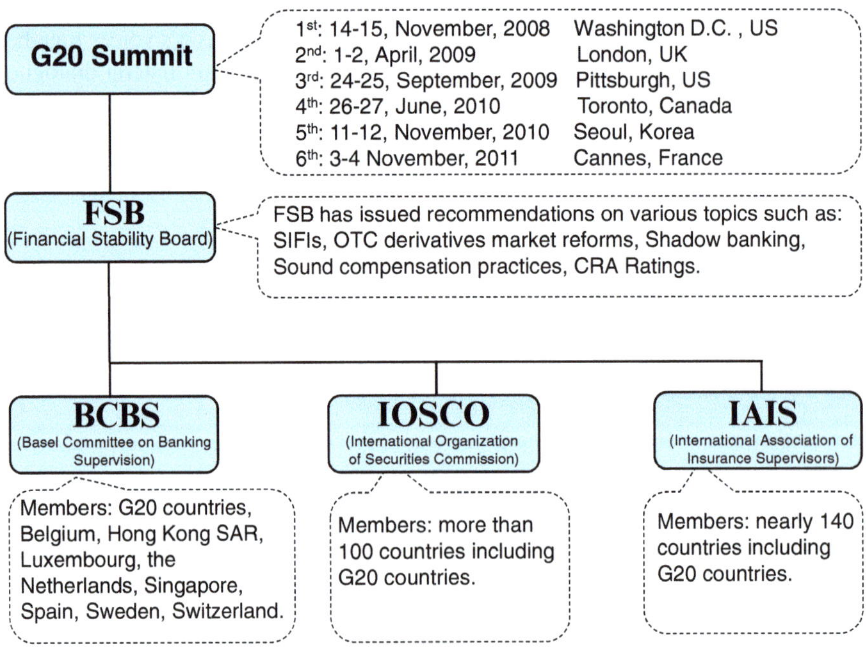


**Fig. 1** International forums on financial regulation and supervision

started in advanced economies, spilling across the globe to emerging economies. Faced with the fact that emerging economies were not the root of the crisis but were certainly affected, and that they were able to support the global economy better than advanced economies, world leaders reached a common understanding that global solutions to the crisis can only be found and implemented through a political forum involving both advanced and emerging economies. This led to the G20 Washington Summit, which met in November 2008 shortly after the Lehman incident. The Washington Summit issued a "Declaration" regarding financial markets and the world economy, as well as an "Action Plan" to implement principles for financial reform. Since then, G20 Leaders have met on several occasions (London Summit, April 2009; Pittsburgh Summit, September 2009; Toronto Summit, June 2010; Seoul Summit, November 2010; and Cannes Summit, November 2011), and the development and implementation of financial regulatory and supervisory reforms have always been at the core of their discussions. The next G20 Summit will be held in Los Cabos, Mexico in June 2012.

## *1.2 FSB*

The FSB was established in April 2009 as the successor to the Financial Stability Forum (FSF). The FSF was founded in 1999 by G7 finance ministers and central bank governors as a new structure to enhance cooperation among various national and international supervisory bodies and international financial institutions to promote stability in the international financial system. At the Washington Summit, the G20 Leaders called for the FSF "to expand urgently to a broader membership of emerging economies" (Declaration of G20 Leaders, Washington Summit), and a broad consensus emerged in the following months towards placing the FSF on stronger institutional ground with an expanded membership. At the G20 London Summit of April 2009, the expanded FSF was re-established as the FSB with a broadened mandate to promote financial stability. Table 1 shows FSB membership.

The mandate of the FSB is to coordinate at the international level the work of national financial authorities and international standard setting bodies, and to develop and promote the implementation of effective regulatory, supervisory and other financial sector policies. The FSB brings together international financial institutions, sector-specific international groupings of regulators and supervisors, and committees of central bank experts. Sector-specific standard setting bodies that are also members of the FSB include the Basel Committee on Banking Supervision (BCBS), International Organization of Securities Commission (IOSCO), and the International Association of Insurance Supervisors (IAIS). The FSB also comprises national and regional authorities responsible for maintaining financial stability in significant international financial centers, namely ministries of finance, central banks, and supervisory and regulatory authorities. Jurisdictions that are members of the FSB have been expanded to include all G20 countries.

**Table 1** FSB membership

| | FSB member* | G20 | | FSB member* | G20 |
|---|---|---|---|---|---|
| *America* | | | *Middle East/Africa* | | |
| United States | ○ | ◎ | Turkey | ● | ◎ |
| Canada | ○ | ◎ | Saudi Arabia | ● | ◎ |
| Brazil | ● | ◎ | South Africa | ● | ◎ |
| Mexico | ● | ◎ | | | |
| Argentina | ● | ◎ | | | |
| *Asia* | | | *International Standard Setting* | | |
| Japan | ○ | ◎ | BCBS | ○ | |
| Australia | ○ | ◎ | IOSCO | ○ | |
| Hong Kong | ○ | | IAIS | ○ | |
| Singapore | ○ | | IASB | ○ | |
| China | ● | ◎ | CGFS | ○ | |
| India | ● | ◎ | CPSS | ○ | |
| Korea | ● | ◎ | | | |
| Indonesia | ● | ◎ | *International Financial Institutions* | | |
| *Europe* | | | BIS | ○ | |
| United Kingdom | ○ | ◎ | ECB | ○ | |
| Germany | ○ | ◎ | IMF | ○ | |
| France | ○ | ◎ | World Bank | ○ | |
| Italy | ○ | ◎ | OECD | ○ | |
| Netherlands | ○ | | | | |
| Switzerland | ○ | | | | |
| Russia | ● | ◎ | | | |
| Spain | ● | | | | |
| European Commission | ● | ◎ | | | |

*○ FSF member, ● New member since 2009
◎ G20 member

## 2 Challenge for Japan and Asia: Speaking as a Single Voice

### *2.1 Greater Representation of Asia in International Forums*

While Japan was (and still is) the only Asian country in the G7, the G20 comprises six countries in the Asian region (Japan, Australia, China, India, Indonesia and Korea). And while the FSF comprised 12 jurisdictions (G7 plus Australia, Hong Kong, The Netherlands, Singapore and Switzerland), of which only 3 were Asian (Japan, Australia and Hong Kong), the expanded FSB covers 24 jurisdictions (all G20 countries, Hong Kong, The Netherlands, Singapore, Spain and Switzerland) of which 8 are Asian (Japan, Australia, China, Hong Kong, India, Indonesia, Korea and Singapore).

At first glance, we may think these changes would reduce the presence and influence of Japan in those international forums; indeed, while Japan represents an Asian voice in the G7 as the only Asian member, it cannot assume the same role in the G20 where several Asian countries are represented. However, if we look from a regional perspective, the recent changes have significantly increased the relative weight of Asia in these important forums: Asian members now occupy around a third of G20/FSB member jurisdictions, a larger share than the Americas and comparable to (if not, is more than) Europe. So the question is now, how can Japan (and other Asian countries) take the best advantage of a larger Asian presence in the G20 and FSB to play a leading role in financial regulatory and supervisory reforms?

### 2.2 *Asia Speaking as One Voice*

Speaking as one voice is easy in theory, but difficult in practice. Even in Europe, where the European Commission plays a significant role in coordinating member countries' positions in international forums such as the G20, the countries do not always share a common view. In the recent G20 discussion on financial regulatory and supervisory reforms, we have seen examples of divergence within EU countries. In Asia, such a regional coordination would be an even greater challenge, not least because Asian countries face a higher degree of divergence among themselves than Europeans. Below are some anecdotal examples:

- According to the statistics of the United Nations shown in Fig. 2, divergence of GDP per capita among Asian countries is much greater than in Europe. This shows that Asian economies are at very different stages of development.
- The same observation can be made if we look at domestic financial assets as a percentage of GDP (using the statistics from the IMF, BIS and World Federal Exchange), shown in Fig. 3. Here again, divergence in Asia is much greater than in Europe, suggesting that Asian financial systems remain at different stages of development.

This divergence among Asian countries clearly poses a difficulty in reaching a single Asian voice. The challenge is how to turn this diversity from a disadvantage to an advantage. Everything has its pros and cons, and while divergence could make coordination across Asian countries more difficult, it could also contribute to a deepened, multi-faceted discussion at a regional level that reflects a wide range of perspectives from countries at different stages of economic and financial development. In fact, we may expect that the outcome of discussions in Asia on any policy issues (including financial regulatory and supervisory reforms) would comprise balanced views from advanced, emerging and developing economies, and thus be an ideal input to discussions at international forums such as the G20 and FSB.

## 3 Asia's Approach: Efforts Towards Regional Coordination

### 3.1 *Multilateral Forums*

There already exists some forums for regional financial supervisors in Asia, and new ones are emerging:

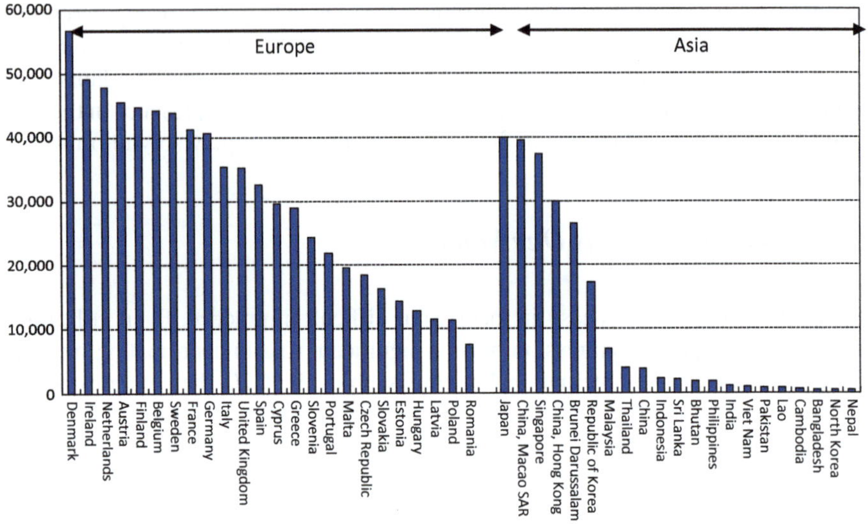


**Fig. 2** Regional differences: GDP per capita (US$) in 2009. Source: United Nations

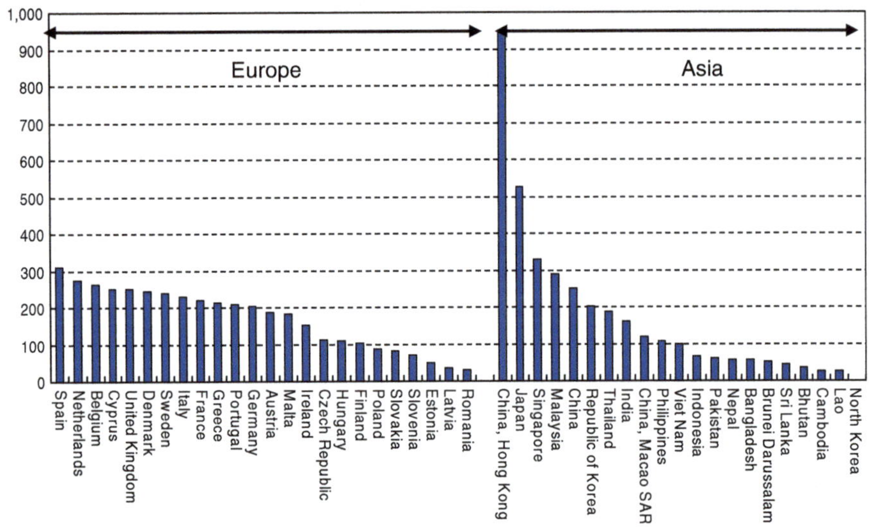


**Fig. 3** Regional differences: domestic financial assets (% of GDP) in 2008. Note: Domestic financial assets: Sum of Currency and deposits, Equity securities, and Domestic debt securities. Source: IMF, BIS and World Federal Exchange

- For example, the Executives' Meeting of East Asia-Pacific Central Banks (EMEAP), a cooperative organization of central banks and monetary authorities in East Asia and Pacific region, has as its sub-group the Working Group on Banking Supervision (WGBS). The WGBS incorporates representatives from the banking supervisory agencies (including non-central bank supervisors) of the region and meets twice a year, in addition to occasional conference calls. Member jurisdictions of the WGBS include: Japan, Australia, China, Hong Kong, Indonesia, Korea, Malaysia, New Zealand, Philippines, Singapore and Thailand. The WGBS is today co-chaired by the Bank of Japan (BOJ) and Bank of Thailand, and the Financial Services Agency of Japan attends WGBS meetings with the BOJ.

- Another example in the securities sector is the Asia Pacific Regional Committee (APRC) of the IOSCO. The IOSCO is the leading international policy forum for securities regulators and is recognized as the global standard setter for securities regulation. The organization's membership regulates more than 95 % of the world's securities markets in 115 jurisdictions. The APRC is one of the regional committees of the IOSCO and includes more than 20 jurisdictions of the Asia and Pacific region.
- Following its re-establishment with expanded membership, the FSB is also making efforts to strengthen its outreach initiatives. The Board has finalized the operational framework for its Regional Consultative Groups (RCGs) and in 2011 established six RCGs covering the Americas, Asia, the Commonwealth of Independent States, Europe, Middle East and North Africa, and Sub-Saharan Africa. The inaugural meeting of the FSB RCG for Asia was held in Seoul in November 2011, followed by a second meeting in Kuala Lumpur in May 2012. The membership of RCGs comprises both FSB member and non-member jurisdictions of the region. In the case of the Asian RCG, eight non-FSB member jurisdictions (Cambodia, Malaysia, New Zealand, Pakistan, Philippines, Sri Lanka, Thailand and Vietnam) have joined the group, in addition to eight FSB member jurisdictions of the region. The Asian RCG is co-chaired by the Bank of Korea and Bank Negara Malaysia.

## *3.2 Other Regional Dialogues*

In addition to multilateral frameworks, as described above, various regional dialogues are also occurring between Japan and its Asian homologues to enhance coordination across the region:

- In 2005, the framework for the China–Korea–Japan Trilateral High-level Meeting was established, together with the Trilateral Financial Supervisory Cooperation Seminar.
- Trilateral dialogues among Japan, China, and Korea are also ongoing in various other forms, such as a conference call among the financial supervisory authorities of the three countries in September 2011.
- The Financial Services Agency also hosted an international conference on "Asian Market Integration and Financial Innovation" in February 2012, at the time of IOSCO meetings in Tokyo.

### *3.3 Need for Emerging and Developing Economies' Perspectives*

Initially, the international agenda of financial regulatory and supervisory reforms largely focused on issues that were of greater interest to advanced economies. This was a natural result of the fact that the recent financial crisis stemmed from these economies, revealing weaknesses in their financial systems. As these reforms achieve progress, issues pertaining specifically to emerging and developing economies are now drawing greater attention. At the Cannes Summit in November 2011, the G20 Leaders called "international bodies to take into account emerging market and developing economies' specific considerations and concerns in designing new international financial standards and policies where appropriate." It is essential that multilateral frameworks and dialogue among Asian jurisdictions be able to contribute to this emerging demand.

## 4 Conclusion

Asia is a region of great diversity. This poses a challenge in the formation of a single voice for Asia; however, this diversity also means that Asia can lead discussions in international forums (such as the G20 and FSB) to well-balanced conclusions.

Regional dialogues within Asia should therefore be enhanced to bring Asia's voices together as one. Japan is actively taking part in various multilateral and bilateral dialogues and forums from this perspective, and will continue to do so.

# Comment Paper to Chapters "The EU's Approach to Improving Financial Regulation" and "Asia's Approach to Improve Financial Regulation"

**Jun Inoue**

Professor Begg described the wide-ranging financial reform that has been occurring in Europe since 2008. Mr. Mimura introduced a web of international forums on financial regulation and supervision, and discussed the increase in memberships from Asian countries in these forums; however, Asia presents a diverse range of models. Both speakers presented the current regulatory developments in Europe and Asia in detail.

Nevertheless, under the concept of "who will provide the next financial model", some further consideration of the regulation models is required. Have Europe and Asia met to discuss the approaches to exchange regulatory ideas? If the answer is yes, which approach appears appropriate for the next model of financial regulation and why?

In that sense, Mr. Mimura's discussions on IMF membership, G20 membership and FSB membership provide clues to understanding the dynamics of the negotiations between both sides. In each international forum, Europe exhibits collective efforts, while Asia exhibits great diversity. Further research on membership and forum discussions will provide deeper insights into the appropriate regulatory model (and possibly, the global standard).

J. Inoue (✉)
Faculty of Comparative Culture, Otsuma Women's University,
Tokyo, Japan
e-mail: jinoue@otsuma.ac.jp

S. Kaji and E. Ogawa (eds.), *Who Will Provide the Next Financial Model?: Asia's Financial Muscle and Europe's Financial Maturity*,
DOI 10.1007/978-4-431-54282-7_3, © Springer Japan 2013

# Comment Paper to Chapters "The EU's Approach to Improving Financial Regulation" and "Asia's Approach to Improve Financial Regulation"

**Satoshi Koibuchi**

Both papers review the current status of financial supervision in the region and argue how to improve financial regulation via regional cooperation.

The first paper by Prof. Iain Begg argues the financial regulatory policy in the EU. It divides the period of crises experienced by European countries after the failure of Lehman Brothers in September 2008 into four phases: the "fire-fighting" phase in the aftermath of the Lehman failure; the "macroeconomic stabilization" phase from late 2008; the "recovery and re-regulation of financial system" phase from early spring 2009; and the "sovereign debt" phase from the autumn of 2009. Under the perception that the governance reforms to deal with systematic risk are important remedies to manage the current crisis and prevent future crises, the four elements of the reforms were already implemented in the EU before the outbreak of its own sovereign debt crises. First, new supervisory architecture consisting of the European System Risk Board and the European System of Financial Supervisors (ESFS) were established and began their duties at the beginning of 2011. Second, the newly constituted European Banking Authority (EBA) under the ESFS became responsible (from the second round stress test, with the results announced in July 2011) for the stress tests on major European banks. Third, new bank resolution procedures were introduced to resolve failed banks without triggering systematic problems. Forth, comprehensive reforms of policy coordination were introduced, assuring macroeconomic stability, and included the intensified surveillance of member states' fiscal policies and structural reforms. The paper also points out that all that remains on the EU reform agenda is the demand for a more consistent decision-making process to accommodate the different interests among the member states, and that the European Central Bank have a more active role in financial stability and macroprudential supervision.

S. Koibuchi (✉)
Faculty of Commerce, Chuo University,
Tokyo, Japan
e-mail: koibuchi@tamacc.chuo-u.ac.jp

S. Kaji and E. Ogawa (eds.), *Who Will Provide the Next Financial Model?: Asia's Financial Muscle and Europe's Financial Maturity*,
DOI 10.1007/978-4-431-54282-7_4, 

This paper provides meaningful insights for researchers and policymakers regarding the main characteristics of EU financial regulatory development since the global financial crisis in 2007–2009. In terms of financial supervision, the global financial crisis provided two lessons: one is the necessity of integrated financial supervisory framework, especially from a macro-prudential viewpoint, which deals with systematic risk spreading through the financial system; the other is the importance of financial supervision on cross-border banking activity, especially cross-border security investments by banks. Because major European banks also suffered from huge direct losses with US subprime loans, almost comparable to those of major US banks, it was quite reasonable that the EU would swiftly begin to deal with reforms in line with the reform agenda before the outbreak of its own sovereign crises. However, as the paper documents, these attempts by the EU were continually hampered by conflict between national and supra-national interests and between Eurozone and non-Eurozone member countries. Because of these political difficulties, the current supervisory framework of the EU remains inadequate and unable to tackle the critical situation of the financial sector hit by the sovereign crises of member countries.

The inadequacy of the EU's financial supervisory framework is characterized by the lack of a truly integrated supervisory authority to cover all EU financial institutions and financial markets. The EBA, which was designed to be responsible for the European banking sector as a whole, still does not have the direct power to order bank rescues or the recapitalization of European banks while each member state's regulatory authority (national central bank) does. According to the paper, the reason for this simply comes from the lack of fiscal integration across member countries, seemingly one of the most difficult policy agendas in the Eurozone, because the cost of bank rescues and recapitalization would be primarily borne by the taxpayers of each member state. This evidence strongly suggests that despite the recent attempts to develop a regional financial regulatory framework in the EU, establishing a truly integrated and coordinated financial regulatory framework across the EU is very difficult. With hindsight, EU member countries were more diversified than the policymakers supposed at the time of the introduction of the single currency, and the degree of diversification has been further intensified during the recent sovereign crises via the widening macroeconomic performances between "peripheral" member countries and others in the Eurozone. The EU and the Eurozone still have many tasks to overcome in the field of financial supervision.

In this sense, although the second paper by Mr. Mimura argues the recent development of policy coordination in Asia in terms of financial supervision, regional cooperation in Asia still remains at the preliminary stage, still seeking a "single voice" in Asia. As the regional differences among Asian countries are considered much broader than across EU countries, as the paper stresses, continuing and accelerated efforts to ensure greater coordinated financial supervision across Asia are imperative because economic integration in Asia will not slow and cross-border banking activities across Asian countries will grow in the coming decades.

# Part II
# Monetary Policy

# The European Central Bank and Implications of the Sovereign Debt Crisis

**Francesco Drudi, Alain Durré, and Francesco Paolo Mongelli**

**Abstract** Since the onset of financial turmoil in August 2007, the main central banks worldwide have implemented extraordinary standard and non-standard monetary measures. Accommodative fiscal measures were also implemented on a large scale. These measures have questioned the sustainability of public finances in various euro area countries, which led to the current sovereign debt crisis. The current sovereign debt crisis is even more challenging as it affects the value of banks' assets and their collateral, and therefore increases risks to the economic outlook. Against this background, this chapter describes the actions of the European Central Bank (and their rationale) while discussing the necessary separation between the responsibilities of central banks and government. Finally, some lessons about the possible adjustment of the roles of central banks and fiscal authorities in the euro area are also addressed.

**Keywords** Crisis • ECB • Eurosystem • Fiscal policy • Monetary policy

---

This chapter was prepared for the international conference of joint research groups "EU Economy" of the EU Studies Institute on "Who will provide the next Financial Model? Asia's Financial Muscle and Europe's Financial Maturity" held in Tokyo on 10 December 2011. It reflects information and data up to mid-November 2011. Special thanks go to Piet Philip Christiansen, Adriana Lojschova and Giovanna De Salvo for their research assistance. The views expressed in this book chapter are solely those of the authors and do not necessarily reflect the views of the ECB or the Eurosystem.

F. Drudi (✉)
European Central Bank, Frankfurt am Main, Germany
e-mail: francesco.drudi@ecb.int

A. Durré
European Central Bank, Frankfurt am Main, Germany

IÉSEG-School of Management (Lille Catholic University), Lille, France
LEM-CNRS (U.M.R. 8179), Lille, France

F.P. Mongelli
European Central Bank, Frankfurt am Main, Germany

Goethe University Frankfurt, Frankfurt am Main, Germany

S. Kaji and E. Ogawa (eds.), *Who Will Provide the Next Financial Model?: Asia's Financial Muscle and Europe's Financial Maturity*,
DOI 10.1007/978-4-431-54282-7_5, 

# 1 Introduction

The financial crisis that began in August 2007 is exceptional in at least three respects: its effects on a wide range of segments of financial markets; the magnitude and speed of its negative spillover; and its mutating nature.

After the money markets dried up in August 2007, setting off financial turmoil, the resulting bankruptcy of Lehman Brothers Ltd. in September 2008 sparked a global financial crisis. This systemic event is unprecedented in terms of financial losses, economic disruption and in its geographical reach across mostly developed economies. From late 2009 to April 2010, a brief respite in the crisis was observed. However, the aftershocks were still to prove severe in Europe: from May 2010, a sovereign debt crisis began spreading across the euro area. This crisis poses severe challenges to the European Central Bank (ECB), which had to address the implications of the crisis to ensure the functioning of the transmission mechanism. The latter was significantly impaired by the malfunctioning of several bond markets. Thus, for over 4 years now the world has endured a mutating financial crisis. While recalling the main phases of the ongoing crisis, this chapter provides some reflection on the link between fiscal policy and monetary policy, and focuses on the response of the ECB, in particular during the period that was most affected by the sovereign debt crisis.

Overall, policy responses were equally exceptional throughout the financial crisis. The main central banks worldwide implemented standard and non-standard monetary measures (often in coordination). Accommodative fiscal policies were also adopted on a large scale to support economic activity and employment, and to recapitalize the financial system. Global regulatory and supervisory systems have been turned around; the G20 has acquired new vigor; and the International Monetary Fund (IMF) was revitalized and is now involved in three adjustment programs in the euro area. Moreover, many established convictions were shattered and perceptions regarding systemic risks changed; thus, many long-held views and various economic paradigms are being revisited, and several important lessons have been learned.

The economic, financial and institutional environment has changed in Europe and will continue to change. The ECB has been among the advocates for structural reforms where needed, tighter fiscal, macro surveillance and more uniform financial regulations. Moreover, it has contributed to the debate on the reform of micro and macro financial supervision as well as the creation of facilities for crisis management and resolution in the euro area. Thus the ECB and the national central banks (NCBs) of the euro area—together representing the Eurosystem—have actively contributed to a dialogue that is pushing forward European integration. Slowly, various pieces of a large puzzle are falling into place. However, the institutional framework is still evolving and several elements will require further work.

This chapter is organized as follows. In Sect. 2 we discuss the interaction between monetary and fiscal dominance against the background of financial stability concerns. In Sect. 3 we review the main phases of the financial crisis. In Sect. 4 we explain the main motivations for the measures undertaken by the ECB. As the crisis remains ongoing, many elements of this chapter are still preliminary. Other caveats will be mentioned throughout the chapter. All in all, the current juncture is one that holds great potentials but still entails diverse risks.

# 2 The Interaction Between Monetary and Fiscal Dominance Against a Background of Financial Stability Concerns

## 2.1 *Theoretical Background*

The interaction between monetary and fiscal authorities has long been debated in academic literature. There are various aspects, from an optimal policy mix to the possible rigidities (and financial costs) that one may have on the other. The latter aspect of the question—which arguably may be seen as the fundamental question of the (monetary vs. fiscal) dominance on a central bank's balance sheet—usually receives growing attention during crisis times. A renewed interest has recently emerged in several economies in light of the magnitude of the exceptional measures undertaken by central banks.

By assuming greater responsibilities, a risk exists that a central bank may go beyond its strict mandate, possibly setting the roots for unstable inflation dynamics through various mechanisms. In practice, this may happen with quasi-fiscal activities undertaken by the central bank, which has historically been associated with macroeconomic instability. In this respect, Hamilton (2009) points out that: *every hyperinflation in history has two ingredients: ... a fiscal debt for which there was no politically feasible ability to pay with tax increases or spending cuts [and] a central bank that was drawn into the task of creating money as the only way to meet the obligations that the fiscal authority could not.*

The likelihood of such non-monetary activities by the central bank might be related to the specific and unique position that central banks usually have as a lender of last resort. As financial crises demand rapid policy responses from existing institutions and endanger financial stability, it is natural to expect the central bank to play an essential role, especially if the crisis at stake is caused by market distortions that ultimately create a liquidity shortage (see also the historical discussion in Goodhart (2011)). The related underlying reasoning, originally stated by Thornton (1802) and further defined by Bagehot (1873), assumes that a fractional/fragmented banking system is even more sensitive to large (liquidity) shocks that can generate panic phenomena, which eventually cause a significant decrease in the money stock, and inducing a collapse in economic activity. In this regard, given their ability to provide an elastic supply of liquidity, central banks are uniquely well placed to avoid such developments by issuing their own monetary liabilities. At the same time, the sentiment according to which central banks may be faster to respond than any other institution has probably been strengthened over time by the shift towards central bank independence (even translated in some cases into legal texts) in the late twentieth century.[1]

By funding these activities, central banks bear risk exposures (and financial costs) that would not necessarily be so in the strict context of monetary policies. Thus, a distinction should be made between liquidity support and solvency support. Pure monetary policies would definitively justify the former (which in turn aims at preserving price stability) while policies supporting the latter contain quasi-fiscal ingredients (which could often be (erroneously) presented as responding to financial stability concerns but would be hardly compatible with the primacy attached to the price stability objective).

In his analysis of the exceptional measures undertaken by the US Federal Reserve, Goodfriend (2011) distinguishes between monetary policy (aiming at controlling the stock of high-power money), interest-on-reserves policy (a novelty for the US central bank but with a long history for European central banks) and credit policy. By credit policy, he refers to portfolio choices on the central bank balance sheet that do not necessarily influence the stock of reserves, e.g., by affecting mostly the composition of the assets held by the central bank. Through this type of policy, Goodfriend (2011) argues that, by acting as an intermediary between private borrowers and lenders, the central bank is engaged in a distributional activity, which exposes itself (and ultimately tax payers and/or money holders) to financial losses. In the latter case, the ability of the central bank to absorb financial losses without altering the conduct of monetary policy then depends on its financial soundness or, to put it differently, the ability of the central bank to have sufficient financial resources over time to pursue its policy.

In the academic literature, two main options are usually discussed in this respect. A first option is that the central bank, benefiting from its monopoly of money issuance, may cover losses by issuing new monetary liabilities, which would dilute the real value of money over time. The second option directly refers to the guarantee (explicit or implicit) that a central bank may receive from its main shareholder, i.e., the government. In this case the central bank would be able to support financial losses from the implementation of risky activities assuming that the government will always recapitalize the central bank in the future when needed. As pointed out by Buiter (2008), both options suffer from limits in practice. On the one hand, it could be reasonably assumed that there is in reality an upper limit to the extraction of resources from an inflation tax. As from a certain point, if monetary liabilities become too large with respect to private agents' needs, the price level will increase and, through expectations of higher inflation in the future, money demand will diminish further, possibly leading to unstable and

[1] This evolution in the thinking on central banking came from growing criticisms by academics in the 1970s and 1980s about political control over central banks (and exploited at large the associated central bank quasi-fiscal powers), which usually led to high inflation and an inefficient allocation of credit to favoured economic sectors. In particular, works initiated by Kydland and Prescott (1977) and Barro and Gordon (1983), and empirically supported by Alesina and Summers (1993), point to possible benefits in terms of macroeconomic performance (notably as regards the level and variability of inflation rate) in case of more independent central banks.

erratic inflation paths.[2] On the other hand, it could also be argued that the taxation power of governments may also face an upper limit, which would erode the credibility of the recapitalization prospects over time. In this context, once economic agents realize that the fiscal limit is reached (i.e., no further possibility of expenditure cuts or tax increases), this may feed into expectations of passive monetary policy, which will imply unstable and volatile inflation rates.[3]

Despite the necessary simplification that such models may contain, their strength lies in the ability to emphasize the significant impact that the interaction between government and the central bank may have on macroeconomic developments. In particular, when the central bank embarks in a variety of activities that may imply the assumption of larger risk, it is likely that its controllability of inflation will be eroded over time; hence, similarly affecting the credibility of its price stability objective. Even within a framework where quasi-fiscal activities might be financed by capitalization of present and future monetary income, there are good reasons to think that the upper non-inflationary limit of these types of activities will be breached at some point.[4]

## 2.2 *Where Do We Stand in the Euro Area?*

### 2.2.1 Treaty Provisions

To avoid any interference with the primary objective of price stability assigned to the ECB, a prohibition of monetary financing and privileged access (of public sector to financial sectors) has been introduced in the Treaty establishing the Functioning of the European Union (TFEU).[5]

By its nature, the prohibition of monetary financing places limits on the scope for central bank action to support governments facing financing problems. It is precisely these limits that protect the integrity of the Eurosystem's balance sheet and thus

---

[2] This first strand of literature refers to models of seignoriage as initially discussed by Cagan (1956).

[3] This second strand of literature refers to works within the fiscal theory of price level framework. See, for instance, Leeper (1991), Sims (1994), Woodford (1995), and more recently Leeper (2010).

[4] On the basis of a New Keynesian DSGE type of model, Durré and Pill (2010) find that a third equilibrium regime (besides a regime of pure monetary dominance and a regime of fiscal dominance) may exist under strict conditions. However, (implicit or explicit) pressures from fiscal authorities may be such that these conditions appear difficult to respect in practice. For a discussion on the risks of financial dominance see BIS (2011) and Borio (2011).

[5] Under Article 123(1) of the TFEU (which prohibits monetary financing), the ECB and the national central banks (NCBs) are prohibited from purchasing debt instruments directly from public sector's institutions or bodies, i.e., debt instruments issued in the primary market. The acquisition by NCBs or the ECB of debt instruments issued by all public sector institutions or bodies in the secondary market is, in principle, allowed. However, in accordance with Recital 7 of Council Regulation (EC) 3603/93, 13 December 1993, specifying definitions for the application of the prohibitions referred to in Articles 104 and 104b (1) of the Treaty (now labeled Articles 123 and 124 of the TFEU), such purchases must not be used to circumvent the objective of Article 123. This qualification also applies to marketable debt instruments issued by all community institutions or bodies.

preserve the independence and credibility of the single monetary policy. In the absence of such institutional safeguards, a danger exists that so-called "fiscal dominance" over the price level may emerge, with monetary policy becoming subservient to the needs of the fiscal authorities, and thus unable to focus on its primary objective of maintaining price stability in the euro area. In this sense, the prohibition of monetary financing supports the credibility of the Eurosystem and the monetary policy of the ECB. Moreover, the prohibition of monetary financing helps to strengthen fiscal discipline and thereby promote the functioning of the Monetary Union. See also Issing (2010), Hodson (2010), and Hodson and Quaglia (2009).

### 2.2.2 The Policy of the ECB

In the implementation of its policy the ECB followed two basic principles to avoid the risk that its policy could be seen as dictated by "fiscal motivation", which could undermine its credibility.

First, regarding the conduct of monetary policy, it remains crucial for the central bank to have a transparent and well-defined policy objective that is perfectly understood and readily accepted by economic agents. The uniqueness of focusing on price stability is from the ECB viewpoint the best way to credibly contribute to growth and economic and financial stability. In this regard, recent experience shows that flexibility and pragmatism remain essential in the assessment of the monetary policy stance to make the right interest rate decisions at the appropriate time. In the case of the ECB, such an assessment is mainly based on two elements: (1) the formation of a view on the medium-term inflation outlook and, in particular, the risks to price stability, based on the interaction of supply and demand in various markets (economic analysis); and (2) the identification of the monetary impulses from current and past monetary policy decisions, taking into account that these impulses are always transmitted to the economy with a certain lag via a thorough assessment of money and credit developments (monetary analysis). While the first perspective (economic analysis) would support the assessment of risks to price stability over a short- to medium-term horizon, the second perspective (monetary analysis) would focus on medium- to long-term horizons.

It is clear that monetary policy decisions may only affect the developments of economic variables in the intended way if financial markets efficiently transmit the initial monetary impulses along the yield curve. This requires the proper functioning of not only the money markets but also certain segments of financial markets. If this condition is not met, timely pragmatism from the central bank will again be needed in the future to ensure that the monetary policy transmission channel continues to work effectively, while at the same time continuing to assess the appropriateness of the monetary policy stance given changes in the economic environment. It is through this prism that the (both standard and non-standard) crisis period measures taken by the ECB must be understood. In exceptional circumstances, when severe distortions in financial markets emerge (reflected, for instance, in volatile and rising money market spreads), a more proactive form of liquidity management by the central bank is required in order not to jeopardize the central bank's main monetary policy objective and the understanding of the monetary policy by economic agents.

Therefore, the first key element required to understand the rationale for the non-standard measures taken by the ECB (as further illustrated in the two following sections) is that these measures were dictated by the need to guarantee that the monetary policy decisions of the ECB were appropriately reflected in the financing conditions of the economy. This is a key pre-requisite to ensure that monetary policy is able to operate and maintain price stability over the medium-term.

A second key feature is the risk management framework, which shapes the implementation of the monetary policy of the ECB. Since its inception, the ECB established a comprehensive risk management framework, which limits the risk taken on the balance sheet of the central bank, in a way that ensures it is equal to its risk-absorbing capacity. The main elements of this framework[6] include the establishment of a list of eligible assets to be used as collateral in central bank refinancing operations, a policy of valuation of collateral that takes into account market and credit risk and, through additional haircuts, liquidity risk. This is complemented by a policy of eligible counterparts that need to satisfy criteria of financial soundness. In the same vein, with regard to outright operations, the ECB limits its purchase to issuers whose risk is contained, as reflected in their rating or on the basis of additional considerations which relate, for example, to the existence of macroeconomic adjustment programs. Finally, the Eurosystem—which designs the operational framework for implementing the monetary policy of the ECB and includes the ECB and the national central banks of the euro area—has substantial financial buffers, such as its capital and reserves. It should also not be forgotten that a large part of the liability of the Eurosystem is in the form of banknotes, which increases the income generating capacity of the Eurosystem.

Overall, the two previous principles (namely a clear policy objective and appropriate risk management), relying on efficient transmission mechanisms, are essential to guarantee the credibility of the ECB and to maintain the effectiveness of its monetary policy.

## 3 A Chronological Bird's Eye View of the 2007–2011 Financial Crisis

The onset of the financial turmoil in August 2007 shocked everybody because of the extreme stability of financial developments during the preceding 10–15 years; a period often labeled as the *great moderation.* Yet, with the benefit of hindsight, one could recognize that this period was in fact characterized by extensive global

[6] For a more detailed review of the collateral rules of the Eurosystem, see ECB (2011), Chapter 6, pp. 45–81.

imbalances, as well as the spread of poorly understood and misused financial innovations. It is likely to be a combination of these dynamics that led to the build-up of global systemic risks, which were particularly intense in the 2004–2007 period.[7] This provided the conditions for an amplification effect after the trigger went off; i.e., the collapse of US sub-prime mortgages. In this regard, it could be argued that there is no single explanation for the financial crisis.

Once the tensions in the euro area money markets emerged, it was natural for the ECB to forcefully intervene as the distribution of liquidity between market participants was severely distorted, and therefore potentially endangered the stability of the whole banking system. One of the striking features of this crisis is its mutating character in the various phases; this affected the liquidity position of the banks in each step through various channels. Consequently, it was necessary for the ECB to adjust over time the nature of its standard and non-standard measures to tackle the roots of the prevailing tensions and their impact.

## 3.1 Financial Turmoil: 9 August 2007–14 September 2008

Concerns over the money markets began to emerge in early 2007, notably with the increase in subprime mortgage defaults in the US in February 2007. Then a severe liquidity crisis in the money markets erupted on 9 August 2007 following the decision of a big euro area money market player, BNP Paribas, to freeze redemptions for three of its investment funds. Towards the end of 2007–early 2008, tensions grew in the financial markets due to write-downs by financial institutions in both the US and Europe, along with concerns about the soundness of monoline insurers and the rescue of Bear Stearns by the US Federal Reserve and JP Morgan Chase (see Brunnermeier 2009 for more details). These events led to widening money market spreads across major economies between unsecured (i.e., InterBank Offered Rates, (BOR))[8] and secured (i.e., Overnight Index Swap, (OIS)) interest rates, reflecting the heightened uncertainty of market participants (Fig. 1). Such a "confidence crisis" among market participants reflected uncertainty about the financial soundness of financial institutions and also uncertainty about the possible impact of tensions on aggregated liquidity availability. Thus, the conditions of a normal liquid market were no longer fulfilled (see McCauley 2009).

Given the possible implications of disrupted trading activity in the money market for the transmission of monetary policy, the ECB promptly intervened by increasing the size and number of its refinancing operations. Even though it took some time

[7] Between 2003 and 2007, the volume of US sub-primes mortgages increased by almost 300%, from $332 billion to $1.3 trillion. Most financial institutions continued believing that US house prices would continue to rise, interests would remain low, and households would continue servicing their mortgages.

[8] Note that this reference interest rate for the unsecured segment of the euro area money market is called the EURo InterBank Offered Rate (EURIBOR) and that of the US and UK money market is called the London InterBank Offered Rate (LIBOR).

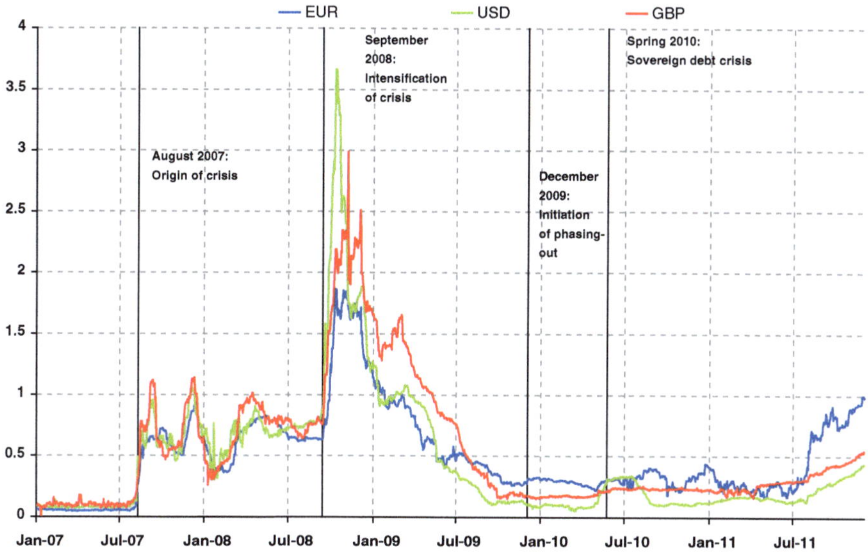


**Fig. 1** Money market spreads in the euro area, UK and US (weekly averages, basis points). Source: Reuters and ECB calculations. Note: Spreads are the difference between the 3-month EURIBOR/LIBOR and the Overnight Index Swap rates

before the ECB formally committed to fully accommodate the liquidity demands of the counterparties, a full allotment procedure was implemented in practice.

The goal of the ECB during this phase was to reassure market participants of their access to liquidity while aiming to steer the Euro OverNight Index Average (EONIA) close to the minimum bid rate in spite of the augmented volatility of money market interest rates. In this regard, the implementation of the ECB monetary policy was mainly based on the so-called front-loading of the fulfillment of the minimum reserve requirements without significant excess liquidity.[9] In practice, this procedure implied a rapid accumulation in reserves at the beginning of the reserve maintenance period on banks' current accounts held at the ECB, with a gradual decrease towards the end of the reserve maintenance period.[10]

[9] The net recourse to the standing facilities (i.e., the difference between the amounts on the marginal lending and on the deposit facility) during this first phase was rather low, i.e., a daily average of approximately EUR 0.25 billion during most of the reserve maintenance period with a peak of EUR 1.5 billion during the final week.

[10] As recalled in Cassola et al. (2008), by reducing the probability of banks' recourse to borrowing at elevated interest rates in the unsecured money market and by increasing the probability of being "locked-in", this procedure contained the upward pressures on the short-term interest rates in the money market. At the same time, liquidity draining fine-tuning operations (FTOs) were conducted during and at the end of the reserve maintenance period to mop up the remaining liquidity surplus and to support the expectations of the overnight interest rate being close to the minimum bid rate, i.e., the main ECB policy rate. Thus, the majority of the FTOs conducted during that period were liquidity-absorbing operations as reported in Cassola et al. (2011).

This first phase of the crisis is also characterized by intense cooperation among major central banks to alleviate tensions in cross-border money markets, in the US and the euro area in particular. Indeed, towards the end of 2007, significant tensions also occurred in the US money markets, partly reflecting a reduced access of EU banks to short-term liquidity in USD. Consequently, euro area banks had a tendency to bid more aggressively for the refinancing operations of the ECB and/or in the euro area money market, when possible, before embarking in FOREX swap transactions to convert the EUR into USD. This also created further tensions in the euro area money market. The ECB and the US Federal Reserve thus decided to take joint action by offering USD funding to Eurosystem counterparties as of 12 December 2007, leading to the establishment of the USD Term Auction Facility against ECB-eligible collateral. Similar actions were also taken at a later date with other central banks, notably the Swiss National Bank.

Last but not least, while the non-standard measures only tackled the distortions in the distribution of liquidity in the money market, the ECB had no compelling reason to change its monetary policy stance during the first phase of the crisis in light of the resilient economic environment.

## *3.2 The Global Financial Crisis: 15 September 2008–7 May 2010*

Tensions in financial markets escalated again with the nationalization of GSE Freddie Mac and Fanny Mae on 7 September 2008, and they exploded with the bankruptcy of the US company Lehman Brothers Ltd. on 15 September 2008. All financial institutions without exception suddenly became vulnerable as the Lehman's collapse destroyed the market's faith in the implicit "too big to fail" warranty. Consequently, market participants in the money markets, especially in Europe and in the US, hoarded massive liquidity to protect their balance sheets and avoid the situation of a liquidity shortage. Major central banks, including the ECB, then significantly increased their intermediation role with the introduction of non-standard measures (in the form of unlimited provision via short- to long-term collateralized refinancing operations) and/or conducted programs of (public and private) securities purchases.[11]

Between September 2008 and November 2009, the ECB took several bold non-standard measures to increase the provision of liquidity and thus restore confidence among market participants. First, a rollover of the supplementary term refinancing operations (conducted on an ad-hoc basis in the previous phase) on top of regular (1-week and 3-month) operations and the introduction of three additional liquidity-providing longer-term refinancing operations (LTROs) with a maturity of 1 year. Second, all refinancing operations were conducted on the basis of a fixed rate with full allotment procedures, and FTOs were discontinued (with the exception of one-day

[11] See among others Reinhart and Reinhart (2010) and Gagnon et al. (2010).

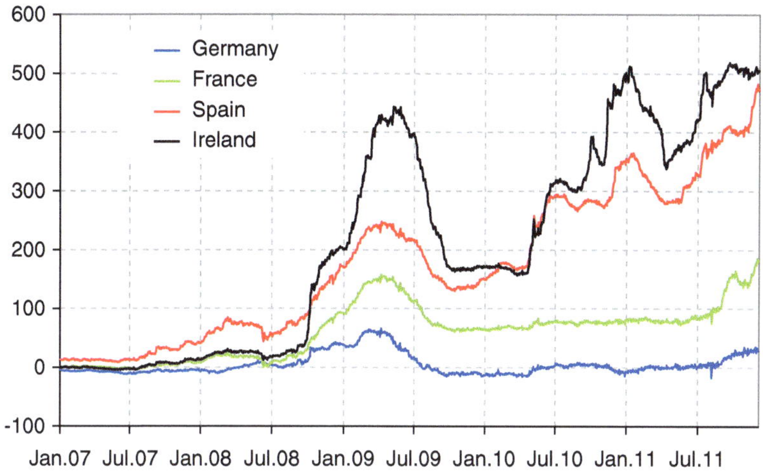


**Fig. 2** Covered bond spreads against 5-year swap rate (daily, basis points). Source: Reuters

liquidity-absorbing FTOs on the last day of the reserve maintenance period). Third, the interest rate corridor of standing facilities was temporarily narrowed (between October 2008 and January 2009). Fourth, the eligibility criteria for collateral were temporarily extended and, in addition, the credit threshold for eligibility was lowered from A- to BBB- for marketable assets (except ABS) and non-marketable assets (with an additional haircut). In the same vein, the list of counterparties was also extended for some operations. Fifth, international coordination with other central banks was reinforced, notably through an increase of swap arrangements and agreements on repurchase transactions. Last but not least, the ECB decided, in light of growing tensions in the covered bank bond market in the euro area (Fig. 2), to establish a monetary policy outright portfolio with the covered bonds purchase program (CBPP) of EUR 60 billion.[12]

At the same time, a sharp fall in trade credits and global trade, the prospect of disorderly deleveraging, bankruptcies and eventually rising financing costs due to market tensions negatively impacted on growth and price expectations, leading to massive revisions of economic projections and inflation expectations (see Fig. 3).

As a result, the ECB decided to change its monetary policy stance using standard measures by reducing the minimum bid rate in a sequence of steps from 4.25% to a record low of 1% between 8 October 2008 and 13 May 2009. Other key ECB interest rates were similarly adjusted while keeping the interest rate on the deposit facility in positive territory (at 0.25%) to allow some interbank activity (Fig. 4).

[12] These tensions were due to the difficulties experienced by some credit institutions, and played an important role in the banks' debt instruments market in the euro area. They materialized through increasing covered bond spreads against the swap rate, reaching a peak in April/May 2009 (see Fig. 2).

**Fig. 3** Break-even inflation rate (daily, % p.a.). Source: Reuters

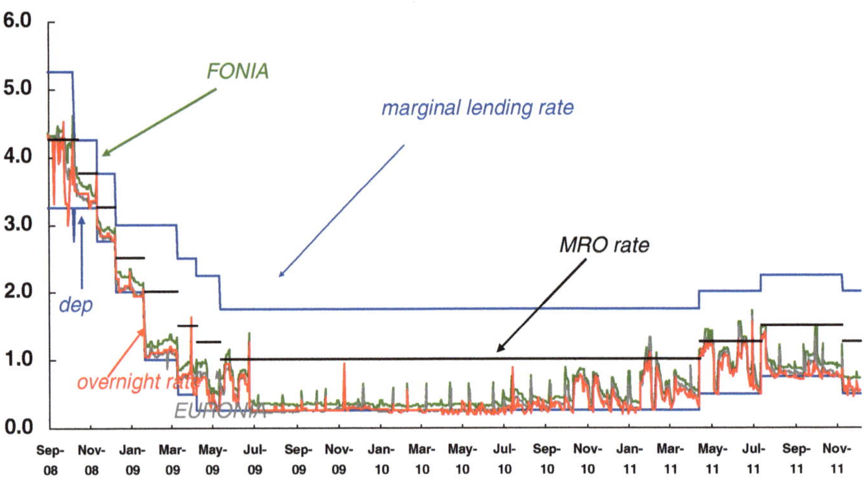


**Fig. 4** ECB interest rates and money market rates (percentages per annum; daily data). Source: ECB, Reuters

During this period, the ECB aimed to reassure market participants regarding their access to liquidity via a further increase of its intermediation role in the money market, and by adjusting its policy stance with the downward revision of growth and price prospects. By making the supply of liquidity endogenous through the full

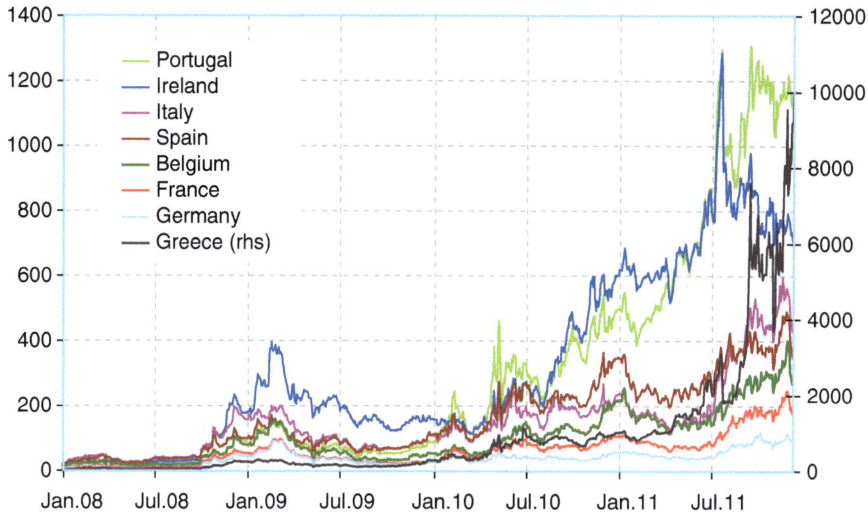


**Fig. 5** Sovereign CDS premium (daily, basis points). Source: Reuters

allotment procedure, the ECB allowed the occurrence of excess liquidity while signaling its monetary policy stance with the level of the key ECB interest rates. As illustrated by Fig. 4, money market interest rates remained at very low levels with the EONIA reaching its lower bound, i.e., very close to the deposit rate.

## 3.3 *Sovereign Debt Crisis: Today*

Yet a new phase of the global financial crisis was brewing. While money market distortions started to recede, tensions regarding the public finances of some euro area countries emerged in November 2009. Eventually such tensions exacerbated in April/May 2010. The roots of these tensions started with Greece where the newly elected government began a huge revision of the public deficit left by the former coalition in early November 2009.[13] Consequently, the Credit Default Swap (CDS) premium for Greece began to pick up in late 2009, together with the spreads between its 10-year government bonds relative to German bonds (Fig. 5). These tensions mainly reflected growing market concerns about the sustainability

---

[13] The previously underestimated Greek public deficit was made possible by off-balance sheet operations and a lack of transparency in budget data. The desire for clarity by the newly elected government led to a revision of the public deficit from 8.2% to 12.5% of Greece's gross domestic product released on 1 November 2009.

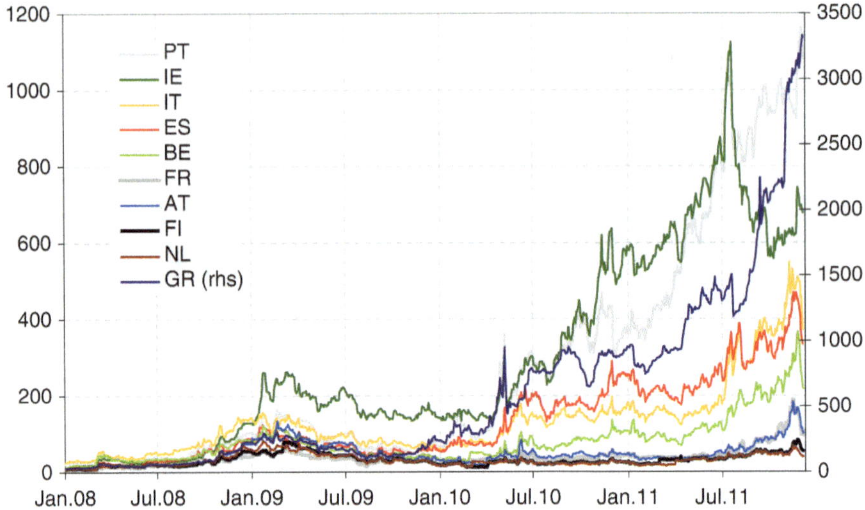


**Fig. 6** Ten-year Government bond spreads against 10-year German bonds (basis points; daily data). Source: Reuters, authors' calculations. Note: The abbreviations denote the following countries: Portugal (PT), Ireland (IE), Italy (IT), Spain (ES), Belgium (BE), France (FR), Austria (AT), Finland (FI), The Netherlands (NL) and Greece (GR). This convention is also applicable to all figures

of public finances in view of rising government deficits and debt. In early 2010 similar concerns affected the bond pricing of other euro area countries leading to similar developments (i.e., increasing sovereign CDS premiums and widening spreads against the corresponding German bond, see Figs. 5 and 6).

As a result, the first financial package (EUR 110 billion) by the EU /IMF to Greece was announced on 2 May 2010.[14] In light of these developments, the ECB decided to temporarily freeze the rating of marketable debt instruments issued or guaranteed by the Greek government and used as eligible collateral in the refinancing operations of the ECB.[15]

On 7 May 2010, spreads against German government bond yields recorded a first high (Fig. 6), whilst CDS premia on euro area government debt peaked (see Fig. 5). Secondary markets for several sovereign bonds dried up, which in turn affected the

[14] At that time, the agreement was that the IMF would provide under a 3-year program EUR 30 billion through the stand-by arrangement while the EU would provide EUR 80 billion over the same period. This program was subject to strong conditions to restore fiscal sustainability and improve the country's competitiveness.
See further details at http://www.imf.org/external/pubs/ft/survey/so/2010/car050210a.htm.

[15] See the decision of the ECB of 6 May 2010 on temporary measures relating to the eligibility of marketable debt instruments issued or guaranteed by the Greek Government (ECB/2010/3), available at http://www.ecb.europa.eu/ecb/legal/date/2010/html/index.en.html.

activity in both the money market and the covered bond market (Figs. 1 and 2). As shown in Figs. 12, 13, 14 and 15 in the Appendix trading volumes in the EONIA and the overnight repo market decreased while the EURIBOR-OIS spreads widened at various maturities, and both short- and long-term volatilities started to pick up again (both for the EURIBOR and OIS segments). Beyond the likely impairment that tensions in the bond markets could cause to the transmission of monetary policy, these particular tensions in the euro area sovereign debt market had the potential to create huge distortions in the liquidity distribution within the banking system in all euro area jurisdictions, notably through the impact of tensions among collateral values used for secured interbank operations. Indeed, the falling prices of several public debt instruments could worsen the financial distress seen in the banks' balance sheets by reducing the value of their asset portfolio, and hence further weakening their financial and liquidity position. This in turn reinforced the uncertainty of market participants regarding the financial soundness of their potential counterparties, and supported an increased recourse to central bank refinancing and liquidity hoarding.

To address the renewed tensions in the money market and to ensure a continued smooth transmission of monetary policy decisions along the yield curve, the ECB decided on 10 May 2010 to conduct interventions in the euro area public and private debt securities markets through secondary market purchases from credit institutions under the Securities Markets Programme (SMP). In addition, some adjustments in the design of the liquidity operations were also adopted.[16] In coordination with other central banks, the temporary liquidity swap arrangements were also reactivated, thus resuming USD liquidity-providing operations on the basis of fixed rate with full allotment procedures against ECB-eligible collateral at terms of seven and eighty-four days. Figure 7 illustrates the evolution of the cumulative SMP purchases since the onset of this measure.

On 9 May 2010, EU finance ministers established the European Financial Stability Facility (EFSF), with a volume of up to EUR 500 billion (EUR 440 billion from the lending capacity of the facility combined with loans up to EUR 60 billion from the European Financial Stabilisation Mechanism), although, to preserve the very high credit standing of the EFSF, the lending capacity was significantly less. The IMF committed an additional EUR 250 billion, bringing the total to EUR 750 billion.[17]

In the reminder of 2010 and in early 2011, tensions escalated further. Bond yields on Irish and Portuguese government bonds reached levels that gradually led to a loss of market access. This, and the difficult public finance situation, led to an agreement

---

[16] In particular, it was decided to conduct fixed-term (i.e., with a maturity of 7 days) liquidity-absorbing FTOs to create incentives among credit institutions to have more active liquidity management. Moreover, it was decided to apply the fixed rate with full allotment procedure to the regular 3-month LTROs to be allotted on 26 May and 30 June (which will be further prolonged until at least the end of January 2011) and to conduct one single 6-month LTRO with full allotment and a fixed rate indexed to the average of the minimum bid rate at the main refinancing operations over the life of the LTRO.

[17] On 10 May the EU announced that the IMF was ready to provide up to EUR 250 billion to supplement its own EUR 500 billion stabilisation fund to support the euro area's weaker Member States.

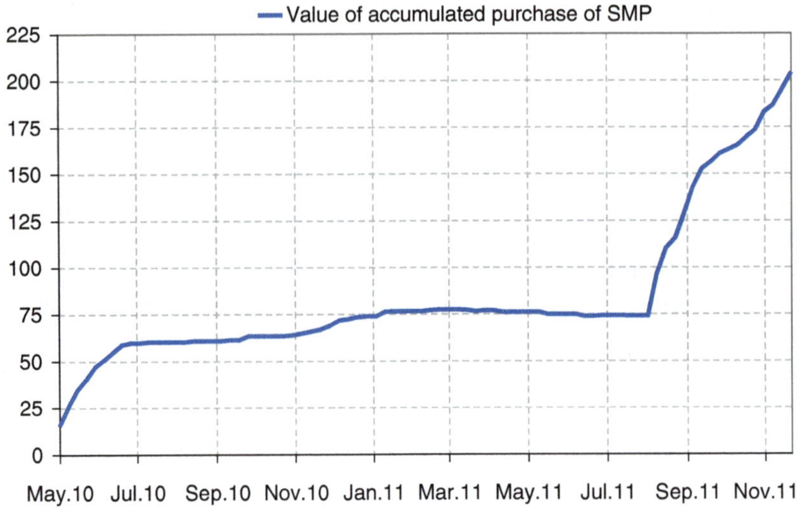


**Fig. 7** Size of securities market programme (SMP). Source: ECB

for two further EU/IMF programs in November 2010 for Ireland and February 2011 for Portugal.

The agreement on the new programs and the general macroeconomic situation in the euro area and elsewhere contributed greatly to the stabilization in financial markets. Interventions under the SMP also were suspended for several months (see Fig. 7). As the assessment of the outlook for price stability gradually pointed to the emergence of upside risks to price stability, the ECB decided to increase its key rate twice, in April and July 2011, each time by 25 basis points.

The tensions regarding the Greek situation, however, did not abate, and slippages in the implementation of the Greek program soon gave rise to concerns as to the sustainability of public finance in Greece. On a political level, the orientation gradually emerged in favor of supporting private sector involvement (PSI) actions with the aim to lengthen the maturity structure of Greek government debt and reduce its cost over time. In this environment, government bond yields increased markedly in several euro area countries and tensions spread to various segments of the financial markets. Figure 8 illustrates the severe fluctuations in equity markets, both in terms of severe gyrations in stock markets indices as well as implied volatilities. In the same vein, volatility in the money market significantly increased again (see Fig. 15 in the Appendix).

On 21 July 2011, to address the difficult situation, the EU Heads of State or Government of the euro area agreed to a more flexible use of the EFSF resources to include secondary market purchases as well the recapitalization of banks.[18] The effective lending capacity of the EFSF was also expanded and broad elements for PSI in Greece were outlined.

[18] On 29 September 2011 the German Parliament approved the strengthened EFSF and a few weeks later the Slovakian Parliament ratified it as well.

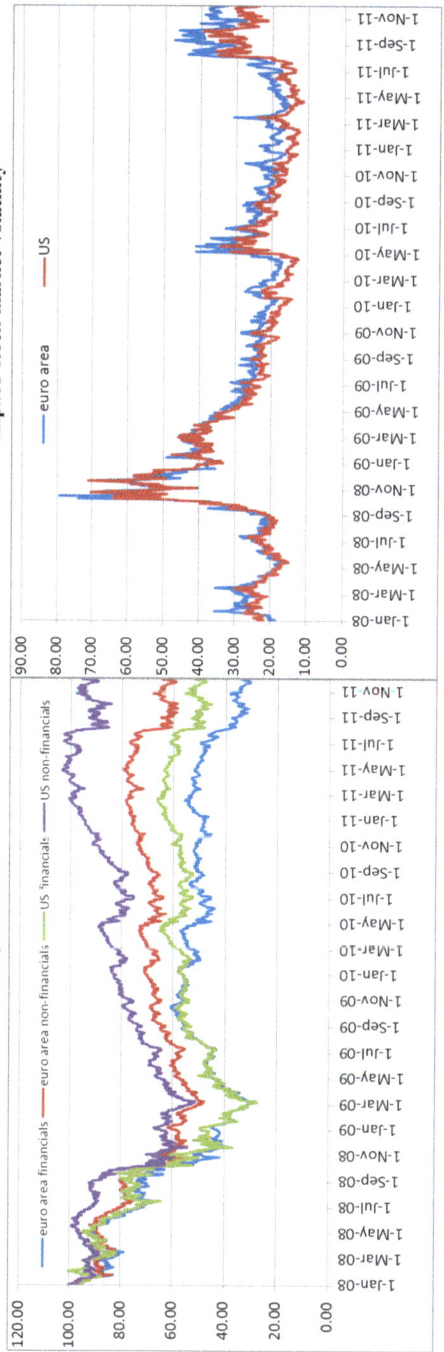


**Fig. 8** Developments in stock markets in the United States and euro area. Source: Datastream, Bloomberg. Note: Stock price indices are rebased on 1 January 2010

These actions were not followed by the stabilization of the financial markets. The ECB, at its regular Governing Council meeting on 4 August 2011, announced a further 6-month refinancing operation and to prolong the allotment of liquidity with a fixed rate full allotment procedure until the end of the fourth quarter of 2011. Three days later, on 7 August 2011 following an extraordinary Governing Council meeting, the ECB announced that it would actively implement the SMP. The pace of purchases significantly increased in the subsequent period; between early August and early December, the size of the weekly fine-tuning operations (which are regularly conducted by the ECB to sterilize the interventions conducted in the context of the SMP and are a good proxy for the amount of overall purchases) increased to over EUR 20 billion.

The further deterioration of the liquidity position of banks during 2011 due to the intensification of tensions in the euro area sovereign debt markets led the ECB to take three further non-standard measures on 6 October 2011. More specifically, the ECB decided to conduct two longer-term refinancing operations (of approximately 12 months and 13 months, respectively) and to implement a second covered bond purchase program (CBPP2) for an intended amount of EUR 40 billion, and the fixed rate tender procedure with full allotment for all refinancing operations was extended to mid-2012.

Finally, amid the deterioration of soft economic indicators and growth expectations during the first half of 2011, the ECB further decided at its meeting on 3 November 2011 to decrease its key interest rates by 25 basis points. A key factor in the reassessment of the outlook for inflation was that the financial market tensions were associated with a tightening in financing conditions in the euro area; this was related in part to the consequences of the sovereign debt crisis.

## 4 What Is the Reasoning Behind the ECB Policy Decisions?

In the face of the challenges posed by the mutating 2007–2011 global financial crisis, major central banks worldwide were innovative in terms of the instruments they used, going beyond traditional and standard monetary policy instruments (i.e., changes to central banks' interest rates). In each country, the nature of the operations reflected the key features of the corresponding banking system.[19]

In the case of the ECB, its actions during the crisis were implemented on the basis of the so-called "separation principle", which allows for a clear distinction of the motivations behind the standard measures and those driving the non-standard ones. In practice, a clear distinction is maintained between standard measures on key policy interest rates (i.e., the determination of the monetary policy

[19] In this regard, it is worth recalling the importance of banks in the external funding of non-financial corporations in the euro area (80% of total funding) in comparison with the US (40%). Consequently, most of the instruments used by the ECB took the form of direct financing to banks whereas the US Federal Reserve implemented several asset purchase programmes in larger amounts.

stance that aims in turn to deliver price stability) and non-standard measures on liquidity refinancing operations (which may also support the functioning of the money market on top of the implementation of the monetary policy stance). Within this framework, the actions of the ECB since August 2007 can be rationalized as outlined below.

Concerning the conduct of monetary policy (standard measures), ECB decisions are resolutely focused on the maintenance of price stability. In this regard, it is essential to conduct a comprehensive assessment of all the factors that impinge upon the prospects for price stability and to act in a manner that best serves its primary objective. Although the decision in July 2008 reflected concerns regarding the reinforcement of upside risks to price stability, decisions since October 2008 were governed by the likelihood that the intensification of tensions in financial markets were likely to have significant implications for the outlook for price developments and thus for the course of the monetary policy.

At the same time, it is essential that monetary policy decisions are transmitted effectively and smoothly to the economy in general, and to private sector price-setting decisions in particular (Goodhart 2011). Given the crucial role of the ECB at the start of the transmission mechanism, the transmission of monetary policy decisions requires well-functioning financial markets, the money market in particular. This latter concern is the main motivation for the introduction of non-standard measures.

Standard and non-standard measures naturally operate together. In the case of wide disruptions in the transmission mechanism, interest rate decisions would not be transmitted to the economy and would hamper the capacity of the ECB to maintain price stability. In this sense, non-standard measures aim to implement the appropriate monetary policy stance, as signaled by key ECB interest rates. This would allow the ECB to keep alive non-standard measures, if needed, while adapting interest rates according to the outlook for price stability over the medium-term.

In regard to the transmission of monetary policy decisions as reported in Fig. 9, the financial crisis that began in August 2007 had the potential to severely impair it through various channels.

First, when the supply of interbank credit becomes scarce as a result of mistrust among market participants, the cost of interbank credit, i.e., the first step in the transmission process, rises above the level that would be consistent with the desired monetary policy stance of the ECB (Fig. 1). In particular, given the crucial benchmarking role of the EURIBOR futures contacts in the determination of retail interest rates, rising costs clearly endangered the effective transmission of the monetary policy stance to banks and, subsequently, the real economy.

Second, as stated in Brousseau et al. (2009), the advent of repo operations and the entry of new players like financial institutions (pension funds, insurance companies) significantly altered the distribution of liquidity in the interbank market and its functioning, shifting from bank-centric financial systems to bank-peripheral financial systems in the wake of the disintermediation of the traditional money market. More specifically, customer deposits have shifted towards the fund management industry whereas banks increasingly borrow from money market funds using

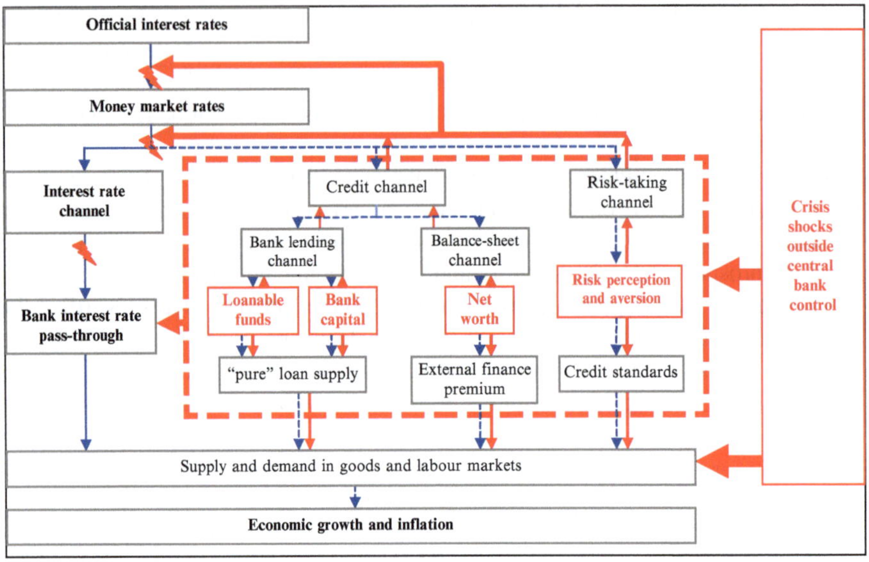


**Fig. 9** The main potential impairments in the monetary transmission mechanism

different vehicles (e.g., certificate of deposits, asset-backed securities, collateralized debt obligation, commercial papers and repo operations, among others). As this type of funding has gradually overtaken the traditional funding model of deposit from rich banks using long cash positions to place funds with interbank counterparts, banks' funding costs, and, hence, retail interest rates, have become more sensitive to developments in the market for structured finance products, the covered bond market and the market for secured interbank lending. In the same vein, with the key role of government bonds in the secured lending market (then considered as a prime source of collateral), abrupt and volatile changes in their value could also imply a sharp deterioration in banks' funding and liquidity conditions, with adverse effects on both the supply of bank loans to the real economy and their prices.

Last but not least, the prospect of a decline in banks' deposits, if not compensated by other sources of funding, may also act as an additional constraint on the asset side of the banks' balance sheets. All these elements (i.e., decreasing (or lack of) value of structured products and other financial assets) increase the likelihood of disorderly deleveraging by banks through, for example, fire sales, which may negatively impact the value of loans to the economy.

With a view to preserve the effectiveness of the interest rate, bank lending and financial asset channels, the ECB has thus increased its intermediation role through a temporary substitution of distorted market segments to ensure a continuation of bank loan provision to the real economy with conditions in line with the monetary policy stance decided by the Governing Council.

This aim has been supported by a number of tools that have been touched upon in Sect. 3, including, prominently, a definition of the collateral list, the adoption of

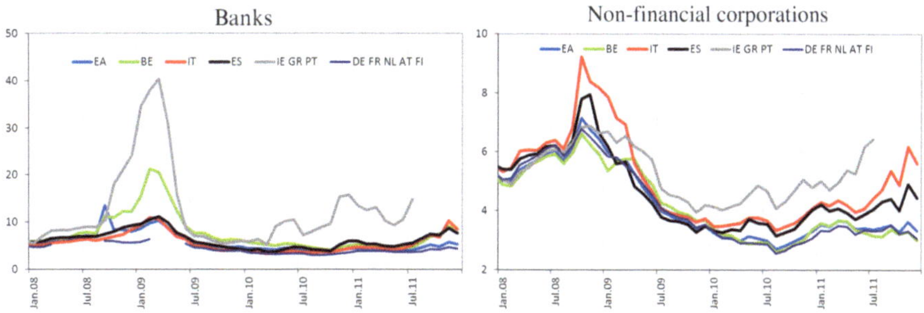


**Fig. 10** Nominal cost of market debt for the corporate sector: investment grade bonds. Source: Merrill Lynch global Index and ECB calculations. Note: Percentage per annum, average yields (January 2008 to November 2011). Country aggregates are calculated using common gross domestic product weights. Investment grade bonds issued by banks are no longer available for GR and IE since July 2010 and for PT since August 2011. Investment grade bonds issued by NFCs are no longer available for GR and IE since July 2010 and for PT since August 2011. The abbreviations denote the following countries or area: euro area (EA), Germany (DE). See also the note attached to Fig. 6

fixed-rated tenders in the allotment of liquidity, the utilization of operations with long maturities and programs for the purchases of private and public sector securities (CBPP, CBPP2 and SMP).

In this respect, it is crucial to fully understand the rationale underlying the SMP regarding what affects the support of the transmission of monetary policy. Government bond markets play a key role in affecting the financing conditions of the economy through a variety of channels. First, government bond prices are often used as a reference to price other private sector securities. Second, movements in government bond prices affect the value of security holdings in the balance sheets of banks and other private sector agents. This could affect the perceived creditworthiness of these agents and their cost of funding. A decline in the value of government bonds would also reduce the collateral available and therefore the access to funding of private sector agents.

Therefore, in the case of malfunctioning in government bond markets, the transmission of monetary policy could be severely impaired. This can be observed with the development in some financial market prices in the period of the sovereign debt crisis, as illustrated by Figs. 8, 10 and 11.

As can be seen notably in Figs. 10 and 11, in the countries most affected by the sovereign debt crisis, the financing conditions of the economy tended to tighten more.

A key question is therefore to what extent are the prices of government bonds indeed affected by malfunctioning in financial markets. This requires sound judgment on the part of the ECB, which regularly conducts a broad based assessment for this purpose. Elements of this assessment include analyses of volumes of transactions, bid-ask spreads, as well as an assessment of current fiscal positions and future ones. As indicated many times in its external communications, the ECB takes note of the commitments of governments to proceed with fiscal consolidation.

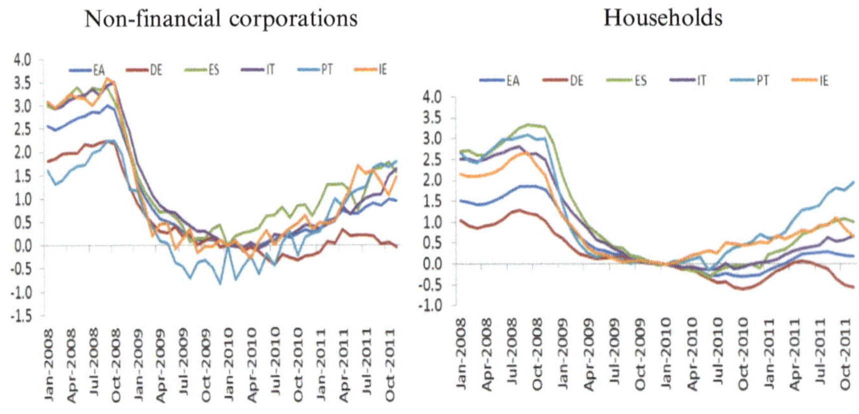


**Fig. 11** Composite bank lending rate. Source: ECB calculations. Note: Percentage per annum, realized values. The composite lending rate is a weighted average based on outstanding volumes of loans and on the assumption of floating rate share in long-term loans

## 5 Some Concluding Remarks

The role of a central bank under any circumstances, and in crisis times in particular, is to inflexibly pursue its main objective, which in the case of the ECB is price-stability. By acting decisively to deliver its main objective while communicating properly about the purpose of the non-standard measures (aimed to restore normal trading conditions without jeopardizing its main policy objective), the central bank should play the key role of an anchor of stability, which appears essential in times of stress. This approach by the central bank (to act appropriately and timely) implies the very careful analysis of any sudden unexpected shocks before it considers a change to its monetary policy stance. In the same vein, it also requires the assessment, in real-time, of the effectiveness and relevance of its actions. In this context, the absence of pre-commitment may allow more flexibility in the conduct of monetary policy by avoiding having to persist with measures that are no longer relevant or necessary. At the same time, it is the duty of the central bank not to assume the responsibilities of third parties, which suggests the removal of non-standard measures when evidence shows that they are no longer needed.

This posits the challenge of appropriately timing the process of phasing out non-conventional policies. In this regard, it is crucial that the withdrawal of support measures does not lead to renewed market tensions, and therefore it may require a gradual approach.

The ongoing sovereign debt crisis of the euro area is particularly challenging. On the one hand, one may argue that the central bank is not alone and that other agents (banks and governments) must also contribute to crisis resolution by acknowledging their responsibilities. In particular, responsible management by both financial institutions and governments is required in the future. On the other hand, in light of the impact of the sovereign debt crisis on the banking system, a gradual and pragmatic approach in addressing the tensions in this segment of financial markets is of utmost importance and represents one of the most challenging situations that the ECB has faced so far.

# Appendix

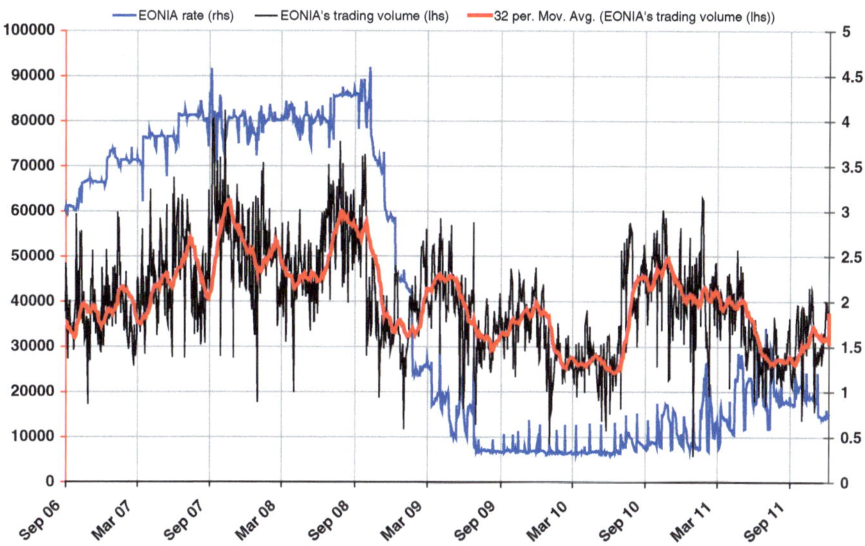


**Fig. 12** Activity and pricing in the EONIA market (daily averages). Source: ECB, Reuters

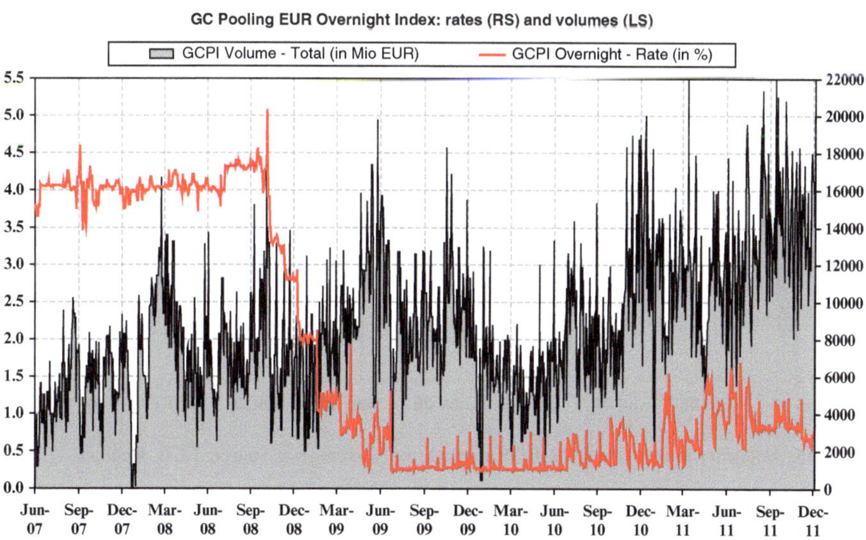


**Fig. 13** Activity and pricing in the overnight Repo market (daily averages). Source: ECB, Reuters

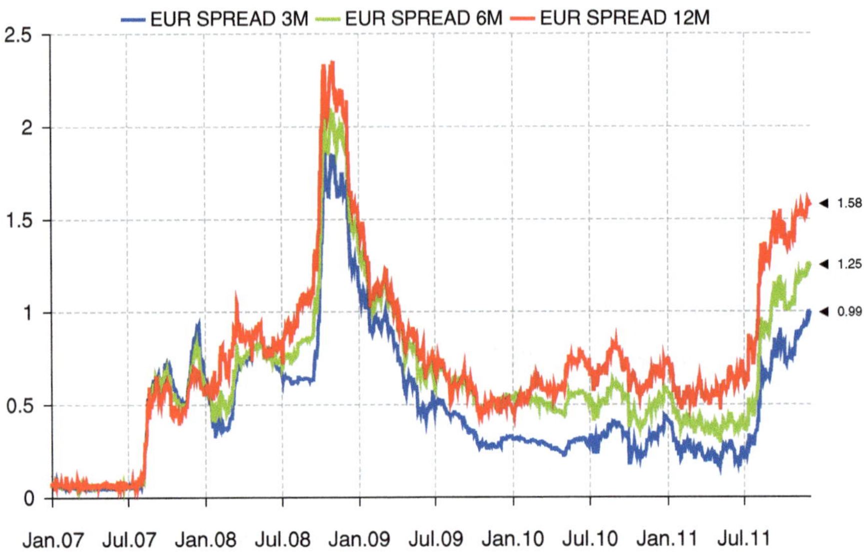


**Fig. 14** Money market spreads between EURIBOR and OIS rates in the euro area. Source: ECB, Reuters

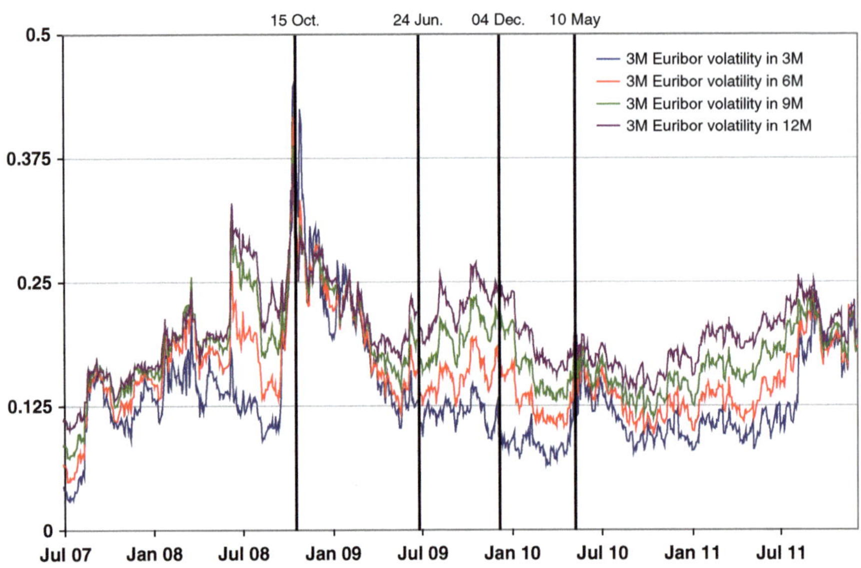


**Fig. 15** Volatility in the term EURIBOR market (daily averages). Source: ECB, Reuters

## References

Alesina A, Summers LH (1993) Central bank independence and macroeconomic performance: some comparative evidence. J Money Credit Bank 25(2):151–162

Bagehot W (1873) Lombard Street, a description of the money market, 3rd ed. Henry S. King & Co, Electronic version, London

Bank for International Settlements (BIS) (2011) Central bank governance and financial stability – a report by a study group, ("Ingves report"), June

Barro RJ, Gordon DB (1983) Rules, discretion and reputation in a model of monetary policy. J Monet Econ 12:101–121

Borio C (2011) Implementing a macroprudential framework: blending boldness and realism. Capitalism and Society 6(1):1–23. doi: 10.2202/1932-0213.1083

Brousseau V, Chailloux A, Durré A (2009) Interbank offered rate: effects of the financial crisis on the information content of the fixing, Document de travail du LEM (2009–17)

Brunnermeier M (2009) Deciphering the liquidity and credit crunch 2007–2008. J Econ Perspect 23(1):77–100

Buiter WH (2008) Central banks and financial crises, discussion paper no 619. Paper presented at the Federal Reserve Bank of Kansas City's symposium on "maintaining stability in a changing financial system", at Jackson Hole, Wyoming, on 21–23 Aug 2008

Cagan P (1956) The monetary dynamics of hyperinflation. In: Friedman M (ed) Studies in the quantity theory of money. University of Chicago Press, Chicago

Cassola N, Holthausen C, Würtz F (2008) Liquidity management under market turmoil: experience of the European Central Bank in the first year of the 2007–2008 financial market crisis. In: Evanoff D, Hartmann P, Kaufman GE (eds) The first credit market turmoil of the 21st century, world scientific studies in international economics, vol 10, World Scientific, New Jersey, pp 195–228

Cassola N, Durré A, Holthausen C (2011) Implementing monetary policy in crisis times: the case of the ECB. In: Jarocinski M, Smets F, Thimann C (eds) Approaches to monetary policy revisited – lessons from the crisis, session 5, European Central Bank, pp 280–321

Durré A, Pill H (2010) Non-standard monetary policy measures, monetary financing and the price level, paper presented at the ECB conference monetary and fiscal policy challenges in times of financial stress

ECB (2011) The implementation of monetary policy in the euro area – General documentation on Eurosystem monetary policy instruments and procedures. February

Gagnon J, Raskin M, Remache J, Sack B (2010) Large-scale asset purchases by the Federal Reserve: did they work? FRB New York staff report no. 441

Goodfriend M (2011) Central banking in the credit turmoil: an assessment of Federal Reserve practice. J Monet Econ 58(1):1–12

Goodhart C (2011) The changing role of central banks. Financial History Review 18(2):135–154

Hamilton J (2009) Concerns about the Fed's new balance sheet. In: Ciorciari J, Taylor J (eds) The road ahead for the Fed. Hoover Institution Press, Stanford, pp 67–84

Hodson D (2010) EMU and political union: what, if anything, have we learned from 10 years of the euro? J Eur Public Policy 16(3):508–526

Hodson D, Quaglia L (2009) European perspectives on the global financial crisis: introduction. J Common Mark Stud 475:939–953

Issing O (2010) The future of the euro: will the success story continue? Revue d'Économie Financière 96(1):27–33

Kydland FE, Prescott EC (1977) Rules rather than discretion: the inconsistency of optimal plans. J Polit Econ 85:473–492

Leeper E (1991) Equilibria under 'active' and 'passive' monetary and fiscal policies. J Monet Econ 27(1):129–147

Leeper E (2010) Monetary science, fiscal alchemy, FRB Kansas City Jackson Hole symposium, Macro-economic policy: post-crisis and risks ahead

McCauley JL (2009) Dynamics of markets – the new financial economics, 2nd edn. Cambridge University Press, Cambridge

Reinhart C, Reinhart V (2010) After the fall, NBER working paper, no. 16334, September

Sims C (1994) A simple model for study of the determination of the price level and the interacion of monetary and fiscal policy. Econ Theory 4(3):381–399

Thornton H (1802) An enquiry into the nature and effects of the paper credit of Great Britain, printed for J. Hatchard, Bookseller to the Queen, Piccadilly, and Messrs. F. and C. Rivington. St Paul's Church Yard, London

Woodford M (1995) Price level determinacy without control of a monetary aggregate. Carn Roch Conf Serie 43:1–46

# Comment Paper to Chapter "The European Central Bank and Implications of the Sovereign Debt Crisis"

**Soko Tanaka**

The paper proposed by Dr. Francesco Drudi, Alain Durré and Francesco Mongelli to the EUSI International Conference (hereafter "the Drudi paper") gives a detailed and skillful explanation on the institutional framework of the Eurosystem and ECB's activities to deal with the euro crisis in the period 2007–2011. The paper especially focuses on the so-called non-standard monetary policy, which has been a controversial issue in advanced countries during the crisis period. It has also been a conflicting issue among EMU countries and even within the ECB. I begin my comments from this new area of central banking and then step into wider issues.

The current sovereign debt crisis has precipitated the values of banks' assets and their collaterals, and thereby aggravated the sovereign crisis itself and the financial crisis at the same time, and the downside risks to the economic outlook. The crisis became truly seismic in autumn 2011 and shook the world economy. In response, the ECB has had to further develop the non-standard monetary policy that was introduced in May 2010. The Drudi paper explains this development in detail.

One of the main purposes of the Drudi paper it seems is to justify the ECB's non-standard policy, which has been geared up step-by-step with the deepening crisis. The crisis severely impaired the transmission of the monetary policy, so explains the paper, and the ECB has been obliged to deepen the non-standard measures to a greater number of spheres, including the money market, interest channels and bank lending.

It is quite persuasive and I believe most people agree. Almost every central bank in developed countries has executed non-traditional policies to counter the severe crises that arose after the Lehman shock. As the euro area crisis is currently the most severe and dangerous in the world, who is against such a policy and its development? Without it, the euro area would break apart.

S. Tanaka (✉)
Chuo University, Tokyo, Japan
e-mail: tanakaso@tamacc.chuo-u.ac.jp

S. Kaji and E. Ogawa (eds.), *Who Will Provide the Next Financial Model?: Asia's Financial Muscle and Europe's Financial Maturity*,
DOI 10.1007/978-4-431-54282-7_6, © Springer Japan 2013

I imagine that the problem lies in the Treaty (now the TFEU). The TFEU prohibits the Eurosystem from taking monetary financing measures under Article 123(1), so it cannot buy sovereign bonds directly from governments. In addition, the Treaty does not give the ECB a duty to maintain financial stability, and thus, the ECB is remarkably limited in its actions to keep financial order in the euro area. This must be why the ECB looks to be hesitant about embarking on large-scale sovereign bond purchases, even during those very critical days with highly volatile bond yields in November 2011.

The Drudi paper explains why such a provision was introduced into the Treaty. Owing to that provision, there was a division of labour. The Eurosystem kept monetary dominance and the public sector carried out fiscal responsibility. However, such beautiful cooperation collapsed in the crisis. Euro area politicians changed de facto the so-called non-bailout clause (Article 125 of the TFEU) during the Greek crisis of 2010 by financing the budget deficits of Greece via the IMF and the established bailout facility. The EFSF was the nest step. The coming ESM will be the third and big step forward.

The crisis showed that the basic concepts of the EMU on central banking in the Maastricht Treaty (now the TFEU) can no longer be maintained.

The Treaty should be revised. I do not expect such a radical view to be stated in the Drudi paper, as central bankers must abide by Central Bank Law and the Treaty.

However, I am not satisfied to read and re-read an article that only justifies the use of non-standard policy of the ECB because it is faced with too many difficult problems that lie partly within and beyond the non-standard policy. How will the TARGET2 balance problem be solved? How will they liquidate the mounting debt of banks as a result of LTROs with 3-year maturities or other rescue plans? In the near future, a large-scale purchase of sovereign bonds will be necessary, which will also bring a liquidation problem. More needs to be done to prevent an escalation of the crisis.

The Drudi paper was very useful to understand the many aspects of the non-standard policy of the ECB. However, it also shows that ECB experts should tell us economists more, and that we have much to discuss for the further successful development of the EMU.

# Evolution of Quantitative Easing

**Shigenori Shiratsuka**

**Abstract** This chapter attempts to shed some light on the evolving nature of quantitative easing, or unconventional monetary policy in general. Confronted with the recent financial crisis, central banks in major economies moved swiftly and aggressively to counter the adverse effects of the malfunctioning financial system. In that process, central banks introduced various unconventional policy measures regarding the range of financial assets being purchased and in the scale of such purchases. As a result, central banks significantly expanded their balance sheets, especially so after the collapse of Lehman Brothers in September 2008. Thereafter, central banks continued to maintain expanded balance sheets by constantly reorganizing their policy strategy in accordance with changes in economic and financial conditions.

**Keywords** Central bank balance sheet • Credit easing • Financial crisis • Quantitative easing • Unconventional monetary policy

This chapter is an update of my previous paper (Shiratsuka 2010). I thank the participants of the 2010 EUSI conference and Toshiki Jinushi for their comments on the preliminary version of my paper. The views expressed in the paper are solely mine and do not necessarily reflect those of the Bank of Japan. Note that central banks, taken up in this chapter, took some additional policy measures after this chapter was finalized.

S. Shiratsuka (✉)
Matsuyama Branch, Bank of Japan, 4-10-2 Sanban-cho,
Matsuyama, Ehime 790-0003, Japan
e-mail: shigenori.shiratsuka@boj.or.jp

S. Kaji and E. Ogawa (eds.), *Who Will Provide the Next Financial Model?: Asia's Financial Muscle and Europe's Financial Maturity*,
DOI 10.1007/978-4-431-54282-7_7, © Springer Japan 2013

# 1 Introduction

In this chapter, I will explore the evolving nature of quantitative easing under the recent financial crisis.[1] In responding to the crisis, central banks in major economies introduced various unconventional policy measures in the range of financial assets being purchased and in the scale of such purchases.[2] Central banks expanded their balance sheets significantly, especially after the collapse of Lehman Brothers in September 2008 (Fig. 1). Thereafter, central banks continued to maintain the expanded balance sheet size by constantly reorganizing their policy strategy in accordance with changes in economic and financial conditions.

In response to the collapse of Lehman Brothers and resultant stress in financial markets, the Federal Reserve (Fed) aggressively intervened in the credit products market and related markets with newly created "credit easing" measures.[3] Thereafter, the Fed also modified its operational framework, depending on the changes in financial and economic conditions as well as various policy constraints: outright purchases of mortgage-backed securities and agency debts, and then long-term government securities, as well as maturity extensions of such securities.

The European Central Bank (ECB) also expanded its balance sheet after the collapse of Lehman Brothers, but employed a different strategy, called enhanced credit support, to impair the transmission channel of monetary policy under a bank-based financial system.[4] The ECB basically implemented various unconventional measures by extending its existing operational framework, although it did change its policy focus as the sovereign debt problem intensified.[5]

---

[1] Following Shiratsuka (2010), I will use quantitative easing and unconventional monetary policy in an equivalent manner. He emphasizes that unconventional monetary policy in reality combines two elements of the central bank balance sheet, size and composition, to enhance overall policy effects, given the economic and financial circumstances and political constraints surrounding central banks.

[2] Borio and Disyatat (2009), Goodfriend (2011), and Ueda (2012) also provide an overall review of unconventional monetary policy in major economies under the recent financial crisis.

[3] Bernanke (2009a) first termed the Fed's approach to "credit easing," stressing a conceptual difference from the quantitative easing policy by the Bank of Japan (BOJ) from 2001 to 2006. Bernanke (2012) provides an overall review on the Fed's policy responses under the recent financial crisis.

Under credit easing, the Fed established various types of credit and liquidity facilities as credit easing measures: Term Auction Facility (TAF) in Dec 2007; Primary Dealer Credit Facility (PDCF) in Mar 2008; Term Securities Lending Facility (TSLF) in Mar 2008; ABCP MMMF Liquidity Facility (AMLF) in Sep 2008; Commercial Paper Funding Facility (CPFF) in Oct 2008; Money Market Investor Funding Facility (MMIFF) in Nov 2008; and Term Asset-Backed Loan Facility (TALF) in Mar 2009. For further details, see the webpage for "credit and liquidity programs and the balance sheet" in the Fed's website (http://www.federalreserve.gov/monetarypolicy/bst.htm).

[4] For further details of enhanced credit support, see, for example, Trichet (2009).

[5] A major innovation of the ECB was the introduction of a full-allotment liquidity provision operation with the significant extension of its maturity in the long-term refinancing operations (LTROs). The maturity of the LTROs was extended to three years in December 2011 as the intensified sovereign debt problem produced a severe stress on money markets in the euro area. See, for example, ECB (2010a, b, 2011).

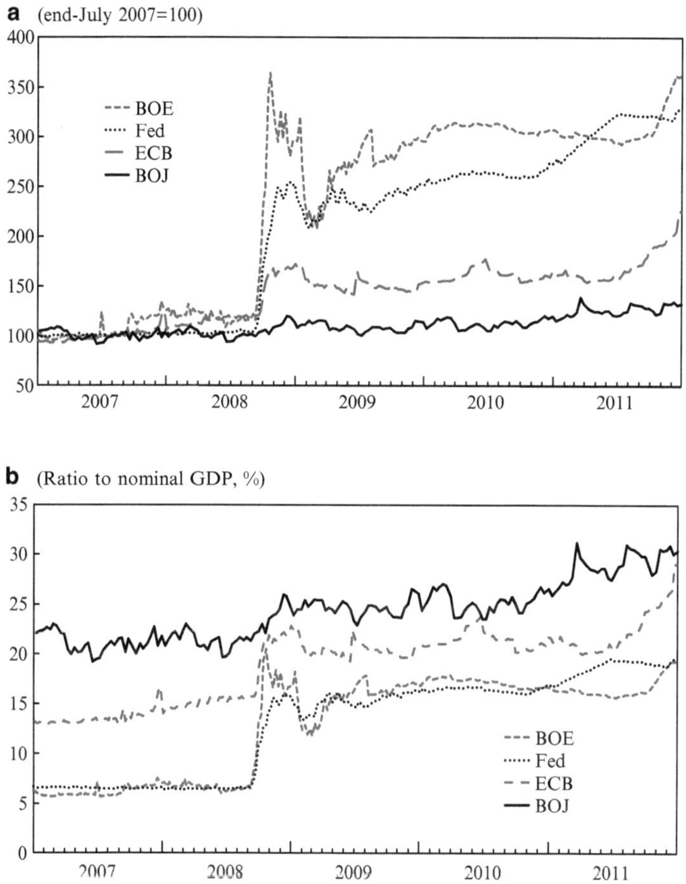


**Fig. 1** Total assets of major central banks. (**a**) Expansion after the financial crisis of 2008, (**b**) Ratio to nominal GDP. Sources: Board of Governors of the Federal Reserve System, "Factors Affecting Reserve Balances"; Bank of England, Monetary & Financial Statistics; European Central Bank, Monthly Bulletin; Bank of Japan, Economic and Financial Statistics Monthly

The Bank of England (BOE) introduced a large-scale asset purchase (LSAP) program, the so-called quantitative easing (QE), in March 2009. The BOE particularly focused on purchasing large amounts of UK government bonds (gilts) from non-bank financial institutions.[6] The BOE finished the program in early 2010, but restarted it in October 2011.

---

The ECB also introduced two security purchase programs on an outright basis: the covered bond purchasing program (CBPP) in May 2009 and the Securities Markets Program (SMP) in May 2010. The second was intended to address the malfunctioning of sovereign bond markets, thereby restoring the monetary policy transmission channel. With that program, the ECB also absorbed the liquidity provided by bond purchases to keep the monetary policy unchanged.

[6] See, for example, Bean (2009), Benford et al. (2009), Cross et al. (2010). Joyce et al. (2010), and Meaning and Zhu (2011) examine the effectiveness of quantitative easing by the BOE.

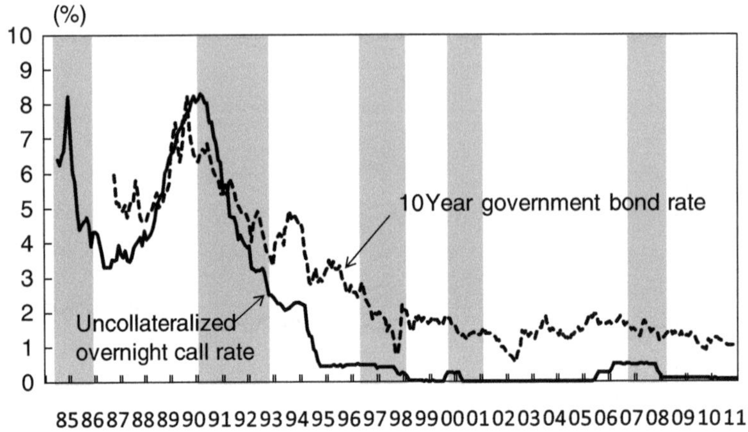


**Fig. 2** Short- and long-term interest rates in Japan. Source: Bank of Japan, Economic and Financial Statistics Monthly

The Bank of Japan (BOJ) has been dealing with financial crisis and deflation since the late 1990s. After the burst of the bubble in the early 1990s, the BOJ sequentially reduced the overnight interest rate (with its high of 8.6 % in 1991) to below 0.5 % (virtually 0 %) in the fall of 1995 (Fig. 2). This implies that Japan has been in a zero interest rate condition for more than 15 years, while the CPI inflation rate became negative in the second half of 1998 (Fig. 3). During that period, the policy responses of the BOJ can be divided into four phases: financial crisis in 1997–1998, a period of zero interest rate policy in 1999–2000, a period of quantitative easing policy from 2001 to 2006, and a period of comprehensive monetary easing from 2009.[7] The BOJ expanded its balance sheet significantly from 10% to 30% of nominal GDP (Fig. 4).

Policy strategies appear to differ from country to country, in terms of the range of financial assets purchased and the magnitude of the expansion of balance sheet size. The distinct difference, however, arises not because central banks have different objectives, but because they face different environments and restrictions, such as the types and origins of the shocks hitting the economy, the structure of the financial system, and institutional arrangements of the central bank. Reflecting the expansion of market-based financial intermediation, many central banks have

[7] Shirakawa (2009c, 2012b) summarizes the policy responses of the BOJ since the second half of 1990s and examine their lessons. For Japan's experience of the financial crisis in 1997–1998, Saito and Shiratsuka (2001) examine the crisis from the viewpoint of the collapse of arbitrage in the financial markets due to the severe liquidity constraints of financial institutions. Regarding the zero interest rate policy from 1999 to 2000, Fujiki et al. (2001) review the conceptual basis for the policy framework. Ugai (2007) provides a comprehensive review of the empirical studies on the effects of the quantitative easing policy from 2001 to 2006.

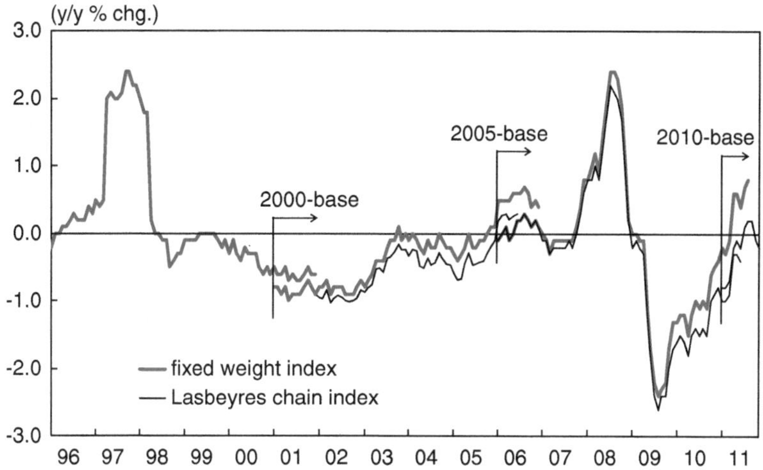


**Fig. 3** Core CPI inflation. Source: Ministry of Internal Affairs and Communications, Consumer Price Index

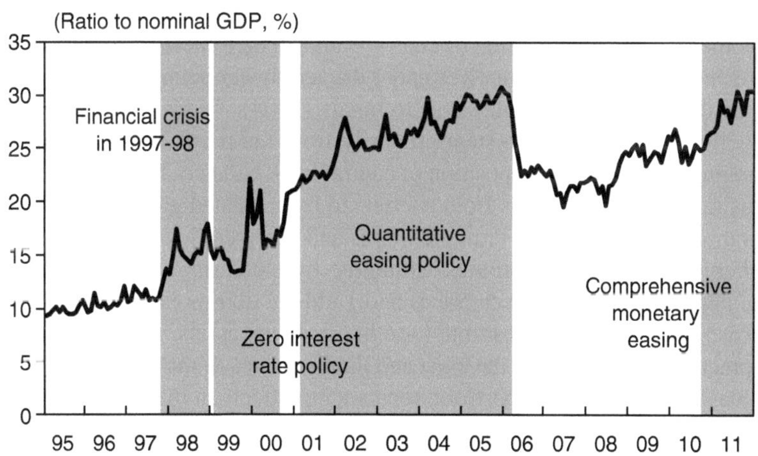


**Fig. 4** Balance sheet size: Bank of Japan. Source: Bank of Japan, Economic and Financial Statistics Monthly

extended the scope of the rescue operations of financial markets beyond the traditional role as lender of last resort, by, for example, the provision of liquidity to non-bank financial institutions and the restoration of market liquidity in credit products and related markets. Given the constraints on policy implementation, central banks combined two elements of their balance sheet, size and composition, to enhance the overall effects of unconventional policy. When viewed from a broad perspective, the responses of the various central banks demonstrate more similarities than differences.[8]

This chapter is organized as follows. Section 2 examines the role of the central bank balance sheet under an unconventional monetary policy by focusing on the link between the two sides of the balance sheet, i.e., the asset side and liability side. Section 3 reviews how central banks in major economies changed the size and composition of their balance sheets to counter the recent financial crisis. Section 4 discusses policy implications. Section 5 provides concluding remarks.

## 2 Role of Central Bank Balance Sheet

In theory, as discussed by Bernanke and Reinhart (2004), unconventional monetary policy can be implemented by combining two elements of the central bank balance sheet, size and composition (Fig. 5).[9] Size corresponds to expanding the balance sheet while keeping its composition unchanged (narrowly-defined quantitative easing). Composition corresponds to changing the composition of the balance sheet while keeping its size unchanged by replacing conventional assets with unconventional assets (narrowly-defined credit easing).

Before the recent financial crisis, unconventional monetary policy measures to change the size and composition of central bank balance sheets were understood to be pure monetary policy alternatives under the zero lower bound of nominal interest rates, as discussed in Bernanke and Reinhart (2004). Given that understanding, policy effects are expected to stem primarily from the portfolio rebalancing effect of changing the size and composition of central bank balance sheets. By shifting the composition of asset holdings from shorter- to longer-dated government securities, a central bank may influence term premiums and the overall yield curve if investors treat them as imperfect substitutes. Similarly, by increasing the monetary base, a central bank may also influence prices and yields of non-money assets if the monetary base is an imperfect substitute for other financial assets.

In practice, however, both the asset and liability sides of the central bank balance sheet play roles beyond the portfolio rebalancing effects in the policy responses to the recent crisis. On the one hand, the asset side works as a substitute for private financial intermediation, for example, through outright purchases of credit products. On the other hand, the liability side, especially expanded excess reserves, functions as a buffer for liquidity risk in the financial markets. In addition, the two sides interact closely with each other because malfunctions in financial intermediation are closely tied to funding liquidity risk of financial institutions, resulting in an increased demand for excess reserves. In that case, the size and composition of the balance sheet depends on the state of the economy, particularly the financial system.

---

[8] Shirakawa (2009a, b) also points out the striking similarities between the policy measures taken by the BOJ since the late 1990s and those currently taken by central banks in the major economies.

[9] This section is based on Shiratsuka (2010).

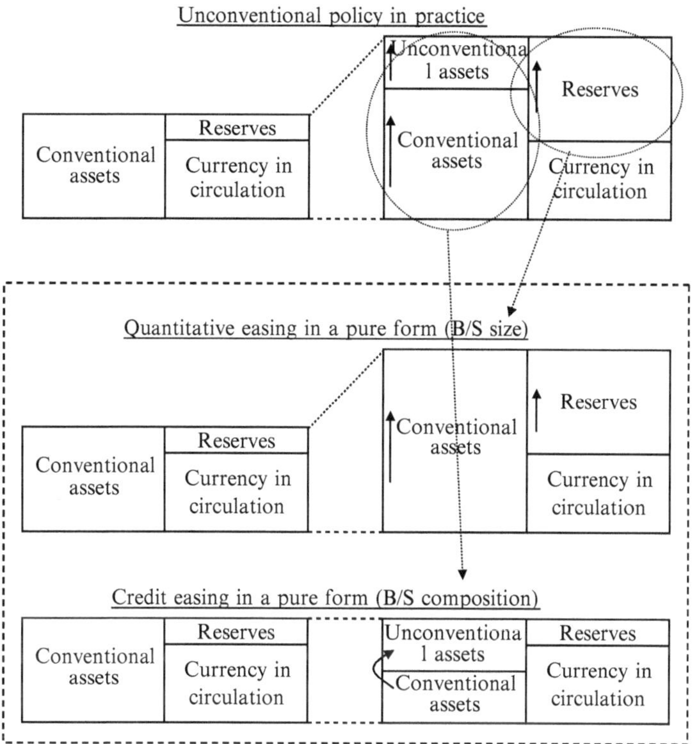


**Fig. 5** Illustration of unconventional policy measures

Central banks' policy responses to the recent financial crisis are therefore not a natural extension of pure monetary policy under the zero lower bound of nominal interest rates, but an emergency operation to rescue financial systems. In particular, many central banks have extended the scope of such rescue operations beyond the traditional role as lender of last resort, for example, the provision of liquidity to non-bank financial institutions and the restoration of market liquidity in credit products and related markets.[10] In that process, central banks combine the two elements of their balance sheet, size and composition, to enhance the overall effects of unconventional policy, taking into account the constraints on their policy implementation. In that respect, quantitative easing, often used in a vague manner, is more suitable as a package of unconventional policy measures, which makes use of both the asset and liability sides of a central bank balance sheet to counter the shocks hitting the economy (broadly-defined quantitative easing).

[10] Kuttner (2008), for example, viewed the recent Fed's policy responses as a lender of last resort, and their effects and costs in detail. In addition, Tucker (2009) discussed three types of last resort operations in a financial crisis: lender of last resort, market maker of last resort, and capital of last resort. He pointed out that the first two operations are the role of a central bank, while the last is that of government.

## 3 Central Bank Balance Sheet Under Financial Crises

The aforementioned role of the central bank balance sheet under a financial crisis is clearly seen in the developments of the size and composition of central bank balance sheets in major economies (Figs. 6, 7, 8, and 9).

Looking first at the liability side, reserves expanded dramatically in all four central banks in the figures, while currency in circulation, a major liability in normal times, remained fairly stable. These observations suggest that, under the recent financial crisis, the accelerated liquidity risk of financial institutions was mitigated by the ample provision of liquidity to money markets.

Looking next at the asset side, in contrast, the sources of increases on the asset side differ significantly between central banks, and over time. The differences in the factors behind the asset side expansion between central banks are closely related to the differences in the financial structure of the economy, including in particular the structure of financial intermediation. Figure 10 illustrates the structures of financial intermediation in four economies. The figure clearly shows that the United States has a primarily market-based financial system, while Japan, the euro area, and even the United Kingdom have largely bank-centered financial systems. As a result, the United States has a stronger incentive to intervene in market-based financial intermediation, including the credit products market, to counter a financial crisis.

Similarly, changes over time are related mainly to changes in the financial and economic conditions, as well as political constraints. The evolving nature of policy focuses over time is clearly seen in the changes in the composition of the Fed balance sheet on the asset side (Fig. 6).[11] The Fed initially took credit-easing measures to intervene aggressively in the credit products markets and other related markets. Such operations can be seen as a rescue operation for market-based financial intermediation by temporarily replacing malfunctioning private financial intermediation with the Fed's own balance sheet. The Fed changed its focus thereafter, putting a greater emphasis on macroeconomic stability rather than financial system stability. More precisely, in November 2008, the Fed launched a LSAP program and started replacing its current balance sheet composition with mortgage backed securities (MBSs) and agency debt, thereby restoring financial flows in housing finance markets. In November 2010, the Fed began expanding its balance sheet again by modifying the LSAP program to purchase large amounts of long-term government securities, the so-called QE2, to boost economic activity.[12] Given that a further expansion of the size of the balance sheet became difficult, the Fed introduced a maturity extension program (MEP) in June 2012, a kind of operation twist, to further stimulate economic activity.

---

[11] Bernanke (2009b) stresses the evolving nature of the important elements of the Fed's balance sheet.

[12] Gagnon et al. (2011), for example, point out that the Fed's large-scale asset purchase program results in significant and long-lasting reductions in premiums in a wide range of securities, including those not directly targeted by the program.

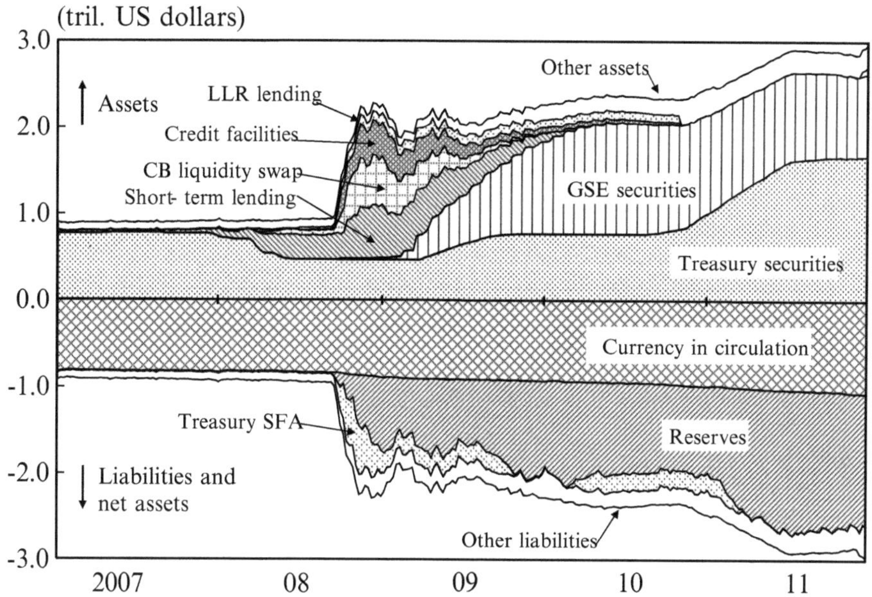


**Fig. 6** Central bank balance sheet (1): the United States. Note: The details of asset components are as follows: short-term lending includes short-term repos, primary credit, secondary credit, seasonal credit, and term auction credit; credit facilities include PDCF, TSLF, AMLF, CPFF, MMIFF, and TALF; LLR lending includes credit extended to AIG, and net portfolio holdings of Maiden Lane I, II, and III. Source: Board of Governors of the Federal Reserve System, "Factors Affecting Reserve Balances"

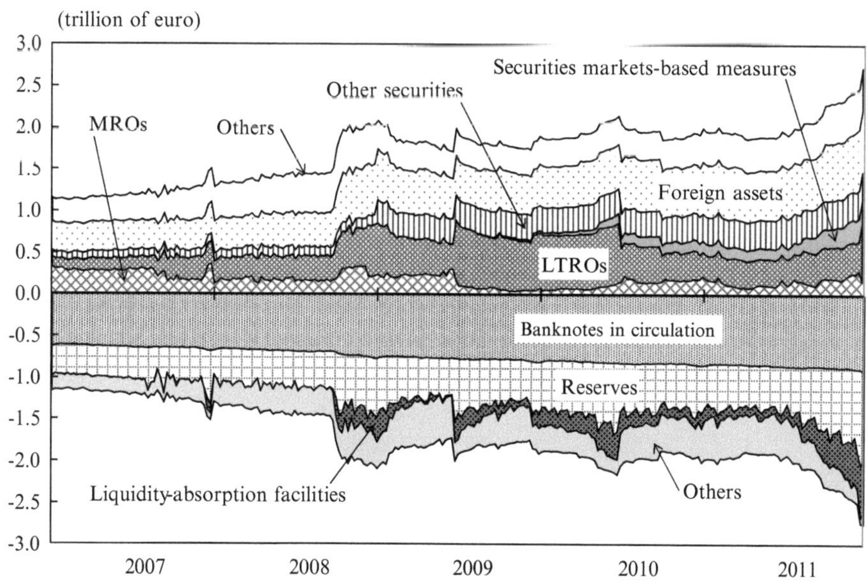


**Fig. 7** Central bank balance sheet (2): Euro Area. Source: European Central Bank, "Consolidated Financial Statement of the Eurosystem"

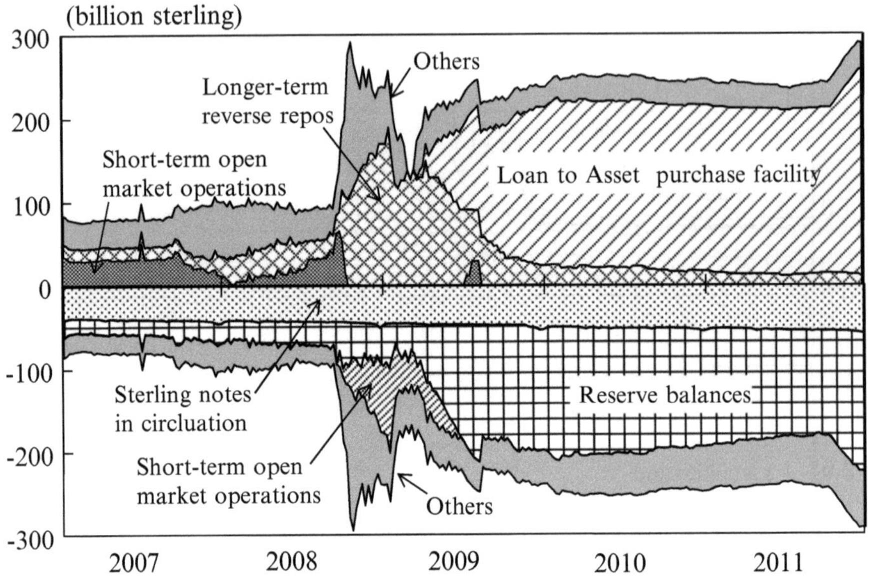


**Fig. 8** Central bank balance sheet (3): the United Kingdom. Note: Since March 2009, the BOE has been using a subsidiary, the Bank of England Asset Purchase Facility Fund, to purchase assets in pursuit of its monetary policy aims. Although the accounts of the fund are not consolidated with those of the BOE, the fund is financed by loans from the BOE. Source: Bank of England, "Bank Return"

By contrast, the three other central banks placed a greater emphasis on macroeconomic stability from the beginning to change the composition of the asset side of their balance sheet (Figs. 7, 8, and 9). The BOJ and the ECB intended to restore monetary policy transmission channels via the banking sector by extending their existing policy framework, resulting in increases in the more conventional assets on the asset side of their balance sheets. The BOE tried to activate an alternative transmission channel by making a detour around the malfunctioning banking sector.

In short, having regard for the economic and financial conditions, the central banks of major economies accommodated the increased demand for reserves to mitigate liquidity risk by purchasing different types of assets. In that sense, quantitative easing is a package of unconventional policy measures that makes use of both the asset and liability sides of the central bank balance sheet, and is designed to absorb various economic shocks. The central banks attempted to combine size expansion and composition change to enhance the overall effects of unconventional monetary policies.

## 4 Discussion

Given the understanding of the evolving nature of quantitative easing discussed so far, this section addresses some questions regarding its implementation.

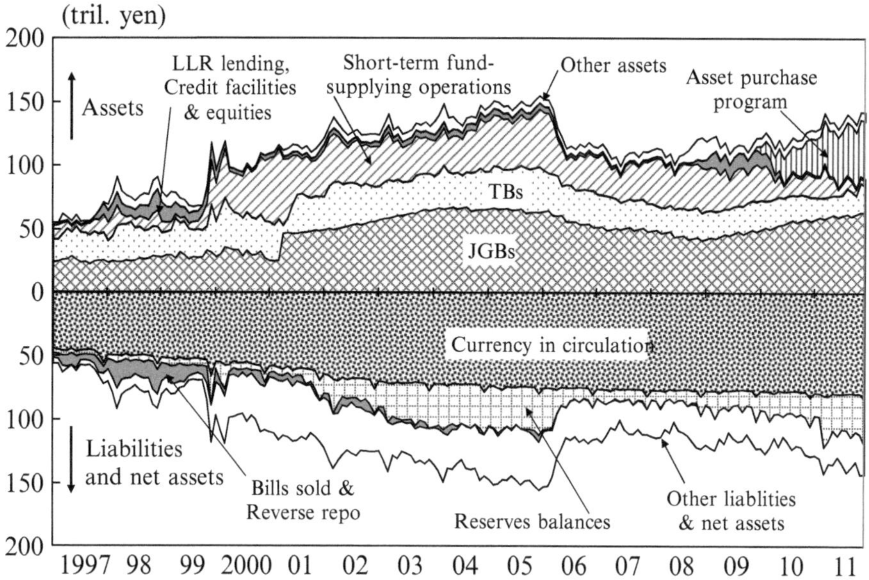


**Fig. 9** Central bank balance sheet (4): Japan. Note: The details of asset components are as follows: short-term funds-supplying operations include funds-supplying operations against pooled collateral, purchase of JGBs and TBs with repurchase agreements, and complementary lending facility; credit facilities and equities include purchases of CPs with repurchase agreements, outright purchase of CPs, and purchase of equities held by commercial banks; LLR lending includes loans based on Article 38 of the BOJ Law, and those to the DIC. Source: Bank of Japan, Economic and Financial Statistics Monthly

## *4.1 Unconventional Policy Versus Policy Commitment*

Bernanke and Reinhart (2004) consider two types of policy options under the zero lower bound constraints of nominal interest rates: changing the composition and size of the central bank balance sheet as well as altering market expectations about the future course of short-term interest rates.[13] In the recent crisis, however, only a

[13] Even under virtually zero nominal interest rates, a central bank can produce further easing effects by making a policy commitment to influence market expectations. This mechanism is called the "policy-duration effect," seen in Fujiki et al. (2001) and Fujiki and Shiratsuka (2002). See, for example, Reifschneider and Williams (2000), Jung, Teranishi, and Watanabe (2005), and Eggertsson and Woodford (2003) for detailed discussions on the policy commitment effect when a central bank faces the zero lower bound of nominal interest rates. Okina and Shiratsuka (2004a) empirically examine the effects of policy commitment, and show that it was highly effective in stabilizing market expectations regarding the future path of short-term interest rates, thereby bringing longer-term interest rates down to flatten the yield curve. Ueda (2005) also reexamines his first-hand experiences as a board member from an academic viewpoint.

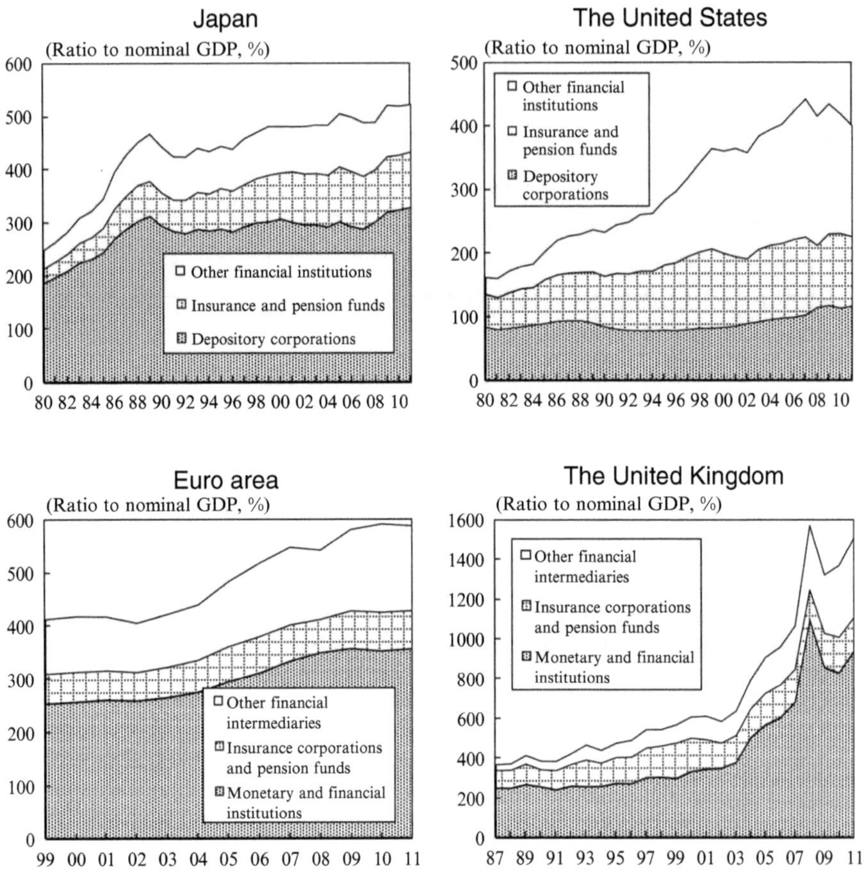


**Fig. 10** Structure of financial intermediations. Note: Other financial institutions in Japan are comprised of securities investment trusts, nonbanks, and financial dealers and brokers. Those in the United States are the sum of investment trusts, financial dealers and brokers, nonbanks, and funding companies. Sources: Japan: Cabinet Office, "National Accounts," Bank of Japan, "Flow of Funds Accounts"; the United States: Bureau of Economic Analysis, "National Economic Accounts," Board of Governors Federal Reserve System, "Flow of Funds Accounts of the United States"; Euro area: Eurostat, "National Accounts," European Central Bank, "Euro Area Accounts"; The United Kingdom: Office for National Statistics, "United Kingdom Economic Accounts"

limited number of central banks employed an explicit policy commitment.[14] In that case, what do we think of the relationship between unconventional monetary policy and policy commitment under zero nominal interest rates?

[14] Some central banks have employed a kind of policy commitment to make clear their policy intention to stabilize longer-term interest rates. For example, the Bank of Canada committed itself to maintaining its target overnight rate at 25 basis points for a certain period of time, based on their inflation projections. In a weaker form of policy commitment, the Fed used forward-looking language: "[The committee] continues to anticipate that economic conditions are likely to warrant an exceptionally low level of the federal funds rates for an extended period."

Financial and economic circumstances that require unconventional policy measures are most likely to accompany an extremely low level of policy interest rates.[15] Under such circumstances, monetary policy is principally directed towards reducing policy interest rates, thereby easing monetary conditions. In that sense, it is inappropriate to consider that unconventional policy measures and policy commitment under zero interest rates are completely separate policy measures.

## *4.2 Portfolio Rebalancing Channel on Yield Curve*

Before the recent crisis, policy arguments on the effectiveness of quantitative easing were based on the portfolio rebalancing effect, generated by changing the composition and size of the central bank balance sheet. Policy effects thus crucially depend on the degree of imperfect substitutability between the financial assets being exchanged.

By shifting the composition of asset holdings from shorter- to longer-dated government securities, a central bank may influence term premiums and the overall yield curve, if investors treat them as imperfect substitutes. However, such policy effects are likely to be weak as far as government securities prices are well arbitraged along a smooth yield curve from short to longer maturity.

A famous precedent for exchanging short- and long-term government securities is "operation twists," which were executed under the Kennedy administration. That experiment was conducted for the purpose of raising short-term interest rates to encourage short-term capital inflow to defend the US dollar, and to lower long-term interest rates to promote domestic corporate investment. In fact, Shiller (1990) concludes in his comprehensive review of empirical literature that the stricter the empirical model, the more subjective the treatment of expectations and the determination of endogenous and exogenous variables. Thus, it is difficult to reach any robust quantitative conclusions.

During financial crises, by contrast, a yield curve is unlikely to be formed smoothly because the behavior of financial institutions is severely limited by their liquidity constraints.[16] Financially stressed financial institutions tend to have serious difficulties with lending, arbitraging, and dealing. As a consequence, policy-targeted interest rates are unlikely to be transmitted to other longer-term interest rates. This implies that the degree of imperfect substitutability between financial assets is higher under financial crisis than in normal times. Nevertheless, it is difficult to expect a strong stimulating effect from central bank interventions to

[15] It should be noted that policy interest rates were maintained marginally above zero under the recent financial crisis, while policy interest rates were reduced to virtually zero in Japan during the ZIRP and the QEP. This is because many central banks adopted an interest payment scheme for excess reserves, thus coming to an understanding that it is unnecessary to guide the policy interest rates to around virtually zero to maintain a certain amount of excess reserves.

[16] Saito and Shiratsuka (2001) examine Japan's experience in the late 1990s.

malfunctioning markets, because such operations are aimed at fixing segmented financial markets, thereby recovering market liquidity and restoring the proper transmission mechanism.

## 4.3 Border with Fiscal Policy

The massive expansion of central bank balance sheets under the recent financial crisis blurred the border between monetary policy and fiscal policy.

The general agreement regarding the traditional role of monetary policy and fiscal policy deems to be as follows. Monetary policy should pursue price stability in the medium- to long-term, while stabilizing short-term economic fluctuations as far as long-term inflation expectations remain well anchored. At the same time, monetary policy is required to be implemented so that it has only limited distributional effects. In contrast, fiscal policy entails strong distributional effects through decisions on taxes and public spending, but needs to be limited to the function of an automatic stabilizer, thus minimizing its discretionary use.

Under the recent financial crisis, however, such general agreement was virtually ignored. Central banks intervened selectively in financial markets, thereby aiming to influence asset prices as well as resource allocations. Such policy interventions have significantly stronger distributional effects than in normal times, thus often being referred to as "quasi-fiscal policy." It should be noted that those policy measures have fiscal policy elements, even though central banks employ such measures to achieve their policy mandate: price stability and financial system stability.

## 4.4 Acute Pain Versus Chronic Illness

Looking at financial and economic conditions after the burst of an economic bubble, acute pain is caused by malfunctioning interbank markets, while chronic illness is caused by balance sheet adjustment associated with structural and persistent effects on the economy.[17] Unconventional monetary policy serves to alleviate malfunctioning interbank markets as a symptomatic therapy for acute pain, and to buy time until substantial progress is made in the balance sheet adjustment. However, no cure-all policy measures exist to resolve chronic illness.

In fact, Japan's economic predicament after the bursting of the asset price bubble in the early 1990s is better understood as a significant downward shift in trend growth, beyond a boom-and-bust cycle (Fig. 11).[18] It was not simply a typical exam-

[17] See, for example, Shirakawa (2010a, b). Dale (2012) also points out the importance of rebalancing the supply side of the economy, and the difficult task of monetary policy to provide short-term support to the economy without stifling the incentives for changes.

[18] See Okina and Shiratsuka (2004b) for a further discussion on monetary policy and the structural implications when the asset price bubble burst.

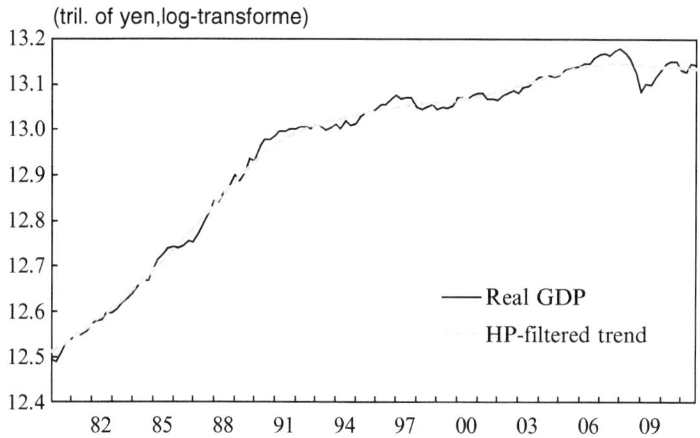


**Fig. 11** GDP trends. Source: Cabinet Office, "National Accounts"

ple of an amplified boom-and-bust cycle of asset prices, producing significant adverse effects on economic activity. These aspects of Japan's asset price bubble, and its consequences for structural adjustments in the 1990s, are especially important because they illustrate the specific environment in which the Bank of Japan had to conduct its monetary policy. This is not a standard stabilization policy around a stable growth trend but unanswered policy questions coupled with hampered sustained growth.[19] Under such circumstances, adverse effects on the economy are generated not by an inter-temporal substitution effect, but by an income effect coming from a declined permanent income associated with a declined trend growth.

In addition, it should be noted that quantitative easing is a temporary policy response. The increase in size and the change in composition of the central bank balance sheet simply buy time until real progress can be made in the balance sheet adjustments of financial institutions, such as the disposal of non-performing assets and recapitalization. Increases in size and changes in composition of central bank balance sheets do not directly lead to an early restoration of financial intermediation function.[20]

[19] To overcome deflation, the BOJ is currently emphasizing the importance of efforts to strengthen the economy's growth potential as well as support from the financial side. The BOJ is implementing two lines of policy measures: one is powerful monetary easing to encourage such efforts, with its virtually zero interest rate policy and the Asset Purchase Program, and the other is a Growth-Supporting Funding Facility. See, for example, Shirakawa (2012a). See also the BOJ website for a further explanation of recent policy actions (http://www.boj.or.jp/en/mopo/outline/sgp.htm).

[20] In addition, quantitative easing is likely to produce side effects, a consequence of the strong policy measures implemented to stabilize the financial system. A massive expansion of the central bank balance sheet is the corollary of public intervention in private financial transactions, potentially distorting incentives and resource allocation in the private sector. In particular, such side effects become more obvious as the duration of quantitative easing progresses.

# 5 Concluding Remarks

In this chapter, I have attempted to shed some light on the evolving nature of quantitative easing, or unconventional monetary policy in general.

Under the recent financial crisis, central banks significantly expanded their balance sheets. Thereafter, central banks have maintained expanded balance sheets by constantly reorganizing their policy strategy in accordance with changes in economic and financial conditions. Such policy responses succeeded in alleviating destabilized financial markets, and, to some extent, stimulating the economy.

It should be noted, however, that such monetary policy responses are not cure-all policy measures, but rather buy-time policy measures before substantial progress is made to resolve the structural problems behind the crisis. Beneath the declining trend growth path, central banks face unanswered policy questions beyond standard stabilization policies under stable growth.

# References


Bean C (2009) Quantitative easing: an interim report. Speech to the London Society of Chartered Accountants. http://www.bankofengland.co.uk/publications/Pages/speeches/2009/405.aspx

Benford J, Berry S, Nikolov K, Young C (2009) Quantitative easing. Bank Engl Q Bull 49(2):90–100

Bernanke BS (2009a) The crisis and the policy response. Speech at the Stamp Lecture, London School of Economics. http://www.federalreserve.gov/news-events/speech/berake20090113a.htm

Bernanke BS (2009b) The Federal Reserve's balance sheet: an update. Speech at the Federal Reserve Board conference on key developments in monetary policy. http://www.federalreserve.gov/newsevents/speech/berake20091008a.htm

Bernanke BS (2012) Some reflections on the crisis and the policy response. Remarks at the conference on "Rethinking finance: perspectives on the crisis." http://www.federalreserve.gov/newsevent/speech/bernanke20120413a.htm

Bernanke BS, Reinhart VR (2004) Conducting monetary policy at very low short-term interest rates. Am Econ Rev 94:85–90

Borio C, Disyatat P (2009) Unconventional monetary policies: an appraisal. BIS Working Paper No. 292

Cross M, Fisher P, Weeken O (2010) The Bank's balance sheet during the crisis. Bank Engl Q Bull 50(1):34–42

Dale S (2012) Rebalancing the supply side of the UK economy: what; how; and issues for monetary policy. Speech to Mark the Centenary of the Department of Economics at the University of Aberystwyth. http://www.bankofengland.co.uk/publications/Pages/speeches/2012/554.aspx

Eggertsson G, Woodford M (2003) The zero bound on interest rates and optimal monetary policy. Brookings Pap Econ Act 1:139–211

European Central Bank (2010a) The ECB's monetary policy stance during the financial crisis. Monthly Bulletin January 63–71

European Central Bank (2010b) The ECB's response to the financial crisis. Monthly Bulletin October 59–74

European Central Bank (2011) The ECB's non-standard measures – impact and phasing-out. Monthly Bulletin July 55–69

Fujiki H, Shiratsuka S (2002) Policy duration effect under the zero interest rate policy in 1999–2000: evidence from Japan's money market data. Monet Econ Stud 20(1):1–31
Fujiki H, Okina K, Shiratsuka S (2001) Monetary policy under zero interest rate: viewpoints of central bank economists. Monet Econ Stud 19(1):89–130
Gagnon J, Raskin M, Remache J, Sack B (2011) Large-scale asset purchases by the Federal Reserve: did they work? Int J Cent Bank 7:3–43
Goodfriend M (2011) Central banking in the credit turmoil: an assessment of Federal Reserve practice. J Monet Econ 58:1–12
Joyce M, Lasaosa A, Stevens I, Matthew T (2010) The financial market impact of quantitative easing. Bank of England Working Paper No. 393
Jung T, Teranishi Y, Watanabe T (2005) Optimal monetary policy at the zero-interest-rate bound. J Money Credit Bank 37:813–835
Kuttner KN (2008) The Federal Reserve as lender of last resort during the panic of 2008. mimeo
Meaning J, Zhu F (2011) The impact of recent central bank asset purchase programmes. BIS Quarterly Review. December
Okina K, Shiratsuka S (2004a) Policy commitment and expectation formation: Japan's experience under zero interest rates. N Am J Econ Finance 15:75–100
Okina K, Shiratsuka S (2004b) Asset price fluctuations, structural adjustments, and sustained economic growth: lessons from Japan's experience since the late 1980s. Monet Econ Stud 22(S-1):143–167
Reifschneider D, Williams JC (2000) Three lessons for monetary policy in a low-inflation era. J Money Credit Bank 32:936–966
Saito M, Shiratsuka S (2001) Financial crises as the failure of arbitrage: implications for monetary policy. Monet Econ Stud 19(S-1):239–276
Shiller R (1990) The term structure of interest rates. Friedman BM, Hahn FH (eds) Handbook of monetary economics, volume 1, Elsevier
Shirakawa M (2009a) Way out of economic and financial crisis: lessons and policy actions. Speech at Japan Society in New York. http://www.boj.or.jp/en/type/press/koen07/ko0904c.htm
Shirakawa M (2009b) Financial system and monetary policy implementation: long and winding evolution in the way of thinking. Opening speech at 2009 international conference hosted by the Institute for Monetary and Economic Studies. http://www.boj.or.jp/en/type/press/koen07/ko0905e.htm
Shirakawa M (2009c) Unconventional monetary policy – central banks: facing the challenges and learning the lessons – remarks at the conference co-hosted by the People's Bank of China and the Bank for International Settlements in Shanghai. http://www.boj.or.jp/en/type/press/koen07/ko0908a.htm
Shirakawa M (2010a) Uniqueness or similarity? – Japans post-bubble experience in monetary policy studies – keynote address at Second IJCB Fall Conference. http://ww.boj.or.jp/en/anouncements/press/koen_2010/ko1009c.htm
Shirakawa M (2010b) Economic policy challenges lying ahead – two years after the crisis – Speech at the 2010 Annual Membership Meeting of the Institute of International Finance. Oct 10. http://www.boj.or.jp//en/announcements/press/koen_2010/ko1010a.htm
Shirakawa M (2012a) The Bank of Japan's efforts toward overcoming deflation. Speech at the Japan National Press Club in Tokyo. Feb 17. http://www.boj.or.jp/en/announcements/press/koen_2012/ko120217a.htm
Shirakawa M (2012b) Central banking: before, during, and after the crisis. Remarks at a conference sponsored by the Federal Reserve Board and the International Journal of Central Banking. Mar 24. http://www.boj.or.jp/en/announcements/press/koen_2012/ko120326a.htm
Shiratsuka S (2010) Size and composition of the central bank balance sheet: revisiting Japan's experience of the quantitative easing policy. Monet Econ Stud 28:79–105
Trichet JC (2009) The ECB's enhanced credit support. Keynote address at the University of Munich. http://www.ecb.int/press/key/date/2009/sp090713.en.html
Tucker P (2009) The repertoire of official sector interventions in the financial system: last resort lending, market-making, and capital. Remarks at 2009 Bank of Japan International Conference. http://www.bankofengland.co.uk/publications/Documents/speeches/2009/speech390.pdf

Ueda K (2005) The bank of Japan's struggle with the zero lower bound on nominal interest rates: exercises in expectations management. Int Finance 8:329–350

Ueda K (2012) The effectiveness of non-traditional monetary policy measures: the case of the bank of Japan. Jpn Econ Rev 63:1–22

Ugai H (2007) Effects of the quantitative easing policy: a survey of empirical analyses. Monet Econ Stud 25(1):1–47

# Comment Paper to Chapter "Evolution of Quantitative Easing"

**Toshiki Jinushi**

Shiratsuka nicely illustrates his understanding of unconventional monetary policy measures based on accumulated experiences. However, I found that he curiously neglected the issue of deflation. In response I write several points regarding my views on the unconventional policy measures of central banks.

I have different interpretations on the US Fed's policy actions. Its Credit Easing (CE) should be categorized into two parts, as they are totally different in their nature. The first part is simply a set of liquidity supply measures for the shadow banking system. Facing financial crisis, liquidity supply is a common policy response, and as such this part should not be valued too highly. We should also not overlook the fact that the Fed did not have the appropriate measures to do so before the crisis.

Its second part is basically a large-scale asset purchase program. Although this program purchased mortgage-related securities as well as Treasury securities, these are not risky assets because their issuers and/or insurers, Fannie Mae and Freddie Mac, were both nationalized institutions. Therefore, in the context of a large-scale asset purchase, the essential distinction between the Fed's CE and the Quantitative Easing (QE) of the Bank of Japan (BOJ) was not whether to buy risky assets, but whether there was a clear intention to influence the relative prices among the broad classes of assets.

The Fed's famous QE2 should be interpreted as a voluntary and partial "monetization" of government bonds to stop deflation. Aside from differences between the financial systems of the two economies, the BOJ's QE targeted the volume of private banks' current account balances at the BOJ, of which laypeople may not be aware, and Fed's QE2 targeted the purchase volume of T-Bonds, which most people understand. This difference seems to reflect the difference between the intentions of the two central banks. The Fed's main aim was to protect against deflation. It wanted

T. Jinushi (✉)
Kobe University, Kobe, Japan
e-mail: jinushi@econ.kobe-u.ac.jp

S. Kaji and E. Ogawa (eds.), *Who Will Provide the Next Financial Model?: Asia's Financial Muscle and Europe's Financial Maturity*,
DOI 10.1007/978-4-431-54282-7_8, © Springer Japan 2013

to shock the market by "monetization" to raise inflation expectations and to lower the external value of the US dollar. The BOJ's main aim was to stabilize the financial system by supplying enough liquidity to banks. It did not want to be mistaken for monetization; it did not want to shock the market.

Regarding Shiratsuka's explanation of the BOJ's QE, I wish to add two points. The first is that the gradual increases of the targeted amount were also important features of the QE. In response to repeated crisis situations, the BOJ raised the targeted amount several times. These actions fulfilled two functions. They stabilized the financial system and tempered the political criticism against the BOJ.

The second is that we should not disregard the BOJ's announcements, "**Understanding** of medium- to long-term **price stability**." These are the BOJ's alternatives to inflation targeting. The "Understanding" defined price stability with a specific level of inflation rates. However, unlike ordinary inflation targeting, the BOJ did not commit to achieve that level of inflation within any particular period of time. There are two versions of the "Understanding" announcements. The old one defined price stability as an inflation rate between 0% and 1%, announced under the QE during the Japanese financial crisis. In retrospect, the financial market seemed to interpret this announcement as BOJ's signal that zero inflation was acceptable. Some market participants wrote that the BOJ acted strongly only when inflation went below −1%.

The new version defined price stability as inflation between 0% and 2%, close to 1%, and was published under the current QE against the world financial crisis. The new version was not to be interpreted in the same way as the old. The BOJ tried to signal that zero inflation was no longer acceptable. Most recently, the BOJ announced an inflation target of essentially 1%.

Shiratsuka correctly points out that unconventional policy measures are only buy-time policies, and not cure-alls. However, those unconventional measures are also aimed at stopping deflation. He also clearly states that monetary policy management under a declined trend growth path is difficult. This is true, but deflation adds further obstacles in the restoration of the trend growth path. I believe that monetary policy should first focus on taking care of deflation!

I think that Shiratsuka has improved his paper by including considerations of the ECB and BOE in his revision of the paper. However, other important policy experiments have been implemented. In Canada, the BOC announced that it would maintain low interest rates for a specified period. In Sweden, the Riksbank began to publish its own forecasted path regarding policy rates. Although these cannot be categorized as quantitative easing, these actions provide us further rich examples of policy measures against the financial crisis. However, by focusing on quantitative easing as policy responses, Shiratsuka provided appropriate and clear illustrations.

To conclude, this paper provides good summaries and considerations of the unconventional monetary policy measures of central banks during this financial crisis. While interested readers will find the paper of value, it does neglect the issue of deflation.

# Lessons Learned, Lessons Not Learned and the Lessons to Be Learned: From the Asian Crisis to the European Crises

**Akira Ariyoshi**

**Abstract** The European sovereign debt crisis erupted a dozen years after the Asian financial crisis of 1997–1998. What is striking are the similarities between the European crisis and the Asian crisis. The case of Greece even bears resemblance to earlier Latin American crises. Why did Europe not draw lessons from history? What can the authorities in Asia learn from the European crisis, so that they too will not ignore the lessons from other countries? This chapter reviews the lessons from the Asian crisis, provides a broad sketch of developments of the euro-zone crisis and considers how Europe could or should have learned from the Asian crisis. It also selectively highlights important lessons for Asia that are emerging from the current crisis in the euro zone.

**Keywords** Asian financial crisis • Crisis prevention • Crisis resolution • Euro crisis • International financial architecture

I am grateful to Professor Masao Kumamoto who served as a discussant for my presentation in conferences, as well as conference participants for their valuable comments. At the time of writing (mid-June 2012), the euro zone crisis was still fluid and evolving, and developments may supersede some of the observations made in this essay.

A. Ariyoshi (✉)
School of International and Public Policy, Hitotsubashi University,
Tokyo, Japan
e-mail: aariyoshi@ics.hit-u.ac.jp

S. Kaji and E. Ogawa (eds.), *Who Will Provide the Next Financial Model?: Asia's Financial Muscle and Europe's Financial Maturity*,
DOI 10.1007/978-4-431-54282-7_9, 

# 1 The Asian Crisis

## *1.1 Causes*

The causes of the Asian crisis are by now well known. While there are some important differences across Asian countries, the broad evolution of the crisis may be summarized as follows[1]: a combination of relatively fixed exchange rates against a backdrop of abundant global liquidity and robust domestic growth resulted in large capital inflows. Due in part to a poor sequencing of capital account and financial sector liberalization, these inflows mainly took the form of short-term inflows channeled through the financial sector, which in turn led to a surge in investment and asset prices. Incentives in the regulatory regime including the assignment of low risk weights to short-term cross-border interbank exposures also encouraged such flows from the supply side. Monetary policy was accommodative, allowing excessive credit expansion to take place. Because of weaknesses in corporate governance and financial supervision, investments were not productive, resulting in large losses for the lender when financial and economic conditions turned negative. The elevated level of investment caused countries to run current account deficits, but these were easily offset by capital inflows. What distinguished the Asian crisis from the earlier Latin American crisis was that unlike the Latin American crisis, the counterpart to the current account deficit was private sector investment, and fiscal accounts were generally in surplus.

Countries thus became vulnerable to sudden reversals of capital inflows, which materialized when confidence was damaged. One trigger for the weakening confidence was decelerating export growth, which reflected a slowing external demand and decline in competitiveness caused by real appreciation. Capital outflows occurred most prominently in the financial sector, which had been the recipient of short-term inflows. The non-rollover of these short-term funds resulted in financial institutions experiencing foreign currency liquidity problems. To prevent failures, the authorities had to intervene to prevent a systemic collapse, initially by supplying foreign currency through foreign exchange market intervention. However, once the reserves were depleted, there was no option but to allow the exchange rate to depreciate, but by then the loss of confidence was such that this would result in a massive depreciation—a currency crisis. The depreciation in turn aggravated the crisis, as it increased the local currency value of foreign currency debt, causing firms with mismatched currency positions in their balance sheets to become insolvent. It should also be noted that authorities concealed the true extent of usable foreign reserves through the use of forward market intervention (particularly in the case of Thailand) and deposits of foreign reserves in overseas subsidiaries of troubled domestic banks (Korea). Confidence was further damaged when the true extent of the reserve loss came to light. The perceived similarities of the fundamentals of the Asian economies in the eyes of foreign investors resulted in contagion across the region.

[1] Sheng (2009) provides a vivid account and thoughtful analysis from the viewpoint of a policymaker involved in the crisis.

A number of factors in the crisis response stage aggravated the crisis. One was the limited financial resources provided in the international effort to manage the crisis. With the United States unable to provide support due to legal constraints and European countries generally taking the position that it was a "crony capitalism" problem that required fixing rather than financial support, the design of the International Monetary Fund (IMF) programs in the early stages of the crisis provided for a relatively modest level of overall financing, relying more heavily on the traditional austerity approach to reduce financing needs and also to restore confidence as well as structural reforms to enhance growth.

The initial response thus failed to grasp the severe contractionary effect of the dual nature of the crisis, financial and currency, which led to much sharper contractions in credit and economic activities than in earlier crises. The deepening recession itself prompted further capital flight, creating an adverse spiral. It is instructive to note that in the case of Korea, the situation only began to stabilize after foreign banks were leaned upon by central banks and the governments of their respective countries to maintain exposure—thus solving a coordination problem between lenders.

The second issue was an excessive focus on structural issues to fix the "crony capitalism" problem and thus promote growth, as well as some questionable implementation of these measures, including in bank resolution. In Indonesia, concern over moral hazard led to a decision to close a number of banks while only providing a partial deposit guarantee. In the context of a fragile banking system, this precipitated a bank run and capital flight that further deepened the crisis.

The IMF programs for the Asian crisis economies included a whole range of structural measures as lending conditionality. While the measures themselves may have had merit, the immediate impact of such measures in restoring confidence or promoting growth was limited. Rather, the wide-ranging imposition of conditionality by the IMF may have damaged confidence by suggesting that the economies faced many severe structural problems,[2] and as a report by the Independent Evaluation Office of the IMF notes,[3] the perceived lack of political ownership for these measures may have further damaged the confidence and credibility in the IMF program and the country, thereby prolonging the crisis.

## 1.2 Lesson Learned

In terms of crisis prevention, the standard lessons drawn from the Asian crisis were to implement greater flexibility in exchange rates, strengthen financial supervision and corporate governance, ensure greater transparency and strengthen surveillance.[4]

[2] Radelet and Sachs (1998).

[3] IMF, Independent Evaluation Office (2003).

[4] See, for example, Lane et al. (1999).

Most of the Asian economies that were hit by the crisis adopted an inflation-targeting framework for monetary policy following the crisis. This meant, in principle, that they would allow exchange rates to float, thereby removing one incentive that encouraged large capital inflows. Asia also made significant efforts to improve their bank supervisory capacity, and by the time the global financial crisis (GFC) hit, most emerging Asian economies had capital ratios that were well in excess of Basel standards and their exposure to toxic assets were minimal.

Asia also undertook significant improvements in providing better economic data and by improving corporate governance. The strengthening of surveillance was a global-level task for the IMF, but Asian countries independently took measures to make their countries less vulnerable, as we shall see later.

In terms of crisis management, the realization dawned that the flows of private capital were much larger and more volatile than could be managed with the traditional ammunition of official resources. This observation led to two lines of initiatives. One was to make official support (IMF financing) much larger in size and faster disbursing. Second was the attempt to create a mechanism for private sector bail-ins, so as to prevent the rapid withdrawal of private capital, and if necessary to require burden sharing in debt reduction.

In the event, the follow up on these issues was minor until the eruption of the 2008 GFC: there had been limited reforms to the IMF lending facilities because of strongly expressed concerns by Germany and other European countries that generous terms could encourage moral hazard and put IMF funds at risk. However, the international community responded rapidly in the wake of the GFC to make IMF lending more flexible and expand the size of individual country lending, as well as making further resources available.

By contrast, a rethink of conditionality in IMF programs did occur. Rather than burdening the program with too many structural conditionality items that could weaken the focus of the program, the IMF made it a general principle to limit conditionality to those that were essential for restoring macroeconomic stability (the so-called macro-critical elements).[5]

Discussions on a sovereign debt restructuring mechanism to bail-in creditors did not go beyond an encouragement to include collective action clauses (CACs) in external debt issues by emerging market borrowers.

Finally, very little was done on the "supply side" of cross-border flows. A Basel Committee study[6] concluded that they did not find conclusive empirical evidence that regulatory risk weights caused distortions that contributed to the crisis. More generally, the dominant view was that poor policies and the vulnerabilities of the countries were the main causes of the crisis.

---

[5] See, for example, "Statement of the IMF Staff: Principles Underlying the Guidelines on Conditionality" (Revised January 9, 2006), paragraphs 6 and 7.

[6] Basel Committee on Banking Supervision (1999).

## 1.3 The Asian View of Lessons Learned

Asian authorities drew lessons that were more focused on the supply side of financing. In a nutshell, they might be summarized as "never rely on Wall Street and Washington." Recognizing the fickle nature of private capital flows (Wall Street) and the perceived social costs of resorting to IMF rescue (Washington), Asian countries built up self-insurance against capital outflows by amassing international reserves. Moreover, conscious of the fact that it was only Asian countries that came to the rescue to co-finance IMF packages in the early phases of the Asian crisis,[7] Asian economies sought to create a regional safety net, which materialized in the form of the Chiang Mai Initiative (CMI). The CMI started off as a network of bilateral foreign currency swap arrangements between the Association of South East Asian Nations (ASEAN) and China, Japan and Korea (ASEAN+3), but has since developed into a centralized reserve-pooling mechanism with committed resources of USD 120 billion.

Another means of "not relying on Wall Street" was to develop local bond markets. The idea behind this was that one cause of the crisis was the risk posed by a "double mismatch" in capital inflows and their ultimate uses; namely, inflows were short-term and dollar-denominated, but the domestic use of the capital was long-term and in domestic currency. As the problem was not that Asia as a whole did not have sufficient savings for finance investment, but rather that savings were intermediated through foreign markets, it was thought that the risks of crisis could be lowered if Asian savings were channeled directly into Asian investment using long-term bonds denominated in local currencies. A well-functioning bond market was also hoped to provide a "spare tyre" for financial intermediation in the event of a banking crisis. This idea developed into a number of initiatives, including the Asian Bond Market Initiative (ABMI) under the auspices of ASEAN+3, and the Asian Bond Fund initiatives driven by the Executives' Meeting of East Asia-Pacific Central Banks (EMEAP). While we have seen a fair degree of expansion in individual national markets, we have not seen the same in "regional" markets, wherein the integration of smaller markets can benefit from greater liquidity brought about by economies of scale.

## 1.4 Applying the Lessons: Coping with Large Post-crisis Capital Inflows

As the Asian economies put the crisis behind them and with the return of benign global financial market conditions, Asia again began to experience a large influx of capital flows from around 2003. This prompted serious concern on the part of the

[7] The first IMF program for Thailand was supported by bilateral support from seven Asian countries and Australia, while Europe and United States did not offer any co-financing.

**Table 1** Cumulative foreign exchange inflows and intervention, 2003–2007 (% of GDP unless noted otherwise)

| | Indonesia | Korea | Phillipines | Thailand | China | Malaysia |
|---|---|---|---|---|---|---|
| Gross capital inflows (A) | 9 | 22 | 15 | 12 | 21 | 24 |
| Current account surplus (B) | 7 | 7 | 10 | 7 | 27 | 53 |
| Reserve accumulation (C) | 5 | 13 | 7 | 16 | 37 | 29 |
| C/A (%) | 62 | 57 | 46 | 136 | 171 | 118 |
| C/(A+B) (%) | 33 | 43 | 28 | 86 | 76 | 37 |

Source: IMF, IFS and author's calculations

Asian authorities: if exchange rates were allowed to appreciate, this may weaken the export sector, which is crucial for economic growth and long-term development, while a sudden reversal of flows may trigger another crisis.

Asian countries, including those that adopted inflation-targeting in monetary policy, chose to intervene fairly aggressively, accompanied by sterilization to limit credit growth and thus temper excess leverage and asset price booms. In part, this action was taken to prepare for a sudden reversal in speculative flows. By absorbing such inflows in the form of foreign reserve build-up, it could be released in the event of the reversal of flows. Between 2003 and 2007, Korea, Indonesia and the Philippines' increases in reserves absorbed roughly half of the gross capital inflows in that period. In Thailand, which also adopted an inflation-targeting regime, its intervention was well in excess of gross capital inflows, with the central bank absorbing a significant part of the current account surplus in addition to gross capital inflows. China and Malaysia, despite having stronger capital control regime, also had to heavily intervene to maintain their relatively fixed exchange rate regime (Table 1). The responses indicate that the fear of losing competitiveness in the export sector, seen as crucial for long-term growth, was also a major factor in their exchange rate policy. The lesson from the Asian crisis that current account deficits financed by capital inflows can result in the build-up of vulnerabilities may have also encouraged these countries to attempt to maintain exchange rate levels to prevent large current account deficits from developing.

Still, the differences in the monetary policy regimes and responses created regional tensions, to the extent that inflation-targeting countries could not focus entirely on exchange rate stabilization. This resulted in large changes in intra-regional exchange rates (Fig. 1). Because of the perceived competition within Asia, not only in exports but also as a destination for foreign direct investment in the manufacturing sector, this intra-regional exchange rate volatility was increasingly seen as a problem by some of the inflation-targeting countries.

Coinciding with the 50th anniversary of the Treaty of Rome in 2007, and the deepening economic integration and cooperation in Asia, these developments led to a growing discussion on the possibility of monetary integration in Asia. Proposals for an "Asian Currency Unit" (ACU) were aired,[8] and reflecting on the success of

[8] Ogawa and Ito (2000) provide an early example of the ACU proposal.

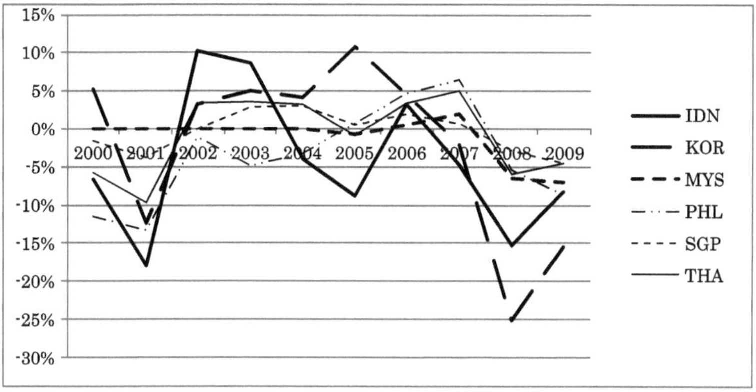


**Fig. 1** Movements of Asian Currencies against Chinese Yuan (Percentage changes in annual average rates)

the euro up to the mid-2000s, many speculated as to when Asia might move to a monetary union. On a less ambitious level but in the nearer term, the possibility of exchange rate coordination within Asia was advocated by some, including using the ACU as a reference to limit variations in individual currency exchange rates.

However, few advances were made regarding regional exchange rate policy coordination, and each country was more or less left to its own devices to manage the surge in capital flows. Sterilized intervention had its limits because of the conflict between inflation-targeting and the impact on the central bank balance sheet: If domestic interest rates had to be raised higher than in the United States to contain inflation, then this would result in a cost of carry for the reserves. Appreciation also resulted in capital losses. Either way, a large level of international reserves posed financial risks for the central bank. It was not only the central bank fearing a possible loss of independence and autonomy if recapitalization were needed to offset mounting losses; the government itself also became wary of too large an accumulation of reserves.

Thus, many countries turned to capital account related measures, including the liberalization of outflows and measures to lengthen the maturity of inflows. Thailand in particular imposed in late 2006 a system of unremunerated reserve requirements to stem short-term inflows, although the ill-designed measures did not function well. Prudential measures relating to capital flows were also used, and became more prominent in Asia after the GFC.[9] The growing use of measures may in part reflect a wider acceptance by the international policy community of macro-prudential measures (as a part of the legitimate tool kit to manage capital flows) to limit vulnerabilities. It may also reflect the higher quasi-fiscal cost of holding reserves in an environment where short-term interest rates of major reserve currencies had become close to zero—as Table 2 shows, the interest rate differences between domestic and foreign

[9] A list of measures taken is provided in "Table 1.2. Capital Flow Management Measures in Asian Economies", IMF (2011a, p. 18).

**Table 2** Estimated cost of carry of international reserves, Q1: 2011

| | Korea | Indonesia | Philippines | Thailand | Malaysia | China |
|---|---|---|---|---|---|---|
| Domestic interest rate (%) | 2.8 | 6.0 | 4.2 | 2.1 | 2.7 | 3.3 |
| Annual cost of carry (in % of GDP)[a] | 0.7 | 0.7 | 1.1 | 1.0 | 1.1 | 1.5 |

[a]Cost of carry is an estimate based on end-2010 reserves and the interests rate differential, divided by 2010 GDP; the interest rate differential is based on the difference between the local money market rate and the U.S. TB rate in 2011, Q1 (0.13%)

interest rates suggest that the cost of carry for many countries had reached approximately 1% of GDP on an annualized basis by early 2011.

The combination of policies helped to contain the build-up of vulnerabilities during the period leading up to the GFC when emerging markets around the world were facing massive inflows of capital. Thus, despite tensions in the final quarter of 2008 and early 2009 caused by the drying up of dollar liquidity, and continuing stress in the global financial markets caused by the sovereign debt crisis in the euro zone, emerging Asia has managed to cope much better than its Eastern European counterparts.

The experience in Asia suggests that the doctrine of the "impossible trinity" requires a more subtle interpretation. Asia has generally taken an eclectic approach to balancing exchange rate stability, monetary policy independence and capital account liberalization. Sterilized intervention allows some breathing space to pursue multiple objectives when inflows are temporary. Macroprudential measures can have the effect of regulating capital flows, but they can also be seen as monetary policy instruments. The current monetary policy framework gives the short-term interest rate a predominant role; however tools like loan-to-value limits on real estate lending and the quantitative control of credit were once the standard tools for monetary policy. These instruments can influence the transmission mechanism of monetary policy, thus adding an extra dimension to monetary policy options. If one can guide exchange rate expectations or influence the risk premium through, for example, fiscal policy frameworks, then this can also decouple exchange rates from movements in interest rates.

# 2 European Crisis

## *2.1 Lessons Not Learned*

The development of the European crisis bears a strong resemblance to the Asian crisis in that many of the warning signs were missed or ignored, and that the crisis response was erroneous or inadequate. Given the similarities, it is surprising that many of the lessons that could have been learned were not, and that actions that may have prevented or mitigated the crisis were not taken.

### 2.1.1 Crisis Prevention

The dangers of a fixed exchange rate and the risks of high levels of current account deficit and domestic investment (and public deficits) financed by large capital inflows were not lost on policymakers. Particularly from around 2003, a combination of benign global financial conditions and strong growth in the European periphery resulted in a sharp increase in capital inflows and a corresponding widening of the current account balance in these regions. Accordingly, the IMF, for example in their Global Financial Stability Report (GFSR), expressed concerns over the capital-inflow-financed current account deficits in Eastern Europe.

However, discussion of these vulnerabilities related solely to emerging market economies, and it appears that the industrialized economies, including those in the euro zone, were largely off the radar. Moreover, it was even argued early on that because much of the financing emerging in Europe was being channeled through local subsidiaries and branches of industrialized Europe's banks that had lasting commitments in the region, these flows were likely to be more stable. Thus, it was argued that the risk of a sudden stop could, in these circumstances, be less than might otherwise be the case.[10] Of course, the GFC and the deterioration of the health of European banks put stop this sort of optimistic view; but even then, the risk of large capital reversals from the euro zone periphery was not really recognized until it happened.

Could euro periphery countries have learned more from the Asian crisis? In terms of lessons regarding crisis prevention, some of the lessons were not implementable given the mechanics of being a member of the euro zone. Obviously, a greater flexibility of exchange rates and interest rate responses to local overheating are not possible. However, rather than riding the boom, if a more critical appraisal of the sustainability of the boom had been made, fiscal measures and banking sector measures to dampen domestic demand and asset price growth could have been taken at an earlier stage. Stronger prudential regulation of financial institutions could have been possible, but the crisis countries at that time were not thought to have particularly weak systems. Indeed, Spain was noted for having introduced a macroprudential tool of counter cyclical capital charges prior to the GFC, although supervision and risk management were much poorer for the savings banks (Caja), which would become a major source of banking stress.

A lesson that was largely ignored but turned out to be critical was related to the incentives created by bank regulations and central bank policies. The zero risk-weighting of euro-denominated sovereign debt in the euro zone and the equal treatment of all euro area sovereign bonds for collateral purposes at the ECB created clear incentives to hold periphery debt if it provided a small yield pick-up over German bunds. Furthermore, the possible spillovers that might result from a materialization of sovereign risk, and the dangers of a systemic crisis, were not really considered.

[10] IMF, GFSR (April 2008).

Greater attention could have been paid to the other set of "lessons" that had been drawn by the IMF from the Asian crisis; namely, greater transparency and stronger surveillance. Failures in these aspects were clearly major causes of the crisis. Just as the disclosure of the true level of international reserves led to a deepening crisis in Thailand in the summer of 1997, the disclosure of misreported fiscal deficit and debt figures in Greece was a major crisis trigger. More fundamentally, the weak enforcement of the Stability and Growth Pact, not least prompted by the relaxation of rules to accommodate non-compliance by core countries Germany and France, led to increasingly vulnerable fiscal accounts in the euro periphery. In that context, the importance of fiscal sustainability appears to have been lost in a period where all euro zone sovereign bonds were viewed equally safe and the easy financing exerted no discipline.

### 2.1.2 Crisis Management

The question that also needs to be asked is why the initial problem in Greece, whose economy only accounts for a few percent of the euro-zone total, developed into a major euro area crisis. A part of the blame must go to the inadequate crisis response, which shared similar failures with that during the Asian crisis.

The initial response to the GFC did seem apply the lessons learned from the Asian crisis. Countries generally undertook an aggressive easing of monetary and fiscal policies, recognizing the highly contractionary effects of a financial crisis. The concerted international support for economies in the European periphery facing balance of payments difficulty was much greater than that during the Asian crisis, with the IMF typically providing credit lines ten times greater than the IMF quota. Governments also undertook to support the financial system by fully guaranteeing the deposits of banks to avoid bank runs.

But whether these lessons were entirely appropriate soon became apparent. In particular, unlike in the Asian crisis countries, some of the banking systems in Europe had assets several times larger than their GDP. This meant that the banking system may be "too big to save", with governments unable to backstop the banking sector with their own credit. When attempts were made, banking liabilities became in effect sovereign liabilities, in some cases leading to a fiscal crisis (as in the case of Ireland). While an unlimited guarantee may be useful in containing systemic runs on the banking system, it would only work where there was sufficient fiscal space for the government to take on such risks. In the same vein, there are also limits regarding the extent to which a government can support demand with expansionary fiscal measures when fiscal conditions are already weak.

As the nature of the crisis in Europe shifted to a fiscal crisis, the crisis response began exhibit the same shortcomings seen during the Asian crisis. One was that even though the resources provided were extremely large by past standards, the level of support was inadequate to restore market confidence. Repeated expansions of the safety net in Europe were not made until the last minute, and were never large enough to completely turn around market sentiment. What was worse was that unlike in the Asian crisis where there was no question of restructuring sovereign debt, the rescue packages openly talked about and eventually included haircuts in privately held sovereign debt. The initial promise that private sector involvement would only be implemented after 2013, gave way to the introduction of a "voluntary" debt exchange in the subsequent package. Despite assurances that only Greece would be subject to such treatment, the lack of sufficient financing to make that promise appear credible resulted in intensifying the contagion across southern Europe. As in the Asian crisis, the power of contagion was underestimated.

A sovereign debt restructuring mechanism built into the euro zone architecture may have been helpful in ensuring an early resolution to the crisis. However, government default was not contemplated in the European Constitution, and the ad hoc introduction of private sector involvement on a voluntary basis in the midst of a crisis was clearly not helpful.

The second related issue is the emphasis on adjustments and the imposition of strict conditionality to ensure the implementation of adjustment measure, in order to resolve the crisis. A strong view held by some creditor countries was that markets for the affected sovereign bonds would only normalize with the implementation of strong structural measures to reduce long-term structural deficits and promote growth. The narrative for Italy, for example, increasingly revolved around the issue of vested interests and the slow pace of reform that suppresses growth and the return to fiscal sustainability, even though Italy has a primary surplus that had been improving.[11] In addition to the short-run demand effect of fiscal retrenchment on growth and its immediate negative consequences for debt dynamics, the excessive focus on governance and the inevitable political delay in implementing such measures was further eroding confidence, as happened in Asia.

Moreover, to restore fiscal sustainability within the typical program timeframe of 3 years, the adjustment programs in the euro periphery built in a rapid and sizeable adjustment in fiscal balance. The logic was that to restore confidence in debt sustainability, there must be a visible improvement in the fiscal balance.[12] To achieve this, the programs relied heavily on tax increases and spending cuts, but this resulted in the withdrawal of demand, which led to further contractions of output and a worsening fiscal balance. In response, further adjustments were imposed to compensate for the slippages, resulting in a further withdrawal of stimulus and more politically difficult reforms. Though it may indeed be the case that the original promises of fiscal and structural reforms were not carried out in full, to strengthen fiscal retrenchment in the face of a larger-than-anticipated fall in output goes against the lessons from the Asian crisis.

---

[11] See, for example, "Italy's Economy: That Sinking Feeling" *The Economist*, November 12, 2011 issue, p. 30.

[12] This is in contrast to a country that is not facing immediate pressures on sovereign debt, where fiscal policies may aim to restore stability in the long-run through the introduction of credible medium-term fiscal consolidation plans, while using active fiscal policy in the short-run to support demand.

This excessive emphasis on adjustment took place notwithstanding the more flexible and generous approach that the IMF had been adopting in response to difficulties in emerging markets in the wake of GFC. This may well reflect the fact that the European Union was effectively leading the program design, contributing two-thirds of the financing package, so that the traditional austerity favored by Germany dominated over the more flexible approach of the IMF.

A third lesson that was not appreciated in full was the adverse spiral between fiscal[13] and financial crisis. It is important to note that the original cause of the sharp deterioration of the fiscal situation was the spillover from the U.S. subprime crisis, both from the holding of toxic assets by European banks and the sharp drop in international trade that resulted in a deep European recession. The inadequate response to the Greek fiscal situation resulted in a widening fiscal crisis throughout the euro periphery. Just as the external (sovereign) crisis and the financial crisis in Asia generated an adverse spiral where countries fell into a "bad equilibrium", the sovereign crisis of the euro zone periphery put strain on bank balance sheets and bank access to liquidity, raising the specter of a credit crunch and further recession throughout the euro zone.

Policymakers tended to focus on fiscal consolidation to restore market sentiment over sovereign risk, and did not do enough to reduce the stress in the financial system. However, a reversal of sentiment takes time, and it is much more important in the short-run to halt adverse feedback through the strengthening of the financial system.

## 2.2 *Lessons to Be Learned*

One of the central lessons to be learned from the crisis in Europe, and more broadly from the series of crises starting in 2008, must be that no country is immune from crisis. Despite being proven wrong by emerging market countries in the Latin American debt crisis of the early 1980s, the sentiment that "countries don't go bust" was continually applied to advanced economies. What has been demonstrated is the potential volatility of market sentiment, and the self-fulfilling nature of financial crises. The risks of fiscal crisis were anticipated in the Delors Report, which set out the roadmap for European currency unification. The Report noted the following[14]:

> To some extent market forces can exert a disciplinary influence. Financial markets… [would] assess [countries'] budgetary and financial positions, penalize deviations from commonly agreed budgetary guidelines or wage settlements, and thus exert pressure for sounder policies. However, *experience suggests that market perceptions do not necessarily provide strong and compelling signals and that access to a large capital market may for*

[13] The Asian crisis can be viewed as an *external* sovereign crisis, and the euro zone crisis may also be thought as a balance of payments crisis for peripheral sovereigns.

[14] Committee for the Study of Economic and Monetary Union (1989), Subsection 30.

> *some time even facilitate the financing of economic imbalances*. Rather than leading to a gradual adaptation of borrowing costs, market views about the creditworthiness of official borrowers tend to change abruptly and result in the closure of access to market financing. The *constraints imposed by market forces might either be too slow and weak or too sudden and disruptive*. Hence countries would have to accept that sharing a common market and a single currency area imposed policy constraints. (*Emphasis added.*)

The success of finance theory and the acceptance of efficient market hypothesis have blinded many from the fact that markets are driven by greed and fear. Therefore, the lesson should be that we must assume that markets can become irrational and dysfunctional at times.

Leaving aside the unique issues related to currency unions, the second lesson relates to the size of the safety net. The liberalization of capital accounts and the size of cross-border flow of capital mean that the potential size of capital movements can be extremely large. The financing structure of banks and sovereigns are similar in that they require a constant rollover of debt and a market's refusal to do so will cause immediate liquidity problems that could quickly translate into solvency issues. The Asian crisis demonstrated that the traditional balance of payments support, where the IMF played a catalytic role in restoring confidence and resuming capital inflows, no longer worked for large and open emerging market economies. A realistic stabilization strategy is for official creditors to provide unlimited liquidity—be it from the central bank, IMF or through bilateral government support—to solvent debtors[15] until sentiment can be turned around. The necessary improvement in sentiment could and should emerge as a response to credible adjustment efforts, but that would also require the passage of time. Moreover, as potential outflows become larger, the support mechanism must similarly be larger. Placing a limit on the support measure that raises doubts about its ability to stabilize the situations is self-defeating and opens the road to contagion.

A corollary is that rather than focusing on net financing requirements and net capital flows, we should pay greater attention to gross financing requirements and gross capital flows, which in turn means paying attention to the stock of assets and liabilities. Even a country with a fiscal surplus or a current account surplus (and net capital inflows) may experience difficulties if gross flows suddenly stop or turn around. A case in point may be that of Belgium. Many initially argued that Belgium was sheltered from contagion despite its large public debt stock because it was a large net creditor in terms of its external investment position. However, as the overall situation deteriorated, doubts about the ability to refinance its debt emerged, and spreads on the Belgian government debt also widened.

[15] A major difficulty is how to distinguish a solvent sovereign, as without the ability to seize assets from the sovereign, long-term solvency relates to the willingness more than the ability to repay out of uncertain future revenue streams. Moreover, in the short-term, much of the repayment ability is based on the ability to refinance existing debt, which in turn is determined by the willingness of investors to hold debt. That critically relies on sentiment, which in turn is influenced strongly by the availability of a strong enough safety net that can step in in times of stress.

## 2.3 Specific Lessons for Asia

The experience in Europe provides additional lessons for Asia; some confirm the lessons from the Asian crisis, while others indicate additional points to heed.

One confirmed lesson is the potential dangers of a fixed exchange rate regime. Immediately after the crisis, a "two corners" view of exchange rate regimes emerged that argued that only a completely fixed exchange rate or a fully floating exchange rate could present viable options to limit the possibility of crisis.[16] The Argentine experience with its currency board had already discredited this view, but the euro zone crisis shows that a completely fixed exchange rate of a common currency does not prevent speculation regarding breaking from a fixed regime.

A fixed exchange rate does in the end force strong adjustments, but the internal devaluation that the process requires is extremely stressful. A common currency would normally act as a commitment mechanism that eliminates any speculation of abandoning the regime, because the exit costs are very high. However, if the cost of adjustment becomes too high, countries might opt to exit, despite the potentially enormous cost of a disorderly exit.

But is a fully flexible regime the answer? The experiences of Iceland and Switzerland suggest no. Switzerland had to resort to setting an upper bound on exchange rates, while in Iceland exchange controls had to be imposed to prevent an excessive depreciation of the exchange rate. While these may be exceptional actions under exceptional circumstances, there are broader implications. Just as a fixed exchange rate encourages strong capital inflows and creates possible asset bubbles, a flexible exchange rate has the potential to create protracted misalignment that could result in the misallocation of resources between tradable and non-tradable sectors.

These observations will no doubt influence long-term thinking on Asian financial integration. Intra-regional exchange rate stability is obviously desirable in promoting intra-regional trade. This is particularly so in the context of a vertical supply-chain network in Asia, as intra-regional exchange rate changes could drastically shift the profitability of each process located in different countries. However, the experiences in Europe, during the period under the European Exchange Rate Mechanism (ERM) and in this crisis, suggest that significant fiscal and political integration is needed to ensure the sustainability of a stable intra-regional exchange rate regime, particularly in Asia where many of the preconditions for an optimal currency area are missing.[17]

The current financial integration initiatives may also need to be rethought. First, the size of recent financing packages indicate that the volume of official financing required in crisis situations, or as a precautionary mechanism to provide assurance

[16] As argued, for example, by Summers (2000).

[17] For a discussion on the extent to which Asia fulfills the conditions for an optimal currency area, see Kawai (2008).

to investors, have become much larger. The individual country access limits under the Multilateralized Chiang Mai Initiative (known as CMIM) are as low as 1.5–2% of GDP in the case of Indonesia and Korea, although that for Korea is supplemented by bilateral swap agreements with Japan and China amounting to approximately 12% of GDP.[18] Considering that the recent IMF packages have provided credit lines of approximately 10% of GDP to emerging markets and that the euro area packages have been closer to 50% of GDP, CMIM would have to be significantly expanded if it is to play a meaningful role in averting or stabilizing a crisis. Furthermore, the activation of CMIM is closely tied to IMF programs. Only 20% of the available credit can be drawn without an IMF program, and the use of the remaining potential credit line requires an IMF program to be in place.

This IMF link has been cited as a major reason why the CMI was not used during the GFC, when some countries may have benefitted from an additional source of liquidity. This is often attributed to the "stigma" that an IMF program carries in Asia, due to the memories of IMF involvement during the Asian crisis. However, the fact that the stigma remains even when IMF introduced up-front lending with virtually no conditionality suggests that there is more to the stigma than the perceived intrusiveness of IMF programs. One likely issue is that IMF is regarded as a crisis management institution, and approaching the IMF may be tantamount to admitting that the country is in crisis. The CMI (and CMIM) also shares the characteristic that it was set up to help countries in crisis, which may also deter potential borrowers. The fact that Korea did not attempt to access CMI or IMF and preferred instead to utilize central bank swap arrangements, which Korea has taken pains to explain are for a "non-crisis situation", attest to the desire to minimize reputational risks of accessing crisis support facilities.

The evolution of the recent crisis where financial market turmoil hit countries with strong fundamentals, and where even major industrialized countries had to resort to bilateral dollar swaps with the Federal Reserve, suggest that facilities that can be activated easily in cases of difficulties caused by external events (rather than through domestic vulnerabilities) are useful. An increased flexibility of CMIM to replicate Federal Reserve swap functions for those countries that are not eligible for the Fed swap would be useful, in addition to supplementing IMF resources in crisis situations.[19]

[18] The swap agreements, which were expanded in October 2011 for a limited period, are comprised of USD 40 billion in dollar-won and USD 30 billion in a yen-won swap with Japan, and a USD 57 billion yuan-won swap with China. The yen-won swap between the central banks is aimed to be used for "stabilizing regional financial markets through supplying short-term liquidity" in a "non-crisis situation", while for China the two sides have agreed "to explore the possibility and extent of converting swap currencies into reserve currencies." (Quotations from central bank press releases).

[19] In May 2012, the ASEAN+3 Finance Ministers and Central Bank Governors announced their intention to strengthen CMIM through, *inter alia*, doubling its resources, increasing the limit for non-IMF linked access, and introducing a precautionary facility.

Second, the bond market initiatives, though useful from a long-run structural viewpoint, also have the possibility of increasing vulnerabilities. Much of the euro zone sovereign debt is held within the euro zone. They are in essence, "local currency bonds held by regional investors". Yet that does not mean that investors can be relied on to hold on to them. Similar caveats could hold for foreign holdings of local currency bonds in Asia.[20] Indonesia, for example, has seen the share of foreign holdings in its government debt rise to over 30%, or close to 10% of GDP. If a sudden outflow were to occur in this sector, this could have serious consequences; even though Indonesia has gross international reserves of 2.5 times its short-term external debt and over 15% of GDP, self-insurance will not be adequate in extreme situations.

Korea is another case where gross flows have mattered. Despite its large holdings of international reserves and current account surplus, Korea was subject to foreign exchange market pressures during the GFC because of its banks' heavy reliance on short-term external funding. More generally, even when net capital inflows are not excessively large, if this were the result of high levels of both gross capital outflows and gross inflows, a sudden stop or reversal of these inflows could pose significant problems.[21]

This is not to say that financial integration should not proceed. The degree of financial integration in Asia, particular in terms of cross-border banking services, is still limited. Despite the large intra-regional trade, the financial services that support it are often provided by non-regional financial institutions and in non-regional currencies. This has resulted in spillovers from non-regional financial turbulence. Though much of the effect appears to have been caused by a sharp contraction of export demand, the credit crunch due to a dollar liquidity shortage during the 2008 crisis negatively affected Asian trade,[22] even though the banking systems in Asia were not directly affected by holding toxic assets. In the European crisis, there is also a growing concern that European banks may have to retrench, thus withdrawing large amounts of financing from Asia.

An expansion of cross-border banking within Asia would help in reducing such vulnerability to external shocks. However, one must also heed the lesson from the euro zone crisis of the dangers of financial contagion through cross-border banking networks. In this regard, strong cross-border cooperation in supervision and in possible resolution is important. A strengthening of regional financial infrastructure,

---

[20] As holdings by foreigners are not confined to regional investors, we cannot assume that these holdings represent investments of regional savings. Indeed, available data suggest that 90% of portfolio investment in Asia comes from non-regional sources (IMF 2011b, Fig. 4.1). Moreover, unlike euro-denominated bonds within the euro zone, it is not clear that even holdings by regional investors benefit from a 'home bias' that would make them more stable.

[21] The *G20 Action Plan to support the Development of Local Currency Bond Market*, published on October 15, 2011, also cautions of possible instability from local bond markets unless supported by a strong domestic investor base and robust institutional and regulatory framework (paragraph 6 of the report).

[22] Coulibaly et al. (2011).

including settlement systems and supervisory systems, would help to both increase integration as well as strengthen resilience.

In terms of fiscal prudence, the euro crisis has shown the wisdom of maintaining adequate fiscal space to cope with crisis. Such space is needed to provide a credible support for the financial sector in the case of financial crisis, as well as to provide stimulus to prevent a potential depression. Asian governments have generally kept their gross government debt within 50% of GDP, and have maintained prudent finances. This allowed them to undertake aggressive fiscal stimulus to counter the global recession following the 2008 global crisis. Yet, the euro zone crisis has shown the all-important role of market confidence, which does not necessarily respond to objective values of debt or other indicators. For Asia, the ability to monetize debt and depreciate currency means that the more important metric may still be external sovereign debt rather than total or local currency debt. Still with an open capital account, the possibility that national government debt crisis can trigger massive devaluation and bank insolvency, resulting in acute consequences, cannot be ignored.

## 2.4 *Not Learning the Wrong Lessons*

It is equally important not to learn the wrong lessons from the crisis. Asia managed to ride through (at least so far) the GFC of 2008 and its second stage in the euro zone crisis. While China's growth has supported Asia, the maintenance of strong external positions and the accumulation of international reserves have no doubt contributed to Asia's resilience. But it would be a mistake to seek to further strengthen Asia's self-insurance. The potential scale of capital flows means that it is not practical to attempt to insulate oneself against shocks by building up large current account surpluses or stocks of reserves. Moreover, even though the building up of reserves is not necessarily a zero sum game as it would be under the gold standard, simultaneous attempts to accumulate reserves could, on a global scale, prove destabilizing. In any event, holding large reserves could incur fiscal costs from the negative carry and capital loss from appreciation, as well as having economic costs in terms of foregoing domestic investment opportunities. In particular, Asia needs to improve its infrastructure to support long-term growth, and domestic savings should be channeled into investment. It would be preferable to work to strengthen the safety net, both on a regional and a global scale, so that sufficient liquidity can be provided in the event of a crisis.

While private financial markets are inherently prone to bouts of instability, recognition of this fact should not lead to an attempt to excessively control financial transactions. Too much faith was placed in the ability of markets to identify and price risk, and to effectively allocate risk. Still, a competitive and reasonably free system for the allocation of credit and the management of risk provides a valuable infrastructure for a modern economy. On the other hand, the belief that appropriate regulation can curb excess and ensure financial stability is too naïve. We would most likely need to employ a wide range of tools to minimize the risk of crisis, including monetary, fiscal, exchange rate and regulatory policies. Asia has so far managed to balance the "impossible trinity" through a measured approach of relying on a variety of tools, and further efforts in that direction seem more promising.

## 3 Concluding Comments

A quote that is attributed to Mark Twain states that "history does not repeat itself, but it rhymes". It is surprising that people often ignore the lessons from others, believing that somehow they are different.

The current European crisis resonates in many ways with the Asian crisis, but its unique turns and variations provide new and additional lessons for Asia. Ultimately, we are faced with the task of how to manage financial activity: Financial activity by nature involve promises about the future. Promises may not be fulfilled, and can result in massive losses from time to time. Yet, it is impossible to do away with financial activity if we are to realize opportunities that lie in the future.

This note provided some preliminary and selective lessons from the European crisis. The crisis has not run its course and we will certainly learn further lessons; perhaps we will also find that some of the lessons we have drawn, if not wrong, only apply under certain circumstances. Asia should not feel complacent from its current position of relative strength, and should seek to learn lessons from Europe, as Europe failed to do from Asia.

## References

Basel Committee on Banking Supervision (1999) Supervisory lessons to be drawn from the Asian crisis. BCBS working papers no 2, June 1999

Committee for the Study of Economic and Monetary Union (1989) Report on economic and monetary union in the European Community. Presented April 17, 1989 (The Delors report)

Coulibaly B, Sapriza H, Zlate A (2011) Trade credit and international trade during the 2008-09 global financial crisis, board of governors of the federal reserve system. International finance discussion papers, number 1020 June 2011

Group of Twenty (2011) G20 action plan to support the development of local currency bond market, 15 Oct 2011

International Monetary Fund, Independent Evaluation Office (2003) IMF and recent capital account crises: Indonesia, Korea, Brazil, 2003. International Monetary Fund

International Monetary Fund (2006) Statement of the IMF staff: principles underlying the guidelines on conditionality (Revised January 9, 2006). Downloaded from http://www.imf.org/external/np/pp/eng/2006/010906.pdf

International Monetary Fund (2008) Global financial stability report, April 2008

International Monetary Fund (2011a) Regional economic outlook: Asia and Pacific, April 2011

International Monetary Fund (2011b) Regional economic outlook: Asia and Pacific, Oct 2011

Kawai M (2008) The role of an Asian currency unit for Asian monetary integration. Paper prepared for the conference, "Beyond Bretton Woods: the transnational economy in search of new institutions," organized by Instituto de Investigaciones Economicas UNAM, Mexico City, the

observatoire de la finance, Geneva, and Pacific Asia Resource Center, Tokyo, held in Mexico City on 15–17 Oct 2008
Lane T et al (1999) IMF-supported programs in Indonesia, Korea, and Thailand: a preliminary assessment. IMF occasional paper no. 178, 1999. International Monetary Fund
Ogawa E, Ito T (2000) On the desirability of a regional basket currency arrangement. Working paper no. 8002. 2000. NBER
Radelet S, Sachs J (1998) The East Asian financial crisis: diagnosis, remedies, prospects. Brookings Pap Econ Act 1:1–74
Sheng A (2009) From Asian crisis to the global financial crisis. Cambridge University Press, Cambridge
Summers LH (2000) International financial crises: causes, prevention, and cures. American Economic Review, Papers and Proceedings 90(2):1–16
The Economist (2011) Italy's economy: that sinking feeling. November 12, 2011 issue, p 30

# Comment Paper to Chapter "Lessons Learned, Lessons Not Learned and the Lessons to Be Learned: From the Asian Crisis to the European Crises"

**Masao Kumamoto**

Professor Ariyoshi's paper states the important lessons that emerging Asian countries have learned from the past Asian currency crisis and should learn from the current European fiscal and financial crisis. While it focuses on the various aspects of these issues, I would like to make two further comments.

The first comment concerns the relationship between financial integration and market discipline. There is some debate on whether financial integration enhances or weakens market discipline [e.g., Manganelli and Wolswijk (2007)]. If financial integration improves market efficiency, then market discipline would provide an accurate assessment of the risk-return profile of assets. As for government bonds, accurate asset pricing implies that governments pursuing unsound fiscal policies will be forced to offer higher yields to attract risk-averse investors. This is market-driven discipline for fiscal policy. However, this was not the case for the euro area government bond markets. For example, in 2007 just before the global financial crisis (GFC), Germany's fiscal balance was at 0.2% surplus, and Greece at 5.1% deficit. However, the yield spread between German and Greek bonds was too small to reflect the differences in fiscal soundness. Therefore, we can say that in euro area countries financial integration might weaken market discipline and eliminate the market's ability or willingness to discriminate in terms of the quality of national fiscal policies. One reason for this is, as pointed out in the paper, the zero-risk-weighting of euro-denominated sovereign debt in the euro area and the equal treatment of all euro area sovereign bonds for collateral purposes by the ECB. A further reason is that, also pointed out in the paper, market perceptions do not necessarily provide strong and compelling signals, as the market can become irrational and dysfunctional at times.

M. Kumamoto (✉)
Faculty of Economics, Tokyo Keizai University,
Tokyo, Japan
e-mail: kumamoto@tku.ac.jp

S. Kaji and E. Ogawa (eds.), *Who Will Provide the Next Financial Model?: Asia's Financial Muscle and Europe's Financial Maturity*,
DOI 10.1007/978-4-431-54282-7_10, © Springer Japan 2013

Capital inflows into Asian emerging countries have been growing again, especially since the GFC, due to excess liquidity and lower interest rates in advanced countries. As a result, not only government bond markets but also other asset markets in most Asian countries have been in boom despite the differences in national fiscal soundness and national economic situations. Therefore, it is important to investigate whether capital inflows into each country would discriminate or reflect the quality of each national fiscal policy and/or national economic situation.

In regard to this point, it is also important to investigate the determinants of capital inflows into Asian countries. Traditional literature classifies the determinants of capital flows into two categories: the push or external factor and the pull or internal factor. The push factor is a common factor that pushes capital towards emerging countries. For example, it includes excess global liquidity and economic growth in advanced countries, foreign interest rates and the risk appetite of foreign investors. In contrast, the pull factor is a factor that attracts capital flows into emerging countries. For example, it includes domestic interest rates, real GDP growth, public sector balance, total exports to GDP ratios, foreign debt service to GDP ratios, and real exchange rates and volatility.

If capital inflows are determined by pull factors, then sound or improving economic policies in emerging countries are a crucial condition for stable development. By contrast, if capital inflows are determined by push factors, then flows are highly unstable and emerging countries are subject to the evolution of macroeconomic and financial conditions in advanced countries. General articles conclude that in the 1990s, push factors explained the majority of capital flows into Latin America, while pull factors explained the majority of capital flows into Asia [e.g., Chuhan et al. (1998)]. However, some literature also shows that the situation in the second half of the 2000s was quite different to the 1997 pre-crisis period. Push factors including interest rate differences with Japan, exchange rates with the dollar, growth in advanced countries, and excess global liquidity and the risk appetite of foreign investors have all played an important role in capital inflow [e.g., Brana and Lahet (2010)]. These results throw doubt on the sustainability of capital inflows into Asian countries. Foreign investors have come to treat each Asian financial markets equally despite the differences in national economic situations, which could mean that if external factors in advanced countries were to improve in the near future, then capital inflows would suddenly stop and/or capital reversals would occur in all Asian countries, even if they had sound or improving economic policies, leading Asian countries into the early phases of new global financial turmoil.

The second comment concerns the monetary policy framework in Asian countries in terms of the "Impossible Trinity". After the Asian currency crisis, Korea introduced inflation targeting in 1998, followed by Thailand and Indonesia in 2000, and the Philippines in 2002. In these countries, the rapid depreciation of their currencies because of speculative pressures in 1997 led to fears of inflation—this action was necessary at the time of the crisis to ensure adequate liquidity in the financial system.

To stabilize inflation expectations, there was a need for a new anchor for monetary policy. The introduction of inflation targeting has contributed to economic recovery by stabilizing inflation expectations, and it has served to promote sound monetary policy by enhancing the transparency and accountability of monetary policy decision-making in these four Asian countries. At the same time, they have aggressively intervened with sterilization to limit credit growth and to temper excess leverage and asset price booms. As pointed out in the paper, Asia has generally taken an eclectic approach to balancing exchange rate stability, monetary policy independence and capital account liberalization. However, sterilized intervention has its limits because of its impact on the central bank balance sheet.

In general, central banks in advanced countries with inflation targeting argue that policy should only respond to exchange rate movements if they threaten the attainment of the inflation objective. However, in emerging countries, some theoretical studies in the literature state that stability is achieved by adding an exchange rate term to their Taylor rule for setting interest rates and by attaching a greater weight to it. This is due to their shallow currency markets, short-history of stable inflation, the importance of the exchange rate as an anchor for expectations and the possibility of currency mismatch [e.g., Amato and Gerlach (2002) and Aghion et al. (2009)]. In contrast, some empirical studies have shown that there is little evidence that monetary policies in inflation targeting Asian countries respond to the movements of exchange rates [e.g., Cavoli (2010) and Aizenman et al. (2011)].

As a result, the movement of exchange rates has been more volatile after the crisis. Because the degree of external or foreign dependence is usually high in emerging market countries, volatile exchange rates would cause volatile inflation rates and would discourage internal trade among Asian countries; especially, as pointed out in the paper, intra-regional exchange rate volatility, which has been increasing and might disturb foreign trade and the destination of foreign direct investments. Therefore, intra-regional exchange rate stability and cooperation is desirable to promote intra-regional trade, and the paper advocates the exchange rate coordination using the ACU as a reference to limit variations in individual currency exchange rates. In this respect, it might be useful for central banks in inflation targeting Asian countries to add the movement of ACU to their monetary policy reaction function.

In addition, there are two controversial arguments on whether the central bank should target asset prices when they conduct monetary policy. One view, the "BIS view" is that the inflation targeting central banks should respond to asset price misalignments because of the damaging effect of asset price booms and busts on the financial system as well as the real economy [e.g., Cecchetti et al. (2003)]. The alternative view, the "FRB view" is that inflation targeting central banks should not respond to asset price fluctuations [e.g., Bernanke and Gertler (2001) and Goodfriend (2003)]. It is difficult to judge which view is appropriate for Asian countries, but this could be an important issue for Asian countries attempting to cope with large capital inflows.

## References

Aghion P, Bacchetta P, Ranciere R, Rogoff K (2009) Exchange rate volatility and productivity growth: the role of financial development. J Monet Econ 56:494–513

Aizenman J, Hutchison M, Noy I (2011) Inflation targeting and real exchange rates in emerging markets. World Dev 39(5):712–724

Amato JD, Gerlach S (2002) Inflation targeting in emerging market and transition economies: lessons after a decade. Eur Econ Rev 46:781–790

Bernanke BS, Gertler M (2001) Should central banks respond to movements in asset prices. Am Econ Rev 91:253–257

Brana S, Lahet D (2010) Determinants of capital inflows into Asia: the relevance of contagion effects as push factors. Emerg Mark Rev 11:273–284

Cavoli T (2010) What drives monetary policy in post-crisis East Asia? Interest rate or exchange rate monetary policy rules. J Asian Econ 21(5):456–465

Cecchetti SG, Genberg H, Wadhwani S (2003) Asset prices in a flexible inflation targeting framework. In: Hunter WC, Kaufman GG, Pomerleano M (eds) Asset price bubbles. MIT Press, Cambridge, MA, pp 427–444

Chuhan P, Claessens S, Mamingi N (1998) Equity and bond flows to Latin America and Asia: the role of global and country factors. J Dev Econ 55:439–463

Goodfriend M (2003) Interest rate policy should not react directly to asset prices. In: Hunter WC, Kaufman GG, Pomerleano M (eds) Asset price bubbles. MIT Press, Cambridge, MA, pp 445–458

Manganelli S, Wolswijk G (2007) Market discipline, financial integration and fiscal rules: what drives spreads in the Euro area government bond market? ECB working paper series, no 745

# Part III
# The Financial Sector

# Is a New Financial Model Necessary for Growth?

**Carlo Altomonte and Lorenzo Saggiorato**

**Abstract** Fostering a country's competitiveness is crucial to provide a viable escape from the current crisis. Using a novel micro-level dataset (EFIGE dataset), this chapter analyzes the relationship between firm-level productivity and the ability of a firm to compete in international markets. Subsequently, the chapter investigates the link between productivity and access to external financing during the crisis. We found that more productive firms are less likely to apply for external financing, but once they do apply for extra credit, they experience a higher probability of obtaining the loan. This selection mechanism is, however, effective only at very low levels of productivity, and creates some friction when firms move up the productivity ladder. This evidence calls for renewed attention by policymakers to ensure that the implementation of new banking regulations is able to guarantee an allocation of credit and access to finance that correlates to firms' underlying productivity.

**Keywords** Credit access • Firm-level heterogeneity • Total factor productivity

## 1 Introduction

The ability to "grow out" of the crisis is currently widely recognized as the only viable long-term option for the sustainability of the EU. The situation in Japan is similar, with signs that economic stagnation and high levels of public debt are

C. Altomonte (✉)
Bocconi University, via Sarfatti 25, 20136, Milano, Italy

Bruegel, Brussels, Belgium
e-mail: carlo.altomonte@unibocconi.it

L. Saggiorato
Bocconi University, via Sarfatti 25, 20136, Milano, Italy
e-mail: lorenzo.saggiorato@unibocconi.it

S. Kaji and E. Ogawa (eds.), *Who Will Provide the Next Financial Model?: Asia's Financial Muscle and Europe's Financial Maturity*,
DOI 10.1007/978-4-431-54282-7_11, © Springer Japan 2013

once again looming. And yet, much of the current policy debate tends to revolve around the short-term aspects of recovery, related to financial stability in the wake of the crisis, be it the collapse of Lehman Brothers or the euro area. While the latter is of paramount importance for the overall sustainability of the world economy, much less emphasis is devoted to the equally important discussion on competitiveness-enhancing "structural" reforms conducive to higher growth and prosperity.

From a political economy perspective, the latter asymmetric behavior is quite rational; the political return on crisis-management policies is larger as governments have a greater ability to use well-known tools (fiscal or monetary policies) that are able to influence, in the short-run, the business cycle. In contrast, the political return on structural reforms is perceived to be low, as the effectiveness of the policy actions is less clear and, if anything, significant changes in competitiveness might take place only in the medium- to long-run. As a result, stability comes first in the political agenda, while structural reforms tend to be postponed to "better times".

The risk of such an approach is that the resulting policy framework implicitly generates a trade-off between stability and competitiveness-enhancing policies, with the former clearly dominating the latter. While the political dividend of such a setup might be relevant in the short-run, over time the resulting institutional framework might impose a straightjacket on growth, with both Europe and Japan possibly being very stable over the next decades but also marginal players in the global arena.

To solve such a conundrum, it is useful to recall a general rule of economic policy, stating that the number of instruments at hand has to be equal to the number of objectives we want to achieve. It then follows that if stability and growth have to be jointly pursued in our quest for a new financial model, one should identify and use a set of tools able to exert effects on both the short- and long-term phase of the cycle. In other words, *mutatis mutandis*, one should complement policy actions envisaged as a short-term reaction to the crisis with regulatory changes in the structural features of the economy (essentially the functioning of labor and capital markets) in ways conducive to the creation of a more competitive economic environment characterized by higher growth rates.

In this chapter we attempt to capitalize on new evidence from a representative set of European firms, to assess the extent to which European financial markets are able to reallocate resources to firms in ways that are conducive to growth. We find a significant degree of heterogeneity across countries with some potentially adverse results in terms of competitiveness, showing a significant scope for policy action to reform the EU financial model to become more conducive to growth.

In particular, Sect. 2 of the chapter presents our dataset and Sect. 3 develops some measures of competitiveness at the firm-level, essentially related to productivity and the ability of firms to export to international markets. Section 4 links the characteristics of these "competitive" firms to the functioning of EU financial markets, while Sect. 5 concludes with some policy implications.

## 2 A Micro-level Approach: Data Description

This analysis relies on the EU-EFIGE/Bruegel-UniCredit dataset (hereafter the EFIGE dataset), a unique firm-level dataset collected within the project *EFIGE—European Firms in a Global Economy: internal policies for external competitiveness*, supported by the Directorate General Research of the European Commission through its 7th Framework Programme.[1] The dataset presents a number of desirable features, as it surveyed approximately 15,000 manufacturing firms of more than ten employees, across seven European countries, and is constructed to obtain representative samples for each country. Table 1 provides an overview of the sample.

The selected firms answered a questionnaire, covering several dimensions of their strategies. The topics of the various survey sections included ownership and managerial structure, labor force, innovation and R&D activities, exposure to international markets, financial relations and business environment. The survey was administrated in 2010 with a focus on the activities of the previous 2 years. However, by merging the dataset to balance sheet information, it was possible to collect balance sheet data for all the surveyed firms for the period 2001–2009, exploiting the information provided by Amadeus, a firm-level dataset by Bureau van Dijk covering firms all over Europe.[2] The latter enabled analysis with a multiple time dimension.

Using the Amadeus data, a measure of firm-level productivity was computed. Among the various indicators of productivity (Unit Labor Cost, Labor Productivity, Total Factor Productivity—TFP), we adopted TFP, consistent with the theory and previous empirical results. As an indicator, TFP considers the impact of different factors of production on output and is easily comparable across sectors with different production functions. The idea behind TFP is that productivity can be thought of

**Table 1** Overview of the sample

| Country | Number of firms |
|---|---|
| Austria | 443 |
| France | 2,973 |
| Germany | 2,935 |
| Hungary | 488 |
| Italy | 3,021 |
| Spain | 2,832 |
| UK | 2,067 |
| Total | 14,759 |

[1] Additional project information can be obtained from the official web site: www.efige.org

[2] See www.bvdinfo.com for further information on the dataset.

**Table 2** Descriptive statistics (averages 2001–2009)

| Country | No. of firms | Avg. No. of employees | Avg. total assets | Avg. revenues | Avg. K/L | Avg. TFP |
|---|---|---|---|---|---|---|
| Austria | 443 | 70.32 | 9,023.63 | 17,282.96 | 135.13 | 1.57 |
| France | 2,973 | 65.1 | 7,427.06 | 11,576.87 | 113.17 | 1.18 |
| Germany | 2,935 | 108.33 | 7,385.32 | 14,067.98 | 130.23 | 1.49 |
| Hungary | 488 | 126.47 | 6,832.29 | 9,750.56 | 79.79 | 1.80 |
| Italy | 3,021 | 50.74 | 9,918.26 | 11,162.72 | 225.76 | 0.90 |
| Spain | 2,832 | 49.32 | 7,675.85 | 8,859.37 | 134.18 | 0.97 |
| UK | 2,067 | 126.92 | 5,801.84 | 21,489.45 | 137.11 | 1.03 |
| Total | 14,759 | 68.3 | 7,809.71 | 11,802.55 | 154.12 | 1.06 |

as a firm's ability to combine inputs to obtain a given output. In other words, one could state that a firm that produces greater outputs, given a certain allocation of inputs, has a higher level of productivity. Thus, productivity is quantitatively captured as the residual term of the estimation of the following production function in Eq. (1):

$$Y_{it} = \alpha K_{it} + \beta L_{it} + \gamma M_{it} + \varepsilon_{it}. \tag{1}$$

Consistent with standard practice in the economic literature, productivity was computed following the approach proposed by Levinsohn and Petrin (Levinsohn and Petrin 2003). The authors provide a measure of Total Factor Productivity that is not affected by the simultaneity bias that might occur with a standard Ordinary Least Square (OLS) estimate of Eq. (1), because the residual term, which the model regards as productivity, is unobserved by the econometrician. However, some part of it might be known to the firm when deciding on the amount of inputs to be used, especially capital and labor. The solution adopted by the authors consists in a semi-parametric estimation of Eq. (1), using the total cost of materials as an instrumental variable to solve the simultaneity bias problem (see Levinsohn and Petrin 2003 for the assumptions behind this choice).

Table 2 shows the descriptive statistics for the sample. Note that the number of firms presented is constant over time, whereas the other figures vary. The table also reports the average value of each variable by country over the considered time span.

The table suggests that there are some relevant structural differences among the sample countries. We notice, for instance, that firms located in Italy and Spain are much smaller in terms of the average number of employees; conversely, firms located in the United Kingdom, Hungary and Germany employ many more workers than the sample average. This difference does not always correspond to a proportional mark-up in terms of TFP.

## 3 Competitiveness Analysis with Firm-Level Data

One of the advantages emerging from the use of firm-level data is that it is much easier to take into account the differentiated impact of policy actions accruing from firm heterogeneity, i.e., the fact (confirmed by a vast body of literature, as in Mayer and Ottaviano 2008) that within an industry or country there are many low-performing firms and just a few high-performers. The point is exemplified in Fig. 1: working at the aggregate-level, i.e., using "average" indicators at a country- or industry-level, would typically imply the assumption of an underlying normal distribution for each firm-level variable, as represented in blue in the figure. However, empirical evidence suggests that any firm performance will be displayed with the majority of firms located on the left-hand side of the distribution and just a few on the right tail. In other words, any performance indicator at an industry or country-level, deriving from the aggregation of heterogeneous firms, will be distributed according to a Pareto-type density function, as depicted in red in Fig. 1. It stands then that working at the aggregate-level would imply a misspecification of reality, because an eventual aggregate performance measure calculated using means risks being biased, most likely upwards, thus delivering a distorted picture of the real underlying competitive position of a given industry or country.

The same will be true if we try to assess the extent to which the structure of a given financial market is conducive for higher levels of competitiveness. In an environment characterized by firm heterogeneity, what really matters is not (only) whether, e.g., credit has been eased or not, on average, in the aftermath of the crisis, but rather whether this increase is in line with firms' productivity. In other words, the general functioning of financial markets has to be assessed with respect to the

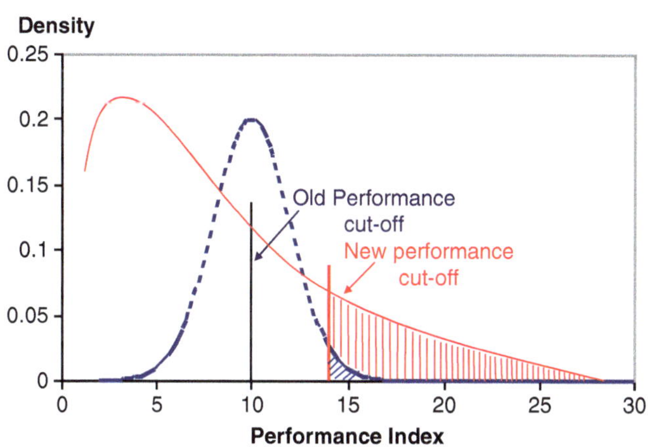


**Fig. 1** Actual distribution of firms. Source: Altomonte et al. (2011)

**Table 3** Distribution of exporters

| Country | Share of exporters |
|---|---|
| Austria | 0.77 |
| France | 0.63 |
| Germany | 0.65 |
| Hungary | 0.7 |
| Italy | 0.74 |
| Spain | 0.63 |
| UK | 0.67 |
| Total | 0.67 |

differentiated impact it will generate on the heterogeneous performance of firms and, via this way, on the economy as a whole. Coming back to the previous example, if there has been a relatively low increase in the cost of credit for the more productive firms, the post-crisis context would set in motion a Schumpeterian selection effect in which less productive firms would find it increasingly difficult to access capital and therefore exit. This produces potential benefits for aggregate productivity. By the same token, a policy seeking to promote corporate access to capital in this context would also result in an efficient (with respect to productivity and growth) allocation of capital across firms.

In contrast, if the functioning of capital markets is such that access to capital is eased for all firms across the board, irrespective of their productivity levels, or, worse still, if the relatively less productive (but better connected) firms end up having better access to finance during and after the crisis, then the effect of the reallocation of capital induced by the crisis (and/or a specific policy in this context) would harm aggregate productivity, as the most competitive firms would be constrained in their growth.

The first step of the research is thus to identify "competitive" firms in our sample, to learn about their relations with financial intermediaries vs. those of relatively less competitive firms. We define competitiveness as the ability of firms to compete in international markets, as the latter is also often cited as a distinctive element of "competitiveness" at the country-level. Moreover, as will be explained in the following analysis, such a definition of competitiveness is strictly linked to each firm's TFP.

We start our analysis by creating a binary variable, giving a value of one to those firms that exported at least part of their output before or during 2008, and otherwise zero. Table 3 provides the shares of exporting firms across the sample countries (the so-called "extensive margin" of exports).

It emerges that there are no structural differences among the considered countries, with the shares of the active firms being very similar to one another. However, in light of the above arguments, it could well be the case that within-country heterogeneity might matter more than across-country heterogeneity.

Figure 2 plots the (log) distribution of TFP for exporting firms vs. non-active abroad firms, which are defined as those that do not operate in any way in international

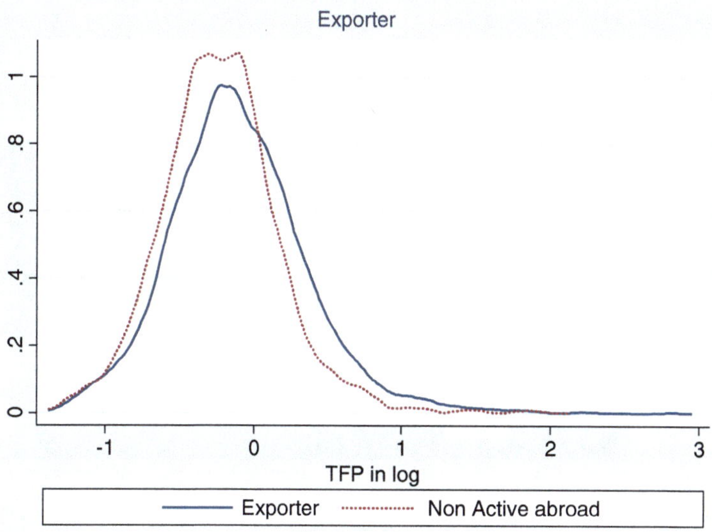


**Fig. 2** TFP density according to international activity

markets (through export, import, outsourcing or foreign direct investment—FDI). It clearly emerges that those firms that are able to compete in international markets have, on average, higher TFP levels, as witnessed by the thicker right tail of the distribution. It also emerges, not surprisingly, that there is a substantial heterogeneity among firms (note that Fig. 2 reports a log-distribution), with a long right tail of very productive firms (even within firms that are non-active abroad) and a clear mass of relatively less productive firms.

Figure 3 provides further evidence supporting this issue, which reports the shares of exporting firms for the various TFP deciles.

It stands clear that after a certain level of productivity, the probability that the firm exports at least some of its products substantially increases, in particular from the 7th decile onward. Referring to the economic literature (e.g., Melitz 2003; Melitz and Ottaviano 2008), the latter can be considered in our sample as the "cut-off" (i.e., the minimum level) for productivity that enables firms to compete in international markets. Those firms that survive but cannot meet the "cut-off" are instead more likely to only operate in the domestic market.

The analyzed relationship is robust regarding econometric evidence, which shows on average a 10% productivity premium of exporting vs. domestic firms across the sample, even controlling for country- or industry-specific characteristics. Furthermore, the identified "cut-off" is significant as it is associated with a 95% probability of exporting when TFP is above the 7th decile of the underlying distribution (and always controlling for country and industry characteristics).

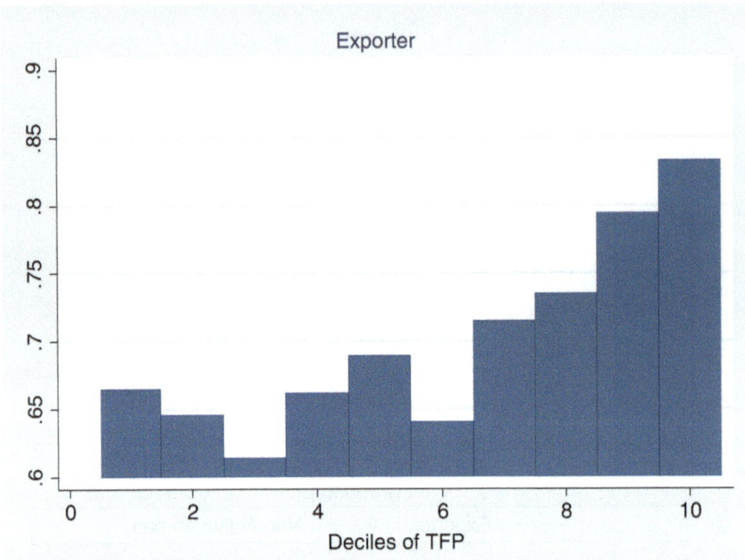


**Fig. 3** Distribution of internationally active firms by TFP deciles

We can therefore conclude that the concept of TFP is a significant proxy of the competitiveness of a firm in international markets, and thus we can use this variable when assessing the functioning of financial institutions in Europe.

## 4 Competitiveness and Capital Markets

In this section we try to establish a link between our proxy of competitiveness and its relationship with the workings of financial markets. In particular, we analyze this interaction along three dimensions: the first relates to the financial characteristics of the firm, measured via a set of variables constructed using Amadeus balance sheet information; the second dimension exploits data provided by EFIGE and analyzes the extent to which firms are credit rationed as a function of their productivity; and finally we analyze the purposes and uses of the extra credit, when obtained.

Six indicators have been created to measure the financial shape of a firm following the growing literature on the link between firm-level performance and capital markets.[3] First, the Financial Independence Index (FII) is computed as the sum of capital and cash flows, divided by total assets; it measures the extent to which a firm

[3] For further information regarding this subject and specifically the indicators used see Kaplan and Zingales (1997), Nickell and Nicolitsas (1999) and Forlani (2010).

self-finances its long-term economic activity. The Cash Ratio (CashR), obtained as the ratio between cash flows and current liabilities, measures the ability of a firm to repay short-term debt just with generated cash flows. The Index of Financial Pressure (IFP) is computed as the ratio between interest payments and the sum of profits, depreciation and interest payments itself; it ranges from zero to one, with one indicating higher financial pressure. The Current Ratio (CurrR), given by current assets over current liabilities, and measures the ability of a firm facing short-term debt with activities to be carried out in the short-term. The Liquidity Ratio (LR), computed as the difference between current assets and current liabilities, divided by total assets, measures the extent to which a firm is able to repay its current asset with short-term liabilities. Last, the Leverage Ratio (LevR), measured as the ratio between total debt and capital, indicates the degree that a company depends on external financial sources.[4]

To correctly assess the relationships between the various financial characteristics and productivity, the following model is estimated:

$$TFP_{it} = \alpha + \beta F_{it} + \overline{\gamma} FE_{it} + \varepsilon_{it}, \qquad (2)$$

where TFP is, as usual, Total Factor Productivity, F is one of the six financial indicators introduced above[5] and FE is a matrix of fixed firm-level controls for a country, the industry of activity (measured as 2-digit NACE revision 1.1), the size of the firm and the year of observation. The introduction of these controls enables the ruling out of a possible compositional effect that might bias the estimation, as some sectors or countries could be characterized by high productivity and better financial shape; controlling for the specified fixed-effects ensures that the estimate obtained is not driven by any compositional effect.

In the light of what emerged in Figs. 1 and 2 concerning the Pareto-shaped distribution of productivity, estimating the model in Eq. (2) via OLS appears inconsistent because this would imply working on average effects; we instead used a quantile regression (Koenker and Bassett 1978), which estimates a linear model for each specified quantile. This method captures the various impacts of the regressors considered at different levels of the dependent variable. Figure 4 provides a graphical representation of the coefficients estimated from Eq. (2), showing all six financial indicators considered for the ten deciles of TFP. Analyzing the figure, it is important to first focus on the vertical axis of each graph and note that each indicator is linked to TFP with a sign indicating that more productive firms are, on average, in better financial shape (with respect to all the indicators considered). This relationship would also have been estimated with an OLS model, as it is represented by the horizontal lines on the graphs indicating the "average" OLS estimated coefficient and its confidence interval. However, the quantile regression approach adopted goes further, providing information on the relationship at different levels of TFP. Indeed, it

[4] Annex shows the equations relative to each indicator.

[5] The indicators are not introduced together in the regression to avoid multicollinearity problems.

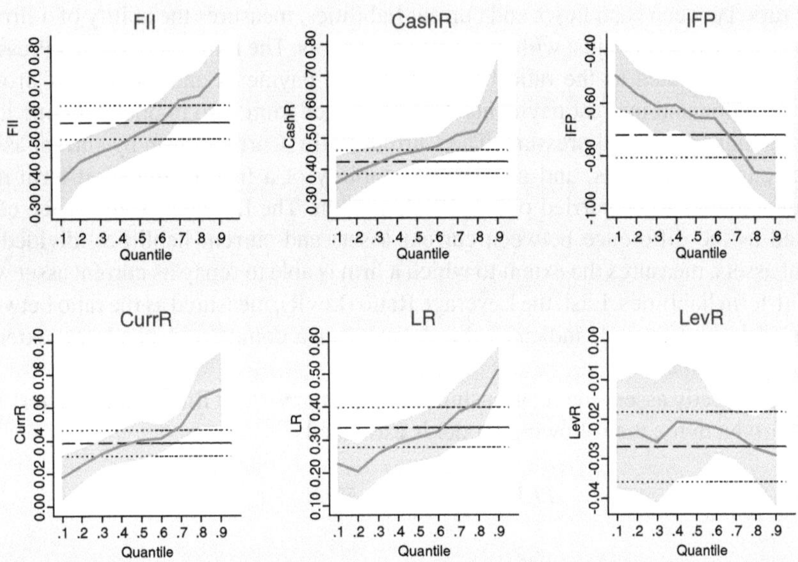


**Fig. 4** Coefficients of financial indicators on TFP deciles

emerges that for all the analyzed indicators, with the exception of LevR, the relationship between TFP and financial well-being is not only positive, but it increases along the deciles of TFP. Thus, at higher levels of productivity, the positive relationship between the financial indicator with TFP is even stronger.[6]

The positive and increasing relationship estimated is consistent with a simple comparison of the averages of the indicators at different levels of productivity, but the former does not suffer from the composition effect that might bias the latter, as discussed above. To provide further evidence, the average value of the FII is 0.36 for firms in the first decile of productivity and 0.66 for those in the last decile; likewise, the average value for Index of Financial Pressure decreases from 0.22 for the first decile to 0.06 for the final one. Comparable patterns were obtained for all indicators. This analysis provides some preliminary insights into the relationship between productivity and capital markets. Indeed, it suggests that there exists a relationship between the financial shape of a firm and its productivity—its ability to compete in international markets.

After identifying a link between productivity and financial well-being, we can now investigate whether more productive firms also have easier access to capital markets, in particular via the banking system. In other words, we wish to investigate the extent to which banks are able to discriminate among firms when dealing with credit requests. Note too that the timing of the survey, conducted in 2010 over the

[6] The relationship estimated with respect to IFP and LevR is negative and decreases with TFP deciles because both indicators have a negative connotation.

**Table 4** Credit rationing across sample countries (%)

| | Credit rationing | | |
|---|---|---|---|
| Country | No rationing | Weak rationing | Strong rationing |
| Austria | 40.0 | 46.0 | 14.0 |
| France | 30.5 | 42.1 | 27.4 |
| Germany | 36.9 | 44.9 | 18.2 |
| Hungary | 14.0 | 48.8 | 37.2 |
| Italy | 24.7 | 36.7 | 38.7 |
| Spain | 22.5 | 46.6 | 30.9 |
| UK | 59.3 | 33.3 | 7.4 |
| Total | 28.2 | 42.2 | 29.5 |

period 2008–2009, enabled us to focus on the effect of the crisis on credit rationing. Using EFIGE data, it was possible to identify 1,997 firms that applied for extra credit in 2008.

These firms have been subsequently classified according to the outcome of the request: firms whose requests were successful and credit granted at the same rate as the previous year were classified as non-rationed; those whose requests were successful but the loans were subject to higher rates than the previous year were classified as weakly credit rationed; and those whose requests for extra credit were denied were classified as strongly credit rationed.[7]

Table 4 provides a snapshot of the issue in the various sample countries.[8] It is evident that in every country, with the exception of the United Kingdom, the most common classification is weak credit rationing, followed by strong rationing.

The table indicates that the issue of strong credit rationing is more likely to occur in southern Europe, especially Italy, where more than one in three firms had their credit applications denied. This percentage decreases until it reaches the value for the United Kingdom, where only 7.4% of the applicant firms were refused. In each country, the percentage of strongly-rationed firms is inversely proportional to that of non-rationed firms. However, it emerges that the vast majority of firms in all countries, with the exception of the United Kingdom, face the serious issue of weak rationing, with a percentage range of 33% (United Kingdom) to 48% (Hungary). This indicates that even if the bank did accept the credit request, the firm had to pay a higher interest rate compared with the previous year.

Figure 5 shows the percentages of the various extents of credit rationing according to the deciles of TFP. On the one hand, a virtuous pattern can be identified when considering together the non-rationed and weakly rationed firms, because the sum of the two categories increases with TFP deciles. The first decile has a value of 60%,

[7] The definitions of weak and strong credit constraints are derived from those proposed by Minetti and Zhu (2011), who worked on a similar variable for Italy.

[8] Note that the percentages are computed over the number of firms that applied for extra credit, by country.

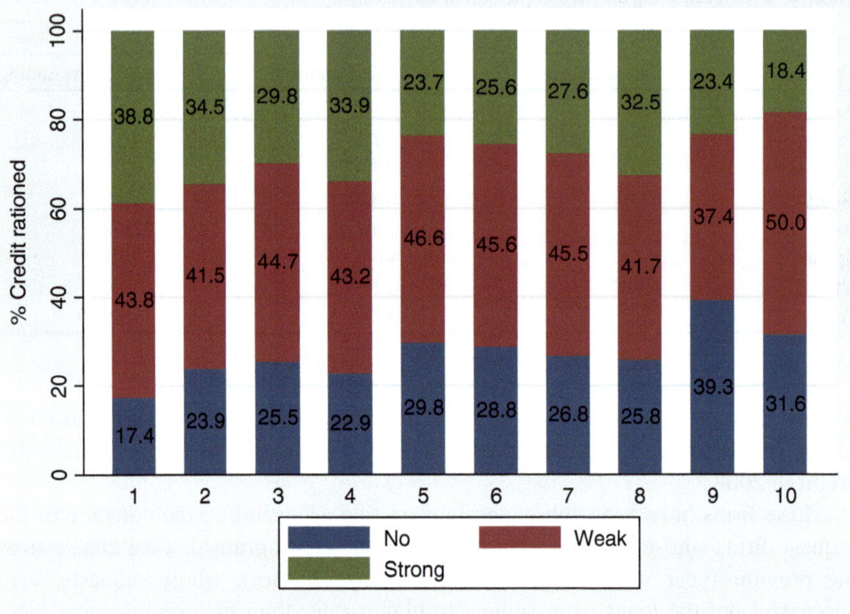


**Fig. 5** Credit rationing across TFP deciles (%)

increasing to 80% for the last one. The latter indicates that firms in the upper deciles of TFP, once they apply for more credit, are more likely to see their request fulfilled, possibly at marginally higher rates with respect to the previous year. Indeed, 39% of the firms in the first decile of productivity that applied for extra credit had their requests denied, while the figure lowers to 18% for firms in the tenth decile of productivity.

However, on the other hand, we notice that some forms of weak rationing persists during the crisis regardless of the TFP decile in which the firm requesting credit is operating. The latter casts a shadow on the ability of the financial markets to provide credit to the "right" firm via adequate forms of screening. Clearly, it is important to bear in mind that the variable on credit rationing is defined only for those firms that actually applied for extra credit, while the vast majority of firms in our sample decided not to follow this road, either because they did not require credit or perhaps due to the fact that they believed that they were unlikely to be successful. For these reasons, Fig. 5 provides a reduced level of information regarding the relationship between access to the capital markets and productivity.

Hence, to obtain a clearer overview of the issue, Table 5 (from which Fig. 5 was generated) presents further evidence regarding credit rationing across TFP deciles.[9]

[9] Take note that the total number of credit rationed firms does not match the figure of 1,997 presented previously. This is because the 2008 TFP value for 736 firms is missing.

**Table 5** Credit rationing across TFP deciles

| | Credit rationing | | | |
|---|---|---|---|---|
| TFP deciles | No | Weak | Strong | Total |
| 1 | 31 | 78 | 69 | 178 |
| 2 | 34 | 59 | 49 | 142 |
| 3 | 36 | 63 | 42 | 141 |
| 4 | 27 | 51 | 40 | 118 |
| 5 | 39 | 61 | 31 | 131 |
| 6 | 36 | 57 | 32 | 125 |
| 7 | 33 | 56 | 34 | 123 |
| 8 | 31 | 50 | 39 | 120 |
| 9 | 42 | 40 | 25 | 107 |
| 10 | 24 | 38 | 14 | 76 |
| Total | 333 | 553 | 375 | 1,261 |

Indeed, the table suggests that the number of firms that apply for extra credit is not irrespective of productivity; as the last column of the table shows, the figure is constantly diminishing with the increase of TFP deciles, indicating that firms in higher deciles of productivity are self-selected, in the sense that, not surprisingly, they are less likely to apply for credit.

This evidence is of major importance with respect to the research question of this analysis, and it is also consistent with the evidence derived from Table 4. More productive firms have a stronger financial structure and rely less on external financing; as a direct implication they are less likely to apply for extra credit, and even if they do, they appear to have easier access to additional loans.

To assess the issue with a robust econometric tool, we estimate a Heckman selection model (Heckman 1976), where the first stage is a probit estimate on the probability of applying for more credit, given the productivity of a firm and the fact that it undertakes, or not, R&D activities.[10] Once the fact that the firm has actually applied for extra credit has been accounted for, the second stage consists in an OLS estimate of the correlation of TFP with three possible outcomes for the variable on credit rationing. The results (not reported here) support what has already emerged: productivity has a negative impact on the probability of requesting credit, but once the additional loan is requested, more productive firms face lower probabilities of seeing the request denied, and also of being charged higher interest rates.

In the next stage of the analysis we focus on assessing the extent to which banks are able to discriminate among firms. It has been shown in Table 4 that there is a strong ongoing relationship between Total Factor Productivity and the financial

[10] The inclusion of R&D in the estimate has the function of exclusion restriction: it is a variable that is correlated with the selection term (probability of requesting extra credit) but not necessarily with the dependent variable of the outcome equation (TFP). Our results show that R&D is slightly positively and significantly correlated with TFP in our sample (+0.0377***), but much more with the probability of requesting credit (+0.2932***). The exclusion restriction helps the strong identification of the selection equation and thus of the model.

shape of a firm. Thus, it seems reasonable to assume that when deciding whether or not to grant a loan, banks are able to observe more easily the financial structure of a firm (and then decide) rather than its productivity.

We rely on this assumption and move to compare the relationship between TFP and the financial characteristics of the firms in the sub-sample of firms that did not apply for credit or applied and received it (both proper non-rationed firms and weakly rationed ones) vs. the sub-sample of strongly rationed firms. In particular, we focus on the two liquidity-related variables, CashR and CurrR, as these indicators do not depend directly on the fact of having received a loan, like FII and LevR, or through the repayment of interests, as with IFP.

If this relationship does not vary from one sub-sample to another, then it implies that banks are not effective in discriminating among firms; conversely, a significant change in the relationship would imply that credit rationed firms are actually different from others. From a more formal viewpoint, a quantile regression is appropriate here, following the model in Eq. (2), and includes an interaction term between the financial indicator (CashR and CurrR) and the binary variable "rationed" (taking a value of one for strongly rationed firms). The resulting equation is as follows:

$$TFP_i = \alpha + \beta F_i + \gamma Rationed_i + \delta Rationed * F_i + \eta FE_i + \varepsilon_i. \quad (3)$$

Table 6 provides the results of the estimate for the coefficients of the financial indicators, for both rationed and non-rationed firms. The analysis on both variables suggests that rationed firms are actually different from non-rationed ones, but only if residing on the extreme left-hand side of the distribution of TFP. Indeed, we notice that in the first deciles of productivity the relationship of both financial variables with TFP for rationed firms is positive and steeper than the one estimated for the remainder of the sample. This implies that firms with low productivity are strongly related to very poor financial structure and for this reason tend to be credit constrained.

However, moving up the TFP deciles, with respect to both indicators, this relationship is weaker and, from the fourth decile onward, the coefficients estimated for the sub-sample of strongly rationed firms are no longer different from the rest of the sample. This indicates that banks are effective in discriminating among credit requests, mainly at very low levels of productivity, which are associated with very poor financial structures. After the 4th decile of productivity no structural difference emerges between the two sub-samples. This finding is important as it highlights the diminishing power of banks to select "good" firms as firms' productivity increases, thus identifying a need for policies that improve access to capital markets.

The last paragraph of this analysis on the link between productivity and capital markets focuses on the uses of external financing. As noted by Rajan and Zingales (1998), in a financial crisis there is a clear link between a firm's performance and its reliance on external finance vs. internal cash flows, with the latter being a better setup in a crisis context. The EFIGE survey data also enable us to explore this issue,

**Table 6** Results of quantile regression, credit rationing interaction

| | (1) | (2) | (3) | (4) | (5) | (6) | (7) | (8) | (9) |
|---|---|---|---|---|---|---|---|---|---|
| Variables | q10 | q20 | q30 | q40 | q50 | q60 | q70 | q80 | q90 |
| CashR | 0.324*** | 0.382*** | 0.395*** | 0.420*** | 0.421*** | 0.460*** | 0.492*** | 0.509*** | 0.505*** |
| | (0.0500) | (0.0356) | (0.0220) | (0.0394) | (0.0510) | (0.0546) | (0.0442) | (0.0412) | (0.0837) |
| CashR*Credit rationing | 1.084*** | 0.795*** | 0.564** | 0.414 | 0.170 | −0.0191 | −0.125 | −0.423 | −0.807** |
| | (0.356) | (0.276) | (0.269) | (0.374) | (0.240) | (0.178) | (0.346) | (0.460) | (0.321) |
| CurrR | 0.0205*** | 0.0211*** | 0.0270*** | 0.0302*** | 0.0355*** | 0.0332*** | 0.0372*** | 0.0434*** | 0.0487*** |
| | (0.00638) | (0.00589) | (0.00763) | (0.00650) | (0.00416) | (0.00556) | (0.00676) | (0.00887) | (0.0146) |
| CurrR*Credit rationing | 0.220*** | 0.0962 | 0.131** | 0.0912 | 0.0824 | 0.0557 | 0.0119 | −0.0184 | −0.100 |
| | (0.0640) | (0.0600) | (0.0562) | (0.0756) | (0.0745) | (0.0854) | (0.0376) | (0.0354) | (0.121) |

Standard errors in parentheses
*** $p<0.01$, ** $p<0.05$, * $p<0.1$

**Table 7** Use and increase of external financing (%)

| Country | % of firms that recurred to ext. financing | of which: % of firms that increased ext. financing |
|---|---|---|
| Austria | 24.17 | 51.72 |
| France | 37.43 | 33.67 |
| Germany | 20.84 | 48.02 |
| Hungary | 48.07 | 44.79 |
| Italy | 60.29 | 40.38 |
| Spain | 66.57 | 48.69 |
| UK | 39.10 | 32.58 |
| Total | 44.68 | 41.75 |

as shown in Table 7, revealing that on average 44.5% of European firms have applied for external finances during the crisis. However, this is a very heterogeneous picture, with figures ranging from as low as 20% for German firms to more than 60% in the case of Italian and Spanish firms. The issue is further deepened by focusing on those firms that actually increased the total amount of external financial resources in 2008–2009. In the second column of the table we see that almost half of the firms that depend on external financing actually increased the amount of the latter during the previous year. This is true for most of the countries with the exception of the United Kingdom and France, where percentages sit around 30%. To obtain a true understanding of the extent of this phenomenon, the figures have to be compared with the percentages provided in the first column of the table.

Moreover, it is of major relevance to understand whether a firm that applied for this external finance and obtained it means to use it to foster investments, to reorganize its financial structure or to fulfill some cash flow needs. Exploiting the richness of the dataset it is possible to identify the main use (one of six categories) of the obtained loans according: investments, M&A operations with related firms, M&A operations with unrelated firms, liquidity needs, optimization of the financial structure or other uses. All the possible usages of the loans listed should be considered favorably, as they all imply a plan of growth for the firm, with the exception of "liquidity needs" because the request of a loan with the scope of fulfilling cash flow needs is in itself an indicator of some malfunctioning of the firm, where it is unable to cope with its current economic activity needs.

Table 8 reports evidence from the sample of the uses of external financing, by country.[11] The main piece of information provided by the table is that loans meant to fulfill liquidity needs are by far the most frequent instance: more than one of every two granted loans are used with this purpose. Furthermore, the figure is

[11] Note that the original question in the survey concerns the use of the increased external finance, including different sources of financing, mainly bank loans and securities; given the purpose of the research we have considered only the firms that financed through the banking system. However, when considering both sources of financing the distribution of uses by TFP deciles is not affected by major structural changes.

**Table 8** Use of increased credit obtained (%)

| Country | Investments | M&A with related firms | M&A with unrelated firms | Liquidity needs | Optimizing financial structure | Other |
|---|---|---|---|---|---|---|
| Austria | 20.55 | 0.00 | 0.00 | 24.66 | 5.48 | 49.32 |
| France | 45.96 | 2.02 | 0.51 | 40.40 | 5.56 | 5.56 |
| Germany | 23.15 | 0.62 | 0.31 | 29.01 | 5.56 | 41.36 |
| Hungary | 26.72 | 2.59 | 0.86 | 18.97 | 3.45 | 47.41 |
| Italy | 23.30 | 1.20 | 0.67 | 57.92 | 10.65 | 6.26 |
| Spain | 23.14 | 1.72 | 0.75 | 66.20 | 3.77 | 4.41 |
| UK | 11.24 | 1.50 | 0.00 | 43.07 | 7.49 | 36.70 |
| Total | 25.32 | 1.47 | 0.56 | 51.09 | 6.41 | 15.16 |

particularly high in some countries, such as Italy and Spain, where the figures are 58% and 66%, respectively, and also the United Kingdom with a share of more than 40%. Data concerning Italy and Spain are particularly relevant if we combine them with the information provided by Table 7. Indeed, we notice that a significant number of firms in these two countries increased their external financing with respect to the rest of the sample, and the vast majority of those firms used the obtained loan to address liquidity deficiencies. Given the relevance of the issue it is important to specify that this figure strongly depends on the role of the banking system in each country. It is also important to bear in mind that the magnitude of the issue could suffer from an upward bias because of the specific timing of the survey (that is, the financial crisis, with all the well-known implications on liquidity). Nevertheless, the results are quite striking.

Consistent with the approach adopted so far, we now consider the destinations of extra credit, taking into account firm-level heterogeneity. Figure 6 shows the percentages of the various uses of external financing using TFP deciles. The first feature reported in the figure is that the share of firms using the extra credit for liquidity needs drops considerably as the TFP deciles increase, decreasing from more than 70% to 35% by the last TFP decile.

Jointly with this effect we also notice a relative increase in the occurrence of other uses of the external financing: mainly investment, optimization of the financial structure and M&A activities with related firms. This piece of information completes the framework of the analysis, from which it emerges that there is, indeed, a strong relationship between competitiveness and access to capital markets.

## 5 Conclusions and Policy Implications

The evidence collected shows a differentiated picture in terms of capital markets functioning in ways that are conducive for growth and competitiveness. First of all, we found that more productive firms are in general less likely to apply for external

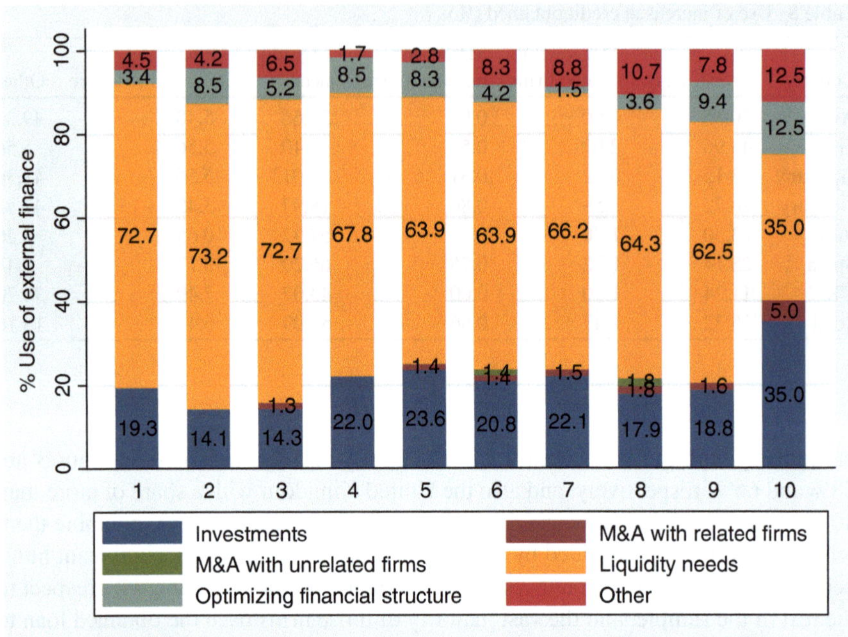


**Fig. 6** Uses of external financing across TFP deciles (%)

financing via bank loans. This is primarily due to their better financial shape, which means that they are less dependent on external resources in both the short- and long-term, but rely mainly on equity and operating cash flows. They are also subject to weaker financial pressure, which means that a smaller part of their economic activity is consumed by interest repayments.

However, it has been assessed that if more productive firms do apply for credit then they are more likely to receive it and to obtain it at the same interest rate as in the previous year. This seemingly trivial issue is, indeed, of major relevance because it suggests that even in a period of crisis with high liquidity constraints, banks in the surveyed countries have been, on average, able to discriminate and offer loans more easily to "good" firms rather than to unproductive ones.

However, we have further deepened this issue by identifying some ambiguity that occurs within this selection mechanism: banks appear significantly more effective in discriminating firms at very low levels of productivity whereas the selection process seems less precise moving up the deciles of productivity, namely from the fourth decile onward. The picture is eventually completed observing that once productive firms are granted extra credit, they are less likely to use it to replace deficiencies of the current economic activity. Rather, they are more likely to use it to foster economic growth through new investments or extraordinary finance operations, or to reorganize their financial structure.

We therefore derive a situation in which the underlying function of credit allocation by financial markets might have changed in some countries during the crisis, in ways not necessarily correlated with the productivity of the firms receiving credit. If the latter situation persists, we could face in some countries a situation in which credit is not allocated in terms of firms' productivity, with detrimental consequences for growth.

The latter outcome clearly calls for renewed attention by policymakers, not only at an EU-level but also (because of the emerging heterogeneity) nationally, making sure that the implementation of new banking regulations is able to ensure an allocation of credit and an access to finance that correlates with the underlying firms' productivity. Incidentally, such a feature of the credit markets does not often arise in the current debate on financial stability and reforms of banking regulation; but it is an issue that requires urgent discussion.

## Appendix: Description of the Financial Indicators

Below is a list of the financial variables created. The subscripts indicate that each indicator is specific for firm $i$ at time $t$.

$$FII_{it} = \frac{Capital_{it} + Cash\,Flows_{it}}{Total\,Assets_{it}}$$

$$CashR_{it} = \frac{Cash\,Flows_{it}}{CurrentLiabilities_{it}}$$

$$IFP_{it} = \frac{Interest\,Payments_{it}}{Profits\,BeforeTaxes_{it} + Depreciation_{it} + Interest\,Payments_{it}}$$

$$CurrR_{it} = \frac{Current\,Assets_{it}}{Current\,Liabilities_{it}}$$

$$LR_{it} = \frac{Current\,Assets_{it} - Current\,Liabilities_{it}}{Total\,Assets_{it}}$$

$$LevR_{it} = \frac{Total\,Debt_{it}}{Capital_{it}}$$

# References

Altomonte C, Barba Navaretti G, di Mauro F, Ottaviano G (2011) Assessing competitiveness: how firm-level data can help. Policy contributions 643, Bruegel

Forlani E (2010) Liquidity constraints and firm's export activity. Development Working Papers 291, Centro Studi Luca d'Agliano, University of Milano

Heckman J (1976) The common structure of statistical models of truncation, sample selection, and limited dependent variables and a simple estimator for such models. Ann Econ Soc Meas 5:475–492

Kaplan S, Zingales L (1997) Do financing constraints explain why investment is correlated with cash flow? Q J Econ 112:169–215

Koenker RW, Bassett G Jr (1978) Regression quantiles. Econometrica, Econometric Society 46(1):33–50

Levinsohn J, Petrin A (2003) Estimating production functions using inputs to control for unobservables. Rev Econ Stud 70(2):317–341

Mayer T, Ottaviano G (2008) The happy few: the internationalisation of European firms. Intereconomics: Review of European Economic Policy 43(3):135–148

Melitz MJ (2003) The impact of trade on intra-industry reallocations and aggregate industry productivity. Econometrica 71(6):1695–1725

Melitz MJ, Ottaviano GIP (2008) Market size, trade, and productivity. Rev Econ Stud 75(1):295–316

Minetti R, Zhu SC (2011) Credit constraints and firm export: microeconomic evidence from Italy. J Int Econ 83(2):109–125

Nickell SJ, Nicolitsas D (1999) How does financial pressure affect firms? Eur Econ Rev 43:1435–1456

Rajan RG, Zingales L (1998) Financial dependence and growth. Am Econ Rev 88(3):559–586

# Comment Paper to Chapter "Is a New Financial Model Necessary for Growth?"

**Hideki Hayashi**

## 1 Macroeconomic Environments

This paper presents the ability to "grow out of debt" as the ideal solution for the current sovereign crisis and shows how this can be achieved under the constraint of financial activities.

Using data representing the internal policies of European firms, a micro-level analysis is conducted to determine the economic behaviors of firms. However, macroeconomic environments may affect the sentiment and behavior of decision-makers, for example, managers and bank managers.

In this sense, macroeconomic environments are important factors in the analysis, especially at a time of financial crisis. This paper examines the factors that affect the ability of the firm, ranging from firm-specific factors (e.g., the sector of activity, size and technology) to macro/institutional factors (e.g., price/cost structure, investment environment and capital markets).

## 2 How Productivity Can Be Enhanced at a Firm-Level

To investigate the relationship between productivity (or competitiveness) and financial constraints, the author used firm-level European data (EFIGE).

Based on this analysis, it may be possible to evaluate whether and to what extent those identified characteristics linked to competitiveness depend on the "health" of financial institutions (banks).

H. Hayashi (✉)
Keio University, Minato, Tokyo, Japan
e-mail: hayashi@eusi.jp

S. Kaji and E. Ogawa (eds.), *Who Will Provide the Next Financial Model?: Asia's Financial Muscle and Europe's Financial Maturity*,
DOI 10.1007/978-4-431-54282-7_12, © Springer Japan 2013

The above-mentioned data covers the activities of small and medium-sized enterprises (SMEs). This is an interesting focus—not only does it enhance the sensitivity of the analysis, but it also is applicable to the productivity of Japanese firms, most of which are SMEs.

## 3 A Micro-foundation of Competitiveness

Based on measures of firm-level performance (e.g., productivity) within an industry or country, there are numerous "bad" firms, and fewer productive ones. Good companies should be provided with greater opportunities for innovation (R&D, human capital, quality certification), and better managerial practices (wages linked to productivity and no family involvement). Furthermore, greater equity appears to be associated to a higher probability of relocation and thus higher competitiveness, while financial indicators typically associated to higher bank involvement are not significant or display a negative correlation.

This conclusion indicates that more productive firms are less affected by the financial constraint of banks. However, under the present financial crisis, the implementation of strict financial regulations to achieve financial stability could financially constrain productive firms.

# European Sovereign Crisis and Its Implications for Japan: Reducing Budget Deficits Without Damaging Recovery

**Mitsuhiro Fukao**

**Abstract** Japanese government bond interest rates remains very low in spite of the very large budget deficit and very high debt-GDP ratio of the Japanese government. The Japan's low interest rates make a stark contrast to very high interest rates in the periphery countries of the Euro-zone such as Greece. This is due to the fact that Japan has an independent central bank, the Bank of Japan, and it can maintain zero-interest policy as long as deflation continues. However, the continuation of the status quo is highly risky because the market confidence in Japanese government is gradually eroding. In order to stabilize Japan's fiscal deficit, it is necessary to raise taxes on a very large scale without hurting the economy recovery. Gradual increase in the indirect taxes with some fiscal investment stimulations and/or the introduction of Gesell tax (thin tax on the balance of safe assets) are proposed as possible policy options.

**Keywords** Euro • Fiscal consolidation • Gesell tax • Sovereign crisis

## 1 Introduction

Developed countries are just as susceptible to repeated financial crises as undeveloped nations. Japan experienced a severe financial crisis in 1997–2002 after real estate and stock market booms in the late 1980. The US and many EU countries also experienced a severe crisis in 2008–2009 after the bankruptcy of Lehman Brothers. This was mainly caused by the excessive securitization of sub-prime mortgage loans

M. Fukao (✉)
Keio University, Minato, Tokyo, Japan
e-mail: fukao@fbc.keio.ac.jp

S. Kaji and E. Ogawa (eds.), *Who Will Provide the Next Financial Model?: Asia's Financial Muscle and Europe's Financial Maturity*,
DOI 10.1007/978-4-431-54282-7_13, 

and excessive risk taking by some financial institutions. Since 2009, euro countries have been experiencing a severe sovereign and banking crisis due to the excessive accumulation of government and private debt in some peripheral euro zone countries. Given the very high public debt of the Japanese government, Japan may yet soon experience a severe sovereign debt crisis.

## 2 Repeating Financial Crises

In the past, financial crises have often been caused by speculative bubbles in real estate and stocks. These bubbles are often generated by the following three factors[1]:

(1) Excessively easy monetary policies
(2) Financial deregulation and financial innovations
(3) Regulatory distortions favoring investment in certain assets such as land or sovereign bonds

This mixture of factors tends to create speculative bubbles in real estate and financial markets. The Japanese financial crisis was caused by these factors, stemming from the real estate bubble of the 1980s. The same mix of factors created a big bubble in the US residential real estate market. The Fed kept real interest rates at a very low level in the early 2000s in the face of a real estate boom, and financial deregulations allowed very high leverages in securitization and derivative markets. Tax incentives induced consumers to spend the equity in their residential property. This environment created twin bubbles in the sub-prime mortgage market and derivatives market, including credit default swaps (CDS). Risky assets were then distributed globally via increasingly integrated financial markets.

The emergence of this financial crisis was apparent in the weakening links of the market by spring 2007, but the real crisis was triggered by the failure of Lehman Brothers on September 15, 2008. The unexpected failure of the fourth largest investment bank created chaos in the world financial markets. The near failure of American International Group, Inc. (AIG), a giant AA rated US insurance company, the following day due to its excessive risk taking in the CDS market exacerbated the crisis. These events started a genuine credit crunch in US and European financial markets.

From the view point of Tokyo, there was a sense of déjà vu—the Japanese financial crisis in 1997 was triggered by the failure of two security companies and a major bank. In November 1997, the failure of Sanyo Securities, Hokkaido Takushoku Bank and Yamaichi Securities substantially contributed to Japan's financial instability. The actual amount of bad loans uncovered at failed financial institutions

[1] See Shigemi (1995).

was far larger than that disclosed prior to the failure. It was this mistrust of financial statements that blocked the domestic call market (which is used for short-term interbank loans), and multiplied the number of cash-pressed financial institutions turning to the Bank of Japan for loans. This credit crunch in turn cut into corporate investment and hiring, increased bankruptcy rates and reduced consumption and housing investments because workers feared losing their jobs.[2]

Rapid responses by major countries, including capital injections to financial institutions, the expansion of the deposit insurance system and public lending activities, aimed to stabilize the financial market. Global zero interest and expansionary fiscal policies limited the downward spiral of expenditures.

Soon after the end of the acute phase of the global financial crisis, the euro zone crisis began to surface. In 2009, peripheral euro zone countries, including Greece, Ireland and Portugal, started to experience gradual rises in government borrowing costs due to their budget and current account deficits. By the summer of 2011, the sovereign crisis of euro zone countries became very serious and the government bond interest rates of Italy, Spain and France started to rise above the interest rates of German bonds. The US-triggered global financial crisis adversely affected European financial institutions and the fiscal balances of euro zone countries. However, the root cause of the euro zone sovereign debt crisis was the premature joining of periphery countries to the monetary union; they joined before achieving a strong and sustained convergence of inflation rates with the core countries of Germany, the Netherlands and France. Moreover, low labor mobility among euro zone countries did not help labor cost adjustments among member countries.

## 3 Financial Crisis in the United States

In the global financial crisis, beginning in 2008, major US investment banks were hit hardest by the turmoil in the securitized mortgage markets. Several reasons have been documented in most analyses of the current crisis:

(1) The Securities and Exchange Commission (SEC) weakened capital requirements on five major investment banks in 2004. The SEC replaced traditional hair cut rules with VaR (value at risk) based capital requirements.
(2) Increase in highly leveraged investment strategies with derivatives and securitization. Increase in the popularity of CDS and securitization of sub-prime loans with special purpose companies (SPCs) and special purpose vehicles (SPVs).
(3) Increase by hedge funds in the use of the prime brokerage services of investment banks. In this service, investment banks could use the deposited assets of its customers to raise their funds. As a result, customers' assets were not

[2] See Fukao (1998, 2003, 2004, 2007) and Nakaso (2001) for detailed explanations of the Japanese financial crisis in 1998–2003.

separated from the assets of the bank. In the case of Lehman Brothers, many customers were not able to recover their deposited securities after the failure.

In my view, the mismanagement of the Lehman failure by the US government and the Fed exacerbated the crisis. After rescuing Bear Sterns, the fifth largest investment bank in March 2008 using public Fed money, the government allowed Lehman Brothers, the fourth largest, to file for Chap. 11 bankruptcy protection in September 2008.[3] This failure was unexpected in the financial market and shook public confidence in major financial institutions. Moreover, the value of Lehman senior debt fell to just 9 cents in the dollar 1 month after the failure. This extremely low market value for a supposedly liquid security company was a shock to many observers.

The bankruptcy of Lehman Brothers induced the following reactions in other important markets.

(1) Several money market funds (MMFs) could not maintain par value due to losses on Lehman commercial papers (CPs). As a result, money was moved from MMFs to other more secure assets such as treasury bills (TBs).
(2) Many funds withdrew assets from their prime broker investment banks such as Morgan Stanley. This response was similar to a bank run.
(3) Lehman Japan failed to deliver government bonds to its counter parties in their repo transactions. Scared Japanese financial institutions halted repo transactions with most foreign financial institutions. As a result, foreign financial institutions could not raise funds, even with Japanese government bond (JGB) collateral.

The following day after the Lehman failure, AIG, the biggest US insurance company, faced a severe liquidity problem and asked the Fed and US government for help. AIG was one of the Forbes top ten US companies in 2007 and maintained an AA rating. Its CPs had the highest credit rating until the crisis. The near collapse of AIG was trigged by its derivative unit in London, AIG Financial Products. AIG financial products sold a massive amount of CDS protection and reported big profits for the group. However, as the housing bubble burst, some of the sub-prime related CDS protection turned sour and AIG's credit rating was downgraded. This triggered a collateral requirement regarding its CDS liabilities to its counterparties. AIG asked the government to lend them a massive amount of cash to function as collateral for its CDS transactions.

AIG sold extensive amounts of CDS protection on bonds with high credit ratings and reported significant profit before the crisis. Because AIG sold protection on senior ABS of sub-prime loans, it incurred heavy losses after the sub-prime loan problem became serious. In effect, AIG underestimated the future cost of sold CDS

[3] See Duffie (2010) for an explanation regarding the failures of major investment banks.

protections. Theoretically speaking, the net present value (NPV) of CDS fees is equal to the NPV of CDS protection costs. Therefore, AIG should have retained most of the CDS fees as reserves against the future costs. However, AIG recognized most of the fees as profit.

This AIG episode also indicates that profits on derivative transactions may be overstated on the financial statements of many market players. If all the derivative transactions are evaluated using a unified evaluation scheme, all the NPVs of derivative transactions should equal zero, because derivative transactions are a zero sum game:

$$\text{CDS protection seller's profit / loss} + \text{CDS protection buyer's profit / loss} = 0$$

The case of AIG implies that the aggregated value of CDS positions for all market participants may be positive rather than zero.

Warren Buffett, the chairman of Berkshire Hathaway, highlighted this problem in early 2003.[4] Berkshire Hathaway purchased General Re, a reinsurance company; this company had a derivative subsidiary, General Re Securities. In the unwinding process of General Re Securities, Buffett found a significant undervaluation of derivative liabilities and an overvaluation of derivative assets. By the time Buffett discovered these hidden losses, the CEOs and traders of General Re Securities had left the company after receiving bonuses. Buffett pointed out that the valuation of the derivative portfolio is not market based but model based. These models can be easily manipulated to show profit in the short run. Buffett wrote, "In extreme cases, mark-to-model degenerates into what I would call mark-to-myth."

## 4 Similarity Between the Japanese and Global Financial Crisis

From the above accounts of the Japanese and US financial crises in Sects. 2 and 3, it is clear that these crises are very similar. The first factor is the loss in confidence in the soundness of major financial institutions. In Japan, public confidence in financial institutions evaporated in the face of the successive failures of Sanyo Securities, Hokkaido Takushoku Bank and Yamaichi Securities in the fall of 1997. In the United States, the successive failures of Lehman Brothers and AIG in September 2008 created a similar environment.

The causes of the failures of major financial institutions were also similar. In Japan there were the real estate loans of banks and the hidden losses of for-

[4] See Warren Buffet (2003)

ward security transactions of Yamaichi Securities. Large losses were hidden in unconsolidated subsidiaries of failed banks. In the United States, these failures were represented by losses in securitized sub-prime mortgages, hidden losses in CDS transactions and unconsolidated SPVs.

Policy reactions were also similar: repeated capital injections to major financial institutions, mergers of large financial institutions, expansion of deposit insurance coverage and increased lending by central banks and government financial institutions.

## 5 The Threat of Sovereign Crisis in Japan

The Japanese government's gross debt to GDP ratio was estimated at 233% as of the end of 2011 (IMF estimate), a level far higher than the 166% in Greece, a nation deep in financial crisis (the figures for Greece are prior to the March 2012 principal reduction of government bonds held by the private sector; the same hereafter). In terms of net debt after deducting financial asset holdings from gross debt, the ratio in Japan is 131%, rapidly approaching that of Greece at 153%. Japan's annual fiscal deficit is also at an extremely high level, and is estimated to have reached approximately ¥48 trillion and 10% of GDP in 2011. Even if Japan's consumption tax were 5 percentage points to 10% as planned by 2015, the tax revenue would amount to around ¥12 trillion, and only reduce the deficit by one quarter. Japan's financial position is becoming worse than that of the European periphery countries, which suffered financial crises and are now receiving financial support. Japan, however, does differ from these countries, and in particular Greece, in several respects.

First looking at the currency system, Greece does not have an independent currency or central bank. Therefore, the government of Greece cannot depend on a central bank as a lender of last resort to raise funds. In contrast, when facing a financial crisis, as a last resort, the Japanese government can maintain payments using borrowings from the Bank of Japan by revising the Bank of Japan Act and other legislation. This has the risk of sparking inflation, but it would happen for the purpose of averting government default.

Conditions are also very different between Japan and Greece in terms of balance of payments. Greece has an ongoing balance of payments deficit, and is a debtor nation. From 2000 to 2010, Greece's cumulative balance of payments deficit was 111% of GDP (IMF statistics; the same hereafter). Moreover, that debt is not denominated in Greece's own currency, but in the common currency of the euro. In contrast, Japan is a creditor nation, and recorded a cumulative balance of payments surplus equivalent to 28% of its GDP over the same decade. Most of Japan's government debt is yen-denominated and held inside Japan. Moreover, because Japan is a creditor nation, even if domestic investors were to consider the credit risk of the Japanese government, sell yen, which are their asset holdings, and purchase foreign currency, the subsequent depreciation of the yen would lead to (yen-denominated) gains by companies, households and financial institutions that hold foreign currency denominated assets. The Japanese government also holds some US$1.3 trillion in foreign currency reserves (as of the end of February 2012), so it would reap substantial gains from yen depreciation.

As the conditions in Japan and Greece are so different, even if Japan's fiscal deficit grows because of the reconstruction costs from the earthquake disaster, there is little likelihood that the Japanese government will fall, in the near future, into a fiscal crisis as in the euro zone. Nevertheless, the following crisis scenarios are conceivable in the long run.

(1) Politicians fear the reaction of the electorate, continue deferring tax increases, and the government's cumulative debt expands. As a result, a rise in interest rates could lead to a growing risk of an increased interest payment burden.
(2) Japan's elderly population, 50 years and older, which owns most of Japan's net financial assets will slowly lose confidence in the Japanese government and transfer their funds from yen to foreign currencies, gold, stocks, real estate, etc.
(3) The prices of long-term Japanese government bonds decline and long-term interest rates begin to rise.
(4) The government, facing an increased interest payment burden from the issuance of new bonds and the rolling over of existing bonds, shortens the maturity structure of issued bonds, and mostly finances deficits with short-term bonds. As long as the Bank of Japan maintains the zero interest rate policy, the government's interest payment burden does not increase and fiscal collapse is avoided. At the same time, however, the shortening of the government bond maturity structure brings a growing risk that future increases in short-term interest rates will suddenly increase the government's interest payments.
(5) The funds shift described in (2) accelerates with a worsening of government finances. In particular, if the current account balance turns to a deficit as the savings rate declines with an aging society and the fiscal deficit expands, there is a growing risk of a large depreciation of the yen. If, in fact, the yen then declines and share prices rise, this could be positive for business conditions and result in a bubble-like economic recovery. In turn, the inflation rate would then begin to rise. An economic recovery would increase tax revenues, and decrease the fiscal deficit. If a major tax increase and deficit reduction could be achieved at that point, it might be possible to avert fiscal collapse. If the government hesitates to raise taxes, however, the economy might enter the following scenario.
(6) If the Bank of Japan raises interest rates to counter rising inflation and implements monetary tightening, this could drastically increase the government's interest payments, and the government's credit could suddenly decline.
(7) If the government intervenes in Bank of Japan monetary policy, forces low interest rates, or forces purchases of government bonds, inflation will accelerate further and government bond prices will plunge.
(8) With the sudden rise in interest rates, banks holding large quantities of long-term government bonds would suffer massive losses, and request financial assistance from the government.

(9) If the government forces the Bank of Japan to underwrite government bonds at low interest rates, the government could avert a sudden increase in government debt from increased interest payments. In this case, just like the inflationary period immediately after Japan's defeat in the Second World War, it would be possible to significantly decrease the real value of government debt by rapid inflation and the government could successfully restore fiscal balance. In terms of income distribution, however, individuals holding government bonds, life insurance, personal pensions and other financial assets would suffer a great loss in terms of their real value. In this case, the government could restore the soundness of government finances through inflation tax.

Therefore, a loss of confidence in the government would bring great confusion to the Japanese economy and financial markets, and could cause severe damage to market functions. The maintenance of "fiscal stability" is a prerequisite to maintaining financial stability.

## 6 Policies to Stimulate the Economy While Increasing Net Tax Revenue

Given the very high levels of debt of the Japanese government, it is necessary to raise taxes or to cut expenditure. However, a tighter fiscal policy is likely to weaken the economy, at least in the short run. The Bank of Japan has kept short-term interest rates at less than 0.5% since 1995 and has almost no room to maneuver to reduce them further. Quantitative easing is very useful in a financial crisis to support banks but not as effective to stimulate final demand to expand the economy. Therefore, it is necessary to raise taxes without help from an expansionary monetary policy.

There are a few possible ways to raise tax without significantly hurting the economy. One such policy is a combination of gradual increases in indirect taxes and gradual reductions in direct taxes such as payroll tax for public pension plans, poll tax and corporate income tax. By pre-announcing a series of increases in consumption tax, the government can raise inflation expectations with front-loading effects on consumption and housing investments.[5] At the same time, by reducing payroll tax, the government can stimulate employment. These combined changes in taxes should be revenue-enhancing. The government can also use green taxes to stimulate the economy. By pre-announcing a gradual increase in carbon emission tax to reduce greenhouse gas, the government can increase inflation expectations. Using some of this tax revenue, the government can cut corporate income tax and provide subsidies for green investment.

[5] Japanese consumption tax is levied on new houses excluding the value of land.

## 7 Stimulating the Economy via a Gesell Tax

The combination of gradual increases in indirect taxes to create an artificial inflation can help to offset the negative effects on demand from increased taxes. However, when the government requires large tax revenues quickly, it may not be possible to offset the negative effects of tax increases by using part of the tax revenue. In this case, we economists have to think hard to come up with policy instruments that will be effective even under deflation. One such instrument is a Gesell tax (a famous stamp duty on money).[6] By levying tax on outstanding government guaranteed financial assets, it is possible to set a nominal return on safe assets at a negative number. In other words, it is possible to overcome the zero lower bound on nominal interest rates by introducing a new tax on some part of financial assets. In the following, I summarize my proposal stated in an earlier paper.[7]

The interest rate on safe assets can be made "negative" by taxing the balance of all government-backed financial assets such as bank deposits, government bonds, postal savings, cash, etc., at a rate that is slightly higher than the deflation rate until deflation is halted. For example, when the trend deflation rate is 1% per annum, the government may levy 2% tax on the outstanding amount of government debts, yen deposits and cash each year until the deflation ends. By pre-announcing this policy, the real interest rate can be made negative. This policy is a modified version of Silvio Gesell's stamp duty on currency as proposed in Gesell (1958).

It is easy to tax yen deposits and government bonds. To levy tax on cash, the Bank of Japan could introduce new banknotes and charge fees for the exchange with old notes. For example, the bank could exchange ¥10,200 in old money for ¥10,000 in new money. In times of deflation, people increase their holdings of cash and bank deposits, because doing so is the safest way to earn a positive real return. The pre-announced introduction of a Gesell tax would encourage investments in stocks and real estate. This negative interest rate policy is expected to decrease savings and stimulate investment. Moreover, this tax will stimulate bank lending and inter-corporate lending. If a bank retains its central bank deposits and government bonds, they will be taxed. To avoid this tax, the bank has to make loans to non-government entities. Companies also extend inter-corporate credits because cash will be taxed while receivables are not. The yen exchange rate would also depreciate against foreign currencies.

The government would also benefit from substantial revenue from this tax. A 2% tax would amount to approximately ¥30 trillion or 6% of Japan's GDP. While such a novel tax might cause some confusion, the government could make use of the tax revenue to reduce its budget deficit, or to improve its anti-unemployment policy.

However, this policy does have some negative side effects.

---

[6] See Chap. 23 of Keynes (1936). Goodfriend (2000) also discussed a possible taxation on currency to fight deflation.

[7] See Fukao (2005) for the details of this proposal.

First, this tax will have a negative effect on the credit rating of Japan's government. For example, Moody's Investors Service states that an imposition of tax on the government liabilities may constitute an event of partial default by the government even though the tax rate would be very low. As deflation in Japan has been less than 2%, the required Gesell tax rate would be at most 3% per annum. This is comparable to a 30% withholding tax on a 10% yield bond.

Second, this tax will impose a tax on the people and institutions (mostly old age retirees and financial institutions) that own a large amount of safe assets. To offset this effect, it would be desirable to provide some fiscal relief measures. Regarding individuals, one possible measure is to distribute lump sum cash to all legal residents in Japan. Assuming a 2% tax rate, the government may give ¥100,000 per person as a one-time grant. The cost of this one-time cash distribution would be approximately ¥13 trillion, less than half of the tax revenue of approximately ¥30 trillion. Regarding institutional investors such as commercial banks and life-insurance companies, a 2% tax on government bonds and Bank of Japan deposits would be a heavy burden. To offset this negative effect, the government could refund this tax with the Gesell tax revenue from bank deposits.

Once deflation is overcome, the nominal interest rate would rise. Even if the real interest rate remains the same, an increase in the nominal interest rate would adversely affect the cash flows of companies and households with large debt. Therefore, the government may have to take policy measures to allow for smooth debt restructuring in the private sector.

A Gesell tax is a powerful but blunt policy instrument, and it would be difficult to pass a law to implement this tax through the Diet. However, if the current deflationary stagnation continues, it would be almost impossible to stabilize Japan's budget deficit running at close to 10% of GDP. A Gesell tax is an unconventional fiscal tool that can simultaneously achieve increased tax revenue and increased private expenditure.

## Appendix on Gesell Tax

To stimulate the economy by raising taxes, it is necessary to levy tax on all government-guaranteed assets including banknotes. In this appendix, we assume that a 2% tax is levied on such assets.

(1) Effective target of the tax: all owners of safe assets.
(2) Implementation of a Gesell tax: this tax is levied by a partial default of government-guaranteed assets. The debt service is cut by 2% by reducing interest payments and the repayment of principal. This debt reduction is treated as tax revenue by the government.
(3) Taxable assets: all government debt, all domestic currency deposits effectively protected by the deposit insurance system or implicit government guarantee, and all liabilities of the central bank including banknotes.

(4) Banks' domestic currency debts are cut by 2%. The profit from debt reduction will be absorbed by the government as tax revenue. As banks will also lose money from government bond investments and the holding of the monetary base, only the net profit from the Gesell tax will be paid to the government.
(5) Taxation on banknotes will be messy. The ideal taxation method is to replace banknotes with stored value cards such as the Japanese Suica or PASMO, or the Oyster card in the UK. At taxation day, 2% of the remaining value of the card will be taxed. If this taxation method cannot be adopted, the central bank has to print new money and exchange it for old at a fee of 2%.
(6) The announcement of this tax will stimulate spending before it is introduced. Money will shift from cash and deposits to stocks, corporate bonds and real estate. Banks will try to extend loans by using a monetary base that will be taxed. Inter-corporate lending will be stimulated because receivables are not taxed but cash will be. The domestic currency tends to depreciate against foreign currencies that are not taxed.

## References


Buffett WE (2003) "Derivatives," Berkshire Hathaway annual report for 2002, Feb 21
Duffie D (2010) The failure mechanics of dealer banks. J Econ Perspect 24(1):51–72
Fukao M (1998) Japanese financial instability and weaknesses in the corporate governance structure. Seoul J Econ 11(4):381–422
Fukao M (2003) Japan's lost decade and weaknesses in its corporate governance structure. In: Stern RM (ed) Japan's economic recovery. Edward Elgar, Northampton, pp 289–327
Fukao M (2004) Weakening market and regulatory discipline in the Japanese financial system. In: Borio C, Hunter WC, Kaufman G, Tsatsaronis K (eds) Market discipline across countries and industries. Cambridge, MIT Press, pp 119–133
Fukao M (2005) The effects of 'Gesell' (currency) taxes in promoting Japan's economic recovery. International Economics & Economic Policy 2(2–3):173–188
Fukao M (2007) Financial crisis and the lost decade. Asian Econ Pol Rev 2(2):273–297
Gesell S (1958) The natural economic order, revised edition. London, Peter Owen
Goodfriend M (2000) "Financial stability, deflation and monetary policy," paper for the ninth international conference at the Institute for Monetary and Economic Studies, Bank of Japan, on the role of monetary policy under low inflation: deflationary shocks and their policy responses, July 2000
Keynes JM (1936) General theory of employment, interest, and money. Macmillan, London
Nakaso H (2001) The financial crisis in Japan during the 1990s: how the Bank of Japan responded and the lessons learnt. BIS papers, no. 6. Bank for International Settlements, October
Shigemi Y (1995) Asset inflation in selected countries. Bank Jpn Monet Econ Stud 13(2):89–130

# Comment Paper to Chapter "European Sovereign Crisis and Its Implications for Japan: Reducing Budget Deficits Without Damaging Recovery"

**Etsuko Katsu**

Japan currently faces a significant amount of outstanding sovereign debt, and to avoid a liquidity crises similar to the European sovereign debt crises, Japan must rapidly engage in fiscal consolidation, including an immediate increase in consumption tax and the reform of its social security system. However, Japan is not yet experiencing the crisis situations seen in Europe (for example in Greece, Italy, and Spain) because of a large pool of domestic savings that has resulted in a substantial current account surplus, and has acted as a breakwater.

Fukao has fairly assessed the existing evidence and has provided an even-handed judgment regarding his comparison study of Japan's financial crises in the 1990s, the recent US financial crises, and the EU sovereign crises.

## 1 US Financial Crises and Japanese Financial Crises of the Mid-1990s

Fukao's paper attempts to explain the differences between the Japanese financial crises in the mid-1990s, the 2008 US financial crises, and the current European sovereign debt crises. He pointed out that the following three factors are similar for the Japan, US, and European financial crises: first, excessively easy monetary policies in advance of crises; second, financial deregulation and financial innovation; and third, regulatory distortions favoring investment in certain assets such as land or sovereign bonds.

Fukao's first explanation, which I found persuasive, is that there are several reasons behind the US financial crises. The first is the behavior of the U.S. Security and

E. Katsu (✉)
Meiji University, Tokyo, Japan
e-mail: etsuko@isc.meiji.ac.jp

S. Kaji and E. Ogawa (eds.), *Who Will Provide the Next Financial Model?: Asia's Financial Muscle and Europe's Financial Maturity*,
DOI 10.1007/978-4-431-54282-7_14, 

Exchange Commission (SEC), which weakened the capital requirements on major investment banks in 2004 and replaced traditional hair-cut rules with Value at Risk (VAR) based capital requirements. He stated the second reason as an increase in the trade of Credit Default Swaps (CDS) or in trade of Collateralized Debt Obligations (CDO) which were securitized with sub-prime loans to increase the liquidity in global markets with leverage. The final reason concerned the behaviour of investment banks—they did not separate customers' assets from their own.

These factors are well explained, and the mismanagement by the US government and the Fed exacerbated the crises, as Fukao pointed out. The sudden bankruptcy of Lehman Brothers resulted in the collapse of market confidence in the Money Market Mutual Funds (MMFs) or repo transactions collateral, and contagion then caused the collapse of American International Group (AIG) and CDS markets. We can say that the US government-led collapse of Lehman Brothers suddenly changed the market equilibrium, making deleverage and repatriation immediately followed.

Loss of confidence is a shared feature of the US and Japanese financial crises, as the author pointed out; however, the form of the loss of confidence differs considerably between the US and Japan. In the US, the loss of confidence occurred in various types of marketable financial products, and in Japan it occurred in the traditional lending market.

## 2 Huge Sovereign Debt in Japan and EU Sovereign Crises

I am broadly sympathetic to the approach taken by Fukao in this paper on the sovereign crisis in the Eurozone countries. The Japanese government's gross debt to GDP was 233% and this figure is larger than the 166% in Greece at the end of 2011. In terms of net debt, Japan's ratio is 131%, gradually approaching the 153% of Greece at the end of same year.

The difference between Japan and EU periphery countries is, as the author pointed out, a position of balance of payments. Japan enjoys the highest net foreign asset position including significant foreign reserves (approximately 1.3 trillion dollars), which is in contrast to Greece's current account deficit that has widened to more than 10% of GDP.

The Eurosystem enabled Greece and other southern European countries to easily borrow euro-denominated funds from abroad, and the result is huge current account deficits and bubble economies in those countries with too easing monetary conditions for them. This is an obvious difference between the case of the EU and Japan's current debt problem, as Japan has its own currency and an autonomous monetary policy.

A further difference between Greece and Japan is the structure of the holders of government bonds. Ninety-five percent of Japan's government bonds are held inside Japan and all are yen-denominated. Furthermore, Japan's foreign assets are dollar-denominated, so creditors such as households, financial institutions, and corporations will profit if the yen depreciates.

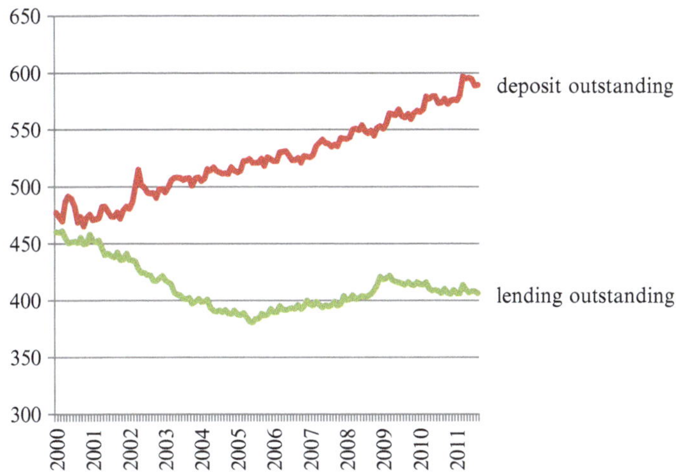


**Fig. 1** Japanese banks' outstanding of deposits and lending (trillion yen). Source: Bank of Japan

As mentioned earlier, Japan has a large pool of domestic savings and a stable investor base (a small portion of foreign investors), which creates low interest rates for Japanese Government Bonds (JGB). Fukao states that approximately 80% of JGB are held by domestic financial institutions. However, regarding domestic savings, corporate financial surpluses, which were around 6% of GDP in 2011, have been an important source of JGB funding. These surpluses though could decline with future economic recovery.

In addition, there is the possibility of a global spill over. JGB yields are sensitive to global risk factors, especially to changes in the US Treasury market. In the JGB futures market, foreign traders account for one-third of all trading, although foreign investors own just 5% of the JGB spot market. Market stress in overseas sovereign debt markets or rating downgrades could also push up the JGB yields.

The most serious problem for Japan is a sudden rise in JGB yields mirrored by suspicions regarding the sustainability of fiscal deficit of Japan. If JGB yields suddenly rise, it will balloon the interest payments of government expenditure and with a decline of bond prices, banks would have large losses that could ultimately create a credit crunch.

In addition, with the increase in outstanding JGB held by commercial banks, Japanese banks will not lend money to private entities with a strict supervision by the Financial Service Authority (FSA) and because of the necessity to meet the standards of the new Basel III which will be implemented in 2013. In contrast, the deposits with Japanese banks are significantly increasing. The financial assets of individuals equal approximately 1,500 trillion yen, but the risk-averse behavior of Japanese individuals has resulted in them shifting their funds to safe capital deposits. As a result, the gap between deposits and bank lending in Japan is increasing and this could contribute to the further stagnation of the Japanese economy (Fig. 1).

## 3 Feasibility of Gesell Tax

Finally, let me turn to the feasibility of a Gesell tax, as raised by Fukao, to remedy the deflation that Japan has experienced for more than 15 years. The author proposed a stamp duty, which is an idea first introduced by Silvio Gesell in 1906, and a tax on safe assets like yen deposits and government bonds. According to Fukao, it would encourage investments in stocks and real estate, and the negative interest rate policy is expected to decrease savings and stimulate investment.

As author pointed out, it would not merely stimulate investment by individuals, it would also stimulate bank lending and inter-corporate lending, which Fig. 1 shows as stagnant in the medium-term. It also suggests that the yen exchange rate would also depreciate against foreign currencies, and the government would benefit from the revenue from this tax.

It sounds like an ideal tax, especially when the economy is experiencing deflation. But it must be asked whether it would pose a possible risk to the financial institutions which currently hold 80% of outstanding of JGB. If the Gesell tax shifts funds from safe assets like deposits and government bonds to risk assets like securities and stocks, it could reduce the outstanding deposits that currently absorb huge amounts of JGB. As a result, the prices for JGB would suddenly decline and those financial institutions that currently hold a substantial amount of JGB would suffer huge losses.

The JGB market is now in no serious situation, but it is sensible to the bold changes. Such moves could effect a sudden change in the market equilibrium of the JGB market. We could go with an orthodox method, or be more forward thinking. While the Gesell tax is notable, it also requires further consideration.

# An Assessment of China's Banking System Reform

**Alicia García-Herrero and Daniel Santabárbara**

**Abstract** China's banking system can be seen as an enigma. It was once considered China's Achilles' heel but has now become an important part of the country's success story. This article reviews and assesses China's banking reforms implemented since 1998. Three key aspects of the reform are reviewed: bank restructuring, financial liberalization and bank regulation. Although improvements have been seen in asset quality and regulation, lasting government intervention and weak corporate governance by way of inadequate incentives could lead to financial stability problems. The involvement of Chinese authorities in increasing bank lending during the global financial crisis reveals that the reform process is far from complete.

**Keywords** Bank regulation • Bank restructuring • China's banking system • Corporate governance • Financial liberalization • Government intervention

## 1 Introduction

Not so long ago, it was generally believed that China's financial system was on the verge of collapse, and that in developed countries, the process of financial innovation had lowered the overall risks of their financial systems. The situation today looks quite different; industrial countries have faced the worst financial crisis of

---

The opinions expressed here are those of the authors and not necessarily those of the institutions they are affiliated with. All remaining errors are solely ours.

A. García-Herrero (✉)
Banco Bilbao Vizcaya Argentaria, Bilbao, Spain

University of Lingnan, Tuen Mun, Hong Kong
e-mail: alicia.garcia-herrero@bbva.com.hk

D. Santabárbara
Banco de España, Madrid, Spain
e-mail: daniel.santabarbara@bde.es

S. Kaji and E. Ogawa (eds.), *Who Will Provide the Next Financial Model?: Asia's Financial Muscle and Europe's Financial Maturity*,
DOI 10.1007/978-4-431-54282-7_15, © Springer Japan 2013

decades and yet China, in contrast, has managed to stave off strong external turbulence and even utilize the banking system to intermediate the largest fiscal stimulus package in the country's history. The consequences of the latter, however, are yet to be seen, as shall develop later.

The reasons for the limited impact of the international financial crisis in China can largely be ascribed to the external isolation of its financial sector and strong public intervention in credit allocation, along with lax monetary and fiscal policies. This relative lack of development, generally a drag on the financial system, has proved to be "timely" on this occasion.

However, the fact that China's banks have avoided the crisis with relative success is not a strong enough reason to unequivocally affirm that the reform of its financial system has been successful. In fact, we must not forget that China has not fully completed its intended financial reform. This paper reviews and evaluates the steps already taken towards reform and also looks into the pending modifications to provide an overall assessment of China's position in terms of its reforms and the soundness of the banking system. In addition, given the sheer size of the fiscal stimulus package and the key role that banks have played in financing it, one key issue for this paper is to evaluate the risk the operation may pose for Chinese banks in terms of asset quality. To that end, we use a simple accounting framework and compare different macroeconomic scenarios and their impact on Chinese banks' asset quality.

This article is composed of the following sections. The first section offers some stylized facts regarding the evolution of China's banking sector since the 1980s. The second deals with the first of the three key areas of reform, namely bank restructuring. The third offers an overview of China's progress with financial liberalization, and Sect. 4 concentrates on measures taken to improve financial regulation. Section 5 evaluates the implications of the extensive lending that stemmed from the 2008–2010 stimuli package. Finally, Sect. 6 provides an overall assessment of the banking reform.

## 2 Description of China's Banking Sector

If financial development were to be measured on quantitative terms only, China would even be ahead of several developed countries (Fig. 1). In fact, bank credit—the main source of financing in developing countries as well as in Europe[1]—is already more than 100% of China's total GDP, which is certainly much higher than most countries with a similar GDP per capita to China (Fig. 2). This apparent paradox is mostly the result of the transition from a state-planned economy to a market economy, as China's banks have long been used as the primary financing vehicle for state-owned companies and local governments. However, a better way to measure financial development is how well bank deposits are intermediated or, in other words, how efficiently bank credit is allocated (Fig. 3) (Dorrucci et al. 2009).

[1] Banking sector assets already represent nearly 70% of the assets of the financial system. The remaining amounts are primarily equities, with less participation in fixed income.

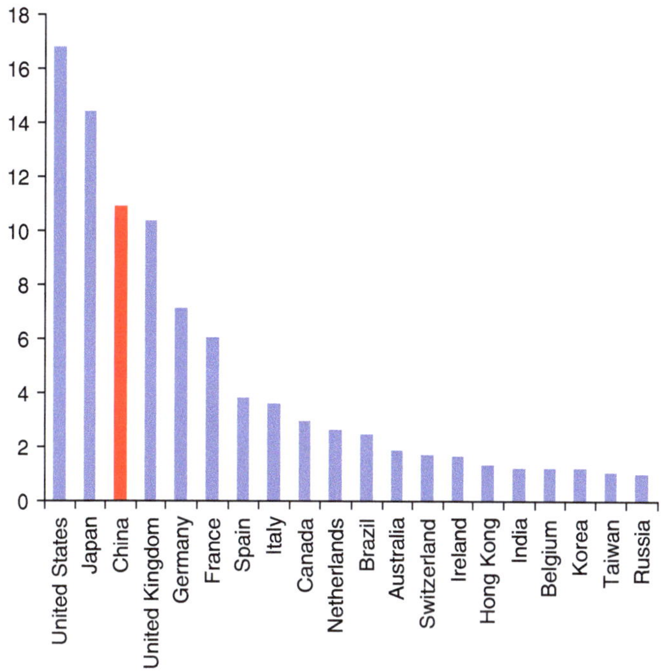


**Fig. 1** Banking system assets (2010, USD bn). Source: Fitch

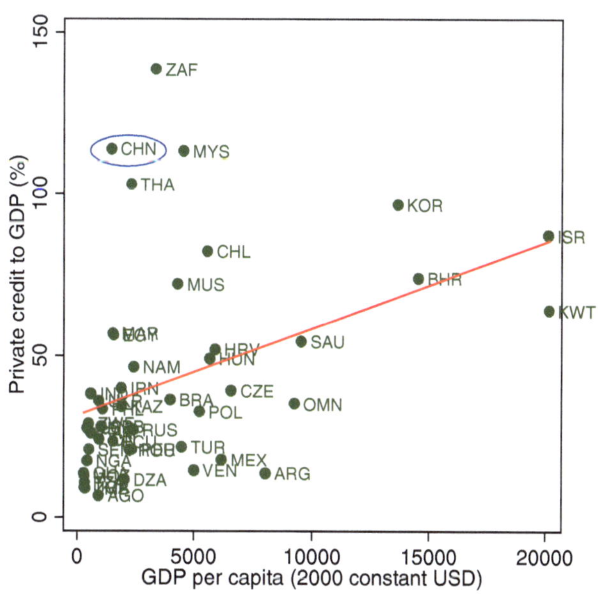


**Fig. 2** Private credit and per capita income, average 2000–2008 (% of GDP, constant 2000 USD). Source: IMF

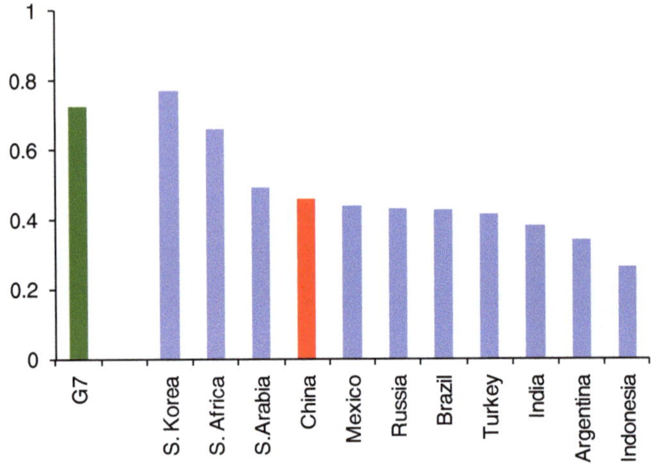


**Fig. 3** Domestic financial development, G20 EMEs (average 2005–2010). Source: Dorrucci et al. (2009)

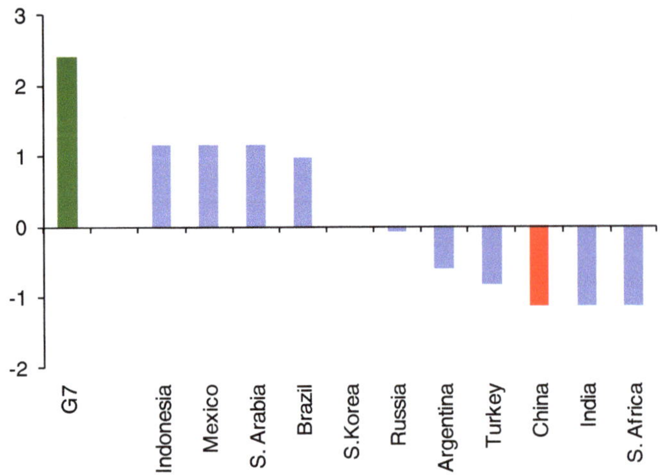


**Fig. 4** "De jure" financial openness, G20 EMEs (average 2005–2009). Source: Chinn and Ito (2008)

In fact, although China's banking system has become bigger and also sounder in terms of solvency and asset quality, it is still characterized by high public intervention in credit allocation and financial repression, both of which substantially reduce competition. This combination of factors makes it very difficult for China's banking system to intermediate credit efficiently, no matter how financially developed it may seem when judgment is based on size. In addition, in terms of financial openness, given the current restrictions on cross-border financial flows, China's banking system is relatively isolated internationally (Fig. 4).

The strong and sustained dynamism of China's economy implies that its financial system has enormous potential but is also in need of a profound transformation. The challenge is how to carry out this transformation without disruptions.

## 3 Bank Restructuring

As was the case with other planned economies, China's banking system in 1979 consisted of a mono-bank, the People's Bank of China (PBC), which acted as the central bank and only commercial bank. After the separation of both functions in the 1980s, the PBC remained in charge of monetary policy and banking regulation. Four state-owned commercial banks (SOCBs) were set up, as well as a series of smaller financial institutions constricted to local or regional business. China's SOCBs specialized in financing areas considered key to economic development. In the 1990s, these institutions started to operate more like commercial banks, a change that was encouraged by the creation of three policy banks, although they continued to accumulate non-performing loans (NPLs) as bank lending grew without an assessment of the underlying risks. Banks were focused on providing funding to state-owned enterprises (SOEs), independent of their repayment capabilities. As a result, and following a sharp reduction in economic growth in the wake of the Asian crisis, almost half of the loans in the banking system were non-performing by 1998.

In 1998, the PBC began what was meant to be a multi-year restructuring process. In 2003, the majority of financial supervision and regulation power was transferred to a new institution, the China Banking Regulatory Commission (CBRC), which continued with the financial reform with even more vigor.

The plan focused on recapitalizing the four SOCBs and clearing the impaired loans from their balance sheets, thereby encouraging the entry of strategic investors and listing them in the stock market. The objective of the CBRC was for these various measures to reinforce each other, as not only capital would be raised but also the corporate governance of banks would be improved through the discipline of protecting private shareholders' value, at least to some extent.

The SOCB restructuring was carried out in four waves, each with four sequential phases (see Fig. 5). The first phase consisted of capital injection by the Ministry of Finance (MoF) and/or the central bank. The second was the write-off of NPLs from the banks' balance sheets and the transfer of the loans to asset management companies (AMCs) or the MoF (see Fig. 5 for details of the entities involved). The other two phases, introduced in 2003 when the CBRC began to lead the reform, were introduced first to ensure more independent management and better risk assessment by allowing foreigners to buy a stake in Chinese banks, and then to list them on the stock market. In any event, the incentives for the change in management were clearly not there since foreign participation was announced to remain below 20% for a single investor (25% for joint foreign ownership), and the percentage of ownership floated in the stock market was never large enough to obtain control.

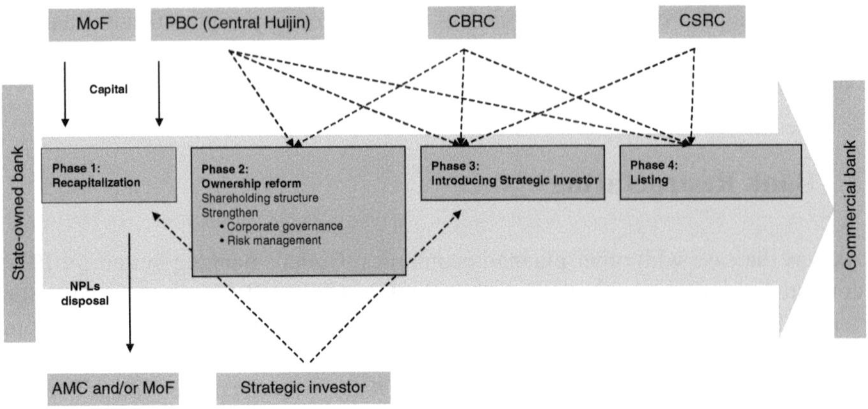


**Fig. 5** Commercial bank reform strategy: participants and phases

The four restructuring waves lasted more than a decade. The first one started in 1998 and was geared towards increasing the capital of the four SOCBs to reach a capital adequacy ratio (CAR) of 8%. To that end NPLs were to be transferred to the AMCs created for that purpose. During the second wave, in 2003, the actions focused on the China Construction Bank (CCB) and the Bank of China (BoC). During the third stage, in 2005, the targeted institution was the Industrial and Commercial Bank of China (ICBC). Last, the restructuring of the weakest systemic institution, the Agricultural Bank of China (ABC), began in 2008 and was finalized in 2010. In constant 2008 dollars, in these four stages, authorities injected approximately US$100 billion in capital and removed approximately US$530 billion from the NPLs (See the Appendix for further details).

## 3.1 *The Role of AMCs in the Restructuring Process*

The first three restructuring waves indicated the relevant role of the AMCs. In essence, AMCs were an accounting instrument to remove NPLs from banks because their capital was too low (RMB 40 billion) to bear the losses derived from the NPLs that they had to manage. In other words, these entities were a useful instrument to postpone the recognition of the liabilities derived when commercial banks were used for public policy purposes. In the meantime, AMCs tried to recover as much of the impaired loans as possible, which so far has amounted to approximately 25% of the value transferred by the NPLs. Ultimately, the residual would be absorbed by the MoF and PBC. In a positive light, significant nominal GDP growth greatly reduced the size of the potential losses.

However, the generosity with which AMCs accepted NPLs from the banks has decreased over time (see Table 1). In the first wave, AMCs acquired outstanding loan portfolios at face value, whereas in the second, a discount of more than 50%

**Table 1** NPLs disposal by AMCs and MoF (RMB bn)

| | | | | Financed by | | | |
|---|---|---|---|---|---|---|---|
| Date | Source bank | Destination AMC | NPLs | AMC bonds | PBC loans | Other | Notes |
| 1999–2000 | ICBC | Huarong | 408 | 313 | 95 | | NPLs purchased at 100% of book value, bond maturity 10 years |
| | ABC | Great Wall | 346 | | 346 | | |
| | CCB | Cinda | 250 | 247 | 3 | | |
| | China Development Bank | Cinda | 100 | 100 | | | |
| | BoC | Oriental | 267 | 151 | 116 | | |
| 2000–2001 | CCB and China Development Bank | Cinda | 45 | | | | |
| 2004 | BoComm | Cinda | 64 | | 161 | | Purchased at 47% of book value, PBC loans to 5 years |
| | CCB | Cinda | 129 | | | | |
| | BoC | Cinda | 150 | | | | |
| | CCB | Cinda | 57 | | | | Transferred at 0% of book value |
| | BoC | Oriental | 142 | | | | |
| 2005 | ICBC | Great Wall | 257 | | 176 | | Purchased at 38% of book value, PBC loans to 5 years |
| | ICBC | Oriental | 121 | | | | |
| | ICBC | Cinda | 58 | | | | |
| | ICBC | Huarong | 23 | | | | |
| | ICBC | | 246 | | | 246 | RMB 246 bn represents a debt recognition by the MoF |
| | Shanghai Bank | Cinda | 3 | | 3 | | Transferred at 0% of book value |
| 2007 | Various banks | Oriental | 5 | | 5 | | |
| | Shenzhen Comm. Bank | Cinda | 4 | | 4 | | |
| 2008 | ABC | | 816 | | 151 | 665 | RMB 665 bn represents a debt recognition by the MoF |

Sources: Dragonomics (2009) and Walter and Howie (2011)

was applied. During the third wave, AMCs acquired NPLs for less than 40% of their face value. Not enough information exists on the fourth and final waves. In addition, in the second and third phases, these acquisitions were accompanied by transfers without counterparts, which implies that the effective discount over the whole NPL package was much higher. In the fourth and last stages, AMCs were not involved and NPLs were transferred to the MoF, implying a more straightforward approach.

AMCs acquired NPLs with a combination of cash payments obtained via a PBC discount loan and from 10-year AMC bonds (which were partly purchased by the commercial banks whose NPLs were removed). Ironically, to some extent, commercial banks swapped default assets for assets from an insolvent entity, the AMC.

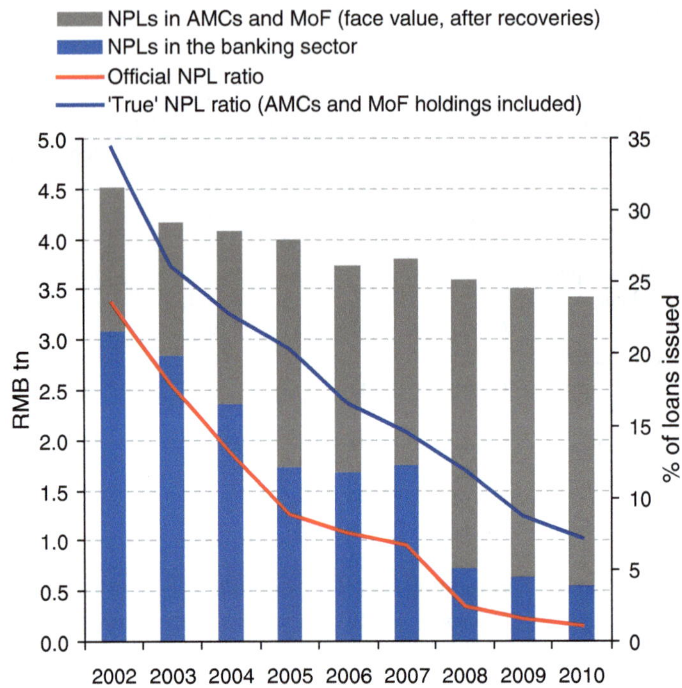


**Fig. 6** NPL ratio (% of outstanding loans). Source: Authors calculations based on Dragonomics (2009) and CEIC

AMCs losses have not been recognized yet and authorities appear willing to further postpone it. In 2009, authorities decided to roll over the 10-year AMC bonds issued in 1999 for another decade, but with a more explicit guarantee from the MoF.

It is important to recall that in the last restructuring wave that approximately 80% of NPLs were transferred to the MoF instead of to AMCs, while the ABC was in charge of their recoveries. This might indicate the authorities' recognition that the AMC model failed and that the losses should be directly borne by the government. Hence, the MoF finally took direct responsibility for the funding and repayment of problem-loan disposals.

## 3.2 *What Is the "True" Size of NPLs?*

China has markedly reduced the NPL ratio of commercial banks during the last decade owing to (1) transfers to AMCs and the MoF, (2) a vast lending expansion and (3) improvements in credit risk assessment and recovery techniques. In 2000, the NPL ratio stood at 41% while in 2010, the CBRC official NPL ratio stood at 1.2%.

However, the latter figure is misleading and not comparable to the former. By including those impaired loans that remain with AMCs and the MoF and have not yet been written-off or recovered, the NPL ratio sat at approximately 7% in 2010 (10% of GDP) (Fig. 6). Hence, the fall in the official NPL ratio is related to transfers of NPLs and the impressive credit growth in the last decade (16% annually).

## 4 Financial Liberalization

The restructuring effort described also conveyed other costs in terms of financial repression (Fig. 7). First, interest rates were set artificially low so that it would be easier to roll over the NPL-related debt. Second, a wide spread between lending and deposit rates was established to sustain bank profitability, but it was accompanied by an inefficient allocation of capital. Third, the development of financial markets was gradually helping to maintain a stable deposit base in banks, but at the expense of very limited investment and financing alternatives. This was accompanied by a high degree of government intervention in credit allocation.

This strategy proved very successful to avoid major financial stress, but bank depositors ended up subsidizing the cleaning up of the banking industry, reflecting a major redistribution of income from households to the financial sector. Lardy

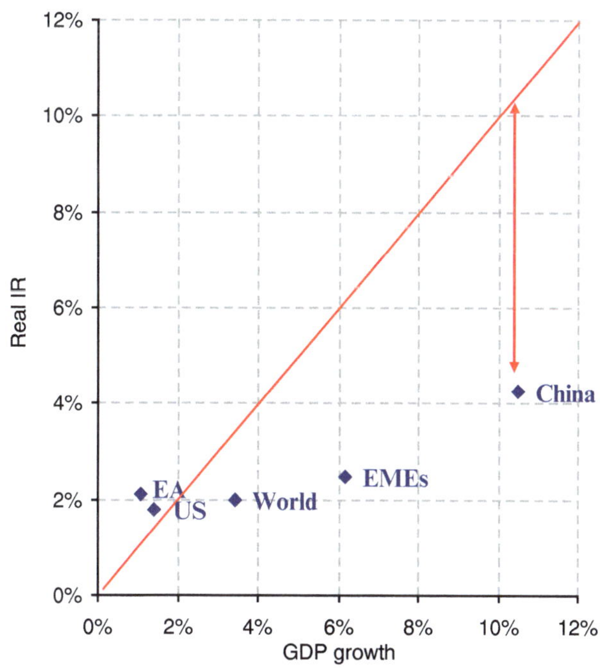


**Fig. 7** Real GDP growth and real long-term interest rates, average 2001–2009 (%). Source: Haver Analytics

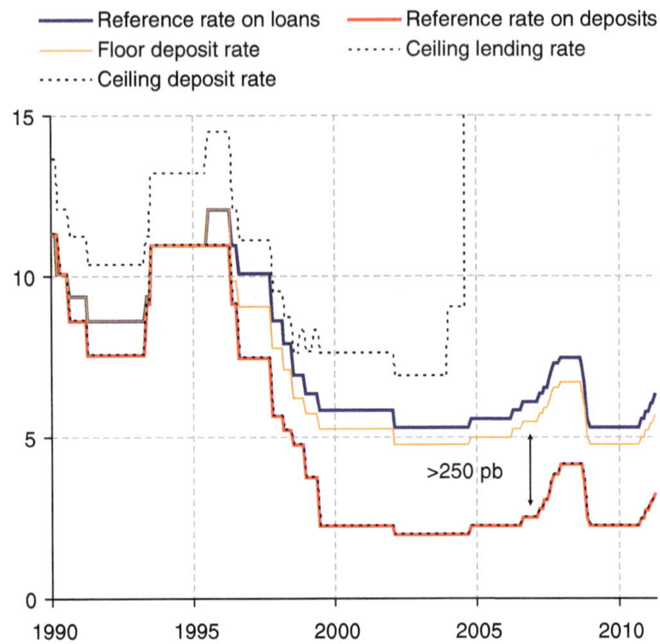


**Fig. 8** Reference lending and deposit rate (%). Source: PBC

(2008) estimates that the implicit tax imposed on households would have reached approximately 4% of GDP at that time.

Financial liberalization policies should eliminate government interference both in terms of determining too low interest rates and credit allocation, as well as the ownership structure of the financial sector.

China's financial liberalization process was based on four pillars: liberalization of interest rates, reduction of entry barriers to promote competition, enhancement of financial innovation and lifting restrictions on cross-border capital flows.

The *liberalization of interest rates* is crucial to encourage a more efficient allocation of resources, as it prevents distortions in investment and savings decisions. In addition, interest rates are the main competitive variable among banking institutions and the current restrictions penalize the most efficient institutions. Last, and maybe even more important for China, the liberalization of interest rates is sine qua non for banks to establish interest rates reflecting the associated credit risk.

The interest rate liberalization process started in 1996 but was halted in 2004. In the first stage, from 1996 to 1999, interest rates were deregulated in monetary and bonds markets. Later, in 2004, ceiling interest rates on loans and floor deposit rates were abolished (Fig. 8). However, a ceiling was maintained on deposit rates and a floor imposed on lending rates (at 90% of the reference rate). This corridor between

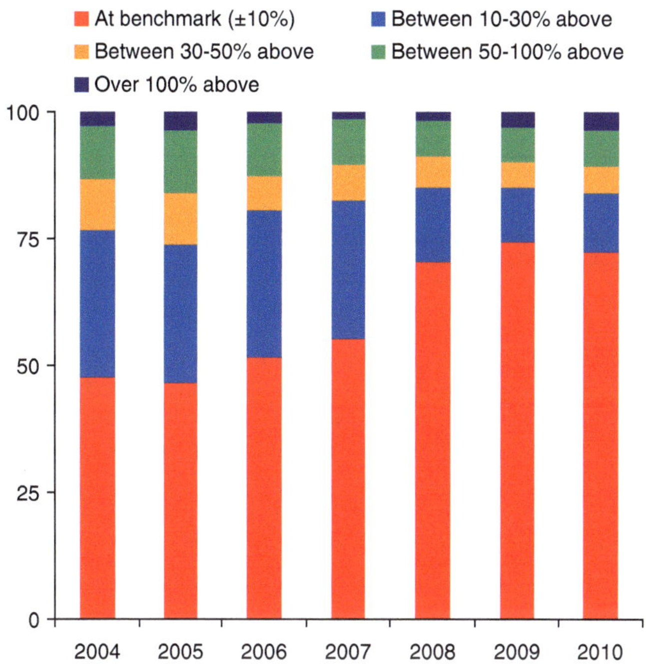


**Fig. 9** Distribution of effective interest rates on loans (% total loans). Source: CBRC

the floor on lending rates and ceiling on deposit rates ensures a safe margin for banking institutions above to 250 basis points, which shields the profitability of commercial banks and discourages competitive pressures. Nonetheless, it also has some negative side effects as it discourages the establishment of necessary risk assessment on credit allocation. In fact, as shown by PBoC surveys on the dispersion of lending rates, SOCBs only negotiated 30% of their loans at rates significantly above the benchmark rate (Fig. 9).

**Box A** Scenario Analysis of the Impact of Interest Rate Liberalization on Banking Sector Profitability

This box aims to assess the impact of fully liberalized interest rates on the profitability of commercial banks. The exercise includes a simulation of the balance sheets and income statements of Chinese banks under the assumption that they enjoy the same net interest margins of commercial banks in (1) emerging Asia (ASEAN and Korea), (2) the US and (3) euro area (Table 2).

(continued)

**Box A** (continued)

**Table 2** Net interest margin in selected areas

| | 2008 | 2007 |
|---|---|---|
| China | 3.02 | 3.02 |
| Asean + Korea commercial banks | 2.70 | 2.92 |
| Euro area commercial banks (average 1994–2008) | 1.45 | 1.45 |
| US large commercial banks | 2.69 | 2.85 |

Source: Bankscope

Chinese commercial banks' balance sheets and income statements are drawn from Bankscope and cover 81% of the assets of the banking system. The interest rates are obtained from the CEIC database for the banking system as a whole (and, hence, are different than those created by each institution). Our exercise uses data up to 2008 to avoid taking into account the effects of the global financial crisis. The major limitation is that the changes in interest rates do not affect the volume of their assets and liabilities or the competitive strategies of commercial banks. It is also implicitly assumed that the effect is monotonic. Likewise, neither the monetary policy nor interbank rates were altered.[2]

The results, summarized in Table 3, point out that the liberalization of interest rates in retail markets does not appear to significantly affect profitability if it does not trigger a competitive reaction in the market and where banks are able to keep their deposit and asset base. If the net interest margin in China converges towards the emerging Asian or US one, then the fall in pre-tax profits would be approximately 22% in 2008, leading to a pre-tax return on average assets (ROAA) of more than 1.20. This reduction would not entail excessive risks to Chinese institutions, especially taking into account the increased profits of Chinese institutions in the last few years. However, because 2007 and 2008 enjoyed abnormally high profitability, this could be an additional limitation of the analysis. Considering the unrealistic and aggressive scenario in which the net interest margin converges to the euro area one (note that the euro area has a very developed banking system confronted with a low interest rate environment, where a significant part of the income is associated with fees and commissions), profits would eventually disappear.

[2] These results should be interpreted with caution given that the assumptions are unrealistic. However, it is likely to offer a better alternative than building an econometric model for bank profitability to determine the effect of past interest rate liberalization and to be used to project the current one. The latter technique will face severe identification problems, as individual bank profitability in each year should be explained with the whole banking system's interest rates (we do not have enough degrees of freedom to estimate this effect in addition to other potential determinants of profitability). See García-Herrero et al. (2009) for further details.

**Table 3** Results of changes in net interest margins on profitability under alternative scenarios

| | Scenario 1 | | Scenario 2 | | Scenario 3 | | Scenario 4 | |
|---|---|---|---|---|---|---|---|---|
| | NIM China equals to ASEAN + Korea through loan rate adjustment | | NIM China equals to ASEAN + Korea through deposit rate adjustment | | NIM China equals to the US large commercial banks average through loan rate adjustment | | NIM China equals to euro area historical average through loan rate adjustment | |
| Results (% changes from 2008 actual data) | 2008 | 2007 | 2008 | 2007 | 2008 | 2007 | 2008 | 2007 |
| Loan average | –10.1 | –5.9 | 0 | 0 | –10.4 | –7.9 | –44.2 | –46.0 |
| Other earning assets revenue | 0 | 0 | 0 | 0 | 0 | 0 | 0 | 0 |
| Deposit expenses | 0 | 0 | 22.2 | 15.0 | 0 | 0 | 0 | 0 |
| Other interest bearing securities expenses | 0 | 0 | 0 | 0 | 0 | 0 | 0 | 0 |
| Net interest margin | –12.0 | –6.9 | –12.0 | –6.9 | –12.3 | –9.2 | –52.6 | –53.6 |
| Profit before taxes | –21.8 | –11.4 | –21.8 | –11.4 | –22.4 | –15.1 | –95.6 | –88.1 |
| Pre-tax ROAA | –24.4 | –17.0 | –24.4 | –17.0 | –25.0 | –20.7 | –98.2 | –93.7 |
| Pro-memoria | | | | | | | | |
| Implicit interest rate on loans | 6.33 | 6.38 | 7.04 | 6.78 | 6.31 | 6.25 | 3.93 | 3.66 |
| Implicit interest rate on deposits | 2.18 | 1.86 | 2.67 | 2.14 | 2.18 | 1.86 | 2.18 | 1.86 |

Source: Authors' calculations based on CEIC and Bankscope data

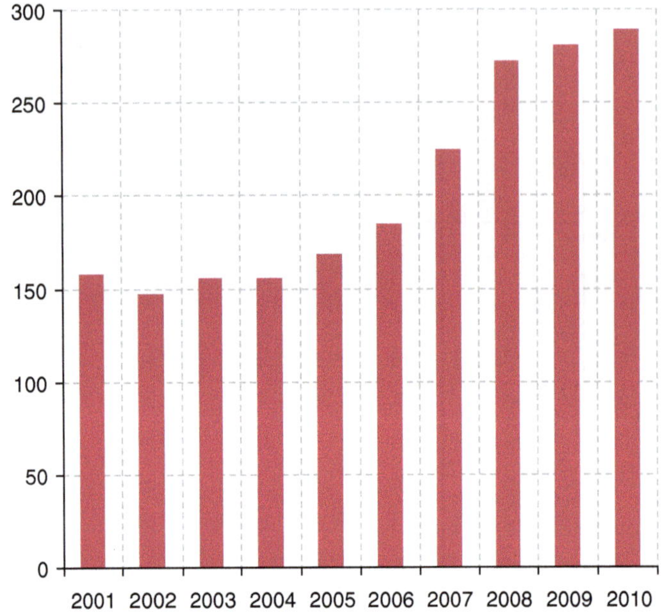


**Fig. 10** Number of foreign institutions. Source: CBRC

With regard to foreign competition, after the big push with China's entry in the WTO in 2001, their role has remained very limited. In fact, their market share has fallen to less than 2% of total bank assets. The WTO agreement stated that foreign banks could enter in a non-discriminatory manner into the Chinese market, and after a transition period of 5 years geographical and business restrictions were gradually eliminated. At the end of 2006, when the 5-year transition period ended, Chinese authorities favored the establishment of subsidiaries over branches, which made it even harder for foreign banks to participate in the Chinese market given the even higher capital requirements. The extensive period (3 years) before a branch or subsidiary can take RMB deposits also makes the process very costly for foreign banks. In addition, the incomplete liberalization of interest rates makes competition difficult in traditional banking operations. Moreover, and in general terms, organic growth does not constitute a credible competitive threat as it is too slow and costly in a country of the size of China. As a result, as of the end of 2009, only 37 foreign institutions were incorporated locally (Fig. 10).

As an alternative to organic growth, non-residents have been authorized to buy non-controlling stakes in Chinese banks since 2003, with a limit of 20% of capital for a single investor (25% for joint foreign investment). As shown in Fig. 11, this has been the route for the majority of foreign capital inflow in the financial sector in recent years, with an accumulated total of approximately US$50 billion. Major foreign investment has been through strategic stakes, which requires involvement with domestic banks by improving their corporate governance, introducing international

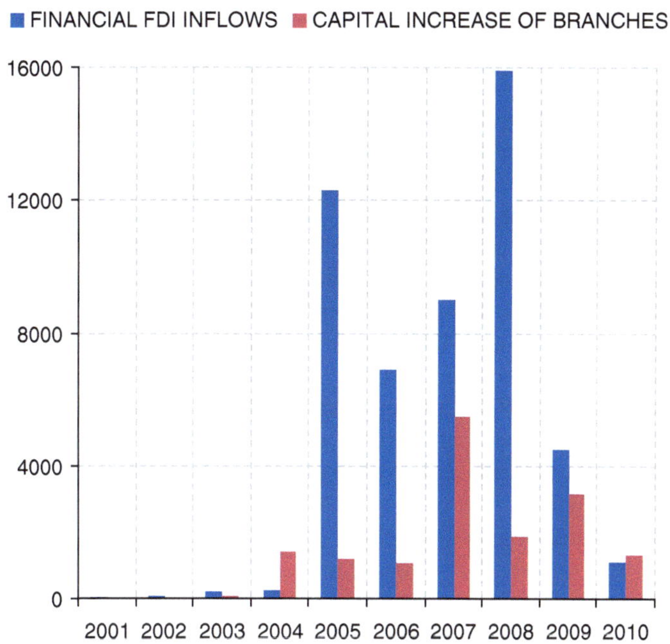


**Fig. 11** Foreign investment in the Chinese banking sector (USD mn). Source: CEIC

practices and transferring risk management techniques (García-Herrero and Santabárbara 2008). This involvement required a 3-year lock up period, which was recently increased to five. Before the global financial crisis, approximately 30 Chinese commercial banks had incorporated foreign investors. However, the financial difficulties suffered by major shareholders during the crisis obliged many of them to disinvest when the lock up period expired.

During 2009 and 2010, Chinese banks were the ones looking for expansion in foreign markets aimed at diversifying their asset bases and benefiting from the opportunities created after the financial crisis. This expansion was articulated either through organic development or mergers and acquisitions. As of the end of 2010, China's five largest commercial banks had set up eighty-nine branches and subsidiaries outside of China. They also acquired or invested in ten foreign banks.

With regard to *financial innovation* in China, it has materialized mainly in two major fields. The first is the bank card business, which includes e-banking and derivatives trading. As of the end of 2009, banking institutions issued 2 billion cards—1.32 cards per citizen—and transactions via bank cards represented 15% of total retail sales. Second, commercial banks further improved the management of wealth management services (US$140 billion). The global crisis, however, brought about a much stronger regulatory grip on such products and delays in the launch of new products, especially derivatives. These tighter regulations, however, did not prevent the growth of extensive shadow banking, especially for private wealth products.

The final aspect of financial liberalization refers to *the liberalization of international capital flows* in China. Without a clear need for financing—being a net creditor in the global economy—the strategy of the liberalization of capital flows was very slow and has since been discontinued. This may be because of the importance that Chinese economic authorities have attached to a predictable exchange rate against the USD (which many consider undervalued) as well as an independent monetary policy.

Broadly speaking, financial flows have been liberalized in terms of FDI whereas tight controls persist on capital flows (be it inflows or overflows).[3] The exceptions are two relatively small windows that have been opened for Chinese capital outflows (QDII) and inflows from foreign investors (QFII). From 2006 onwards, given the mounting pressures on the RMB, larger capital outflows were allowed but this process was halted during the financial crisis. The recent initiatives to promote a wider international use of the RMB are complicating the control of capital inflows under the current macroeconomic set-up. This acceleration of the liberalization makes it all the more urgent and necessary to complete the restructuring of the financial system, as liberalization will not only open the doors to cross-border flows but also to new risks for the banking sector.

## 5 Regulation and Supervision

The reform process has also been accompanied by an improvement in regulation, both making it stricter and aligning it with international standards. With the creation of the CBRC in 2003, this reform was accelerated in several areas: asset quality, regulatory capital and supervision.

With regard to *asset quality*, the first steps in this direction were taken in 2002 when the PBoC—the banking regulator at that time—established a five-tier credit classification system according to the probability of default, and similar to that used internationally. At the end of 2005, all banks were required to classify their loans according to the standard classification system and in 2009 banks were finally required to completely provision their impaired loans. In 2009, the CBRC increased the provisioning coverage ratio to 150% of impaired loans.

Parallel to the improvement of bank regulations, bankruptcy procedures were also improved. A new bankruptcy law was introduced in 2006 and in 2007 a new private property law established a safer legal framework for collateral guarantees. In 2010, the CBRC organized a countrywide intensive review of bank loans to local government financing vehicles (LGFVs) (see the following section) and, on this basis, a series of measures were implemented to keep the growth of LGFV loans in check and mitigate potential associated risks.

[3] For a detailed account of the restrictions see Yongding (2009).

From a *regulatory capital* standpoint, the CBRC introduced regulations in 2003 similar to those of Basel I, which were satisfied by all banks by the end of 2008. These measures have proven very effective. In 2008, the Basel II framework based on internal models was adopted with the intention of making it operational by the end of 2010 or, if the banks were unable to obtain the required regulatory capital by that time, 2013. In late 2010, the CBRC introduced a new toolbox of capital requirements drawing from the new Basel III framework. This included strengthened capital adequacy requirements, leverage ratios, dynamic provisioning and new liquidity measures.

*Supervision* was also reinforced thanks to the legal protection of supervisors, in situ inspection mechanisms, infrastructure for the immediate surveillance of banking activities and a greater coordination among the supervisors of the different segments of financial markets.

During the post-financial crisis era, the CBRC began to attach greater importance to the *protection of depositors and financial consumers' rights* and interests. In 2010, the CBRC continued to strengthen supervision regarding the compliance of banking institutions' marketing and disclosure activities, and issued a number of regulatory documents to this end. However, no explicit deposit insurance has been introduced so far.

In addition, efforts have been made to improve the *corporate governance* of banks by creating boards of shareholders with independent members and, as mentioned previously, through strategic investors. Finally, with the objective of increasing *transparency*, external auditors were introduced with international accounting standards.

Notwithstanding the progress made, the weakest point continues to be *enforcement*. Enforcement in China is even more difficult than usual because of the pervasive public interference in lending. The lack of enforcement means that nominal improvements in corporate governance, such as the appointment of external board members, ends up being ineffective as they are political appointees. Strong public interference also complicates risk management as banks prefer to grant credit to SOEs or entities with strong political contacts. This explains why lending rates continue to be aligned with benchmark rates and no higher (Fig. 6).

## 6 The Way Forward: What Are the Risks Derived from the 2008–2010 Credit Expansion?

Since 2008, when the global crisis started, the balance sheets of Chinese banks have expanded at an extraordinary pace. This has been instrumental in government stimuli. Indeed, credit growth in China in the last 2 years has been the fastest in the world, in contrast with their low CAR (Figs. 12 and 13). For many observers, these facts indicate that financial vulnerabilities might be rising.

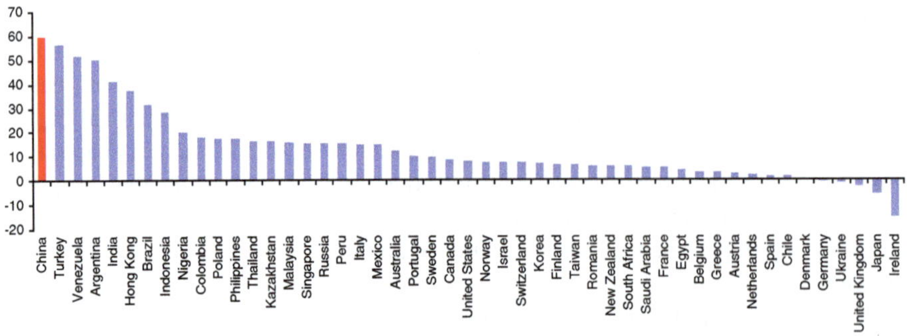


**Fig. 12** Cumulative loan growth 2009–2010 (%)

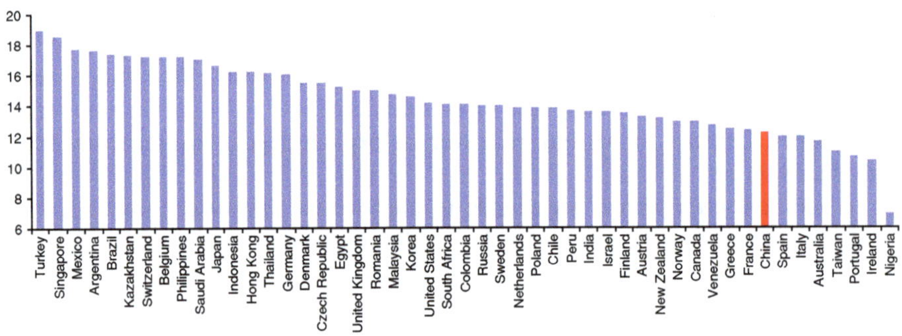


**Fig. 13** Capital adequacy ratio 2010 (%). Source: Fitch

## 6.1 *Risks Resulting from the Stimuli Policies*

As an essential part of the stimuli package implemented in China in late 2008, the Chinese authorities urged banks to finance those local governments in charge of executing a large part of the package, namely investments in infrastructure.[4] This phenomenon, and to a lesser extent the expansion of household borrowing, explains the huge increase in credit in China. In fact, total domestic credit increased as much as RMB 22.4 trillion (28.6 trillion including off-balance sheet lending) for 2008–2010 (approximately 70% of 2008 GDP, 90% of GDP including off-balance sheet lending).

A lending breakdown shows that most of the loans were medium- to long-term credits (Fig. 14) extended to SOEs and LGFVs. In fact, LGFVs were basically created to circumvent the zero budget constraints of the local governments. The size of LGFV lending is uncertain. On the one hand, according to the PBC, LGFV-related

[4] On 9 November 2008, China's State Council announced a stimulus package for 2009–2010 amounting to RMB 4 trillion (US$586 billion) to stimulate domestic demand. However, the OECD estimates that the real size of the package was far bigger, owing to thousands of local government-sponsored projects taking place outside of the main plan. While the announced measures covered a wide range of areas, the main focus was clearly on infrastructure investment.

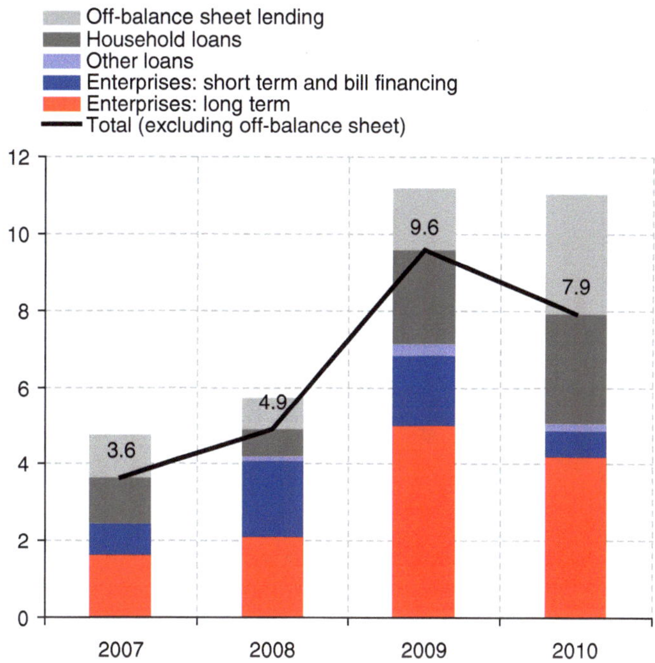


**Fig. 14** Changes in outstanding loans (RMB trn). Source: CEIC

lending accounted for less than RMB 14.4 trillion of the outstanding loans as of the end of 2010 (36% GDP). On the other hand, the National Audit Office, accounting only LGFV borrowing directly backed by local government, reported that they stood at RMB 8.5 trillion (21% GDP).[5] Despite the implicit state guarantee, loans granted to these vehicles could be risky because their capital is low and paid in terms of land value (hence being sensitive to property price movements).

A major concern is that most of the loan growth has been associated with very loose credit standards, with loan pricing not properly assessed and implicit guarantees not enforceable. In addition, given that local government revenues are limited and their expenses are increasing (Fig. 15), negative developments in local government finances or in the property market would also hit the asset quality of the banking system.[6]

[5] The National Audit Office survey only covered LGFV engaged in public works and in commercial projects directly guaranteed by the local government. This definition is too narrow to capture all the contingent liabilities arising from LGFV borrowing.

[6] Chinese local governments share a small portion in tax income, but assume major responsibility in the infrastructure build-out and social economic development-related expenses. In fact, local government budgetary revenue has accounted for only 50–60% of budgetary expenditure since the late 1990s. Local governments consistently face a shortage of funding, relying heavily on central government transfers, tax rebates and land sales, because up until 2009, they were legally forbidden from running budget deficits. In addition, they could not formally borrow from banks and were authorized to issue debt in 2009. Thus, the solution has been to set up local government backed vehicles that also hide their actual debt burden.

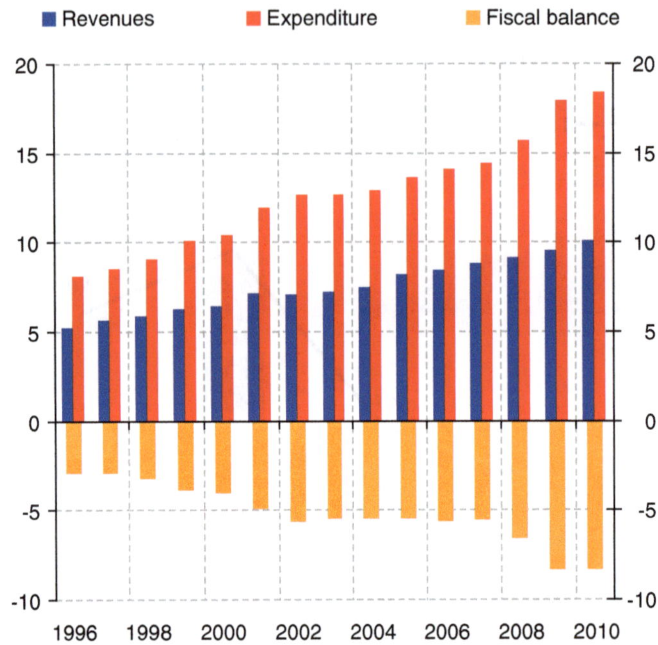


**Fig. 15** Local government revenues and expenses (% of GDP). Source: CEIC

Authorities have sought to mitigate this problem by increasing provisioning and capital requirements, by ordering local government to explicitly recognize debts and by extending the maturity of loans. Banks have also recently raised large amounts of capital. The biggest banks planned to raise RMB 100 billion in 2010 and approximately 500 billion over the following 4 years, but it is unclear to what extent they have achieved this.

The authorities have already recognized the risk derived from LGFV borrowing. The *China Securities Journal*, a government-sponsored magazine, reported that up to 76% of LGFV loans could face repayment problems because underlying projects are unable to generate enough cash flow. In particular, 26% of LGFV loans will be very difficult to recover and another 50% will only be repaid using external sources of finance. Markets also reacted to these concerns and the equity prices of Chinese banks dropped by 38% in the first 9 months of 2011.

### 6.1.1 The Extent of LGFV Lending Issues

One immediate question is to what degree will the current credit expansion negatively affect either local government finances or the banks' asset quality in the mid-term? To determine the extent of bad loans, we built three scenarios based on alternative assumptions of default loss rates and nominal GDP growth.

**Table 4** Impact of loan financing on stimuli package (RMB trn, otherwise indicated)

| | Official data | | Scenario A | Scenario B | Scenario C |
|---|---|---|---|---|---|
| | PBC | National Audit Office | Optimistic | Baseline | Pessimistic |
| Assumptions | | | | | |
| Recognized loans to LGFVs (as of Dec-2010) | 14.4 | 8.5 | 14.4 | 14.4 | 14.4 |
| Default ratio (% of LGFV loans) | 26 | 26 | 26 | 39 | 50 |
| Nominal GDP growth (%) (2010–2020) | 11 | 11 | 16 | 13 | 9 |
| Results | | | | | |
| Loans default | 3.7 | 2.2 | 3.7 | 5.5 | 7.2 |
| Loans default (USD bn) | 551 | 325 | 551 | 815 | 1059 |
| New NPLs (% 2010 GDP) | 9.4 | 5.6 | 9.4 | 13.9 | 18.1 |
| New NPLs (% 2020 GDP) | 3.3 | 2.0 | 2.1 | 4.1 | 7.6 |
| ΔNPL ratio (2015) | 4.6 | 2.7 | 3.7 | 6.3 | 9.8 |
| ΔNPL ratio (2020) | 2.8 | 1.6 | 1.8 | 3.4 | 6.3 |

Given China's current excellent situation, the most optimistic scenario, in terms of smaller losses, should in principle be the most likely. However, such simple extrapolations mask many significant uncertainties.

The assumptions of this exercise are as follows. The default ratio is assumed to range between 26% and 39% of the loans to LGFVs, which is in line with the figures stated by the *China Securities Journal*. In addition, nominal GDP growth will determine the basis for which the NPL ratio can be reduced over time. To that end, the exercise assumes that nominal GDP growth in the next decade will range between 9% (deflationary pressures and low real GDP growth) and 16% (inflation and fast growth) (Table 4).

This simple exercise shows that under scenarios that are not considered extreme, the burden would be between 9% and 14% of 2010 GDP. In any event, as has happened in the past, the problem of bad loans will shrink as a consequence of the high nominal GDP growth. In 2020, the burden of new default loans will be approximately 2–4% of GDP and the NPL ratio will increase from 2% to 3%, which is significant but manageable. Even in a pessimistic environment, new NPLs would be below 8% of GDP in 2020. However, as shown in Table 5, the current level of provisioning and capital seem to be insufficient to bear these losses.

While the root of the current problems is the lack of funding of local governments and the stimuli-driven nature of lending, it is unlikely that the burden will be borne solely by commercial banks. To avoid financial and real spillovers, the central government may guarantee these debts or remove them from the balance sheets of commercial banks. Therefore, the most likely scenario in the event of crisis would be that the central government would either provide local governments with additional sources/revenues or transfer the LGFV loans from banks' balance sheets to some entity or "bad bank" as it did in earlier restructuring.

**Table 5** Loan loss provisions of major commercial banks (RMB bn)

| | 2002 | 2003 | 2004 | 2005 | 2006 | 2007 | 2008 | 2009 | 2010 |
|---|---|---|---|---|---|---|---|---|---|
| Loan loss provision | 158 | 415 | 243 | 303 | 401 | 471 | 574 | 663 | 803 |
| Outstanding balance of NPLs | 2,279 | 2,104 | 1,718 | 1,220 | 1,170 | 1,201 | 487 | 426 | 369 |
| Total loans | 13,129 | 15,900 | 17,820 | 19,469 | 22,535 | 26,169 | 30,339 | 39,968 | 47,920 |
| Provision coverage ratio (%) | 7 | 20 | 14 | 25 | 34 | 39 | 118 | 155 | 218 |
| Provision over total loans (%) | 1.2 | 2.6 | 1.4 | 1.6 | 1.8 | 1.8 | 1.9 | 1.7 | 1.7 |

Sources: CBRC and PBC

This is why, in our central scenario, the government will support local governments and their LGFVs so that no deterioration in bank assets will remain on their balance sheets. However, as China has a more open and developed banking system than in the previous stress episode, such an episode is bound to profoundly damage the credibility of the policies and the modernization of the banking system.

On the other hand, public finances appear to be robust enough to deal with this problem. The official debt to GDP ratio is relatively low (17% at the end of 2010), but it only includes debt issued by the central government. If all contingent government liabilities are included, public debt could rise to approximately 80% of GDP (Fig. 16), which is not so large taking into account China's fast rate of growth.

## 6.2 *Risks from the Property Sector*

The second vulnerability is related to monetary policy and too low interest rates produced by financial repression (Fig. 17). In this regard, evidence points to the fact that loose monetary conditions fuel rises in asset prices (Ahuja et al. 2010; de Bondt et al. 2010; Glindro et al. 2008; Santabárbara 2011 and Wu et al. 2010).

On the determinants of house prices, Santabárbara (2011) built an empirical model for house prices as a function of structural determinants (income per capita and urbanization), financial conditions (loans per capita, interest rates) and speculative behaviors (lag of the log of stock of houses). The model showed that (1) very favorable financing conditions have become increasingly relevant in explaining house prices, which implies that the loose monetary stance in China has decisively contributed to house price increases; (2) structural factors, namely income growth and the urbanization process, have accounted for a "natural" annual real growth of

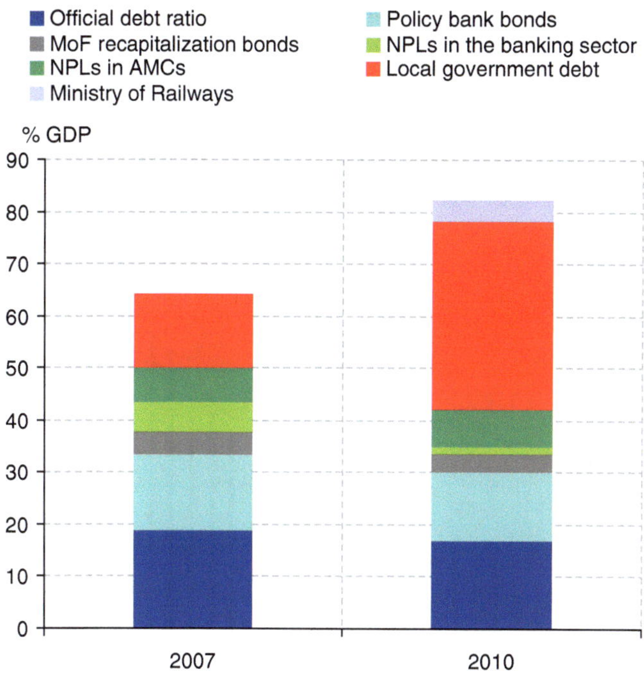


**Fig. 16** Public sector liabilities (% of GDP). Source: Authors' calculations based on PBC, National Audit Office and Dragonomics

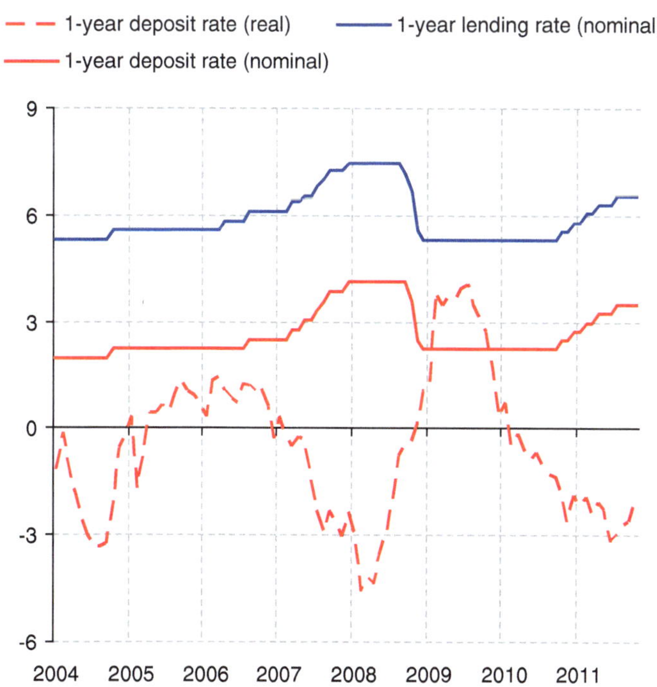


**Fig. 17** One-year reference deposit and lending rates (%). Source: CEIC

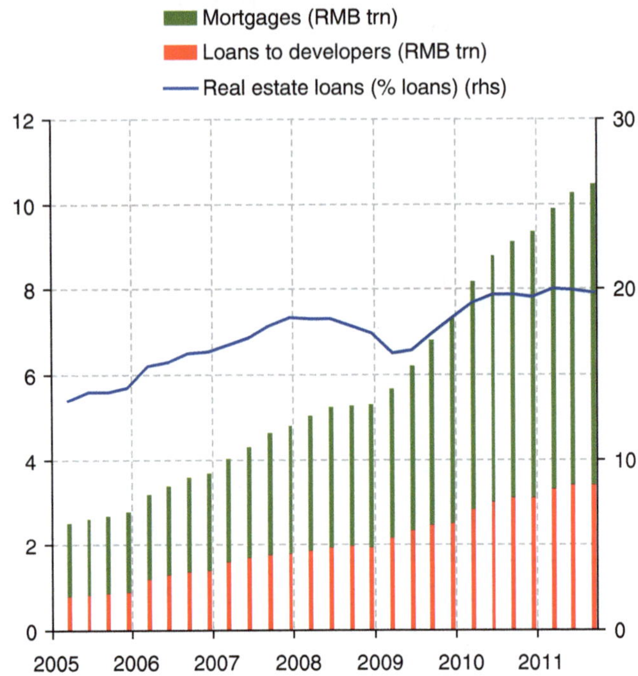


**Fig. 18** Real estate loans (RMB trn, %). Source: CEIC

house prices by 6%; and (3) there is no clear sign of a nation-wide property bubble, but property prices could be overvalued by 10% on average and several large cities (RHS), including Beijing and Shanghai, show an overvaluation of more than 35%.

Authorities have been very active in the property market to avert the risk of price bubbles and to maintain housing affordability mainly through a regulatory approach. Indeed, the policies implemented from April 2010 onwards were aimed at stabilizing housing prices by restricting speculative demand while, at the same time, increasing social housing supply to sustain residential investment.

Property market developments are a threat to bank asset quality as it permeates nearly every aspect of the economy. In China, however, it is generally the more indirect channels that are relevant. Indeed, the direct exposure of banks to the property market is relatively contained. Real estate loans increased by RMB 4.5 trillion from 2008 to 2010 and accounted for approximately 20% of total loans in 2010. However, this phenomenon is seen more as a reflection of financial development than as a source of risk (Fig. 18). Household indebtedness stood at approximately 40% of disposable income in 2010 (well below international standards) and household mortgages (13% of loans) have been granted with effective loan-to-value ratios below 50%, implying that the collateral is large enough to buffer major falls in prices. The riskier aspect is related to the loans given to property developers, which account for 6% of total lending.

As stated above, indirect channels appear to be much more relevant. A housing market collapse would have a sizable impact on economic activity and by extension the credit quality of bank loans. The impact on real economic activity stems from the strong linkages between the real estate sector and other industries. The real estate sector accounts for 5.6% of GDP, and its performance directly affects related industries such as construction (6.6% of GDP), steel, cement, and furniture. On the other hand, financial spillovers might be related to loans that have been made using properties as collateral, such as LGFVs. Therefore, a sharp drop in property prices would likely have a negative impact on local government revenues and their ability to repay these vehicles' loans.

## 7 Appraisal and Conclusions

China's banking system, despite its survival of the international financial crisis and its progress after the reforms, continues to present particular weaknesses that require decisive and straightforward measures. We will now summarize the most significant weaknesses as well as several measures we consider useful to promote their reform.

*Perhaps the most important weakness is the continuation of excessive public intervention and weak corporate governance.* Public ownership has impeded the establishment of a commercially driven financial system—banks continue to be used to pursue broader policy goals. Moreover, although significant steps have been made in the regulation of the financial system and to improve corporate governance, its enforcement is still limited. All these are partly because of a lack of independence of bank managers and even regulators. Bank lending continues to be dependent on the interests of the public sector. A clear case is the bank financing of the fiscal stimulus package, which could pose severe financial stability vulnerabilities. Until public interference in credit allocation is eliminated, commercial banks will be exposed to solvency problems. However, central and local governments do not appear willing to renounce the use of banks as powerful policy tools. This will require a substantial reform of public finances, which includes the relationship between central and local governments.

*To continue the financial liberalization process*, which is currently at a standstill, it is necessary to restructure the banks and improve supervision. A complete restructuring should be accompanied by an increase in the efficiency of China's banks, and not just regarding solvency. On the other hand, liberalization without a comprehensive reform—which has to include a change in the incentive structure—could be even more dangerous than a situation of ample liquidity, such as the current state. Further market-oriented monetary policy instruments and an increase of the cost of capital will help to promote an effective use of interest rates. In addition, assessing interest and exchange risks will become more relevant as financial liberalization develops. Indeed, the rapid increase in exposure in the last few years clearly hints at growing risks as cross-border financial flows increase and capital account liberalization progresses.

Authorities should propose a clear roadmap to promote financial reform and define a sequence for exchange rate reform, monetary policy market-based instrumentation, interest rate liberalization, and the opening up of the capital account.

On the other hand, *the regulatory improvement that has been seen in recent years requires a greater commitment toward enforcement.* To do so, both the independence of the regulator and the improvement of corporate governance are key. Knowledge of the banking business should also be actively promoted, especially with regard to risk management. In addition, as the financial sector is becoming more complex, the perimeter of financial supervision and regulation has to be expanded.

One of the *main reasons for weak corporate governance* is the fact that banks remain a key way for the Chinese government to control the economy. The enlarged role of the state hampers incentives to assess the true level of risk, and also opportunities. With regard to risk measurement, the progress made in credit risk is to be applauded but it is not enough—operational and market risks are also very important. In this sense, the development of hedging instruments is essential. The Chinese authorities have started to move in this direction after a pause during the crisis.

Last, *effective competition in the market is low*, especially between the largest banks, and competition must be encouraged. A system with such a high degree of intervention—with tight control over interest rates, credit quotas, licenses and a small aperture for foreign banks—does not provide a favorable economic environment for either competition or efficiency. Ensuring real competition does not require the privatization of the banking system, although it would obviously facilitate the process.

If the process of reform is not completed or a new stress episode occurs, authorities will be tempted to maintain the current *financial repression*. In the last decade, financial repression was used to mitigate banking sector stress at the expense of passing the final costs of bank restructuring to depositors. This strategy could be successful to avoid major financial stress, but it reflects a major redistribution of income from households to the rest of the economy. As a result, the major risk of the vast expansion of bank lending from period 2008 to 2010 is that the costs will fall on the household sector (as occurred in the past) through higher taxes or continued financial repression that will constrain household income, with obvious implications for the desired rebalancing of the Chinese economy. Indeed, the growing shadow banking system indicates that it is increasingly difficult to maintain financial repression.

Last but not least, from a *macroeconomic point of view*, financial underdevelopment and financial repression have distorted saving and investment decisions affecting China's macroeconomic imbalances. Therefore, if China is willing to attain a more sustainable growth model based on private domestic demand, especially consumption, then further financial reform is crucial to reach these objectives. The low cost of capital and a captive bank deposit base have boosted government-guided investment (although its efficiency is low) and the lack of funding alternatives has encouraged private savings, especially from enterprises. China's financial sector, therefore, is pivotal in explaining the major imbalances of the economy such as the investment-led growth model and a persistent current account surplus.

As a general conclusion, China's financial system is strong enough to take advantage of the opportunities provided by the current crisis, *if* it completes its reform and quickly establishes further market-oriented incentives. The areas that are the longest overdue are a reduction in state intervention and improvements in corporate governance. Moreover, banks have to be encouraged to operate in an environment with less intervention and more competition, as only competition and profits from efficiency can ensure the continuation of a banking system that intermediates savings effectively and efficiently without causing tensions in financial stability. Ownership reform, through more private ownership, will definitely help in this regard. The authorities should not forget that the transformation towards a market economy has been crucial for the economic development of China; therefore, they should continue their efforts in that direction, but in this case, in the financial sector.

## Appendix: Further Details on the Fourth Wave of Bank Restructuring

The first wave started in 1998 with the overall idea to allow SOCBs to operate as commercial institutions. It was implemented by a capital injection of US$33 billion in local currency (Table 6) to raise their CAR to 8% and by transferring their NPLs to several "bad banks," the AMCs. The operation started with a reduction of the PBoC reserve requirements that freed fresh money used by SOCBs to purchase MoF bonds. Just thereafter, the government injected the funds, collected as capital, into the four SOCBs. In 2000, US$170 billion worth of NPLs belonging to the SOCBs were transferred to AMCs at face value, in exchange for bonds issued by the four AMCs (created purposely to recover the debt of each SOCB) and with PBoC loans valued at US$73 billion. At that stage, the amount transferred accounted for more than 15% of GDP and was unable to be borne by China's weak public finances.

The second stage was aimed at allowing the two best performing SOCBs, the CCB and the BoC, to attract foreign strategic investors and to go public. On 31 December 2003, each bank employed all their pre-existing capital (US$11 billion) to write-off the NPLs while the central bank used its investment arm—Central Huijin—to inject US$22.5 billion from international reserves into each bank. As a result, Central Huijin became the main shareholder. To prevent potential pressure

**Table 6** Capital injections into the SOCBs

| | | Amount | | | |
|---|---|---|---|---|---|
| Date | Bank | RMB bn | USD bn | Financed by: | Currency |
| 1998–1999 | SOCBs | 275 | 33 | Ministry of Finance | RMB |
| 2003–2004 | CCB | 186 | 22.5 | PBC (Central Huijin) | USD (FX reserves) |
| | BoC | 186 | 22.5 | | |
| 2005 | ICBC | 124 | 15 | PBC (Central Huijin) | USD (FX reserves) |
| 2008 | ABC | 130 | 19 | CIC (Central Huijin) | USD (FX reserves) |

on the exchange rate and domestic liquidity conditions, the capital had to be maintained in foreign currency. The collateral effect of this measure was an increase in the foreign currency exposure of domestic institutions. Further along, in May and June 2004, the outstanding NPLs of the CCB and BoC were sold at 47% of their face value to the AMCs for US$16 billion and US$18 billion, respectively. Later in 2004, was an additional US$7 billion and US$17 billion, was transferred, respectively, without involving the other two AMCs, Cinda and Oriental. Moreover, the CCB and BoC increased their regulatory capital by issuing subordinate debt for a total of US$4.8 billion and US$7.3 billion, respectively. Subsequently, both banks incorporated strategic investors to improve their management and to diversify their ownership. In June 2005, the CCB selected the Bank of America as a strategic partner, which paid approximately US$2.5 billion for 9% of its capital. In August 2005, 10% of BoC capital was purchased by a consortium led by the Royal Bank of Scotland for US$3.1 billion. Afterwards both banks went public. In October 2005, the CCB raised more than US$9 billion in Hong Kong, and in May 2006, the BoC nearly US$10 billion.

The third round of restructuring focused on the ICBC in 2006. In April 2005, Central Huijin injected US$15 billion into the ICBC. Although the default rates of this bank were higher than those of the banks mentioned previously, only US$9 billion of its capital was used to write-off impaired loans. The major difference with the previous restructuring wave is that not all pre-existing capital was used to write-off NPLs, but that the MoF safeguarded a stake of US$10 billion. As a result, the MoF and PBoC each held 50% of the equity. In June 2005, the ICBC issued US$12 billion in subordinate debt. At that time, it also auctioned US$56 billion to the AMCs at 38% of its face value. Later, an additional US$30 billion was exchanged by a receivable of the MoF. In March 2006, a consortium led by Goldman Sachs, as a strategic investor, acquired 8.5% of the capital for US$3.8 billion. Like the CCB and BOC, the ICBC also went public, simultaneously in Hong Kong and Shanghai, obtaining US$19 billion—the largest IPO in the world at that time.

In October 2008, the fourth restructuring wave began targeting the ABC, the weakest systemic bank because of its focus on rural areas and its large volume of NPLs (US$120 billion). The major difference with previous restructuring waves is that the AMCs did not take part in the process and the MoF extended a higher influence in the restructuring process than previously. As a first step, approximately 80% of the NPLs were exchanged on a full book value basis via an unfounded obligation of the MoF, to be paid in 15 years. Subsequently, Central Huijin—already transferred to the sovereign investment fund (CIC)—injected US$19 billion in exchange for 50% of the capital, whereby the MoF and CIC were the only shareholders. Although the NPLs were transferred to the MoF, the ABC is in charge of their management. With regard to the inclusion of a strategic investor, for the first time the investor was domestic, the National Social Security Fund. ABC went public in July 2010 and raised US$22 billion in a dual listing in Shanghai and Hong Kong.

## References

Ahuja A, Cheung L, Han G, Porter NJ, Zhang W (2010) Are house prices rising too fast in China? IMF working papers, December, WP/10/274

Chinn MD, Ito H (2008) A new measure of financial openness. Journal of Comparative Policy Analysis 10(3):309–322

de Bondt GJ, Peltonen TA, Santabárbara D (2010) Booms and busts in China's stock market: estimates based on fundamentals. Working paper series, 1190, European Central Bank

Dorrucci E, Meyer-Cirkel A, Santabárbara D (2009) Domestic financial development in emerging market economies: evidence and implications. ECB occasional paper no. 102

Dragonomics (2009) The magical debt-shrinking machine, 30 September, mimeo

García-Herrero A, Santabárbara D (2008) Does the Chinese banking system benefit from foreign investors? BOFIT discussion papers, 11, Bank of Finland, Institute for Economies in Transition

García-Herrero A, Gavilá S, Santabárbara D (2009) What explains the low profitability of Chinese banks? J Bank Finance 33(11):2080–2092

Glindro ET, Subhanij T, Szeto J, Zhu H (2008) Determinants of house prices in nine Asia-Pacific economies. BIS working paper, 263

Lardy NR (2008) Financial repression in China, policy brief, 08-8, Peterson Institute for International Economy

Santabárbara D (2011) Are house prices in China explained by its fundamentals. ECB, mimeo

Walter CE, Howie FJT (2011) Red capitalism: the fragile financial foundation of China's extraordinary rise. Wiley, Singapore

Wu J, Gyourko J, Deng Y (2010) Evaluating conditions in major Chinese housing markets. NBER working paper, 16189, National Bureau of Economic Research, MA, July

Yongding Y (2009) The management of cross border capital flows and macroeconomic stability in China. Third world network global economic series

# Comment Paper to Chapter "An Assessment of China's Banking System Reform"

**Tomoyuki Fukumoto**

## 1 The Paper Offers a Precise Review of the Reform of the Banking System

For more than a decade, the Chinese authorities have taken various measures to improve their banking system. I think the authors have been very precise in their chronological description of the actions the Chinese authorities and banks to reform the banking system. Three key aspects of reform are reviewed: bank restructuring, financial liberalization and bank regulation. I understand how challenging it is to obtain accurate and detailed information of this type concerning China. I admire the authors' great efforts to put those facts in order.

However, that said, I think this paper could be improved if the authors incorporate the following points.

## 2 The Paper Would Be Improved if the Claim that the Governance of Chinese Banks Remains Weak Is Reinforced and Supported

After depicting various reform measures to change bank governance, the authors conclude that the most important weakness is the continuation of excessive public intervention and weak corporate governance. Intuitively, I tend to agree with this conclusion. However, it would increase the value of this paper if the authors could present stronger evidence.

T. Fukumoto (✉)
International Department, The Bank of Japan, Tokyo, Japan
e-mail: tomoyuki.fukumoto@boj.or.jp

S. Kaji and E. Ogawa (eds.), *Who Will Provide the Next Financial Model?: Asia's Financial Muscle and Europe's Financial Maturity*,
DOI 10.1007/978-4-431-54282-7_16, 

First, it might be desirable for the authors to articulate what has truly changed, and what has not, in bank governance through the past reform measures. As the authors explain, banks have enhanced transparency by listing their shares and introducing foreign strategic investors. In addition, the Chinese Banking Regulatory Committee (CBRC) has made painstaking efforts to beef up the supervision of banking activities. Through these reform measures, to what extent have Chinese banks become less susceptible to local government intervention? To what extent have their lending decisions become economically rational? It would be beneficial for the authors to elaborate these points.

Second, the authors seem to attribute the evidence of weak governance to the government's guidance to aggressively lend loans to support the government's stimuli in 2009 and the sudden surge in bank lending.

However, I am not sure to what extent banks were forced to extend loans against their will. Because of the stringent window guidance by the People's Bank of China (PBOC), banks could not increase loan volume as much as they could in 2007 and 2008. In the fourth quarter of 2008, the PBOC removed the limit of bank lending increase, which enabled banks to extend loans to potentially profitable projects. For Chinese commercial banks, the sudden surge in lending in 2009, to some extent, may be voluntary, not involuntary. If the authors find it difficult to show quantitative evidence that proves the causal relationship between government intervention and bank lending, then detailed anecdotal evidence regarding events in 2009 would be helpful.

## 3 The Sequence of the Banking System Reform and Future Financial Liberalization Should Be Articulated

In terms of financial liberalization, the authors state that liberalization without comprehensive reform could be even more dangerous than a situation of ample liquidity such as the current one. I totally agree.

At the same time, I would like to ask the authors if they believe that the Chinese banking system has improved enough for the Chinese government to reinitiate financial liberalization, or that financial liberalization should not be reinitiated because further reforms are required. It would help the paper for the authors to articulate the sequence of the banking system reform and future financial liberalization.

Let me explain my point. Chinese banking reform has been conducted for more than a decade. Though there is still much room for improvement in terms of governance and competitiveness, the Chinese banking system as a whole has passed the tipping point where China can reinitiate financial liberalization. The regulated interest rates are not only perversely transferring wealth from depositors to banks, but also expanding shadow banking. Financial liberalization could be reinitiated in tandem with the banking system reform.

## 4 To What Extent Will Ownership Reform Improve Bank Governance?

The authors say that ownership reform, via more private ownership, will definitely help. I agree.

But the authors could elaborate further on how it would help. In this regard, comparison in governance between joint stock commercial banks (JSCBs) and state-owned commercial banks (SOCBs) might be helpful.

As regards SOCBs, the Chinese government emphatically states that they will maintain the majority of ownership in SOCBs. Therefore, it would be difficult for SOCBs to be privatized in the short-term. Do the authors consider that more private ownership under a state majority is sufficient? Or do they believe that full private ownership is necessary?

## 5 Regarding the Chinese Banking System as a Whole, It Would Be Beneficial for the Authors to Touch on the Reform of China's Regional Banks

The authors focus on the reform of state-owned commercial banks. However, as the title of the paper is "An assessment of China's banking system reform", I think the authors should assess China's banking system as a whole. They could expand the scope of their assessment.

It is true that China's four or five big SOCBs have a dominant market share in the Chinese banking system. However, their market share is gradually declining, and other nationwide joint-stock commercial banks are rapidly developing. In addition, there are local urban commercial banks and rural cooperatives. These categories of financial institutions have undergone their own reform.

In particular, when assessing the impact of loans to local financial investment vehicles (LFIV) on loan quality, it would be better to assess the impact on financial institutions by bank category. It is believed that the impact on local urban commercial banks will be much larger than that on nationwide banks for the following two reasons. First, local urban commercial banks are more susceptible to the intervention of local governments. Second, those LFIVs that borrowed loans from local urban commercial banks are smaller and generally their financial strength is compromised.

# Part IV
# Exchange Rate Systems

# Is the European Monetary Union Sustainable? The Role of Real Convergence

**Helmut Wagner**

**Abstract** The founders of the European Union and European Monetary Union foresaw or assumed that the monetary union would only be sustainable if there was a convergence of living standards across member countries, and that the endogenous convergence in living standards was only possible if there was sufficient institutional and structural convergence. However, their view that there may be a kind of endogenous institutional-structural convergence process within a monetary union with structurally heterogeneous member countries has not proved well founded. Convergence (in living standards as well as in institutional and structural development) seems possible only if this process is accompanied by *conditional* aid from those more developed member countries and with a strict surveillance of the implementation of these conditionalities. Without these preconditions, convergence in living standards across member countries in the European Monetary Union will occur only if higher debt ratios are accepted in the member countries. Over-indebtedness in some member countries, however, can lead to a sovereign debt crisis and create contagious effects on other, even further-developed, member countries. This has become apparent in the European Monetary Union during the past few years.

**Keywords** Convergence • European integration • Sovereign debt

## 1 Introduction

Real convergence is an original goal of the European integration process. A major goal of the European treaties in 1957 was to "strengthen the unity of [the] economies [of the member states] and to ensure their harmonious development by reducing the

H. Wagner (✉)
University of Hagen, Hagen, Germany
e-mail: Helmut.Wagner@fernuni-hagen.de

S. Kaji and E. Ogawa (eds.), *Who Will Provide the Next Financial Model?: Asia's Financial Muscle and Europe's Financial Maturity*,
DOI 10.1007/978-4-431-54282-7_17, 

differences existing between the various regions and the backwardness of the less favoured" (preamble of the Treaty establishing the European Community (EC Treaty), 1957).

This goal of real convergence was confirmed in the preamble of the Treaty of Maastricht in the context of establishing a monetary union in Europe. Within that treaty, the correlation of this aim of real convergence with monetary integration was formulated, in that the contracting states declared their resolve to "achieve the strengthening and the convergence of their economies and to establish an economic and monetary union, including, in accordance with the provisions of this treaty, a single and stable currency". Article 2 of the EC Treaty in particular expresses the view that the monetary union was seen as an instrument for achieving the aim of real convergence by stating that the aim of convergence, among other things, was to be pursued "by establishing a common market and an economic and monetary union".

The question arises then whether a monetary union truly does favor real convergence among its members. Economic literature on this point is rather mixed. The fact that *economic* integration fosters real convergence is undisputed. However, whether monetary integration is also favorable for the catching up goal of emerging European Monetary Union member countries is not clear. This will be analyzed in more detail in this paper.

It will be shown that a monetary union can foster real convergence, however only under very restrictive politico-economic conditions. If construction failures are incorporated in a monetary union system, the result may even be real divergence. It will be shown in this paper that in the European Monetary Union (treaties) there were definite construction failures that hindered the monetary union in reaching its goal of real convergence across member states. The two main construction failures include: (1) the politically driven selection of new members, and (2) a lack of incentives to save and/or to reform (towards institutional convergence) and to follow through with commitments due to a lack of sanction mechanisms to deal with the violation of contracts.[1] If these construction failures are not remedied, the sustainability of the European Monetary Union may be in danger.

The paper is organized as follows: in part 2 I will present the concepts of "European (Monetary) Union (E(M)U) integration" and "real convergence" as used in this paper. In part 3, I shall describe the theoretical arguments behind the hypothesis that E(M)U integration fosters "real convergence". In part 4, I ask whether the empirical results corroborate the above hypothesis. In part 5, I shall discuss the danger of "real divergence" in a monetary union with heterogeneity and construction failures, using an example of the European Monetary Union. In part 6, I shall draw some policy implications and conclude the paper.

[1] Another conclusion of this paper is that the larger the development (real convergence) gap between an accession country and the incumbents of a monetary union, the greater the danger of ending up with low or even negative net real growth effects from accession, at least for some period of time. This has proven true for some euro area countries like Greece and Portugal, and may also prove true for other less developed member countries.

## 2 Concepts of "E(M)U Integration" and "Real Convergence"

I understand *European integration* to represent an attempt to build unity among European countries and peoples. Within the European Union (EU) this means that countries pool their resources and make many decisions jointly; this joint decision-making takes place through interaction between EU institutions (for example, the Parliament, Council and Commission). European integration developed after World War II along the following prescribed "evolutionary" steps: (1) commercial league, (2) customs union, (3) common market, (4) economic union and (5) monetary union.

The last step (5) is sometimes considered the "crowning glory" of the European (economic) integration process.

"New Member States" is abbreviated here to NMS; this term encompasses member countries that have joined the EU but have not yet joined the monetary union. They are accession countries to the euro area (EA) with the *right, but at the same time also the obligation* to join the monetary union as soon as they fulfill the Maastricht (nominal convergence) criteria (but at the earliest 2 years after entry into the EU).[2]

Further, Greece, Italy, Ireland, Portugal and Spain is denoted by *GIIPS*, and GIPS encompasses the same country-group with the exception of Italy.

*Real convergence* is a term that represents catching up in terms of Gross National Income (GNI) per capita as well as convergence in institutions and socio-economic structures (as a type of precondition).[3]

Convergence in the sense of *catching up in GNI or Gross National Product (GNP)*[4] *per capita* aims at an alignment of standards of living at a high level in the participating states,[5] which was a main target of the process of European integration from the beginning (as mentioned above). This can be viewed as a long-term economic goal of the integration process in Europe.

However, even if data shows GNI per capita convergence over one or even two decades, this does not guarantee that this process of convergence is sustainable—whether this is the case depends upon institutional and structural convergence (which can be considered as a precondition not only for sustainability, but also for implementation and ensuring a high level of GNI per capita convergence).

---

[2] This requirement does not apply to Great Britain and Denmark; these two countries negotiated early on an opting out clause so that they do not have to join the euro area.

[3] See, for example, Papademos (2006).

[4] Here I treat *GNI* and *GNP* the same measure. GNI is identical to GNP as previously used in national accounts generally (Eurostat's Concepts and Definitions Database).

[5] Various convergence hypotheses have been developed and tested econometrically (see Sala-i-Martin 1996, Galor 1996, Barro and Sala-i-Martin 1995, Chap. 11). Here, catching up is understood to decrease the dispersion of real GNP per capita in the EU countries (see also Grosser 1992, p. 404; European Commission 1996, p. 175). This measure serves as a rough indicator for the alignment of standards of living, an aim of the treaties on which the EU is based. A necessary condition for this convergence is that the "backward" countries grow faster than the richer countries. In the terminology used by Sala-i-Martin (1996) this means that β-convergence is a necessary condition for σ-convergence.

*Institutional convergence* describes the assimilation of institutions and rules within a union, whereas *structural convergence* denotes the alignment of socio-economic structures in the union member countries (be it in labor or product markets, or with respect to judicial efficiency and administrative capacity or political governance).

This institutional and structural convergence can also be considered as a precondition for the goal of business cycle synchronization: one precondition required to produce the desired effects of a currency union (e.g., a quick catch up in GNI per capita) is that the business cycles of participant countries must be largely synchronized. Otherwise, the one-size-fits-all monetary policy in the currency union would be less effective, i.e., too loose for fast-growing, booming economies and too tight for others.

In terms of the theory of optimum currency areas (OCA), this translates into the question of whether the OCA rating of currency-area countries has improved.[6]

## 3 Does E(M)U-Integration Foster "Real Convergence"?—Theory[7]

*Economic integration* fosters "real convergence" mainly via the four developments and/or benefits a less developed country can expect to receive (free of charge) when entering the EU:

(1) *An increase in international trade with other member countries* (driven by (i) a better allocation of resources, (ii) access to better technologies, inputs and intermediary goods, (iii) increased possibilities to profit from economies of scale, (iv) growth externalities like the transfer of know-how and (v) a reorganization of the industry, which can create a Schumpeterian growth-favoring environment (e.g., see Wagner 1997, p. 113);
(2) *An increase in foreign direct investment* (triggering a technology transfer, including advice and technical help, transported together with the direct investments);
(3) *An increase in transfer payments* (from the EU budget to emerging accession countries; for more detail see Wagner 2006); and
(4) *An import of political stability* (through the obligation to adopt many *useful* regulations and rules prescribed in the EU, such as in the so-called *acquis communautaire*[8]).

[6] OCA theory was originally developed in the 1960s; however, it now requires further development against a background of the globalization process that has occurred since then. For a survey of the theory of OCA see, for example, Mongelli (2008).

[7] This section partly leans on Wagner (2001) and Wagner (1995).

[8] The term *acquis communautaire* is used in EU law to refer to the total body of EU law accumulated thus far.

This implies that EU integration forces entrants to align (some of) their institutions to that of the incumbents (or the requirements laid down in the EU treaties), as EU integration ensures some institutional convergence within the union (endogenous convergence). In particular, the size of benefit (2) above is strongly dependent upon the institutional conditions within a recipient country.

With regard to the impact of *monetary integration* on real convergence, we can only find mixed results in the theoretical literature. The *expectation for a positive effect* of (European) monetary integration on the catch up by new entrants is supported on the one hand by the expectation of the strengthening of the above effects, i.e.:

- The hope for *greater* international trade among euro area countries;
- The hope for *greater* capital inflows (particularly Foreign Direct Investments (FDI)) and their effective use;
- The hope for *greater* transfer payments (due to club solidarity); and
- The hope for *greater* political stability via the handing over of monetary policy decision-power to the European Central Bank (ECB).[9]

On the other hand, a further (direct) way in which a monetary union can contribute to GNI per capita convergence is via financial market integration and the elimination of the exchange risk premium. This tends to lead to lower real interest rates and easier access to credit feeding directly into domestic asset markets.[10]

Furthermore, there has been an expectation of healthy discipline imposed by the Maastricht criteria. These criteria demand the achievement of defined nominal convergence criteria, including fiscal criteria that are supposed to remain binding on participants even after they join the monetary union. In abiding by such criteria, member states prove a sufficient degree of economic harmonization and show the seriousness with which the aims of a stable community are being pursued. This applies above all to the less developed member states, in the face of the need for high public investment in infrastructure during the process of catching up.[11]

The disciplining factor is expected to become effective immediately, to reinforce the serious and credible intention. This is supported by appropriate controls, and in combination with visible successes, to fulfill the Maastricht criteria by means of a restrictive monetary and fiscal policy. Those criteria that refer to fiscal policy aspects demand the removal or renunciation of excessive budgetary policies because excessive deficits or debts are considered unsustainable in the long term. This type of unsound budgetary policy would tend to have unfavorable, interest-raising effects

[9] See Wagner (1997).

[10] This can be seen in the development of bond spreads after the (announcement of the) establishment of the euro area in the mid- to late-1990s. See Fig. 4.

[11] The compulsion of a restrictive fiscal policy means that in certain circumstances a high level of unemployment and the fact that important infrastructural investments cannot be financed must be accepted to fulfil the interest parity condition of a monetary union.

on the capital market, which would have a not inconsiderable negative effect on investment decisions.

Because the compulsion for a restrictive fiscal policy also facilitates the implementation of a price-stabilizing monetary policy,[12] the fiscal Maastricht criteria can contribute to diminishing the danger of a monetary bailout by the ECB. This would be expressed in low inflation expectations of market actors, which would lead to positive effects on investments, and therefore on growth.

Of course, *counter-effects* are also highlighted in theoretical studies on monetary unions that favor the view that European monetary integration may instead slow or limit real convergence. These counter-effects are triggered by

(i) The loss of seigniorage[13];
(ii) The danger of internal and external imbalances; and
(iii) Austere fiscal policies (induced by the attempt to fulfill the Maastricht convergence criteria as a precondition for EA entry).
Furthermore, it is feared that the run-up to European monetary integration will lead (for a significant period) to
(iv) Business cycle desynchronization;
(v) An anticipatory recession; and
(vi) Unintended contagion effects.

This would have a negative effect not only on NMS but also incumbent euro area countries.[14]

While the loss of seigniorage only arises after a country has entered the currency area, the other effects (ii–vi) emerge in the run-up phase of euro adoption. I shall discuss these counter-effects in detail in part 5.[15] In part 4 I shall, however, first present the empirical experiences of NMS and EA member countries, particularly GIIPS, with regard to real convergence.

[12] This discipline is seen as particularly important on the road towards an European Monetary Union. See Wagner (2005a).

[13] The establishment of the European Monetary Union means the separation of monetary and fiscal policies in the member states. The opportunity to autonomously procure revenues from seigniorage disappears. Within the monetary union there will still be profits from the creation of money, but these will go to the ECB, which will return the profits to the individual states. However, the profits for those countries that previously had high rates of inflation will probably become significantly lower, because an independent ECB will be likely to considerably restrict the possibility of seigniorage revenues. This could result in substantial budgetary policy problems for some of the less developed member states. This loss of revenue will have to be compensated for by tax increases or reductions in expenditure. However, as a result of the general reduction in rates of inflation in the 1990s this problem appears now to be considerably lessened for the present circle of member states. See Wagner (2006).

[14] At this stage most politicians and economists consider that the benefits would outweigh the costs of European monetary integration (the question is however, is this the case for all members, and at which time horizon).

[15] Another potential counter-argument to the long-term real effects of monetary integration is, however, misleading, and refers to the hypothesis of neutrality of monetary policy (see Wagner 2001).

# 4 Has E(M)U Fostered "Real Convergence"?—Empirics

In the following I shall provide some evidence on whether there has been an alignment of GNI per capita and the institutional and structural fundamentals over the past decade. Furthermore, I also test for an alignment of the Maastricht criteria (See the following graphs and figures in this part and the Appendix).

## 4.1 *GNI Per Capita*

I have focused on the alignment of GNI per capita in NMS-10 during and after 2004 and in GIIPS, compared with the EU-27 and the EA-17.[16] Furthermore, I have calculated σ-convergence in EU-27 and EA-17.

Figure 1 shows that there had been β-convergence in NMS-10 up till the financial crisis, insofar as the growth rates in NMS-10 were higher than the EU-27 average. Figure 2 indicates that this applies also to GIPS, however to a lesser degree.[17] Table 1 shows that there was also σ-convergence in the E(M)U in the decade before the financial crisis, but not among EA-11 (the first-round entrants).

Other studies in the empirical literature on the real convergence of EU members also reach similar conclusions. In a parametric framework, Christodoulakis (2009) estimated the β-convergence parameter for members of the European Monetary Union, and found that the speed of β-convergence weakened between pre- and post-Euro periods. Along the same lines, the σ-income-convergence between members of the monetary union slowed down or even substantially reversed. The only signs of progress can be observed in the synchronization of business cycles that improve the viability of common monetary policy. Thus, business cycles have become more symmetric and less intensive after the establishment of the single currency, at least until 2008.

Raileanu Szeles (2011) applied a nonparametric framework for NMS, which detects convergence clubs and distinguishes between long-term and short-term absolute convergence. Her findings indicate a lack of real convergence in the long-term in favor of short periods of convergence and divergence. Comparing these results with the standard parametric approach to detect β-convergence, the β-parameter is weakly significant.

Emphasizing the role of alternative indicators for real structural convergence, Marelli and Signorelli (2010) estimated β-convergence in productivity levels and labor market performance indicators in the EU-27. The evidence for convergence in

[16] NMS-10 represents the ten former post-communist countries that joined the EU between 2004 and 2007, and the EA-17 currently includes 17 member countries in the euro area.

[17] This may be disappointing for GIPS if compared with NMS-10. However, the *level* of GNI per capita is still higher in GIPS compared with NMS-10 (see Table 4 in the Appendix).

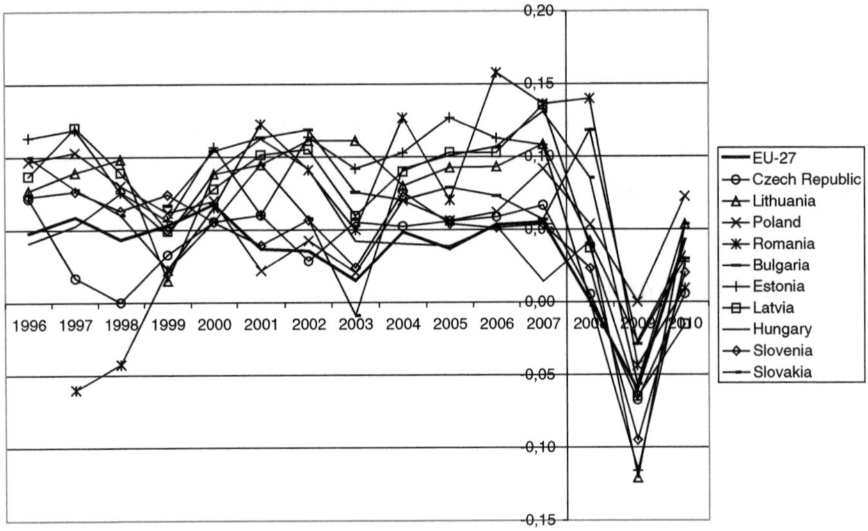


**Fig. 1** GNI per capita growth in NMS. Data source: Eurostat. Notes: Gross national income at market prices in purchasing power standard per inhabitant; year-to-year growth rates

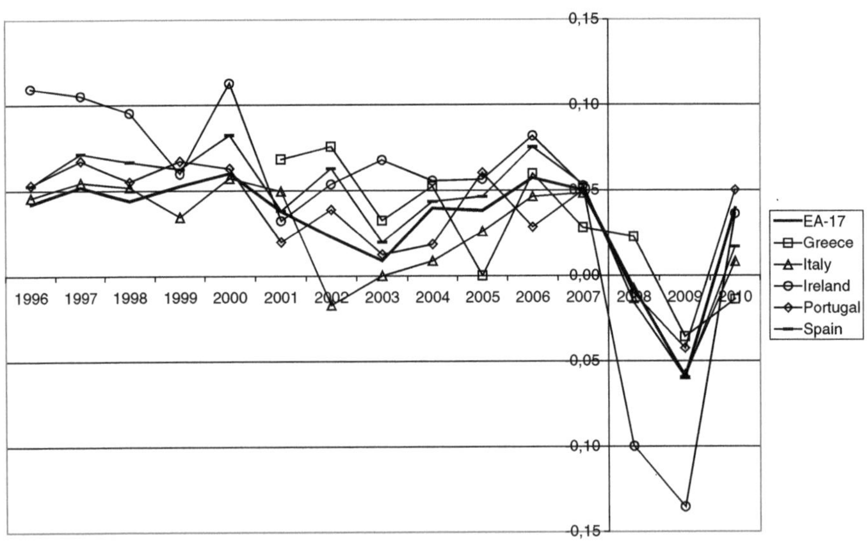


**Fig. 2** GNI per capita growth in GIIPS. Data source: Eurostat. Notes: Gross national income at market prices in purchasing power standard per inhabitant; year-to-year growth rates

**Table 1** σ-Convergence in the European Union and the euro area

| | 1995 | 1996 | 1997 | 1998 | 1999 | 2000 | 2001 | 2002 | 2003 | 2004 | 2005 | 2006 | 2007 | 2008 | 2009 | 2010 |
|---|---|---|---|---|---|---|---|---|---|---|---|---|---|---|---|---|
| $\sigma^2_{\log y,t}$ of EU27 | 0.24 | 0.25 | 0.25 | 0.29 | 0.30 | 0.28 | 0.25 | 0.23 | 0.21 | 0.21 | 0.19 | 0.17 | 0.16 | 0.14 | 0.12 | 0.13 |
| $\sigma^2_{\log y,t}$ of EA17 | 0.16 | 0.15 | 0.14 | 0.13 | 0.14 | 0.14 | 0.12 | 0.11 | 0.10 | 0.11 | 0.10 | 0.09 | 0.09 | 0.07 | 0.06 | 0.07 |
| $\sigma^2_{\log y,t}$ of EA11 | 0.06 | 0.06 | 0.05 | 0.05 | 0.05 | 0.05 | 0.05 | 0.05 | 0.04 | 0.06 | 0.06 | 0.05 | 0.06 | 0.05 | 0.04 | 0.05 |

Data source: Eurostat

Notes: $\sigma^2_{\log y,t}$ denotes the variance across $i$ of $\log y_{i,t}$ ; $y$ is the gross national income at market prices in purchasing power standard per inhabitant industrial specialization is less clear for euro area members. Trade integration increased due to institutional integration in the monetary union and EU. Assessing the σ-convergence of these indicators and Gross Domestic Product (GDP) per capita, strong convergence can be found in labor market performance indicators, but none in productivity and GDP per capita for EA-12. In contrast, NMS experienced strong σ-convergence in GDP per capita and productivity.[18]

This may appear as if the E(M)U clearly leads to GNI per capita convergence across its member countries. However, one has to confess that first, this only applies, if at all, to the decade(s) before the financial crisis and we do not know whether the convergence process will soon be revived against the background of the large structural problems in the less developed member countries. Second, it is difficult to separate the E(M)U integration effect from other effects that also have influenced the convergence process. It might therefore be better to argue so-called "collateral effects", meaning that (expected) E(M)U entrance has encouraged institutional and structural convergence (e.g., enforced by EU regulations in *acquis communautaire* and other requirements) and via this endogenous institutional convergence, GNI per capita convergence has occurred by, for example, increasing the attractiveness of FDIs (for more on the concept of collateral effects see Kose et al. 2006). This might indicate that the level of real convergence is high before and for a short period after E(M)U entrance, and that it slows down soon afterwards.

However, as we will see in Sect. 2, there was no uniform institutional and structural convergence process within the E(M)U. Moreover, the GNI per capita convergence process before the financial crisis was heavily accompanied or fostered by massive financial aid from the richer to the poorer member countries (mainly in the context of an EU "structural aid" program). Thus, the convergence process could be assessed as "artificial".

## 4.2 Structural and Institutional Fundamentals

There are several relevant indicators for structural and institutional convergence that show the same direction of development. In the following figure I show three governance indicators, namely political stability, regulatory quality and rule of law. I have listed them for GIIPS and NMS, and compare them with Germany as a benchmark of the developed EA core (Fig. 3).

We see that there has been institutional *di*vergence in GIIPS after entry into the monetary union (and before the financial crisis!). In contrast, there has been institutional *con*vergence in NMS-10 (before entry into the monetary union).

[18] In sum, empirical evidence appears to advocate in favor of convergence during the initial stage of becoming a member of the European Monetary Union. Once a country has joined the common currency, the process of convergence slows down.

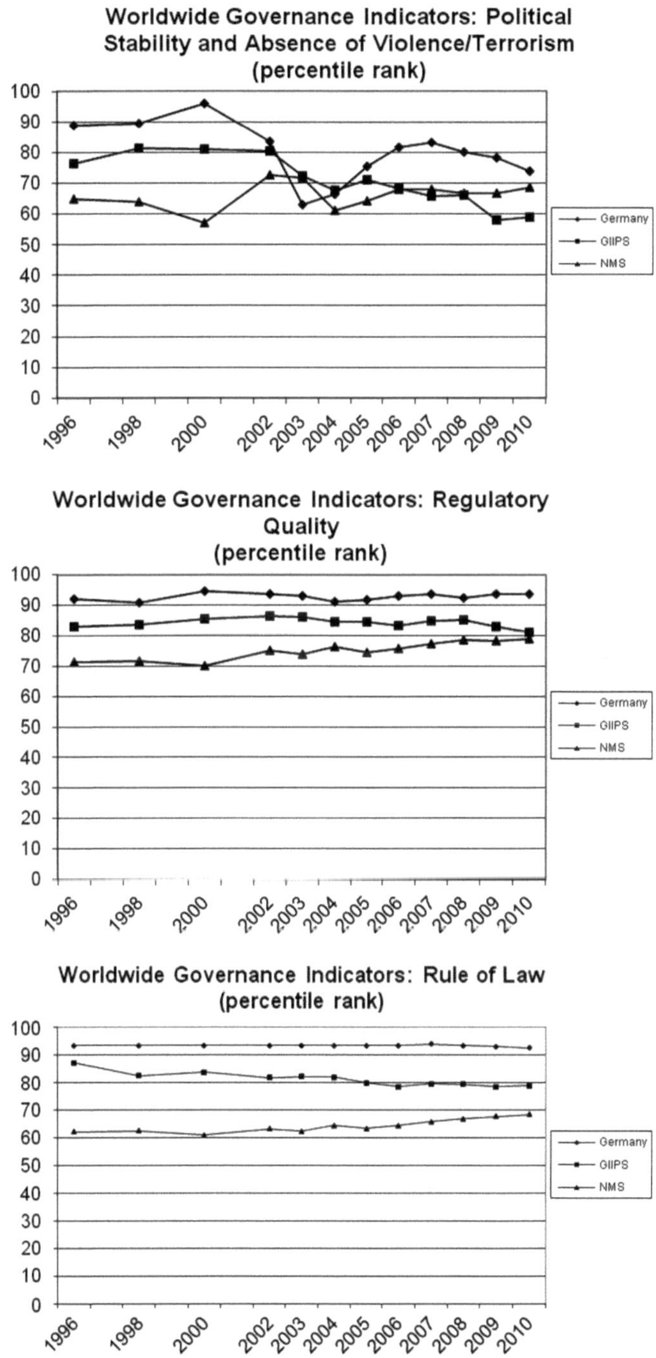


**Fig. 3** Some governance indicators. Data source: World Bank, Worldwide Governance Indicators

In summing up, as a general tendency institutional-structural convergence can only be observed before accession to the European Monetary Union. After accession, institutional-structural convergence appears to slow down or even becomes divergence in some countries (particularly with emerging markets).

### *4.3 Maastricht Criteria*

Finally we ask whether we can observe an alignment to the Maastricht criteria or a violation of the same. We here focus on GIIPS and three NMS (Estonia, Hungary and Poland).

Table 2 shows that before the financial crisis there had been relative convergence with regard to the Maastricht criteria in most GIPS and NMS-10 countries in the sense that the majority could avoid a significant violation of these criteria. The exceptions are Greece and Hungary, both of which committed serious violations before the crisis emerged.

On the whole, the above presentations appear to show that there has been a clear alignment of GNI per capita and the fulfilling of some Maastricht criteria in a majority of the E(M)U member countries. However, there was real divergence with respect to institutional and structural alignment in some of the GIIPS countries after accession to the monetary union. This may be seen as problematic as institutional-structural convergence is often regarded (by the ECB, the Bundesbank and others) as a precondition for sustainable avoidance of violations of the Maastricht criteria, and hence for an efficient monetary policy in the currency union.

Moreover, one can argue that the alignment of GNI per capita and the attainment of some of the Maastricht criteria have been "artificial" for some member countries. The reason for this qualification is that this convergence was only possible against a background of unconditional financial aid and non-credible commitments (due to erroneous or inefficient incentives and sanction mechanisms). This will be explained in more detail in the following part, but it can also be seen in the differences of structural and institutional fundamentals among the various member countries.

## 5 Tendency Towards "Real Divergence" in a Monetary Union with Heterogeneity and Construction Failures: The European Monetary Union as an Example

Looking back, it appears that monetary integration in Europe worked reasonably well in stable (normal) times, however it failed its first big test with respect to mastering a deep financial crisis and its aftermath. It could be argued that it was bad luck and the emergence of a rare shock event—a once-in-a-century event—came too early; however, the true failure was in weak risk management.

**Table 2** Violation of Maastricht criteria: deviations from reference values in percentage points

| | | Price stability | Government budgetary position | | Long-term interest rate |
|---|---|---|---|---|---|
| | | HIPC inflation | General government net lending (+)/net borrowing (–) | General government consolidated gross debt | EA convergence criterion bond yields |
| Germany | 1997 | — | — | — | — |
| | 2002 | — | –0.8 | 0.7 | — |
| | 2008 | — | — | 6.7 | — |
| Ireland | 1997 | — | — | 3.7 | — |
| | 2002 | 1.6 | — | — | — |
| | 2008 | — | –4.3 | — | — |
| Greece | 1997 | 2.7 | : | 36.6 | 2.18 |
| | 2002 | 0.8 | –1.8 | 41.7 | — |
| | 2008 | 0.1 | –6.8 | 53.0 | — |
| Spain | 1997 | — | –1.0 | 6.1 | — |
| | 2002 | 0.5 | — | — | — |
| | 2008 | 0.0 | –1.5 | — | — |
| Italy | 1997 | — | — | 57.4 | — |
| | 2002 | — | –0.1 | 45.1 | — |
| | 2008 | — | — | 45.8 | — |
| Portugal | 1997 | — | –0.4 | — | — |
| | 2002 | 0.6 | — | — | — |
| | 2008 | — | –0.6 | 11.6 | — |
| Estonia | 1997 | 6.6 | — | — | : |
| | 2002 | 0.5 | — | — | : |
| | 2008 | 6.5 | — | — | : |
| Hungary | 1997 | 15.8 | –3.0 | 2.9 | : |
| | 2002 | 2.1 | –6.0 | — | 0.2 |
| | 2008 | 1.9 | –0.7 | 12.9 | 2.0 |

(continued)

**Table 2** (continued)

| | | Price stability | Government budgetary position | | Long-term interest rate |
|---|---|---|---|---|---|
| | | HIPC inflation | General government net lending (+)/net borrowing (–) | General government consolidated gross debt | EA convergence criterion bond yields |
| Poland | 1997 | 12.3 | –1.6 | — | : |
| | 2002 | — | –2.0 | — | 0.5 |
| | 2008 | 0.1 | –0.7 | — | — |

Data source: Eurostat

Notes: "—" indicates no violation of the Maastricht criteria; ":" indicates unavailable data; reference values and boundaries according to the Maastricht Treaty

The key reasons for this disappointing outcome were two construction failures within the E(M)U and its contract:

1. The politically driven selection of new member countries; and
2. Weak incentives and sanction mechanisms (bad risk management)

In the following I shall mainly focus on construction failure 1 and, against the background of space limitation, provide just a brief description of failure 2.

## 5.1 *Political Selection of New Member Countries: Pitfalls of Rapid Monetary Integration*

European integration has developed in several stages. There were just six founding countries (Belgium, France, Germany, Italy, Luxembourg and the Netherlands) in the European Economic Community (EEC) in 1957, and with various common institutions during the 1960s, the first round of enlargement occurred in 1973 when Denmark, Ireland and the United Kingdom decided to join. A second round of enlargement occurred during the 1980s when three former dictatorial countries, which had shaken off their dictatorships by the mid-1970s, pursued an early entry into the EEC to thereby stabilize their young democracies. These countries were Greece (it joined the EEC in 1981), Portugal and Spain (1986). In a third round in 1995 (after the collapse of the Eastern bloc), Austria, Finland and Sweden (formerly so-called "neutral" border countries to the Eastern bloc) acceded to the EEC, which in the meantime was renamed the EU. Finally, in the first decade of the 2000s, 12 more countries were allowed to enter into the EU, namely Bulgaria, Cyprus, the Czech Republic, Estonia, Hungary, Latvia, Lithuania, Malta, Poland, Romania, the Slovak Republic and Slovenia. Ten of these twelve countries (NMS-10) were former communist, dictatorial states that aspired to stabilize their new democracies and grow faster by joining the EU.

Thus, the driving forces behind the enlargement of the E(M)U from 1980 onwards have been largely political, driven by an anxiety that former dictatorial states (such as Spain, Portugal and Greece in the 1970s and 1980s, and the Eastern post-communist NMS-10 in the 1990s and 2000–2009) could destabilize the political landscape in Europe (or turn again to Russia) if they were not integrated in the E(M)U club. The result of this anxiety was, from an economic perspective, that some of the emerging GIPS and NMS-10 countries with weak governance structures were let into E(M)U too early.

In addition, we have seen a cluster of accessions over the past two decades. The EU has almost doubled the number of its member countries during the last decade. Consequently, the pitfalls of enlargement have also increased, in particular when the EA was created. In the last century, countries stayed in the EU for many years before entering the EA (however, the EA was only established in 1999); in contrast, those entering the EU now (since 2000) can join the monetary union immediately, i.e., just after 2 years membership. And most entrants have flirted with this idea. For example, in 2003, the year before the EU entrance of 10 new member countries, all designated NMS announced that they also wanted to become members of the EA as soon as possible (within 2 or 3 years), even though 8 of them had, just 15 years before, been communist-planned economies without any experience regarding western-style markets and political institutions, and were considered to be emerging economies. This then created some nervousness, particularly among the ECB and the incumbents' central banks, as well as among academic experts. Further, it led to many "marketing" and "educational" exercises to convince the post-communist-NMS politicians to pause to think twice whether this rush would really be a good idea.[19] In the end, after some persuasion and some disillusions with regard to fiscal problems[20] in particular, most NMS-10 governments caved in and postponed the planned euro adoption to year-to-year decision—even today only 3 of the 10 post-communist NMS (Slovenia, Slovakia, Estonia) have chosen the step of euro adoption. Latvia, Lithuania, Poland, Czech Republic, Hungary, Bulgaria and Romania remain in a wait-and-see position. However, after the recent financial and economic crisis, many of these NMS have again become more inclined to adopt the euro as soon as possible. Indeed, the cooling down of domestic and external imbalances associated with the recession after the financial crisis seemed to increase the chances of the rest of the NMS-10 to meet the Maastricht criteria within a time frame of 3 years. The question, however, remains whether it is a good option for these countries to try to rush their entry into the EA.

### 5.1.1 General Aspects

There is a series of potential dangers that newcomers face in joining the European Monetary Union. (As stated above, legally they have no choice because they cannot opt-out. Consequently, they are obliged to apply for euro adoption as soon as they think they are able to fulfill the Maastricht criteria within the minimum 2-year period under Exchange Rate Mechanism II (ERM II). In practice, however, they can easily postpone euro adoption, and even ERM II entry, for an extensive period if desired.)

The loss of the nominal exchange rate as an instrument of adjustment to country-specific shocks is often regarded as the greatest economic disadvantage for a country entering the monetary union. This loss is all the more serious within

[19] This nervousness could also be explained by the risky actions taken by the incumbents by allowing less developed EU members (such as Greece and Portugal) prematurely into the euro area. There were concerns not to overload the newly-founded European Monetary Union and particularly the ECB with uncertain or risky challenges.

[20] On fiscal issues of post-communist NMS-10, see Wagner (2006).

the integration area if wages and prices are less flexible, and where labor mobility is lower.[21]

However, I shall focus now on the "other effects" mentioned previously in part 3, which could result in a slowing down or even the (temporary) reversion of the envisaged real convergence process, before and after euro adoption.

The general political implication of this part is that the premature accession (with imperfect or weak institutions) of less developed emerging countries into an economic and/or monetary union that mainly consists of more highly developed industrial countries may be costly not only for the accession countries but also for the incumbents. If candidate countries with weak (imperfect) institutions decide to enter a monetary union, then they must accept the risk that they may not achieve (stronger) positive growth effects and may have a lower ability to adjust to shocks and cope with secular changes.[22] Thus, they will achieve lower growth effects than they would have had if they entered with stronger institutions. This cost or risk of lower growth in the case of early accession has to be balanced by (concerns regarding) the cost or risk of waiting, in the case of euro area enlargement, which mainly consists of the risk of financial instability (speculation), particularly during the ERM II qualification period,[23] and the loss or weakening of a key anchor for the domestic policy agenda in the candidate countries.[24] Nevertheless, with regard to EA accession countries, we will see that it may be better for some of them (namely the economically, technologically and institutionally less devel-

---

[21] The counter-argument is often based on the endogeneity hypothesis that an exchange rate instrument would in any case not be as necessary within a monetary union because the typical cases for its application would endogenously tend to disappear or be reduced. *First,* the increasing integration resulting from the founding of the European Monetary Union would lead to changes in industrial structures in the sense of greater turnover and investment relations within industries. This means that most countries will both export and import the products from many branches ("intra-industrial trade"). As a result, sector-specific shocks will hit different countries more similarly than previously. *Second,* a credible monetary union would influence the behavior of both sides of industry to the extent that they would pay more attention to remaining competitive, because the alternative of devaluation no longer exists. Thus, wage and price flexibility becomes greater, which reduces the significance or the benefit of exchange rate adjustment as a shock absorption instrument. *Third,* the European Monetary Union will eliminate an important category of country-specific shocks that have their origins in exchange rate movements themselves and in an imperfectly coordinated monetary policy. See Emerson et al. (1992), p. 24.

[22] Another critical point or cost associated with premature accession is that the accession of less developed emerging economies into an economic and/or monetary union that consists mainly of more highly developed industrial countries increases the asymmetries in the macroeconomic structures of the union. These asymmetries create challenges or strains for common central banks as the common monetary policy *(one-size-fits-all policy)* then creates different adjustment reactions in individual member countries. Different business cycles and tensions within the union are then predetermined.

[23] See Wagner (2002a).

[24] The International Monetary Fund (IMF), for example, emphasized that accession aspirations should "help these countries maintain the momentum of progress that is needed with fiscal reforms, privatization, other structural improvements, and environmental clean ups" (IMF 2002, p. 39).

oped) to wait and maintain flexible exchange rates after EU accession, and use that time to improve their institutional fundamentals.[25] Importantly, however, this choice should be left to the candidate countries to avoid significantly slowing down the momentum of reform progress in these countries (although one should not forget that the incumbents may also be hurt by the inappropriate timing of NMS entry into the euro area).

In general, the risks and the costs of E(M)U enlargement are dependent upon the starting position of the accession countries when joining the EU; these are greater the larger the gap in development among the accession countries and incumbents.

As stated earlier, countries that have joined the EU have the "right" (and even an obligation) to join the euro club after a minimum of 2 years if they fulfill the Maastricht criteria and have stayed in the ERM II for 2 years (see European Commission 2000). Using this right immediately, however, can be dangerous if the country's starting position is not "optimal" in terms of development.

### 5.1.2 Pitfalls That Slow Real Convergence

Newcomers have various choices on entering the EU; all these choices have potential economic pitfalls, and are especially dependent on the initial stance of development or convergence, and on the chosen exchange rate system. These pitfalls have become even more complex and costly over the recent decades (when comparing first-round, second-round and third-round newcomers) as globalization and the integration of financial markets, together with obligations associated with EA entry, have fundamentally changed the environment in which the catching up process for newcomer countries is managed. I shall briefly provide some examples of the economic pitfalls that today's newcomers may experience if they join the EA too early:

- Excessive external imbalances
- *Endogenously-enforced* austere fiscal policy
- (Fear of) contagion
- Business cycle asymmetries
- Anticipatory recession

I shall concentrate on the first two pitfalls, particularly on the danger of real divergence or a slowdown of economic (GNI per capita) convergence in the case of inappropriate timing of EA entry. Discussions regarding the remaining three effects will be brief.[26]

---

[25] Or as the European Commission pointed out: "the priority should remain on improving the functioning of the budgeting process, carrying out structural reforms, implementing the *acquis communautaire*, and supporting catching up" (European Commission 2002, p. 126).

[26] For further pitfalls, see Landmann (2012) and Wagner (2002a).

(1) External imbalances

There are key risks and challenges that all newcomers face on the road to euro adoption and beyond; these are associated with the exposure to large and volatile capital flows and the danger of overheating due to credit booms.

Capital inflows

All new member countries of an economic union can expect considerable net capital inflows in the form of FDI, portfolio capital and other forms of capital. The most serious risks lie in non-FDI capital flows, which are sensitive to interest rate differentials and risk premiums. Most recent newcomers experience strong non-FDI capital inflows after EU entry. Non-FDI net capital inflows have been particularly large in pegged economies, for instance, at approximately 15% in Lithuania, 20% in Estonia and 30% of GDP in Latvia in 2006–2007 (before the financial crisis). These large inflows of capital entail several risks: (i) they boost domestic demand and thus can lead to overheating and large current account deficits and high inflation (e.g., as then in the Baltic countries); (ii) they can put undue pressure on exchange rates in countries with floating rates; (iii) they expose countries to sudden reversals of capital flows when there is a shift in the markets' assessment of a country's vulnerability; and (iv) they may delay essential reform adjustments.[27]

Credit booms and overheating

Large capital inflows, before and after the 2004 EU enlargement, generated by expectations of fast convergence, have contributed to very high levels of external debt in some newcomer countries. Many of them experienced excessive credit and domestic demand growth, an appreciating real exchange rate and inflationary pressures in the years after EU entry (The fastest growing segments of the credit market were household loans, particularly mortgage loans). Excessive credit growth raised concerns about overheating, widening external imbalances and increasing balance sheet risks in some newcomer countries, particularly in those where domestic borrowers contracted loans in euros and other foreign currencies, leading to an increase in currency mismatches in the private sector balance sheets. The latter made the private sector vulnerable to exchange rate depreciation.

Excessive credit growth can also erode competitiveness if it feeds inflation and wage growth, and so derail real convergence. Another danger arises if rapid growth in mortgage credit leads to sharp rises in house prices in real terms, further boosting credit expansion by increasing the value of collateral.[28] Moreover, by fuelling consumption, rapid credit growth keeps savings low and increases the investment-saving gap. The then five less developed newcomers with the fastest credit growth showed very large current account deficits, from approximately 15% in Estonia to approximately 24% in Latvia. In the Baltic countries, most of the deficits were

[27] For further details see, e.g., Darvas and Szapary (2008).

[28] For example, see Funke et al. (2006) and Berger et al. (2007).

financed by debt, mainly foreign borrowing by banks and enterprises.[29] Such high deficits, however, increase the exposure of countries to capital flow reversal that can create a recession and eventually a banking crisis (this became apparent in the post-crisis period 2009–2010). Financial and banking crises have often been preceded by rapid credit expansion in the private sector, and thus, strong real exchange rate appreciation and large current account deficits are usually observed, as was the case in several East Asian countries preceding the 1997 crisis, in Finland and Sweden preceding the 1992 crisis, and last but not least, in GIPS preceding the 2008 financial crisis. These countries will continue to sit on powder kegs if they do not follow fiscal policies that counter balance the credit growth and retard wage inflation.

(2) Austere fiscal policy *endogenously enforced*

It remains open as to whether the economic pitfall with respect to a slowdown of real convergence is greater with exchange rate pegging or with a floating rate in an inflation-targeting regime.

However, irrespective of whether newcomers choose the pegging or floating option, emerging newcomers face a danger of falling behind in real convergence when pushing too hard to attain the Maastricht criteria as a precondition of early EA entry. This can be derived (and already has in some cases) as an indirect effect of the above-discussed channel of (1) "external imbalances". (See also Sect. 5.1.3 below for further detail.)

(3) (Fear of) contagion

As part of the Maastricht convergence criteria contained in Article 109j and defined in Protocol 6 of the Maastricht Treaty, newcomers have to participate in the ERM II of the European Monetary System within the normal fluctuation margin, and without severe tensions, for at least 2 years (Hochreiter and Wagner 2002). That is, as "euro area members with a derogation" they have to stay in a waiting position for a period within the ERM to prove that they are strong enough to withstand severe exogenous shocks. During this period, where they follow a type of "weak" currency pegging (soft peg), the danger of speculative attacks is particularly severe. In particular, if their institutions are not yet strong enough, they can easily be confronted with a capital outflow triggering the devaluation of its currency and therefore with an increase of their external (foreign currency-denominated) debts. Worse yet, even if these newcomer countries follow a solid economic policy, they can unwantedly import such crises via contagion from neighboring countries. As has been shown previously (Berger and Wagner 2005), not only actual devaluations but an increas-

[29] Latvia, for example, increased its external debt to 139% of GDP in 2008. Domestic lending relative to GDP expanded between 2000 and 2008 from 23% to 89%. In Estonia, domestic lending was also boosted from 34% of GDP in 2000 to 98% in 2008, where most of the expansion was not covered by domestic savings. Therefore, external debt also increased from 45% of GDP in 2000 to 108% of GDP in 2008. Despite these high external imbalances, Estonia (in contrast to Latvia) then managed to keep domestic overheating within tolerable limits due to a sound fiscal policy with budget surpluses between 2002 and 2007.

ing crisis probability in one country may trigger currency crises elsewhere. Here both fundamental weakness and spontaneous shifts in market sentiment may play a role in the transmission of currency crises.[30]

However, there are also dangers of real divergence *within* a monetary union.

(4) Business cycle asymmetries

As described above, excessive credit growth and domestic demand growth leads to inflationary pressures in emerging market economies. Within a monetary union this would result in strong asymmetry in the form of real interest rate differences. This, in turn, could destabilize the union as a whole as it brings inefficiency into the union as the ECB targets averages, thus missing optimal national levels the more the wider the variance is. This again may trigger transitory real convergence, however it often ends up in bubbles and an eventual counter-development towards real divergence (currently seen for example, in some of the GIIPS countries).

(5) Anticipatory recession

If financial markets develop (i) expectations of real divergence as the likely outcome over the following years, and (ii) the expectation that core countries will react and try to stop the divergence process (to stabilize and save the economic and monetary union), then an EU-wide increase in interest rates may immediately arise unless the ECB monetarily accommodates this process. See the model analysis in Wagner (1995, 2002a).[31]

A justification for the feared pitfalls derived above for newcomers seeking quick euro membership can also be derived from the recent experiences of countries like Greece, Portugal, Ireland and Spain. The euro adoption of these countries meant a rapid leveling of the interest rate (a rapid reduction of risk premiums). The latter has been used by (private and/or public sectors of) these countries to raise their indebtedness and produce an unhealthy boom, which was proved during and after the financial crisis when risk premiums rose again and accumulated debts could no longer be serviced. Thus, emerging countries like Greece, Portugal and Spain could run into trouble as the risk premiums representing their emerging market economy status were artificially reduced by their early entrance into the EA. The same could happen in the future to countries with emerging market economies seeking to join the EA.

### 5.1.3 A Model of Real Divergence

In earlier papers (Wagner 2002a, b) I showed that the then emerging NMS-10 could have resulted in real divergence with their early entry into the EA.

[30] The debt crisis in the euro area may also be contagious for newcomers if capital flows are drying up and countries with large current account deficits rely on these.

[31] Moreover, in some euro area countries interest rates or spreads on government bonds may increase due to country-specific risk premiums, as the current development shows.

There, I presented a model that provided one channel along which attempts to satisfy the nominal Maastricht convergence criteria could have negative impacts on real convergence between the incumbents and accession countries of a monetary union.[32] The key arguments are based on (1) the fact that less developed accession countries have relatively high optimal public investment levels in comparison to developed incumbents, and (2) that the nominal Maastricht convergence or entry criteria, which were elaborated for the original incumbents, may put pressure on today's accession countries to deviate from their relatively high optimal public investment levels (sooner or later). This pressure is higher for less developed accession countries, due to fact (1). Hence, the real convergence process could be slowed down due to negative growth effects. I argued in the above papers that in the beginning these negative effects could outweigh the positive effects (especially technology spillovers), as the latter requires time and institutional quality. Overall, my results imply that a sufficient degree of real convergence should be seen as a precondition for a promising accession to a monetary union and not as a hoped-for endogenous result of early accession.

### 5.1.4 Current and Future Adverse External Conditions That Impede Convergence

In Sect. 5.1.2 above, I discussed several channels through which a slowdown of real convergence, or even real divergence, can result if a country pushes (too) hard for early euro adoption (see also the Balassa–Samuelson effect in the context with the fulfillment of the Maastricht convergence criteria and other structural differences). Furthermore, there are *additional pitfalls* or *hindrances*, which may slow the real convergence process in accession countries in the coming years. These pitfalls come mainly from exogenous developments that further restrict current and future NMS in their effort for a rapid catch up to the core countries. I shall briefly discuss the three major developments:

(i) Globalization;
(ii) Aging population; and
(iii) Increasing frequency of financial crises.

I have analyzed the general growth effects of the first two developments for NMS in previous research (see in particular Wagner 2005b; 2006). I shall also briefly sketch the effects of these structural developments in the model outlined above in Sect. 5.1.3.

(i) Globalization

Globalization leads to locational competition, particularly tax competition (even within the E(M)U, which is a form of regional globalization as member countries

---

[32] Due to space limitations I will not replicate the model here and shall only highlight the results of the model analysis.

have to comply with the obligation to open up all markets). This implies that the disposable amount for additional public investment is limited or reduced and hence additional growth (catching up) is limited or reduced (see Wagner 2006).

Such tax competition may lead to a reduction of tax levels in both the incumbent countries and in NMS. In the abovementioned model (Wagner 2002a, b), there are two outcomes of such tax competition depending on two alternative strategies: (1) if the pressure to lower the tax rate leads to more efficient public expenditure systems (by cutting "unnecessary" public expenditure), then no growth effects occur in the model; (2) however, if the government reacts to tax competition by cutting (productive) public investments, lower growth rates occur. The latter case is the same as a (downward) deviation from the optimal tax rates in the model above (Wagner 2002a, b). Regarding the convergence process in the European Monetary Union, this situation translates as follows: if the incumbents act according to strategy (1), i.e., by cutting "unnecessary" public expenditure, and if NMS act according to strategy (2), namely cutting productive public investments, then the convergence process (between the incumbents and the NMS) is slowed. As the model above predicts that NMS have relatively high optimal public spending levels (and as the incumbents need not necessarily satisfy the Maastricht criteria; see Sect. 5.2.3 below), a deviation from the optimal public spending levels seems to be more "probable" in NMS than in incumbent countries. In the model above, this means that the tax rate of NMS will (be likely to) deviate from the optimal tax rate; however, the tax rate of the incumbents will (probably) not deviate from the optimal tax rate; hence, there is divergence.[33]

(ii) Aging population

Aging populations are larger in some NMS than in the rest of the EU, resulting in greater public expenditure and lower taxable incomes. This leads to an increase in the deficit ratio, which may exceed the 3% limit (see Wagner 2006; 2005c).

Aging leads to slower convergence between the incumbents and NMS, provided that the aging population is bigger in the NMS than in the incumbent countries and that it puts some pressure on the government budget, e.g., via increasing pension payments, which forces the government to cut spending in other areas, namely productive public investment. In the model above this means again that *only* NMS governments deviate from their optimal tax-rate, yielding divergence (see Wagner 2006).

(iii) Costly financial crises

Costly crisis management to tackle the feared negative effects of (which are more frequent due to financial globalization) financial and economic crises leads, and will lead in the aftermath, to increasing debt and deficit ratios for years to come,

[33] If, however, the incumbents also follow strategy (2), and moreover if the NMS are assumed to be "large" countries there may also be a strong(er) negative growth effect in the core countries (for more on the fiscal issues and challenges in NMS under globalization see Wagner 2006). But even then the goal of "real convergence" is violated if we regard it as a combination of different convergence sub-goals, also including convergence to an absolute level of living standard.

and possible long-term higher ratios in all EU countries. It is likely that these ratios will exceed the 60% (for public debt) and 3% (for deficit) limits in most EU countries. However, only NMS wishing to enter the EA in the next few years will have to strictly comply with these limits. That is, it will be the acceding NMS in particular who may have to follow such (more) austere fiscal policies (than in other EU countries) for some time if they want to adopt the euro. This procedure could not only slow down the catching up process but also reverse it for a substantial period.

Thus, a reduction of (productive) public investment spending seems more probable in NMS than in the incumbent countries for the following reasons: (1) costly crisis management puts pressure on government budgets, (2) NMS must strictly comply with euro area budget-discipline criteria (due to the Maastricht criteria) and (3) optimal public investment levels are higher in NMS than in incumbent countries. Again, in the model above this translates to a deviation from the optimal tax rate in NMS.

## 5.2 *Weak Incentives and Sanction Mechanisms*

The second construction failure in the European Monetary Union is the lack of incentives to save and/or reform (towards institutional convergence) the emerging economies, including weak commitment by members, because of a lack of sanction mechanisms in the EA regarding the violation of contracts. To understand the weak incentives and sanction mechanisms in the E(M)U, it is useful to take a brief look at its development stages.

### 5.2.1 Vision for an European Monetary Union and Its Incorporation into the Maastricht Treaty

When the EU treaty was drafted and the monetary integration process begun in the late 1980s, the installation of legal regulations and institutions was considered sufficient to guarantee and stabilize the monetary union.[34] The main objective was meant to be taken care of by a private financial market mechanism: if government debt and deficit per GDP exceed the respective *fiscal convergence criteria* or limits

[34] A set of formal entry criteria was supposed to serve as a useful test of prospective members' ability to follow disciplined policies. One of the rationales for fiscal entry criteria or constraints has been that spillovers of fiscal policy may be strengthened within a monetary union due to fiscal free riding. Such free riding tends to generate too expansive fiscal policies. This imposition of restrictions on government deficits and debt is to be seen against the background that, in contrast to monetary policy, fiscal policy has remained a national competency within the European Monetary Union.

(60% and 3%, respectively) in a member country,[35] the risk premium in the interest rate was to increase for that country so that the spreads of government bonds would also increase and have a disciplinary effect on its fiscal policy or government.

In addition, the *"no bailout" clause* in the Maastricht Treaty was supposed to (together with the fiscal convergence criteria) be effective, so that the fiscal discipline of the member countries and their governments would be enforced. This "no bailout" clause in Art. 125 of the Treaty on the Functioning of the European Union (TFEU) states that neither the ECB nor national governments can be coerced to bailout other E(M)U member countries.[36]

Last not least, by constructing ECB law along the lines of German Bundesbank law—codifying the personal and institutional independence of the ECB, focusing on the single goal of price stability, and prohibiting the direct financing of public entities' deficits by national central banks and the privileged access of public entities to financial institutions[37]—the monetary stability of the euro as the new common currency was expected to be ensured.

### 5.2.2 Early Doubts

From early on in the process there have been doubts (among economists and politicians) that the legal and institutional preconditions laid down in the Maastricht Treaty and the Stability and Growth Pact would be effective.[38] On the one hand, it was argued that constituting *fiscal convergence criteria* without ensuring that these criteria would be strictly observed was not an efficient method. Therefore, early on Germany called for automatic sanction mechanisms. It demanded that the sanctions be severe enough to ensure that the Maastricht criteria were adhered to. Further, Germany stated that the sanctions should be introduced automatically to avoid intergovernmental majorities of violators voting against these sanctions. There were attempts to implement the demand for stronger sanctions in the so-called "Stability and Growth Pact" of 1997 when Germany forced the other members to renegotiate the Maastricht Treaty in this respect. However, the changes to the sanctions were insufficient and, even more importantly, Germany also failed to persuade the other members to install automatic sanctions.[39]

[35] These criteria are contained in Article 109j of the Maastricht Treaty establishing the European Community and defined in Protocol 6 of that treaty.

[36] "The Union …[as well as] A Member State shall not be liable for or assume the commitments of central governments, regional, local or other public authorities, other bodies governed by public law, or public under-takings of another Member State, without prejudice to mutual financial guarantees for the joint execution of a specific project."

[37] This is laid down in Protocol No 4 of the Treaty of Lisbon.

[38] In particular, Germany was scared that the constraints of the European treaties would lose their bite once a country was admitted into the monetary union, as no member country can be forced out again.

[39] However, it should be noted that, ironically, it was Germany that first violated the Stability and Growth Pact in the first decade of the 2000s.

On the other hand, many economists in academia and the financial markets were not convinced that the "no bailout" clause in Article 104b of the Maastricht Treaty would be binding in the case of severe financial crises because even this clause could be levered out by intergovernmental majority decisions appealing to "exceptional occurrences" (Art. 122 TFEU).

Finally, even the ECB treaty, as strict as it seemed to be, has its loopholes. The "independent" members of the ECB council were officially to attend to European interests only, however, the members also have their own personal interests, particularly as nationals and with respect to their own potential political career in their home country after they have served on the ECB council. This makes political influence possible and likely influences the expectations of actors in the financial markets.

### 5.2.3 Before and After the Introduction of the Euro

Against the background of the doubts expressed above, private markets from the outset believed neither in the binding nature of the no-bailout clause nor in the bite of the Stability and Growth Pact. This was reflected in the development of leveling government bond spreads from 1995 to 2008 (see Fig. 4). This reflected the mistrust not only against the binding nature of the no-bailout clause but also against the endogeneity hypothesis. This hypothesis claimed that due to the mere fact that a country enters the EA, that it would be encouraged or coerced to further adjust its institutions to those of the incumbents.[40] That is, the process of entry and membership may influence the incentive to conduct structural reforms. This was and is definitely the case after entry into the EU, because the new EU members intend to join the EA (this is what they are expected to). To prepare for this, they have a strong incentive to reform their structures and align their institutions. However, this incentive reduces or even stops after these countries enter the EA, as new members cannot be forced out. Hence, the expectation that with the early inclusion of emerging market economies (of the 1990s) like Greece, Portugal or Spain into the monetary union these countries would institutionally and structurally converge more rapidly towards the core EA proved wrong (see Sect. 4.2 above). For instance, entry into the European Monetary Union does not appear to have sped up either labor market reforms or governance reforms in these countries.

In Fig. 4, it is apparent that the spreads of government bonds among the EA member countries began to level out from the mid-1990s. The reason for this early leveling was the announcement effect or "halo" effect, i.e., the effect of the early announcement regarding the participating countries (already several years before the actual start of monetary union in 1999–2001).

[40] Particularly the "New OCA Theory" emphasized the endogeneity of cyclical correlations with respect to the decision to join a monetary union (cf. Frankel and Rose 1997, and Frankel 2005; see also de Grauwe and Mongelli 2005). However, others have emphasized the endogeneity of structural and institutional convergence in a broader sense (see Wagner 2012a).

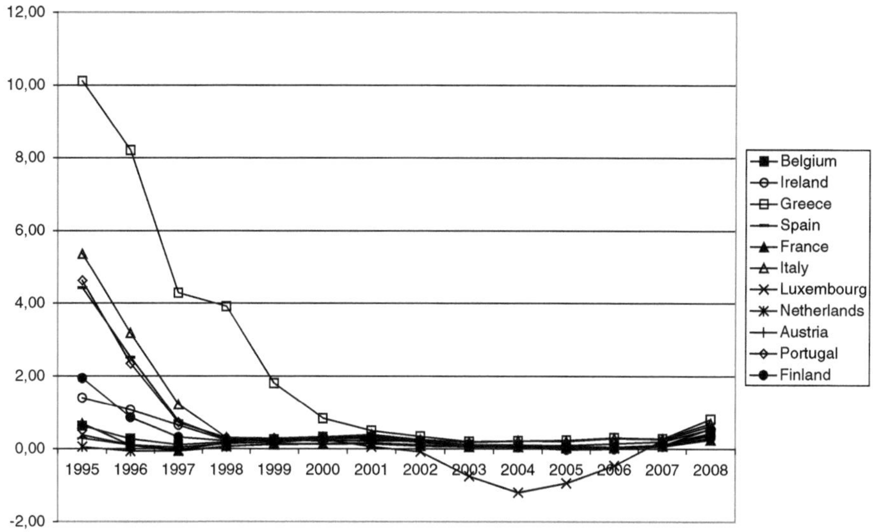


**Fig. 4** EA convergence criterion bond yield spreads vis-à-vis Germany (EA12). Data source: Eurostat

### 5.2.4 After the Financial Crisis

After the eruption of the financial crisis in September 2008 following the default by Lehman Brothers, credit conditions tightened as the solvency of established banks was questioned and there was a significant increase in perceived counterparty risks. Banks refused to lend, inducing a disorderly deleveraging process. Liquid assets were sold at fire-sale prices and credit lines to leveraged financial intermediaries in the shadow banking system were significantly reduced. Business and consumer confidence collapsed as doubts about economic prospects increased and uncertainty regarding policy responses became widespread (for further detail see IMF 2009).

Governments had to intervene to save the financial system and the market economic system as a whole (see Wagner 2010, 2012b). This crisis management by governments was associated with increases in public deficit and debt, particularly in GIIPS (see Figs. 5 and 6). Hence, in the EA bond spreads widened sharply again (see Fig. 7) and the flow of trade finance was interrupted. Banks tightened lending standards and refused to lend to each other when equity prices plummeted. Housing price booms occurred, particularly in Ireland and Spain, created a bubble, and burst as a consequence of the financial crisis. This drew the banking system, and with it the Spanish and Irish economies, into a severe crisis. The rescue measures by the respective governments led the public household from a surplus to a huge deficit (particularly in Ireland) and consequently the bond spreads rose drastically in each country.

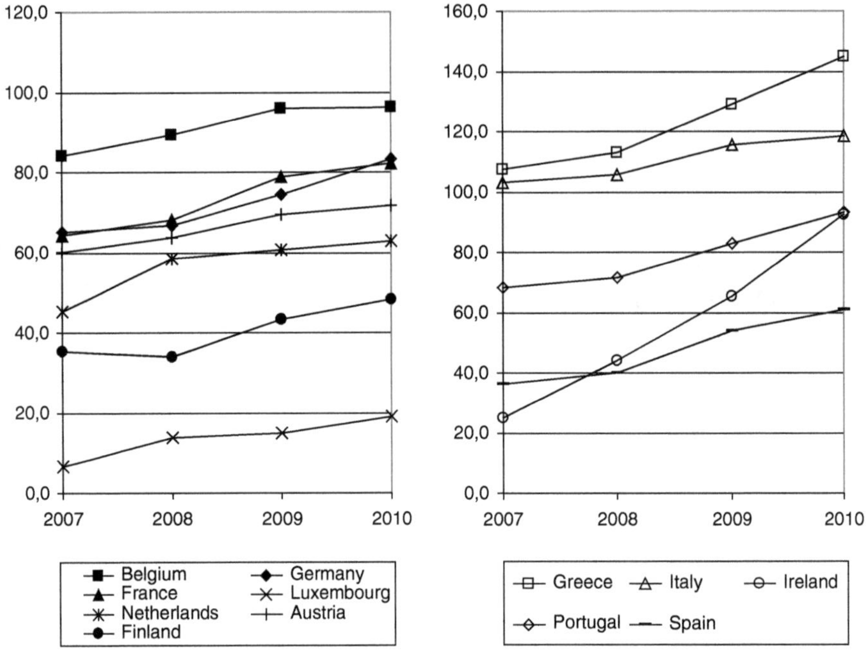


**Fig. 5** Government consolidated gross debt (as percentage of GDP). Data source: Eurostat. Notes: General government consolidated gross debt

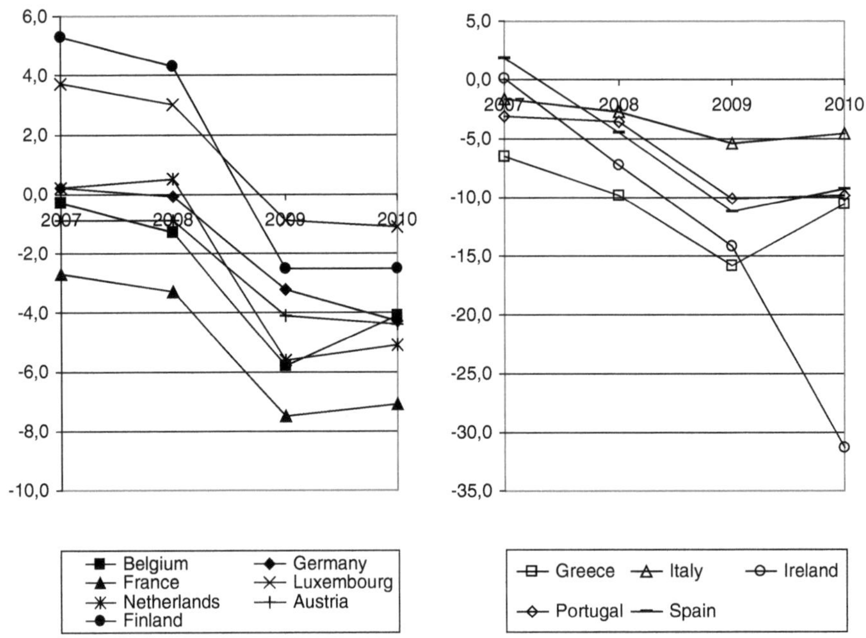


**Fig. 6** Government consolidated gross deficit (as percentage of GDP). Data source: Eurostat. Notes: General government consolidated gross deficit

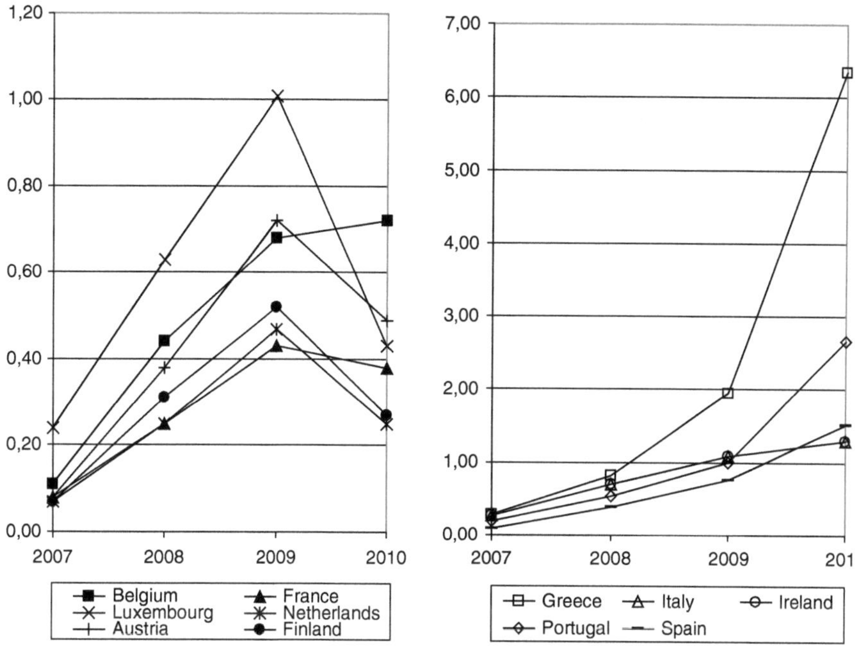


**Fig. 7** EA convergence criterion bond yield spreads vis-à-vis Germany (EA12). Data source: Eurostat

The housing price boom in the above-mentioned countries developed along with strong domestic consumption growth because euro adoption meant the rapid leveling of interest rates (reflecting a rapid reduction of the risk premiums against the background of private markets' expectations of a bailout of member countries in the case of a looming insolvency). Lower interest rates were used by GIPS to raise their consumption expenditures and produce an unhealthy boom with rising unit wage costs, current account deficits and increasing public deficit and private and public debt, thus weakening their international competitiveness. After the financial and economic crisis of 2008–2009, GIPS entered into a sovereign debt crisis and again, as before in the mid-1990s, to higher risk premiums (wider bond spreads). Most of the (previously healthy) EA members that provided financial help (rescue measures) also ended up on the edge of the abyss via the production of significantly higher deficits and debt.

### 5.2.5 Approaches to the Sovereign Debt Problem

There have been several attempts by E(M)U leaders to manage the sovereign debt problem in GIIPS and thus to stabilize the EA. However, these attempts, from the beginning of the sovereign debt crisis until end 2011, have been small-step solutions. Consequently, they have proved to be insufficient again and again (Table 3).

**Table 3** EA sovereign debt crisis policy chronology

| | |
|---|---|
| Sept. 2008 | Greece is put under surveillance after the fall of Lehman Brothers |
| 11 Nov 2009 | European Commission: Greece did not take adequate action to reduce its deficits (Greece being in an excessive deficit procedure) |
| 11 Feb 2010 | "Euro area Member states will take determined and coordinated action, if needed, to safeguard financial stability in the euro area as a whole. The Greek government has not requested any financial support". (official press statement by the heads of state or government of the EU) |
| 25–26 Mar 2010 | European Council: agreement to provide bilateral loans (supported by IMF) to Greece; requires unanimity subject to strong conditionality, based on assessment by European Commission and ECB; financing at non-concessional interest rates; |
| | JM Barroso: "We have solved this in the European family" |
| 23 Apr 2010 | Greece requests for activation of the new financial support mechanism |
| 02 May 2010 | Agreement for granting financial assistance to Greece |
| | €110bn = €80bn by EU + €30bn by IMF in the form of bilateral loans |
| 03 May 2010 | ECB suspends application of minimum credit rating threshold for Greek government debt instruments |
| 07 May 2010 | Implementation of the €110bn Greek rescue package |
| 09 May 2010 | Agreement on a temporary European safety net - the European Financial Stability Mechanism (EFSM): €750bn = €60bn EU + €440bn via EFSF + €250bn by IMF |
| 10 May 2010 | Implementation of the EFSM and the creation of the European Financial Stability Facility (EFSF), a special purpose vehicle for the channeling of the rescue loans |
| | ECB announces further unconventional measures |
| 18 May 2010 | 1 day before the refinancing of a large amount of Greek debt is due: EU provides 1st disbursement for Greece |
| 04 Aug 2010 | EFSF becomes operational |
| 19 Oct 2010 | Agreement to create a permanent European safety net in near future |
| 21 Nov 2010 | Ireland requests financial support from EFSM |
| 28 Nov 2010 | Agreement on granting financial assistance to Ireland |
| 11 Mar 2011 | Decision to reduce the interest rates and extend maturities of the loans for Greece |
| 24–25 Mar 2011 | Agreement that the lending capacity of the EFSF should be increased |
| 31 Mar 2011 | ECB suspends application of minimum credit rating threshold for Irish government debt instruments |
| 07 Apr 2011 | Portugal requests financial support from EFSM |
| 17 May 2011 | Agreement on granting financial assistance to Portugal |
| 07 July 2011 | ECB suspends application of minimum credit rating threshold for Portuguese government debt instruments |
| 21 July 2011 | To reduce the interest rates and extend maturities of the EFSF loans; agreement to provide further financial assistance to Greece via the safety net and a "voluntary" contribution of the private sector |

Only the Brussels summit in December 2011 appeared to have made any real progress: European leaders took a first step towards a EA fiscal "compact", with binding rules on public finances and backed by automatic sanctions. However, this was then overshadowed by the controversy over Britain's veto of a European-wide treaty backing the fiscal compact. Therefore, Germany's goal of finalizing the compact by forcing all 27 EU members to include it in their constitutions failed and hence the renewed attempt to introduce effective automatic and credible (binding) sanction mechanisms failed again.

Furthermore, this fiscal pact was watered down soon after its proposal and decision by the complaints and interventions of single member countries, and now only an intergovernmental solution seems possible.[41] However, experience with intergovernmental solutions creates doubts with respect to the stability and/or effectiveness of such a solution—there are fears that it might turn out to be merely a short-term solution and not able to ensure mid- to long-term stability in the EA.

## 6 Conclusions

A monetary union can only be expected to be truly sustainable if it does not experience endogenous real divergence among its member countries. First, populations in the poorer (emerging) acceding countries expect a certain kind of convergence among "club" members with respect to living standards. Second, populations in richer admitting countries expect that they will not have to continually bear more and more financial burden to subsidize the poorer member countries (which would be the case if real divergence occurred). Thus, the legitimacy of a monetary union is likely to be dependent upon a certain kind of endogenous real convergence within the union. Third, the functioning of a monetary union is dependent upon institutional-structural convergence among member countries so that business cycle asymmetry is not too large within the union, because otherwise the common central bank cannot work efficiently with its one-size-for-all interest rate policy.

In this paper I have asked whether there are theoretical and empirical indicators that a monetary union, in particular the European Monetary Union, leads or has led to real convergence across its member countries. While the theory on this question is rather quiet, empirical evidence shows that over a certain period of time (before and after entry into the monetary union) convergence has occurred. However, as soon as a large-scale global crisis emerged, convergence stopped and divergence arose; the question is for how long? The reason for this reversal was, among other things, construction failures within the European Monetary Union.

[41] And even this solution would likely be a weak compromise. As we often experienced, it is unlikely that reform decisions will eventually be completely implemented. There will be pressure from lobby groups as well as a natural slowdown of reform efforts as soon the crisis weakens.

These construction failures meant that sanction mechanisms regarding violations were never anticipated to be strong. Therefore, private markets did not expect the "no bailout" to be binding, and this resulted in a leveling of interest rates (due to a reduction of spreads) among heterogeneous member countries before and after the date of entry into the European Monetary Union. Lower interest rates (cheap credit) were used by some of the emerging new member countries to raise their consumption expenditure and to produce excessive credit booms, thus creating inflation pressures and an asset price bubble. When this bubble burst, these countries[42] were left with significant debts and deficits (together with rising interest rates due to again-rising spreads, as soon as the financial markets recognized that an easy bailout was not possible). This eventually produced economic divergence *and* political tensions between the poorer emerging and the richer member countries with growing bailout demands against richer member countries; thus, the legitimacy of the European Monetary Union was also reduced in donor countries.

Therefore, the main message is this: before entry into the monetary union, there is a high incentive to reform to meet the entry criteria. However, this reforming zeal apparently stops soon after entry. This can only be overcome by (i) a change in the construction principles of the European Monetary Union towards implementing strict fiscal rules and (quasi-) automatic sanction mechanisms and (ii) a shift away from accepting new union members for solely foreign policy reasons.

On the whole, although there is no specific model that can be followed to establish a successful economic and monetary union, certain pitfalls and precautions can be taken into account. In this paper, I have identified some of them—as a lesson from the current European debt crisis. As a conclusion, I come to the following suggestions:

First: do not create an economic and/or monetary union solely for foreign policy reasons; such a construction is not stable or sustainable.

Second: think twice before you try to establish a union consisting of structurally heterogeneous countries.[43] However, if you do, then the third recommendation is particularly important.

Third: ensure that you have the appropriate incentive mechanisms installed. These include strict rules and (quasi-) automatic sanction mechanisms.

## Appendix

See Table 4.

[42] And also other emerging member countries were affected via contagion.

[43] That is, the more heterogeneous an economic union is with respect to the development stage of its potential members, the more dangerous or costly is the step towards establishing a monetary union.

**Table 4** GNI per capita

| | Average growth rates and variance of growth rates of GNI per capita | | | | GNI per capita in % of EEC6 | | |
|---|---|---|---|---|---|---|---|
| | Average growth rate | | Variance of growth rate | | | | |
| | 1980–1994 | 1995–2008 | 1980–1994 | 1995–2008 | 1980 | 1995 | 2008 |
| EEC6 | 0.064 | 0.041 | 0.00055 | 0.00024 | 100.000 | 100.000 | 100.000 |
| GIPS | 0.064 | 0.055 | 0.00059 | 0.00031 | 69.506 | 71.836 | 85.343 |
| Greece | 0.040 | 0.050 | 0.00052 | 0.00065 | 86.290 | 69.699 | 79.429 |
| Ireland | 0.064 | 0.067 | 0.00107 | 0.00177 | 64.626 | 76.376 | 102.456 |
| Portugal | 0.065 | 0.047 | 0.00147 | 0.00025 | 54.002 | 63.101 | 66.776 |
| Spain | 0.059 | 0.056 | 0.00049 | 0.00038 | 69.634 | 74.222 | 89.459 |
| Estonia | : | 0.090 | : | 0.00096 | : | 29.313 | 58.231 |
| Hungary | : | 0.059 | : | 0.00093 | : | 40.600 | 53.098 |
| Poland | : | 0.070 | : | 0.00044 | : | 34.440 | 66.776 |

Data source: OECD

Notes: Annual gross national income per head in US$ at current prices and current Purchasing Power Parity (PPP); for Estonia, the average growth rate and variance of growth rate of GNI per capita refer to the period 1996–2008; ":" indicates unavailable data; EEC6 refers to the six founding member states: Germany, France, Italy, the Netherlands, Belgium and Luxembourg of the EEC

# References


Barro R, Sala-i-Martin X (1995) Economic growth. McGraw-Hill, New York

Berger W, Wagner H (2005) Interdependent expectations and the spread of currency crises. IMF Staff Papers 52(1):41–54

Berger W, Kißmer F, Wagner H (2007) Monetary policy and asset prices: more bad news for 'benign neglect'. Int Finance 10(1):1–20

Christodoulakis N (2009) Ten years of EMU: convergence, divergence and new policy priorities. Natl Inst Econ Rev 208:86–100

Darvas Z, Szapary G (2008) Euro area enlargement and Euro adoption strategies. In: European economy economic papers 304, European Commission, Brussels

De Grauwe P, Mongelli FP (2005) Endogeneities of optimum currency areas: what brings countries sharing a single currency closer together? ECB, Working paper no. 468

Emerson M et al (1992) One market, one money. An evaluation of the potential benefits and costs of forming an economic and monetary union. Oxford University Press, Oxford

European Commission (1996) Economic evaluation of the internal market. European Economy: Reports and Studies 4/96

European Commission (2000) Exchange rate strategies for EU candidate countries. European Commission ECOFIN (521/2000-EN), Brussels

European Commission (2002) Report on macroeconomic and financial sector stability developments in candidate countries, by directorate-general for economic and financial affairs of the European commission. European Economy no. 8, ISSN 1608–9022

Frankel JA (2005) Real convergence and euro adoption in central and eastern Europe: trade business cycle correlations as endogenous criteria for joining EMU. In: Euro adoption in the accession countries – opportunities and challenges. IMF, Washington, DC

Frankel JA, Rose AK (1997) Is EMU more justifiable ex post than ex ante? Eur Econ Rev 41(3–5):753–760

Funke N, Kißmer F, Wagner H (2006) International lessons for the property price boom in South Africa. S Afr J Econ 74(2):205–214

Galor O (1996) Convergence? Inferences from theoretical models. Econ J 106:1056–1069

Grosser D (1992) Ordnungspolitische Orientierungen und wirtschaftliche Entwicklungen. In: Gabriel WO (ed) Die EG-Staaten im Vergleich. Opladen, pp 382–413

Hochreiter E, Wagner H (2002) The road to the Euro - exchange rate arrangements in transition economies. Ann Am Acad Polit Soc Sci 579:168–182

IMF (2002) Recessions and recoveries. International Monetary Fund: world economic outlook, Washington, DC

IMF (2009) World economic and financial surveys: crisis and recovery (04/09) International Monetary Fund: world economic outlook, Washington, DC

Kose MA et al (2006) Financial globalization: a reappraisal. NBER working paper no. 12484, Cambridge, MA

Landmann O (2012) Rotating slumps in a monetary union. Open Econ Rev 23(2):303–317

Marelli E, Signorelli M (2010) Institutional, nominal and real convergence in Europe. Banks Bank Syst 5(2):140–155

Mongelli FP (2008) European economic and monetary integration, and the optimum currency area theory. European economy – economic papers 302, directorate general economic and monetary affairs, European Commission

Papademos L (2006) On the road to the euro: progress and prospects of the new member states. Speech at conference "The ECB and its watchers VIII", 5 May 2006

Raileanu Szeles M (2011) Exploring the economic convergence in the EU new member states by using nonparametric models. Institut für Wirtschaftsforschung, Halle

Sala-i-Martin X (1996) The classical approach to convergence analysis. Econ J 106:1019–1036

Wagner H (1995) Europäische Wirtschaftspolitik. Perspektiven einer Europäischen Wirtschafts- und Währungsunion (EWWU). Springer, Berlin

Wagner H (1997) Wachstum und Entwicklung. Theorie der Entwicklungspolitik. Oldenbourg Verlag, 2nd ed. Munich and Vienna

Wagner H (2001) Monetary integration and real convergence. In: The European economic and monetary union: regional and global challenges. Nomos, Baden-Baden, pp 79–95

Wagner H (2002a) Pitfalls in the European enlargement process – financial instability and real divergence. Discussion Paper 06/02, Economic Research Centre of the Deutsche Bundesbank, Frankfurt/M

Wagner H (2002b) Growth effects of 'heterogeneous' economic integration: the example of EMU-enlargement. J Econ Integrat 17(4):623–649

Wagner H (2005a) Comments on "Euro adoption in the accession countries: vulnerabilities and strategies". In: Euro adoption in central and eastern Europe, IMF, Washington, DC

Wagner H (2005b) Globalization and financial instability. Int J Soc Econ 32(7):616–638

Wagner H (2005c) Reform in the new EU member states - will a 3-pillar pension system work? E Eur Econ 43:27–51

Wagner H (2006) Fiscal issues in the new EU-member countries – prospects and challenges. SUERF Studies 2006/1, Vienna

Wagner H (2010) The causes of the recent financial crisis and the role of central banks in avoiding the next one. Int Econ Econ Pol 7(1):63–82

Wagner H (2012a) Is there an endogenous convergence in a monetary union? OCA-theory vs empirical evidence. Working paper (mimeo), University of Hagen

Wagner H (2012b) Is harmonization of legal rules an appropriate target? Lessons from global financial crisis. Eur J Law Econ 33(2):541–564

# Comment Paper to Chapter "Is the European Monetary Union Sustainable? The Role of Real Convergence"

**Eiji Okano**

## 1 Motivation

This paper questions whether a monetary union truly favors real convergence. Even if per capita GDP converges over one or two decades, it cannot be necessarily said that the process of convergence is sustainable. Institutional convergence and structural convergence are essential to attain real convergence. There are four elements in the development of real convergence as follows:

1. An encouragement of international trade among EU countries
2. An increase in foreign direct investment
3. An increase in transfer
4. An import of political stability.

## 2 Results

The results of the convergence thus far are as follows: the alignment of per capita GNP; the attainment of some convergence criteria have been artificial for some member countries; politically driven selection of new member countries; and weak incentives and sanction mechanism failures in the European (Monetary) Union.

E. Okano (✉)
Chiba Keizai University, Chiba, Japan
e-mail: e.okano@cku.ac.jp

S. Kaji and E. Ogawa (eds.), *Who Will Provide the Next Financial Model?: Asia's Financial Muscle and Europe's Financial Maturity*,
DOI 10.1007/978-4-431-54282-7_18, 

## 3 Impression

The argument of convergence criteria discussed in this paper is plausible. The introduction of nominal convergence criteria into the model and the claim that these can have negative impacts on real convergence is interesting and ambitious.

## 4 Comments

Focusing on the role of policy authorities is an important agenda and many readers are interested in such an agenda. If there is room to introduce policy authorities in the model, the author should do so. As many papers have pointed out previously, approximately half of all consumption goods are non-tradable items. In that case, the role of fiscal policy may be important. It is also vital to consider the policy interaction between fiscal authorities and the central bank. For example, a fine policy mix may stop defaults, as shown by Uribe (2006).

Another comment is how political stability is measured in the model. The developments mentioned in the former section are very interesting and important. However, the model does not include an explicit measurement of political stability. Introducing this factor may be difficult; however, doing so will enhance the sophistication of the model.

## Reference

Uribe M (2006) A fiscal theory of sovereign risk. Journal of Monetary Economics 53: 1857–1875

# Regional Monetary Cooperation in Asia

**Eiji Ogawa**

**Abstract** This paper focused on the asymmetric responses or misalignments of Asian currencies before and after the global financial crisis. Regional monetary cooperation is necessary for reducing such misalignments. Policy proposals for strengthening regional monetary cooperation in Asia after the global financial crisis are as follows: first, the monetary authorities should use an AMU and AMU Deviation Indicators to make policy dialogue regarding intra-regional exchange rate stability to solve the "coordination failure" of currency policy among Asian countries. Thus intra-regional exchange rates among Asian currencies can be stabilized. Second, the monetary authorities should introduce the surveillance of not only macroeconomic variables but also exchange rates into the surveillance process under the CMI. In addition, fiscal deficits should also be included in the surveillance process, especially after the lessons learnt from Europe Third, the monetary authorities should reduce or eliminate the IMF link to ensure effective currency swap arrangements under the CMI. Moreover, they should offer the AMRO the tasks of surveillance and the implementation of currency swap arrangements to eliminate CMI dependence on IMF surveillance.

**Keywords** Asian currencies • Asian monetary unit • CMI • IMF • Regional monetary cooperation

---

This paper is a revised version of that presented at the international conference "Who will provide the next Financial Model? Asia's Financial Muscle and Europe's Financial Maturity" of the Joint Research Group "EU Economy" of EUSI in Tokyo, held at Keio University on December 10, 2011. The author is grateful for the helpful comments of Mei Kudo (Tsuda College) and other conference participants.

E. Ogawa (✉)
EU Studies Institute in Tokyo, Tokyo, Japan

Graduate School of Commerce and Management,
Hitotsubashi University, Tokyo, Japan
e-mail: eiji.ogawa@r.hit-u.ac.jp


DOI 10.1007/978-4-431-54282-7_19, 

# 1 Introduction

The global financial crisis, which originated in US financial institutions, seemed to erode confidence in the US dollar and, in turn, resulted in depreciating impacts on the US dollar against the euro, the pound sterling, and Japanese yen. However, both the euro and the pound sterling depreciated against the US dollar during the crisis. Moreover, the fiscal crisis in some countries of the euro zone also resulted in depreciating impacts on the euro against the US dollar and the Japanese yen.

The first objective of this paper is to consider how the global financial crisis has affected Asian currencies, including the Japanese yen and the Chinese yuan. We can find asymmetric responses of Asian currencies to the global financial crisis when we look at the movements of various Asian currencies. Thus, these asymmetric responses have resulted in the misalignment of intra-regional exchange rates among Asian currencies, which, in turn, had adverse effects on international trade and foreign direct investments in established Asian production networks. We need to mitigate such misalignments to prevent adverse effects on international trade and foreign direct investments in Asia and therefore in the misallocation of resources in Asia.

The second objective of this paper is to consider how Asian countries can establish regional monetary cooperation while learning from European experiences. One lesson from the euro zone is that it is necessary to hold a sound fiscal position under confident fiscal authorities to maintain the value of the euro, even under economic convergence criteria for the introduction of the euro into each euro zone country.

# 2 Asymmetric Responses of Asian Currencies to the Global Financial Crisis

When we look at the movement of exchange rates for the euro since its inception as a settlement currency in 1999, we can see that it continued with an upward trend for several years following the 2001 collapse of the information technology bubble in the United States. In particular, the euro appreciated after September 2005, namely during the period in the run-up to the global financial crisis. This occurred because the European Central Bank (ECB) was slow to switch from its tightening stance against inflation to an easing stance for the global financial crisis. While the US Federal Reserve Board (FRB) began to ease its monetary policy in response to the outbreak of the subprime mortgage problem, the ECB remained focused on stopping inflation until the bankruptcy of Lehman Brothers on September 15, 2008.

This led to a buildup of US dollar carry trades, with investors borrowing funds in US currency and investing in euro-denominated assets offering higher returns. Massive capital inflows into the euro zone drove up the value of the euro, which in turn led to the further acceleration of capital inflows. The euro continued appreciating despite the fact that European financial institutions were directly hit by the US-triggered financial crisis—they were saddled with massive amounts of subprime

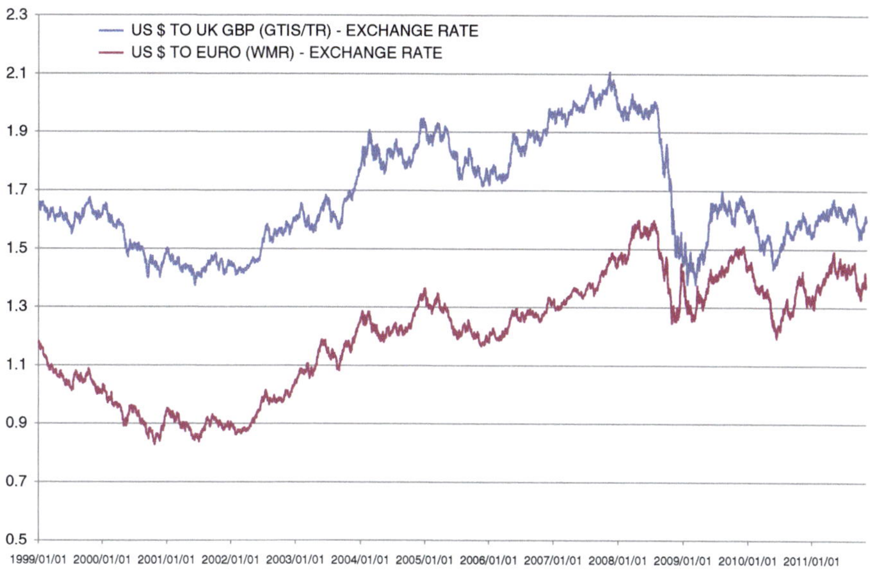


**Fig. 1** Exchange rates; US dollar to Euro and UK GBP. Data: Datastream

mortgage-backed securities. The appreciation of the euro was nothing but a case of a bubble detached from underlying economic fundamentals. Thus, the burst of the euro bubble was inevitable.

The euro bubble collapsed twice as shown in Fig. 1. The first collapse began about a month before the failure of Lehman Brothers. Amid growing uncertainty over the degree of European financial institutions' exposure to subprime mortgage-backed securities, the default risk for those financial institutions—or counterparty risk assumed by those on the other side of transactions—heightened. As a result, some European financial institutions failed to maintain sufficient US dollar liquidity and the euro fell sharply against the US dollar. Subsequently, the ECB managed to end the downward spiral of the euro by securing the provision of US currency from the FRB through a currency swap agreement, and provided US dollar liquidity to financial institutions in Europe (Fig. 1).

Figure 2 shows that the Asian Monetary Unit (AMU)[1] had been gradually depreciating against the currency basket of the US dollar and the euro before May 2003 when the AMU depreciated approximately 10% compared with the benchmark years of 2000 and 2001. However, it reversed its upward trend and returned

[1] The AMU is the weighted average of East Asian currencies where weights on currencies are based on shares of intra-regional trade and GDP measured at Purchasing Power Parity (PPP). Table 1 shows shares and weights of East Asian currencies. See Ogawa and Shimizu (2008) for the detailed explanation. Daily and monthly data are available at a website of RIETI (http://www.rieti.go.jp/users/amu/en/index.html#data). Kawai (2009a, b) and Kuroda and Kawai (2002) propose Asian Currency Unit (ACU) as well. Moon et al. (2006) propose Regional Currency Unit (RCU).

**Fig. 2** Movements of AMU against US dollar and Euro (benchmark year = 2000/2001, basket weight = 2004–2006). Data: RIETI (http://www.rieti.go.jp/users/amu/en/index.html#figures)

to almost the same level as the benchmark years before the end of 2008. Since then it has kept appreciating against the US dollar and euro currency basket over time. In other words, the AMU is relatively more stable with an appreciating trend after the global financial crisis. On one hand, the AMU has an appreciating trend against the US dollar and the euro during and after the global financial crisis. However, it has been fluctuating against the two because the euro turmoil related to the global financial crisis and European fiscal crisis caused significant fluctuations in the exchange rate between the euro and US dollar.

Figure 3 shows movements in an AMU deviation indicator for each Asian currency, that is, movements in each Asian currency against the AMU in terms of nominal exchange rates compared with the benchmark years. It is clear that Asian currencies have had deviating tendencies since 2005. Moreover, some Asian currencies, including the Japanese yen as a typical currency, have remained overvalued since the Lehman shock while other Asian currencies, for example the Korean won, have remained undervalued over time. The Korean won and Japanese yen, especially, displayed characteristic and asymmetric movements before and after the global financial crisis. The Korean won was overvalued (by more than 20% compared with the benchmark years, especially from March 2006 to July 2007) against the AMU from the end of 2004 to early 2008. However, since the end of 2007 the Korean won has been rapidly depreciating. In comparison, the yen has displayed asymmetric movements against the won.

**Table 1** AMU shares and weights of East Asian currencies (revised in 10/2011[a], benchmark year = 2000/2001)

| | Trade volume[b](%) | GDP measured at PPP[c](%) | Arithmetic average shares (%) (a) | Benchmark exchange rate[d](b) | AMU weights (a)/(b) |
|---|---|---|---|---|---|
| Brunei | 0.35 | 0.12 | 0.23 | 0.589114 | 0.0040 |
| Cambodia | 0.18 | 0.16 | 0.17 | 0.000270 | 6.2017 |
| China | 27.14 | 49.84 | 38.49 | 0.125109 | 3.0765 |
| Indonesia | 5.42 | 5.25 | 5.34 | 0.000113 | 472.2701 |
| Japan | 21.89 | 26.30 | 24.10 | 0.009065 | 26.5817 |
| South Korea | 13.46 | 7.87 | 10.66 | 0.000859 | 124.1471 |
| Laos | 0.14 | 0.08 | 0.11 | 0.000117 | 9.4017 |
| Malaysia | 7.21 | 2.21 | 4.71 | 0.272534 | 0.1729 |
| Myanmar | 0.42 | 0.24 | 0.33 | 0.159215 | 0.0208 |
| Philippines | 2.08 | 1.97 | 2.03 | 0.021903 | 0.9247 |
| Singapore | 12.27 | 1.45 | 6.86 | 0.589160 | 0.1165 |
| Thailand | 6.53 | 3.11 | 4.82 | 0.024543 | 1.9639 |
| Vietnam | 2.91 | 1.39 | 2.15 | 0.000072 | 298.7892 |

Source: RIETI (http://www.rieti.go.jp/users/amu/en/detail.html)

[a]AMU shares and weights were revised in Oct 2011. This is the 7th version

[b]The trade volume is calculated as the average of total export and import volumes in 2007, 2008, and 2009 taken from DOTS (IMF)

[c]GDP measured at Purchasing Power Parity (PPP) in the average of GDP measured at PPP in 2007, 2008, and 2009 taken from the World Development Report, World Bank. For Myanmar's share of GDP measured at PPP, we use the data for 2006 because of the data constraint

[d]The benchmark exchange rate ($-euro/currency) is the average of the daily exchange rate in terms of US$-euro in 2000 and 2001

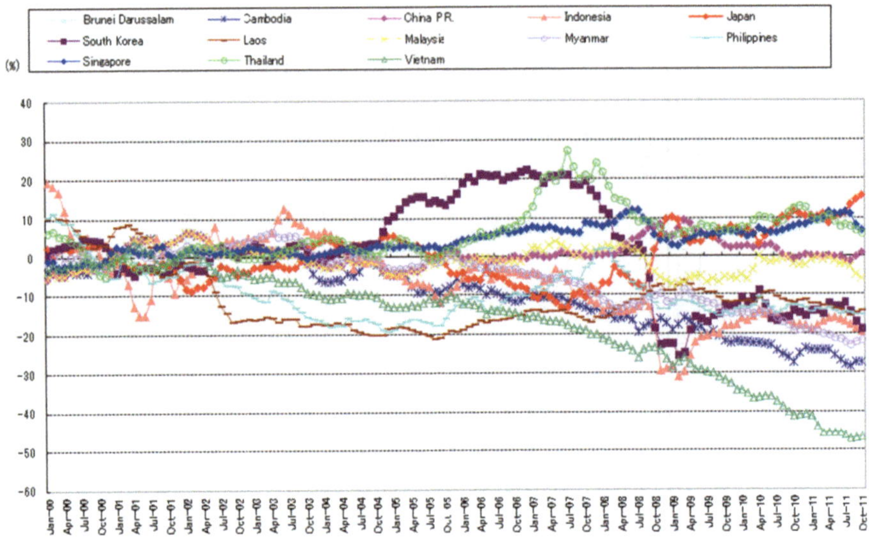


**Fig. 3** Nominal AMU deviation indicators (benchmark year = 2000/2001, basket weight = 2004–2006, monthly). Data: RIETI (http://www.rieti.go.jp/users/amu/en/index.html#figures)

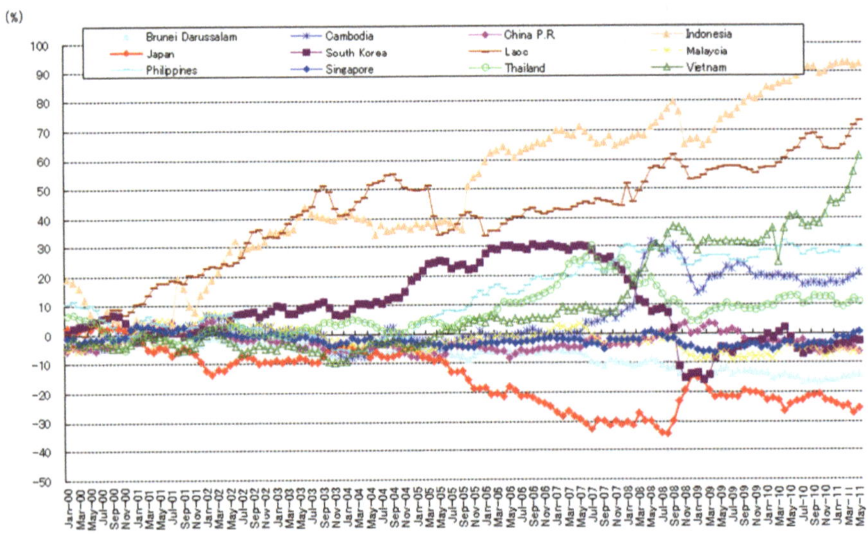


**Fig. 4** Real AMU deviation indicators (benchmark year = 2000/2001, basket weight = 2004–2006, monthly). Data: RIETI (http://www.rieti.go.jp/users/amu/en/index.html#figures)

Figure 4 shows the movements of deviations of Asian currencies against the AMU in terms of real exchange rates compared with the benchmark years. The Real AMU Deviation Indicators of Asian currencies were limited within plus 20% and minus 10% during the period 2000 to 2001. The Indonesia rupiah and the Lao kip appreciated against the AMU in terms of real exchange rates because of higher inflation since 2003. In addition, the Vietnamese dong has been rapidly appreciating since 2010 because of higher inflation, which exceeds its devaluation. The Korean won was overvalued against the AMU also in terms of real exchange rates due to the appreciation of the nominal exchange rate from the end of 2004 to October 2007; although, it has been rapidly depreciating due to the depreciation of nominal exchange rate. In contrast, the Japanese yen has been depreciating because of a combination of yen depreciation in terms of nominal exchange rates and deflation in prices from January 2005 to July 2007; in July 2007 it was undervalued by 30% compared with the benchmark years. However, the Japanese yen has been appreciating in terms of real exchange rates since August 2007.

Ogawa and Yoshimi (2010) focused on recent events, including the reform of the Chinese yuan and the global financial crisis, to statistically investigate recent diverging trends among Asian currencies. For that purpose, data on AMU Deviation Indicators were used to analyze both $\beta$ and $\sigma$ convergences of Asian currencies. Their analytical results showed that the monetary authority of China only maintained a stable exchange rate for the Chinese yuan against the US dollar, even though it announced the adoption of a managed floating exchange rate system for currencies. Analytical results regarding $\beta$ and $\sigma$ convergences show that deviations among Asian currencies have been diverging in recent years, especially after 2005. The widening deviations do not reflect the reform of the Chinese yuan but rather the recent international capital flows and the global financial crisis. In addition, it is important to note as background that the monetary authorities of Asian countries are adopting a variety of exchange rate systems. In other words, a coordination failure in the adoption of exchange rate systems among these monetary authorities has increased volatility and the misalignment of intra-regional exchange rates in Asia.

Figure 5 shows that the weighted average of the Nominal AMU Deviation Indicator rapidly decreased after it recorded 3.5% in January 2002. It stayed at a lower level, between 0.5% and 2.0%, from May 2002 to December 2004. However, it began increasing in January 2005 and it reached 4.7% in July 2007. It then decreased to 1.3% in March 2008, and then rapidly increased, recording its highest level, 5.1% in November 2008.

Figure 6 shows that the weighted average of the Real AMU Deviation Indicator briefly decreased after it recorded 4.0% in February 2002. It stayed between 2.5% and 3.2% from 2002 to 2004. However, it has been increasing since the end of 2004 and recorded its highest level, 9.3%, in July 2007. These results imply that deviations of Asian currencies from the AMU in terms of both nominal and real exchange rates have been, on average, increasing. However, we have to also formally check the diverging trend of the AMU because the Nominal and Real AMU Deviation Indicators decreased from mid-2007 to mid-2008 and July 2007, respectively.

There are two background factors to the asymmetric reactions of Asian currencies. The first is that different exchange rate systems were adopted among Asian countries. Ogawa and Ito (2002) explained that the situation was caused by a "coordination failure" in currency policy among the Asian monetary authorities. The monetary authorities of Japan and Korea adopted flexible rate systems, while China

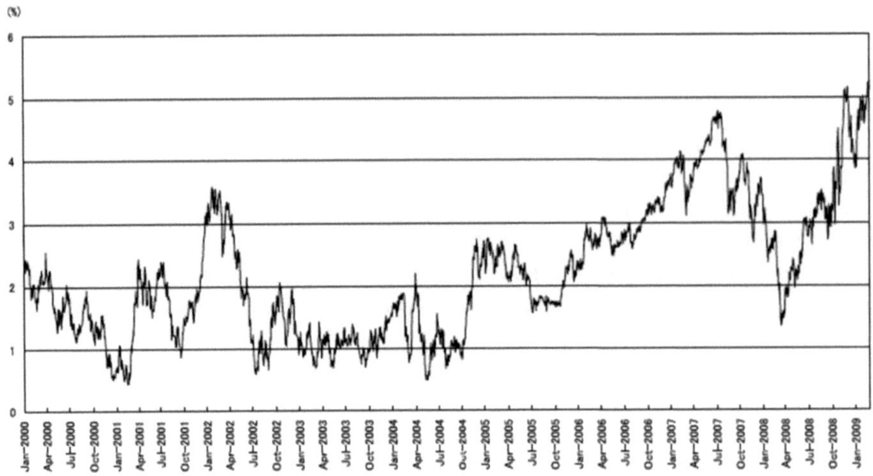


**Fig. 5** Weighted average of nominal AMU deviation indicators (daily). Source: Ogawa and Yoshimi (2010)

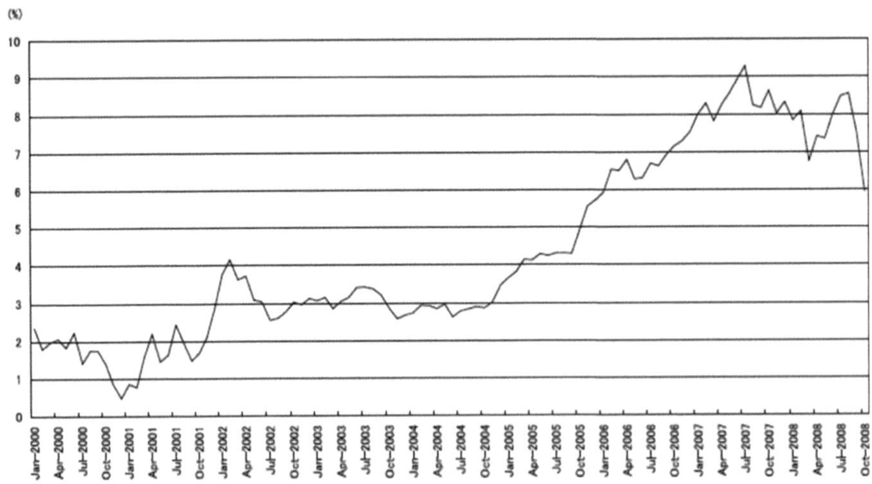


**Fig. 6** Weighted average of real AMU deviation indicators (monthly). Source: Ogawa and Yoshimi (2010)

fixed the Chinese yuan to the US dollar in July 2008 (although it had made announcements that it was to adopt a managed floating rate system with reference to a currency basket), while some ASEAN countries tried to stabilize their domestic currencies against a currency basket.

The second factor is active intra-regional capital flows. United States and European financial institutions conducted yen carry trades by borrowing yen and investing in Korean won before the global financial crisis. During the crisis they closed the yen carry trade and Korea faced sudden stops in capital flow, and then backward flows.

## 3 Coordination Failure in Currency Policy Among Asian Countries

Ogawa and Yoshimi (2010) used the methodology of Frankel and Wei (1994) to investigate actual exchange rate systems and policies conducted by the monetary authorities of Asian countries from 1999 to 2007. This section focuses on the above-mentioned events related to exchange rates during an extended sample period to early 2009. The empirical analysis was conducted to investigate the actual linkage trends of each Asian currency with three major currencies: the US dollar, the euro, and the Japanese yen. For this purpose, the empirical analytical method of Frankel and Wei (1994) was used to analyze these linkages for five sub-sample periods. The ASEAN10 (Brunei, Cambodia, Indonesia, Laos, Malaysia, Myanmar, the Philippines, Singapore, Thailand, and Vietnam), China, and South Korea are included in the analysis, although the sample periods for Cambodia, Laos, and Myanmar cover only 2003 to early 2009 due to data constraints.

Ogawa and Yoshimi (2010) followed the assumption in Frankel and Wei (1994) that the Swiss franc is used as a numéraire in the denomination of exchange rates. Daily data on exchange rates were used to conduct regressions of log differences of a local currency (in terms of the Swiss franc), on the log differences of the three major currencies (in terms of the Swiss franc) for each sub-sample period. The regression for each sub-sample period shows linkages of each Asian currency with the three major currencies during the period. The regression equation is as follows:

$$\Delta \log e^{HOME/SFR} = a_0 + a_1 \Delta \log e^{USD/SFR} + a_2 \Delta \log e^{EURO/SFR} + a_3 \Delta \log e^{JPY/SFR} + \varepsilon_t .$$

where $e^{home/SFR}$ is the exchange rate of a home currency in terms of the Swiss franc, $e^{USD/SFR}$ is the exchange rate of the US dollar in terms of the Swiss franc, $e^{EURO/SFR}$ is the exchange rate of the euro in terms of the Swiss franc, $e^{JPY/SFR}$ is the exchange rate of the Japanese yen in terms of the Swiss franc.

Table 2 shows the linkages regarding the Chinese yuan and the Korean won with the three major currencies.

On July 21, 2005, the Chinese government announced that it would change the Chinese exchange rate system from a dollar peg system to a managed floating system with reference to a currency basket. The Chinese yuan was completely fixed with the US dollar before the announcement, as shown by the coefficients of the US dollar of 1.0002 in Period 1 and 0.9998 in Period 2. The linkage with the US dollar decreased to 0.9541 in Period 3. Further, the coefficients of the euro and the

**Table 2** Linkages of Chinese yuan and Korean won with major currencies

| Chinese yuan | US dollar | Euro | Japanese yen | AdjR2 |
|---|---|---|---|---|
| Full samples | 0.9864[a] | 0.0079 | 0.0026 | 0.988 |
| | (0.0030) | (0.0058) | (0.0025) | |
| Period 1 | 1.0002[a] | −0.0002 | −0.0001 | 1.000 |
| | (0.0002) | (0.0004) | (0.0001) | |
| Period 2 | 0.9998[a] | 0.0001 | 0.0002 | 1.000 |
| | (0.0002) | (0.0006) | (0.0002) | |
| Period 3 | 0.9541[a] | 0.0125 | 0.0279[a] | 0.955 |
| | (0.0121) | (0.0313) | (0.0108) | |
| Period 4 | 0.9652[a] | −0.0128 | 0.0030 | 0.963 |
| | (0.0151) | (0.0251) | (0.0122) | |
| Period 5 | 0.9882[a] | 0.0320[b] | −0.0099 | 0.990 |
| | (0.0122) | (0.0165) | (0.0086) | |
| **South Korean won** | **US dollar** | **Euro** | **Japanese yen** | **AdjR2** |
| Full samples | 0.7843[a] | 0.5669[a] | 0.0529[c] | 0.434 |
| | (0.0293) | (0.0563) | (0.0242) | |
| Period 1 | 0.8037[a] | −0.0083 | 0.2361[a] | 0.635 |
| | (0.0287) | (0.0643) | (0.0246) | |
| Period 2 | 0.5128[a] | 0.0285 | 0.1963[b] | 0.478 |
| | (0.0826) | (0.2258) | (0.0878) | |
| Period 3 | 0.7430[a] | 0.3056[a] | 0.0900[a] | 0.634 |
| | (0.0371) | (0.0965) | (0.0332) | |
| Period 4 | 0.9392[a] | 0.5535[a] | −0.0802 | 0.576 |
| | (0.0761) | (0.1266) | (0.0615) | |
| Period 5 | 0.6409[a] | 1.1006[a] | −0.1729 | 0.200 |
| | (0.2341) | (0.3161) | (0.1645) | |

Standard deviations are reported between parentheses
Full samples: 1/3/2000–2/27/2009, Period 1: 1/3/2000–1/13/2005, Period 2: 1/14/2005–7/20/2005, Period 3: 7/21/2005–8/7/2007, Period 4: 8/8/2007–9/14/2008, Period 5: 9/15/2008–2/27/2009
Source: Ogawa and Yoshimi (2010)
[a]Significant level of 1%
[b]Significant level of 10%
[c]Significant level of 5%

Japanese yen increased in Period 3, although the linkage with the euro was not significantly estimated. The coefficients (between 0.9541 and 1.0002) were much higher than China's trade shares (approximately 15%) with the United States in recent years. The linkages of the Chinese yuan with the euro and the Japanese yen were statistically insignificant despite the Chinese government's announcement of the exchange rate system reform—China's monetary authority has yet to implement the exchange rate system reform announcement by the Chinese government.

Linkage of the Korean won with the US dollar decreased in Period 2. Though the linkage increased after Period 2, the linkage with the US dollar decreased, with a value of 0.6409 in Period 5. In Period 3, linkage with the euro significantly increased. Further, linkage with the Japanese yen is statistically significant in first three subsample periods although estimated coefficients are very low.

# 4 Effects of the Chinese Yuan on China and Neighboring Countries

Ogawa and Iwatsubo (2009) examined whether a revaluation of the Chinese yuan would improve current account imbalances in Asia. This link depends on whether the trade structures between China and other Asian countries are substitutes or complementary. If they are substitutes, a revaluation of the Chinese yuan will improve the current accounts of other Asian countries. In this case other Asian currencies should also be revalued or allowed to appreciate to reduce global current account imbalances. However, if trade structures are complementary, a revaluation of the Chinese yuan will deteriorate the current accounts of other Asian countries. It is going too far to say that a revaluation of the Chinese yuan alone would be enough to solve global current account imbalances. Therefore, it is necessary to conduct an empirical analysis on effects of the real effective exchange rate for the Chinese yuan on the current accounts of Asian countries.

Structural VAR models with contemporaneous restrictions based on the neo-classical and Keynesian theories were used to investigate effect of the Chinese yuan exchange rate on current account of not only China but also Japan and Korea. They included five macroeconomic variables (both real domestic GDP ($y$) and Chinese GDP ($y^*$), the real effective exchange rates of the home currency ($e$) and the Chinese yuan ($e^*$), and the current account in terms of domestic GDP ($CA$)) as endogenous variables.

The estimated VAR models were used to analyze the impulse responses of the current accounts of Asian countries to a real effective exchange rate shock in the Chinese yuan. The sample period covered 1994: Q1 to 2006: Q4.

The real effective exchange rate for the home currency is expected to have a negative effect on the current account of the home country. The real effective exchange rate for the Chinese yuan is expected to have a positive direct effect on the current account of the home country if the trade structures of China and other Asian countries are substitutes. However, the real effective exchange rate of the Chinese yuan is expected to have a negative direct effect on the current account of the home country if trade structures are complements.

The indirect effect of the Chinese yuan on the current account of the home country in the VAR model can be explained as follows. Assume that the trade structures of the home country and China are substitutes. A revaluation of the Chinese yuan (an increase in the real effective exchange rate of the Chinese yuan) induces a demand shift from Chinese products to home products. This shift increases the GDP of the home country and, at the same time, decreases Chinese GDP. In turn, home imports increase (caused by the increase in GDP of the home country) and home exports decrease (caused by the decrease in Chinese GDP). Thus, the real effective exchange rate of the Chinese yuan has a negative indirect effect on the current account of the home country where trade structures are substitutes. Accordingly, the total effect of the real effective exchange rate of the Chinese yuan on the current account is the sum of the positive direct effect and the negative indirect effect in the five-variable VAR model. The sign of the total effect will depend on which is larger, the direct or the indirect effect.

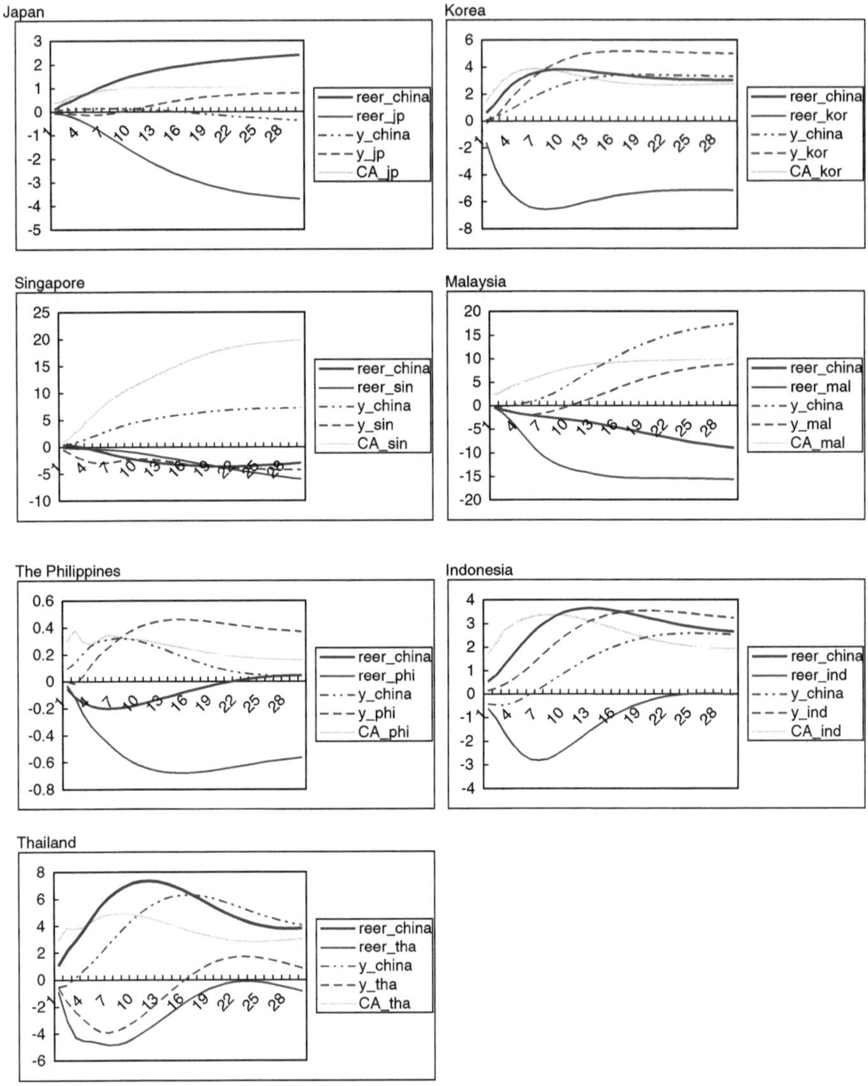


**Fig. 7** Accumulated impulse responses of current account to Cholesky one S.D. innovations. Source: Ogawa and Iwatsubo (2009)

Ogawa and Iwatsubo (2009) obtained the following analytical results. The panels in Fig. 7 show the accumulated impulse responses of the five economic variables to a shock (one standard deviation innovations) in the real effective exchange rate of the Chinese yuan ($e^*$). The real effective exchange rate of the home currency had a negative effect on the current account of the home country for all of the sample countries. The real effective exchange rate of the Chinese yuan had a positive total effect on the current account of the home country for Japan, Korea, Indonesia, and Thailand.

In contrast, the real effective exchange rate for the Chinese yuan had a negative total effect on the current account of the home country for Singapore and Malaysia. The accumulated response of the Philippine current account to the Chinese yuan shock was small and fluctuated over time. Thus, the Chinese yuan revaluation improved the current accounts of Japan, Korea, Indonesia, and Thailand. This evidence implies that the countries' trade structures are substitutable with that of China. However, the Chinese yuan revaluation deteriorated the current accounts of Singapore and Malaysia because the negative indirect effect through GDP is larger than the direct effect.

In sum, the results of the five-variable VAR analysis show that a revaluation of the Chinese yuan would improve the current accounts of other Asian countries, including Japan, Korea, Indonesia, and Thailand. Leading Asian countries such as Japan and Korea and some ASEAN member countries would see an improvement in their current accounts as a result of a revaluation of the Chinese yuan.

## 5 Regional Monetary Cooperation

The monetary authorities of Asian countries, especially ASEAN (Association of South East Asian Nations)+3 (Japan, China, and South Korea), have been strengthening their regional monetary cooperation since the Asian currency crisis in 1997. They established the Chiang Mai Initiative (CMI) in an effort to prevent and resolve the financial and currency crisis of 2000. Under the CMI, the monetary authorities of ASEAN+3 countries established a network of bilateral swap arrangements for managing the currency crisis in the member countries as well as a surveillance process for macroeconomic variables including GDP growth rates, inflation rates, and the soundness of banking sectors.

In May 2009 in Bali, Indonesia, the finance ministers and central bank governors of ASEAN+3 and the monetary authority of Hong Kong announced the signing of the Chiang Mai Initiative Multilateralization (CMIM) Agreement, which came into effect on March 24, 2010. The CMIM has strengthened Asia's ability to safeguard against increased risks and challenges in the global economy, as well as providing financial support (US$240 billion) through currency swap arrangements to CMIM participants facing balance of payments and short-term liquidity difficulties.

The CMIM, a multilateral currency swap arrangement which covers all ASEAN+3 members, was developed from the current CMI bilateral swap network to facilitate prompt and simultaneous currency swap arrangements via a common decision-making mechanism under a single contract. The CMIM has two major objectives: (1) to address balance of payments and short-term liquidity difficulties in Asia and (2) to supplement existing international financial arrangements. Each CMIM member is entitled, in accordance with procedures and conditions set out in the CMIM agreement, to swap its local currency for US currency, up to the amount of its contribution multiplied by its purchasing multiplier.

Moreover, a surveillance office was established in Singapore in 2011, named the ASEAN+3 Macroeconomic Research Office (AMRO). The AMRO performs a key regional surveillance function as part of the US$120 billion CMIM currency swap facility. The finance ministers of ASEAN+3 now have to ensure that any technical issues are ironed out. To support CMIM, AMRO is tasked with monitoring and analyzing macroeconomic situations and the financial soundness of the ASEAN+3 countries, which will contribute to the early detection of possible currency crises, the swift implementation of remedial actions, and effective decision-making in the region.

Under this framework, the monetary authorities should engage in a surveillance process to prevent any future currency crisis. However, the monetary authorities have previously had no standing institution for carrying out any surveillance process in Asia. Instead, the ASEAN+3 deputy finance ministers regularly hold so-called Economic Review and Policy Dialogues as a means of surveillance regarding their macroeconomic performance.

Asian monetary authorities need to prevent biased changes in relative prices caused by US dollar depreciation under their various exchange rate systems. Thus, they need to coordinate their choice of exchange rate systems and exchange rate policies.

Kawai et al. (2004) suggested the following recommendations concerning exchange rate policy in Asia. First, the monetary authorities of ASEAN+3 should discuss the exchange rate issue as a part of the surveillance process. They need to focus on the exchange rate issue, as well as domestic macroeconomic policies and the soundness of their financial sectors; the exchange rates of home currencies against neighboring countries' are indeed linked by terms of trade and competitive prices.

Each Asian country has strong economic relationships with other regional countries, as well as with the United States and European countries. Movements in intra-regional exchange rates among regional currencies affect economic activities in each Asian country via intra-regional trade, investment, and finance. The monetary authorities should not only monitor the account movements of exchange rates but also their deviations from regional averages and, in turn, their exchange rate policies per se.

The surveillance process in itself might not be sufficiently solid to preserve regional policy coordination in the long run because the monetary authorities from each country are not committed to policy coordination; however, they can make a limited contribution to policy coordination. Thus, it is necessary to have a mechanism that will preserve regional coordination in the long run by compelling the monetary authorities to commit to such coordination.

On one hand, the monetary authorities of ASEAN+3 are limited by the CMI, including the so-called IMF link, where currency swap arrangements will only be implemented after the IMF decides to give financial assistance to a crisis-hit country. For example, the Korean government did not implement any currency swap arrangements under the CMI due to the IMF link when the Korean economy experienced a sudden depreciation of the won during the global financial crisis. The Bank of Korea concluded a new currency swap arrangement with the FRB in 2008 and promptly implemented it. Moreover, the Bank of Korea concluded a currency swap arrangement in terms of yen/won with the Bank of Japan because the Korean economy experienced severe conditions under the strict conditionality of the IMF during the Asian crisis of 1997–1998. In 2009, the IMF improved its lending policy, creating a Flexible Credit Line (FCL) as well as modernizing conditionality. The Korean government did not request any financial assistance from the IMF, despite the inclusion of the FCL.

It is necessary to reduce or eliminate the IMF link in the currency swap arrangement under CMI so that CMI can be effective in regional monetary cooperation in Asia. At the same time, it is necessary to establish a secretariat to monitor Asian countries and implement currency swap arrangements, to lessen or eliminate CMI dependence on IMF surveillance. Thus, a secretariat emerged with the AMRO in 2011. The monetary authorities of ASEAN+3 should now focus on their own intra-regional exchange rates under the surveillance of CMI. For that purpose, the AMU and AMU deviation indicators will be useful surveillance tools.

## 6 Roadmap Toward AMU

A roadmap to introduce an AMU was proposed at ASEAN+3 finance ministers' meetings in 2007 and 2008 as shown in Institute for International Monetary Affairs (IIMA) (2007, 2008). IIMA (2007, 2008) pointed out that the roadmap had two paths: one toward surveillance, and one toward transactions. An AMU for surveillance would be used for macroeconomic surveillance, and include the currencies of all member countries. In contrast, an AMU for transactions would represent a composite currency for financial products, especially Asian bonds, taking into account the Asian Bond Market Initiative and Asian Bond Fund Initiative. Only currencies that meet several criteria, including convertibility, should be included. The two paths would eventually converge into one, with sufficient regional economic and financial integration achieved in the long-term.

The development of the two paths would also facilitate regional economic and financial integration. An AMU for surveillance, as a strengthened mechanism for regional surveillance, would help to avoid misalignment and excess volatility in intra-regional exchange rates among Asian currencies. A reduction in misalignment and volatility would lead to facilitating regional economic integration. An AMU for transactions would offer financial products for the diversification of foreign exchange risks with the weighted average interest rates of their component currencies. It would promote intra-regional financial intermediation (a bridge between savings and investment) within the region and simultaneously facilitate regional financial integration in Asia. Thus, the two paths of the AMU and regional economic and financial integration are complementary.

We now focus on an AMU for surveillance, to discuss regional monetary cooperation in Asia. An AMU for surveillance on intra-regional exchange rates could begin immediately; it would be an appropriate tool to identify misalignment and excess volatility in intra-regional exchange rates. The need for such an instrument has increased since the global financial crisis of 2008 and the Asian currency crisis of 1997. It is recommended that the monetary authorities reach an agreement to define the AMU for surveillance, declare a daily AMU value, and monitor AMU deviation indicators of Asian currencies to check for sudden changes in intra-regional exchange rates in Economic Review and Policy Dialogue of ASEAN+3.

Initially the role of the AMU should be solely the surveillance of intra-regional exchange rates. If one currency deviates from the average value of regional currencies it could have an adverse effect on the real economy where production networks are being established. It may be judged that its depreciation reflects not only macroeconomic policy failure but also the country's economic and political health.

Deviation of a currency from the average of regional currencies can be explained by the medium-term trend that may reflect productivity differences or growth potential—a benign deviation or a malicious deviation. For example, deviation toward appreciation may be benign if the appreciation is based on productivity growth and capital inflows that correctly evaluate the growth potential of the economy. Appreciation due to foreign direct investments is most likely benign, while appreciation due to short-term capital inflows may be a sign of accumulating vulnerability. Deviation toward depreciation could also be one of two types. If depreciation is associated with deteriorating domestic demands and relaxed monetary policy, it may stimulate exports in the near future, which is not worrisome. However, if the speed of depreciation accelerates, this may be cause for concern, and the reason for the depreciation should be carefully examined. Therefore, the deviation indicator is only one of several variables that should be used in surveillance; at the very least, it is useful as a flag that indicates when to look further into depreciation.

From a long-term perspective, several stages of a surveillance path are proposed.

The first stage (a tool of macroeconomic surveillance) can be implemented now. ASEAN+3 finance ministers' meetings provide a surveillance function and can ensure that AMRO use an AMU for surveillance. Thus, AMRO can be regarded as the first stage. The test of the current framework, as the second stage (a signal in an early warning system), is whether the surveillance mechanism can identify the warning signs of a future crisis.

The third stage will extend surveillance functions to particular actions, for example, using monetary and fiscal policy to correct deviations in the exchange rate from the basket value. The third stage uses monetary policy coordination and jointly coordinated intervention in foreign exchange markets to keep the deviation within a band (cf. the Exchange Rate Mechanism of the European Monetary System). However, the group has to be quite comfortable, when entering this stage, in judging the deviation of the exchange rate as a warning signal. The economic development of the member countries should be at similar levels by this stage of surveillance.

## 7 Conclusion

This paper focused on the asymmetric responses or misalignments of Asian currencies before and after the global financial crisis. Regional monetary cooperation is necessary for reducing such misalignments. Policy proposals for strengthening regional monetary cooperation in Asia after the global financial crisis are as follows: first, the monetary authorities should use an AMU and AMU Deviation Indicators to make policy dialogue regarding intra-regional exchange rate stability to solve the "coordination failure" of currency policy among Asian countries. Thus intra-regional exchange rates among Asian currencies can be stabilized. Second, the monetary authorities should introduce the surveillance of not only macroeconomic variables but also exchange rates into the surveillance process under the CMI. In addition, fiscal deficits should also be included in the surveillance process, especially after the lessons learnt from Europe where the fiscal crisis damaged European financial institutions and depreciated the euro. Third, the monetary authorities should reduce or eliminate the IMF link to ensure effective currency swap arrangements under the CMI. Moreover, they should offer the AMRO the tasks of surveillance and the implementation of currency swap arrangements to eliminate CMI dependence on IMF surveillance.

## References


Institute for International Monetary Affairs (2007) Toward greater financial stability in the Asian region: exploring steps to create regional monetary units (RMUs), ASEAN+3 Finance Ministers Research Group

Institute for International Monetary Affairs (2008) Toward greater financial stability in the Asian region: measures for possible use of regional monetary units for surveillance and transaction, ASEAN+3 Finance Ministers Research Group

Jeffrey F, Wei SJ (1994) Yen bloc or dollar bloc? Exchange rate policies of the East Asian economies. In: Ito T, Krueger AO (eds) Macroeconomic linkage: savings, exchange rates, and capital flows. University of Chicago Press, Chicago, pp 295–355

Kawai M, Ogawa E, Ito T (2004) Developing a new regional financial architecture: a proposal. Mimeo, Tokyo

Kawai M (2009a) The role of an Asian currency unit. In: Hamada K, Reszat B, Volz U (eds) Towards monetary and financial integration in East Asia. Edward Elgar Publishing, pp 304–322

Kawai M (2009b) An Asian currency unit for regional exchange-rate policy coordination. In: Chung D-K, Eichengreen BJ (eds) Fostering monetary & financial cooperation in East Asia. World Scientific Publishing, Singapore, pp 73–112

Kuroda H, Kawai M (2002) Strengthening regional financial cooperation. Pac Econ Pap 332:1–35

Moon W, Rhee Y, Yoon D (2006) Regional currency unit in Asia: property and perspective, KIEP working paper, 06–03

Ogawa E, Ito T (2002) On the desirability of a regional basket currency arrangement. J Jpn Int Econ 16(3):317–334

Ogawa E, Iwatsubo K (2009) External adjustments and coordinated exchange rate policy in Asia. J Asian Econ 20(3):225–239

Ogawa E, Shimizu J (2008) A role of the Japanese yen in a multi-step process toward a common currency in east Asia. Fukino discussion paper series, 3

Ogawa E, Yoshimi T (2010) Analysis on β and σ convergences of East Asian currencies. Int J Intell Technol Appl Stat 3(5):237–263

# Comment Paper to Chapter "Regional Monetary Cooperation in Asia"

**Mei Kudo**

Barry Eichengreen concluded in his volume of 1994 that a floating exchange rate system was more appropriate for Asia than a monetary union because insufficient preparation had been undertaken for economic integration (Eichengreen 1994). More than 10 years have passed since then, and in light of the enlargement of intra-Asian trade and the monetary crisis, the idea of monetary union or single currency in Asia appears a realistic choice for Asia. While the recent euro crisis has posed difficult questions as to the management of the regional monetary union, a crisis prevention measure via the establishment of a regional monetary union has not lost its impetus. Ogawa's plan for an AMU is one where common currency indicators are introduced into Asia, and this will finally lead to regional integration. Although this idea is interesting and of value in the current unstable international economic situation, I wish to further explain some points that were not fully discussed.

(1) Current status regarding economic convergence in Asian countries

Under an AMU, the intended members include members of ASEAN (Indonesia, Malaysia, The Philippines, Singapore, Thailand, Brunci, Vietnam, Laos, Myanmar, Cambodia) plus 3 (China, Korea, Japan), all with significantly different levels of economic development, and varied economic, political and social conditions. Therefore, I ask first of all, whether there is any economic convergence among these countries, such as inflation, proportion of the budget deficit or public debt to GDP, as employed by the euro countries, in preparation for the introduction of the AMU indicator.

Or, would convergence automatically be brought about by implementing surveillance under the AMU indicator? From the experience of Europe, it is clear that automatic economic convergence can never be achieved by the mere setting of a single

M. Kudo (✉)
Institute of International and Cultural Studies, Tsuda College,
Tokyo, Japan
e-mail: kudo@tsuda.ac.jp

S. Kaji and E. Ogawa (eds.), *Who Will Provide the Next Financial Model?: Asia's Financial Muscle and Europe's Financial Maturity*,
DOI 10.1007/978-4-431-54282-7_20, © Springer Japan 2013

indicator. The European Currency Unit, the forerunner of the euro, was introduced independent to the economic convergence occurring in the member countries. The achievement of criteria prior to the adoption of the euro was a result of political will. After the euro was introduced in 1999, budget deficits emerged again, invalidating the existence of the Stability and Growth Pact, a major issue in Europe today.

Looking again to Asia, as its economic, political, and social diversity is much wider than that in Europe, the realization of economic convergence seems a much more difficult task.

(2) Monetary stability vs. domestic stability

The second point concerns a problem that could arise when a divergence from the AMU indicator occurs. This problem especially relates to the third stage of the three-stage process required to introduce an AMU. In the third stage, it is assumed that the AMU surveillance mechanism requires an actual commitment to correct the divergence from the AMU via budgetary or monetary policy, or intervention in the exchange market—an Asian version of the "European Monetary System" (EMS). According to Ogawa, in this stage, the economic convergence of the member countries would have already been achieved.

However, as already noted above, it is not realistic to assume that economic convergence among AMU countries can be automatically brought about, especially if we refer to the history of the "Snake" and the early years of the EMS. Even assuming such a convergence could automatically occur, how long would it take? We already know that, in certain cases, policies to keep exchange rates within a certain margin of basket currency parity (when economic development, policy goals or economic cycles differ from each other) can be inappropriate to the domestic situations of the member countries. In the early years of EMS, a policy of disinflationary high interest rates by Germany often conflicted with those countries (e.g., France) that gave more weight to economic growth than price stability. After a decision by France to change its policy priority from growth to monetary stability, the convergence of "policy goals" spread among EMS countries; however, such a change of policy goals is not a natural result of a basket currency—it was a political decision. The 1992 EMS crisis forced the pound sterling and other currencies to withdraw from the EMS, and stability in Europe after 1992 was brought about by a widening of parity. Therefore, although economic policy management, which centers on the AMU indicator, is effective to contain inflation and stabilize monetary value, some permanent measures to alleviate the deflationary effects are also required.

Today, although the necessity of a sound budget for the sake of monetary stability is achieving greater legitimacy in Europe, Japan, and America—in the EU consensus has been reached regarding budgetary surveillance rules among 26 countries, including non-euro countries—it must be not forgotten that it is not just monetary stability that ensures a stable international monetary system.[1]

[1] Member countries' agreement on the budgetary rule is based on the situation as at the end of January 2012.

Under the classical gold standard, policy priorities had focused on monetary stability, but after the First World War, with the widening of the franchise, the monetary authority was no longer able to ignore the domestic impact of monetary policy, and had to consider the social impact of monetary policy to a certain degree. The adjustable peg exchange rate under the Bretton Woods system was the result of recognizing such social requirements (Polanyi 1944; Ruggie 1982).[2] Despite the fact that we have already seen the demise of the Bretton Woods system, the importance of balancing monetary stability and domestic stability is still applicable to any monetary system, whether it is global or regional. In an AMU too, a budgetary rule is necessary, but some buffer is also required.

(3) How far?

If greater policy co-ordination is required in implementing the AMU, we will face the question of how far we are prepared to proceed in integration. According to Ogawa, the two paths of the AMU—surveillance and indicator—will result in regional integration in Asia. However, while it is certain that his aim is to achieve regional financial integration in Asia—he mentioned that the "two paths could converge into one, with sufficient regional economic and financial integration achieved in the longer-term"—it is still not certain whether the goal is only financial integration or regional integration beyond financial integration. If the aim is regional integration beyond financial integration, we are not sure of the existence of enough collective interest in regional integration in Asia.

The EU today is the result of more than 50 years of effort by member countries. Further, the philosophy of "integration" is the intellectual product of more than a century and European citizens know first-hand that "integration" means the transfer to some degree of national sovereignty and policy-making rights. In contrast, there exists neither a century-old concept of "Asian integration", nor are we ready to abandon policy objectives for the sake of other Asian countries. At the start of the European integration too, there existed opposition to the transfer of sovereignty, but such an opposition was overcome as Europeans were facing difficulties that could not be solved by one country alone, only able to be resolved by committing to a common European framework via integration (Milward 1992).[3] For example, it is in

[2] The Bretton Woods period (from 1945 to 1971) is sometimes called the era of "embedded liberalism" as the Bretton Woods institutions offered various devices—adjustable peg, short-term lending, an exemption clause from the liberalization obligation during the transitional period in the IMF, and escape clauses in the GATT—which made it possible for member countries to pursue domestic intervention while accomplishing international cooperation based on the liberalization of trade and exchange. John Ruggie developed this concept of "embedded liberalism" regarding the Bretton Woods period, inspired by Karl Polanyi who viewed the market economy under the classical gold standard as "disembedded" from society.

[3] The analytical framework regarding economic integration in European as a way to achieve national goals of economic reconstruction and the recovery of political legitimacy was proposed by Milward (1992).

the interest of France and other smaller European countries to impose collective European controls on the rearmament of Germany to prevent the resurgence of a military threat, and to allow the revival of Germany as a European import hub, which will lead to the expansion of the exports of neighboring countries (Boussaut 1997). For Germany, to participate in the integration of Europe by transferring national sovereignty paradoxically meant a return to the international society as a sovereign country (Küsters 1994).

In Asia today, does there exist enough collective interest for an AMU? An AMU as a crisis prevention measure does not seem a valid reason to ensure generation of collective interest, to persuade all members to agree to abandon their policy discretion.

Thus, as we have seen above, an AMU and regional integration in Asia needs to be supplemented by three elements. First, greater economic convergence among members must be achieved. Second, in addition to a sound currency and budget, certain measures to assure social stability are necessary. Last, collective interest and understanding as to regional integration in Asia must be further developed.

## References

Boussaut G (1997) L'Europe des Français. Paris

Eichengreen B (1994) International monetary arrangements for the 21st century. The Brookings Institution, Washington, DC [Translation by Fujii Y (1997) Iwanami-shoten, p 157]

Küsters HJ (1994) West Germany's foreign policy in Western Europe, 1949–58: the art of the possible. In: Wurm C (ed) Western Europe and Germany: the beginning of European integration 1945–1960. Berg Publishers, Oxford, p 55

Milward AS (1992) The European rescue of the nation-state. Routledge, London

Polanyi K (1944) The great transformation. Rinehart, New York

Ruggie JG (1982) International regimes, transactions, and change: embedded liberalism in the postwar economic order. Int Organ 36:379–415

# Europe's Unresolved Crisis

**Paola Subacchi and Stephen Pickford**

**Abstract** The euro crisis has exposed the structural weaknesses of Europe's model of growth and the differences within the region, and has made evident the deficiencies in the governance of EMU. Countries in the euro periphery have been suffering from long-standing fiscal problems, under-performing economies and imbalances, and a widening gap in competitiveness against "core" countries. They face problems which require a combination of urgent priorities and long-term measures. In the immediate future they have to convince markets that their fiscal plans will reduce debt but without a collapse in growth, and to normalise their banks' access to market funding. In the longer term they need to achieve sustainable increases in growth, and to improve competitiveness and their external payments positions. Structural measures to address the long-term challenges of rebalancing the euro economy, dealing with regional growth differentials and supporting GDP growth are necessary for the future survival and stability of the euro. Changes to the governance of the euro are also required so that countries follow policies that are consistent with the requirements of a common currency, and so that the burden of policy adjustment is borne more equitably.

**Keywords** Competitiveness • Europe • Exchange rate • Sovereign debt crisis

---

This article is drawn from *"Broken forever? Addressing Europe's multiple crises," Chatham House briefing paper March 2012*. An earlier version of this paper was published in the Nomura Foundation series and presented at the Nomura Foundation conference "Challenges for the global economy after the Tohoku earthquake" held in Tokyo on 7 November 2011. The authors would like to thank conference participants, in particular Barry Bosworth and Christopher Allsopp, for their comments, and Richard Varghese for research support. The support of the Nomura Foundation is gratefully acknowledged.

P. Subacchi (✉) • S. Pickford
Chatham House, London, UK
e-mail: psubacchi@chathamhouse.org

S. Kaji and E. Ogawa (eds.), *Who Will Provide the Next Financial Model?: Asia's Financial Muscle and Europe's Financial Maturity*,
DOI 10.1007/978-4-431-54282-7_21, © Springer Japan 2013

## 1 Introduction

Despite Greece's repeated bailouts, Europe's sovereign debt crisis, which began in 2010, remains the biggest threat to the global economy. Rooted in the financial and economic imbalances within Europe, the structural weaknesses of its model of growth and the differences within the region, the crisis has exposed the deficiencies in the governance of the European Economic and Monetary Union (EMU) and shown the limits of its framework of policy cooperation.

The euro crisis did not develop overnight, but incubated over a number of years. Since the EMU's inception, the political nature of European integration has taken priority over economic principles. It has always been clear that Europe falls short of the requirements for an optimal currency area as envisaged in economic theory.[1] A monetary union that was not accompanied by a fiscal union could only succeed by putting in place robust governance and strong rules. Yet for many years rules in the euro area have been disregarded for the sake of politics.

Two of the countries at the center of the sovereign debt crisis, Greece and Italy, were admitted to the single currency union with public debts well in excess of the 60% of GDP limit laid down in the Maastricht Treaty. However, Italy, one of the signatories of the Treaty of Rome in 1957 and one of Europe's largest economies, was deemed necessary to the economic and political success of the euro, and was therefore admitted on the assumption of future fiscal consolidation. Greece's bid for membership came during the preparations for the 2004 Olympics when massive investments had boosted its economic growth. In any event, as it only accounted for approximately 2% of the total euro area economy, Greece was believed to be too small to have any significant impact on the stability of the currency union.[2]

The other countries primarily affected by the crisis—Ireland, Portugal and Spain—were faced with interest rates set by the European Central Bank (ECB) that were inappropriate for the pace of their economic growth and their credit conditions. Monetary policy at the eurozone level was too loose for these countries and needed to be offset by suitable domestic policies, but this did not happen. Instead, credit growth and private-sector borrowing remained excessive, and current account deficits widened, signaling the build-up of large imbalances.

In the aftermath of the collapse of Lehman Brothers in September 2008, most European governments intervened to rescue their banking systems and to support economic growth. As a result, public deficits and debt widened, and Ireland, Spain and Portugal ended up joining the group of countries with long-term public finance problems. For Europe as a whole, the banking crisis morphed into a sovereign debt crisis.

---

[1] For a detailed discussion on optimal currency areas, see Mundell (1961, 1963, 1973a, b). In addition, for a discussion on Mundell's work, the euro and optimal currency areas see McKinnon (2000).

[2] Unless otherwise mentioned, the data used in this paper are from the International Monetary Fund's *World Economic Outlook* (IMF WEO), April 2012.

The last two years have seen numerous attempts at the European level to address the crisis. However, as well as taking effective steps to deal with the immediate problems, it is necessary to address the longer-term issues that lie at the origin of the protracted build-up of imbalances within the euro area. In addition, there are significant issues regarding the future governance of the euro area (and the EU as a whole) that need to be addressed if the euro is to survive.

This chapter argues that structural measures to address the long-term challenges of rebalancing the euro economy, dealing with regional growth differentials and supporting GDP growth are required for the future survival and stability of the euro. Changes to the governance of the euro are also required so that countries follow policies that are consistent with the requirements of a common currency, and so that the burden of policy adjustment is borne more equitably.

## 2 The Critical Outlook for the Euro Periphery

The sovereign debt crisis has widened the divide between European countries that are well adapted to survive and prosper within the monetary union and those that are not. Countries in the periphery with problematic debt positions have seen sharp rises in government borrowing costs since the crisis erupted and at each critical point in its development (Fig. 1). Before January 2010, the periphery countries were able to borrow at a similar cost as Germany. However, the euro crisis has exacerbated fundamental macroeconomic imbalances and eroded market confidence, and therefore significantly increased the risk of sovereign default within EMU. Since Greece agreed a write-down on its privately-held debt, this has spilled over to other countries, such as Spain and Italy, with problematic but not critical positions. Most of all, massive capital outflows from problematic countries into "safe" countries have worsened the already existing imbalances.

Earlier in 2012, following elections in Greece and France, the emphasis in the debate within the eurozone has shifted from "austerity" to "growth". Also the ECB's Long Term Refinancing Operation (LTRO) facility succeeded in stabilizing markets for a while and buying time.[3] Cheap loans with a maturity of 3 years provided by the ECB eased the funding pressures experienced by banks in the single currency area and contributed to a bond rally in early 2012. Italy, in particular, benefited from the LTRO and the austerity plan adopted by the new government led by Mario Monti. But the crisis has continued, as investors concluded that the necessary long-term measures were not being taken at the political level, in individual countries and at the eurozone level.

[3] To support bank lending and liquidity in the euro area money market, the ECB undertook two LTROs with a maturity of 3 years and an option of early repayment after 1 year on 21 December 2011 and 28 February 2012. Take-up by banks totaled over one trillion euros in the two operations.

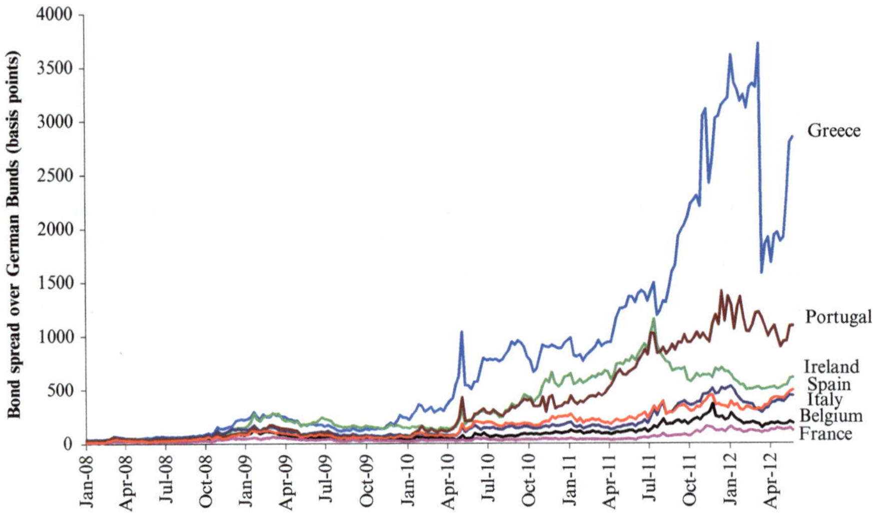


**Fig. 1** The cost of government borrowing. Note: Based on 10-year government bond yields. Source: Financial Times

Greece, however, continues to be the major concern despite the bailout package from the EU and the International Monetary Fund (IMF), and a deep "haircut" on private holdings of Greek debt. Its fiscal problems remain grave and are exarcebated by continuing recession. With GDP growth estimated to contract by 5.3% in 2012 and 1.3% in 2013, there is little scope for improvement in revenues, while a further dose of fiscal austerity is not feasible, both economically and politically. Therefore, the goal of reducing Greece's debt to GDP ratio to 120% by 2020 looks very ambitious and more likely unattainable.

## 3 The Long Genesis of the Sovereign Crisis

In the immediate aftermath of Lehman Brothers' collapse in September 2008, it seemed possible that Europe could escape the worst effects of the global financial crisis. Initially, only those European countries that were exposed through their banking and financial system, such as the United Kingdom, Ireland and Spain, were affected. Excessive credit growth in these countries, fuelled by foreign capital flows, had created imbalances that became unsustainable in the aftermath of the Lehman collapse. When the United States financial and banking system clogged up, foreign capital flows were halted. Struggling parent banks cut back funding to their local subsidiaries through tightened credit or higher costs of borrowing (Subacchi 2011).

As the crisis deepened, more countries were forced to use both monetary and fiscal measures to bail out troubled banks and to support weakening economies. The banking sector was the main recipient of government and central bank money to ensure that credit flows were not frozen and thus avoid a possible banking collapse. Troubled financial institutions were supported via capital injections, guarantees or partial nationalization. Interventions in support of the real economy were also

**Table 1** Sovereign debt, Euro area (% of GDP)

| Euro area | 2007 | 2011 |
|---|---|---|
| Ireland | 24.9 | 105.0 |
| Finland | 35.2 | 48.6 |
| Spain | 36.3 | 68.5 |
| Netherlands | 45.3 | 66.2 |
| Austria | 60.7 | 72.2 |
| France | 64.2 | 86.3 |
| Germany | 65.0 | 81.5 |
| Portugal | 68.3 | 106.8 |
| Belgium | 84.1 | 98.5 |
| Italy | 103.1 | 120.1 |
| Greece | 105.4 | 160.8 |
| *International comparison* | | |
| United Kingdom | 43.9 | 82.5 |
| United States | 67.2 | 102.9 |
| Japan | 183.0 | 229.8 |

Source: IMF WEO, April 2012

substantial,[4] even in countries such as Germany that were reluctant to use fiscal policy to stimulate their economies.[5]

Fiscal stimulus, alongside falling tax revenues and the impact of automatic stabilizers, resulted in an increase in debt-to-GDP ratios for European countries, from a pre-crisis average of around 61–74% in 2009. The fiscal position of some in the periphery deteriorated even more rapidly owing to a number of country-specific factors. These included high pre-existing levels of debt (Italy), large current spending with little scope for "easy" cuts and efficiency gains (Greece), a rapid drop in GDP growth and consequent impact on fiscal revenues (Spain and Portugal), and large bank bailouts (Ireland). Given the pattern of public indebtedness, problems seemed to be concentrated in euro area countries that had fast but unsustainable growth in the pre-crisis years or that had pre-existing critical fiscal positions, or both (see Table 1).

## 4 The Build-Up of Imbalances

Problematic fiscal positions, under-performing economies and imbalances are long-standing weaknesses of the eurozone periphery, and they all predate the global financial crisis. Those countries that have been hit by the sovereign debt crisis—

[4] The size of the stimulus packages varied across Europe, from 3.8% of GDP in Spain to 0.2% of GDP in Sweden.

[5] Countries with a large export sectors, such as Germany and Japan, which up to then had been almost unscathed by the financial crisis, were severely hit by a sudden and sharp drop in their exports.

Greece, Ireland, Portugal, Spain and Italy—share a common problem of competitiveness, especially in terms of labor costs, which have been significantly rising since 1990 (Fig. 2). Consumer prices also grew faster in periphery countries than in Germany (Fig. 3). In Ireland and Spain, this reflected strong growth and overheating economies, in particular the housing sector, supported by low interest rates at the euro area level. In Greece, Portugal and Italy, high inflation was more a reflection of inefficiencies and distortions in labor and product markets.

The widening competitiveness gap between the euro periphery and Germany, and the emergence of large intra-EMU imbalances, are reflected in real exchange rates (Fig. 4). Since the early 2000s, Italy, Spain, Portugal, Greece and Ireland have been losing competitiveness vis-à-vis Germany.

These problems also show up in current account imbalances within the euro area. Although the euro area, taken as a whole, ran a modest current account surplus (0.3% of its total GDP in 2011), the figure masks large underlying imbalances across the region. With the exception of Ireland, all European economies facing severe fiscal problems are running current account deficits. This partly reflects the weaker export competitiveness of the euro periphery relative to the economies at the "core", which are mostly running current account surpluses (Fig. 5).

However, current account imbalances also signal problems in the capital market. Cross-border capital movements following the creation of the euro contributed to worsening capital account deficits of countries—such as Ireland, Spain and Portugal—that were the recipients of large capital inflows in the pre-crisis years. In contrast, Germany, which had experienced capital outflows, began to accumulate current account surpluses, rising from 2.8% of GDP in 2001–2005 to 6.3% in 2006–2010.

Even though the current account balances of the euro periphery have improved since 2008, for countries such as Greece and Portugal they are significant enough to suggest persistent imbalances that, far from being corrected by a slowdown in GDP growth, as in the United States, indicate structural problems in attracting capital flows. These countries are no longer able to finance their external imbalances through the capital market. As a result these countries, and their banks, have relied increasingly on financing from other euro area countries—in particular from the governments, central banks and official institutions. These structural imbalances have resulted in a build-up of inter-country imbalances in the settlement system. The large increase in Target 2 balances at the Bundesbank is yet another manifestation of the current account surpluses run by Germany.[6] More worryingly, the size and persistence of deficits in the periphery countries suggests longer-term structural problems in financing through capital markets.

---

[6] TARGET stands for Trans-European Automated Real-time Gross settlement Express Transfer system. TARGET 2 is the second generation of this system, which is owned and operated by the Eurosystem—the European Central Bank and the central banks of the member states that belong to the euro area—and which offers a cross-border payment service in the European Union. For further details, see the ECB website, Payments & Markets.

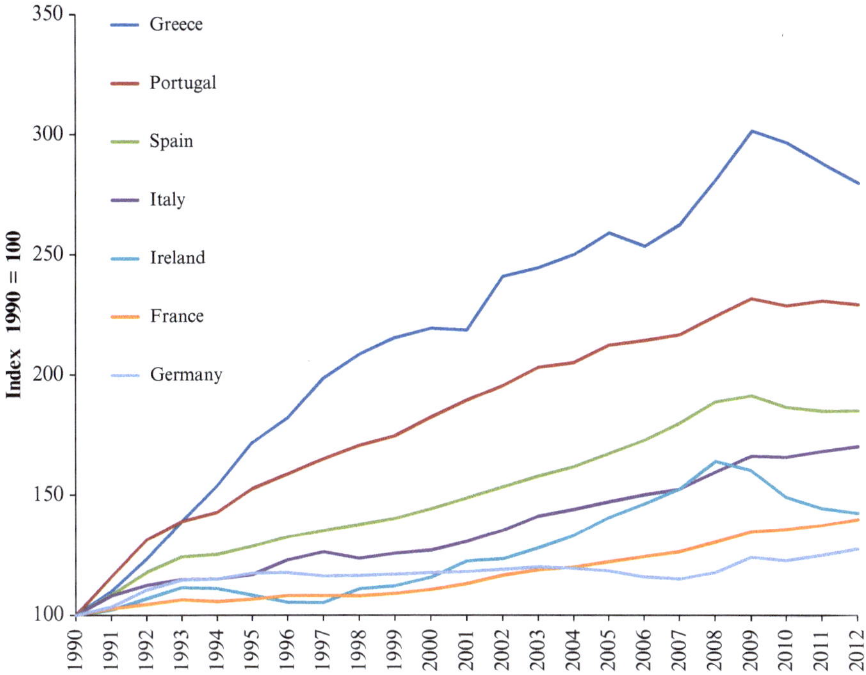


**Fig. 2** Nominal unit labor costs (compensation per employee to real GDP per person employed) Source: AMECO

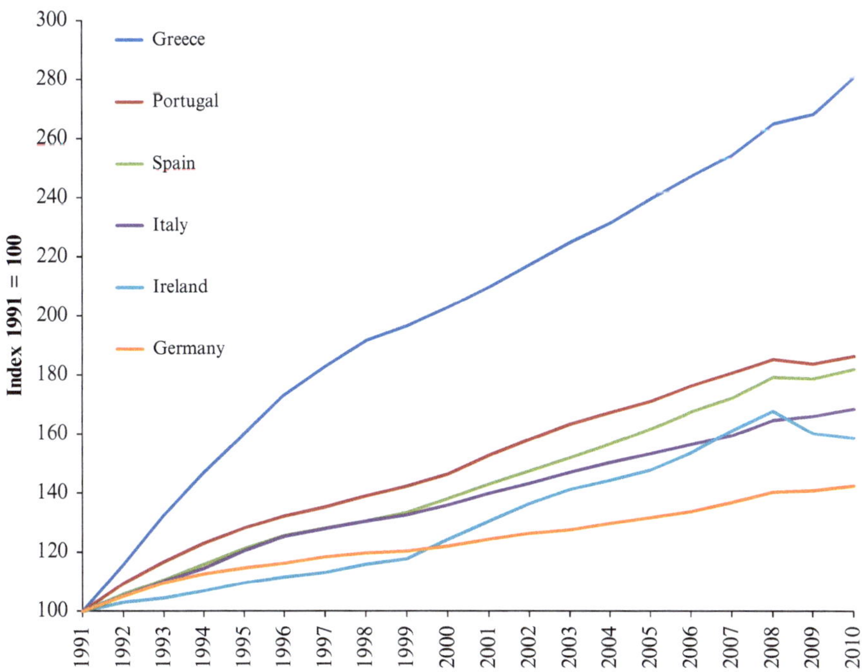


**Fig. 3** Inflation in the euro area (Consumer Prices Index, 1991 = 100) Source: OECD

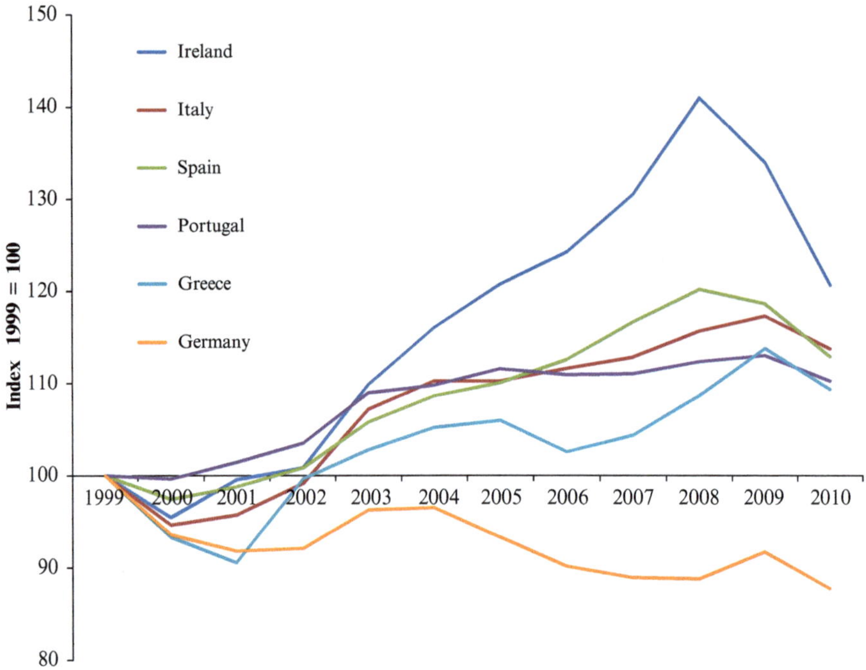


**Fig. 4** Real effective exchange rates

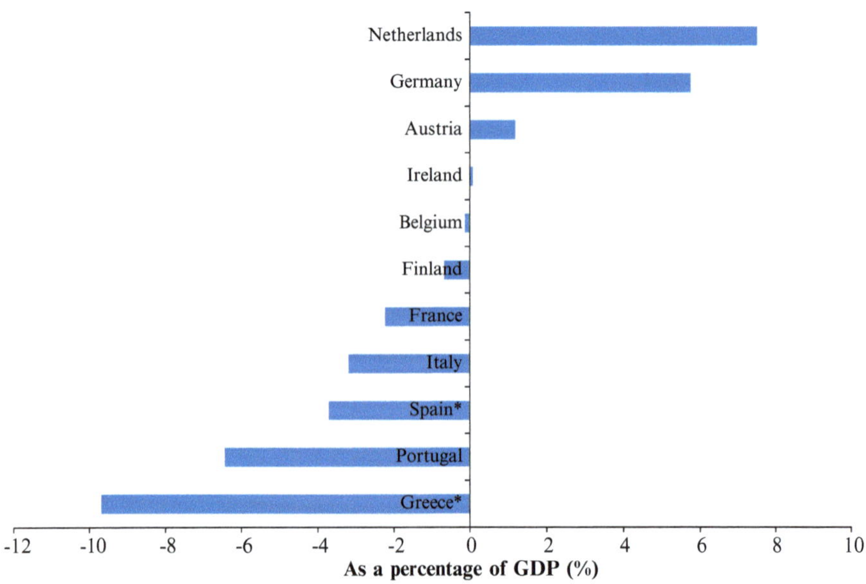


**Fig. 5** Current account balances, Euro area, 2011. Source: IMF WEO

## 5 A "Two-Speed" Europe?

Significant differences have also emerged in the growth performance of different European countries. In large part, the phenomenon of a "two-speed" Europe exposes the difference between those countries that can live within the constraints imposed by the single currency and those that cannot.[7] A number of countries in the periphery (in particular, Greece, Portugal, Spain and Italy) are experiencing relatively low growth and high inflation, which is exacerbating their already problematic debt positions.

The growth problems of the periphery have also showed up in high unemployment rates. Again, Greece, Portugal, Spain and Italy have high and persistent unemployment, especially among youth, and with significant regional differences. Latest labor market figures show youth unemployment in Spain and Greece to be at 51.1% and 51.2%, respectively (Fig. 6). With German youth unemployment running at just below 8%, this again underscores the stark differences within the euro area and the practical consequences of a "two-speed" Europe.

The challenges for those countries in the euro periphery are a mix of urgent priorities and long-term measures. In the immediate future they have to convince markets that their public debts are getting back onto a sustainable track,

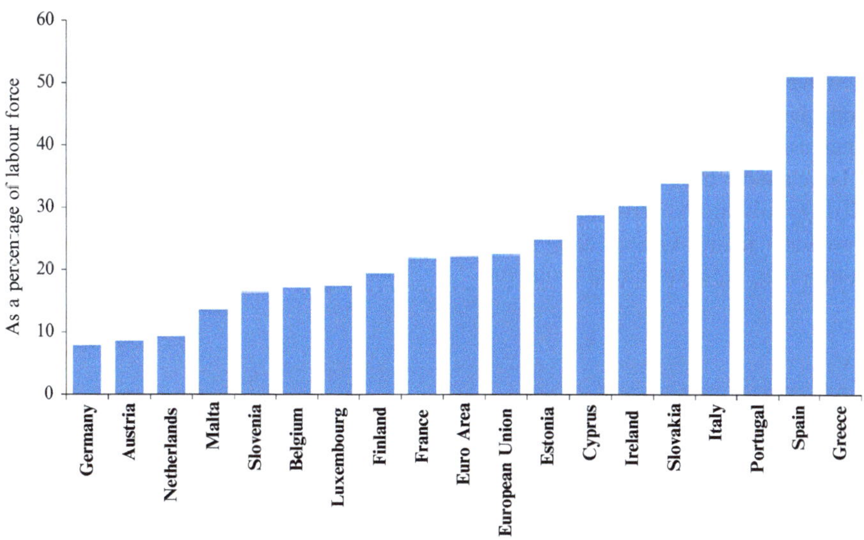


**Fig. 6** Youth unemployment, Euro area, March 2012. Source: Eurostat

[7] This does not necessarily imply, however, that the latter should leave the EMU; however, they need to implement the necessary adjustments and resolve the mismatch.

which means not only credible fiscal consolidation plans but also stronger GDP growth. They also have to normalize the access of banks to market funding, reform their failing banks, and improve their external payments position. In the longer term the challenge is to achieve sustainable increases in growth and to improve competitiveness. However, none of these will be easy, in particular within the constraints of the single currency and its existing governance structure.

## 6 Lasting Solutions to the Euro Crisis

The euro crisis began in 2010. Since then numerous summits have been held and new institutions set up, a new treaty has been proposed to strengthen the oversight of national fiscal policies[8] and the eurozone countries have agreed to move towards a "European banking union".[9] However, throughout the crisis policy-makers have focused on dealing with the symptoms of the problem through a series of short-term fixes, taking decisions based primarily on political priorities and considerations. For instance, the strong resistance to the ECB acting as the lender of last resort or to issuing common bonds by the member countries primarily reflects domestic political priorities in Germany. In addition, the level of austerity imposed on the countries requiring financial assistance is partly to placate the electorates in creditor countries.

The result has been a deepening of the crisis, as the underlying structural problems have remained unaddressed. Not only have countries in the periphery found it increasingly difficult to finance their deficits at sustainable interest rates, but also markets have been questioning the survival of the euro in its current form (Buiter 2011). Solving the crisis of the euro requires not only dealing with the immediate problems facing Greece and other troubled countries in the periphery, but also addressing these structural problems.

[8] Leaders agreed at their December 2011 and March 2012 summits to enhance *ex ante* fiscal surveillance and budgetary processes in the euro area. More importantly, they agreed on an intergovernmental treaty of 25 governments (excluding the United Kingdom and Czech Republic) to support recommendations the Commission makes in the framework of the Excessive Deficit Procedure, leading to greater automaticity and a balanced budget rule at constitutional or equivalent level, and to recognize the jurisdiction of the Court of Justice on these issues. Furthermore, to ensure the financial stability of the euro area, the leaders agreed that the European Stability Mechanism (ESM) should enter into force in July 2012 instead of July 2013, and that urgent decisions in the ESM can be taken by qualified majority voting.

[9] At the Brussels summit in late June, European leaders decided to establish a banking supervisor as a way to contain the crisis, but also to address a shortfall in the design of the currency union. Centralised banking oversight is seen by Germany as the necessary condition for allowing the European Stability Mechanism to recapitalise banks directly.

There are three sets of long-term issues that need to be tackled:

- Helping countries in the periphery to live within the constraints of the single currency
- Adapting the governance of the euro to provide stronger sanctions but a fairer adjustment mechanism
- Adopting a growth model that allows the euro area as a whole and its constituent members to grow.

## 6.1 In the Short-Term: A Lender of Last Resort

It is still essential to implement short-term measures to stabilize the situation in a number of periphery countries to stabilize their fiscal positions and their banking systems. While the financial support for Greece, together with a write-down of privately held debt, helped to stabilize the Greek economy for a while, in the longer term it is far from clear that relying on fiscal austerity to improve Greece's competitiveness is politically sustainable.

Moreover, markets have still not been convinced that enough has been done to provide the resources that would constitute an effective firewall against contagion to other euro area countries. The European Financial Stability Facility (EFSF) and its successor institution, the European Stability Mechanism (ESM), will be stretched to cope with the support for Spanish banks agreed in June. The IMF too would need additional resources if it were to co-finance assistance packages for big euro area countries, but non-European countries are insisting that expansion of the EFSF/ESM is necessary if IMF resources are to be increased.[10]

The ECB also moved decisively to provide significant amounts of liquidity at longer maturities to ensure that European banks had sufficient liquidity to cope with the Greek debt crisis. However, the ECB has also made it clear that this is not its permanent role. Further, the Maastricht Treaty prohibition on monetary financing prevents the ECB from acting as a fully-fledged lender of last resort to countries in crisis. Changing that provision is almost certainly impossible, not only because of the political capital invested in it, but also because in a monetary union (and a banking union)

[10] The G20 finance ministers and central bank governors meeting held in late February 2012 insisted that the European nations had to build a more credible firewall before seeking help from the international community. Their Communiqué states: 'Euro area countries will reassess the strength of their support facilities in March. This will provide an essential input in our ongoing consideration to mobilize resources to the IMF' (G20, 2012). In March, the Eurozone increased its liquidity capacity. Then in June at the G20 summit in Los Cabos the G20 leaders agreed to increase the assets available to the IMF to more than $450 billion dollars, thus doubling the Fund's lending capacity.

it raises very difficult issues of burden sharing between the member countries. This means that it is even more important to press ahead with other longer-term measures to improve the functioning of the single currency.

## 6.2 *Living Within the Euro*

Membership of the single currency means that countries no longer have control over monetary policy, one of their main policy levers. That imposes additional constraints on fiscal and structural policies to maintain competitiveness, and macroeconomic balance (both internal and external). At present the single currency also places most of the responsibility for policy adjustment on countries with current account and fiscal deficits.

One of the biggest problems faced by periphery countries in recent years has been the persistent loss of competitiveness. In the absence of exchange-rate flexibility, countries have to rely more on fiscal policy and structural measures to achieve adjustments in relative prices and wages. At the European level, the Stability and Growth Pact (SGP) and the Lisbon process have provided frameworks to monitor and assist the necessary adjustments. In practice, though, neither has provided sufficient pressure to achieve policy adjustments at the national level. Strengthening the incentives for member countries to adjust their policies to maintain competitiveness is a priority.

The balance of responsibilities between deficit and surplus countries also needs to be re-thought. At present almost all responsibility lies on deficit countries to cut their fiscal deficits and to apply downward pressure on wages and prices. At the aggregate level this creates a bias towards deflationary policies. In theory, the ECB's monetary policy should adjust in response. However, there is currently little or no room for further reductions in interest rates. And this deflationary bias makes it harder for deficit countries to make the fiscal adjustments that are required.

With more effective fiscal control in countries with large deficits, European policy-makers would therefore face harder questions about the appropriate mix of macroeconomic policies at the aggregate level, including the possibility that countries with stronger fiscal positions should run more expansionary policies. The euro area, as a whole, is a large and relatively closed economy with substantial interconnections between its members. Running too tight an overall fiscal policy would have adverse effects on growth, at least in the short-term, especially in current conditions when growth is slow in other parts of the global economy.

## 6.3 *Adapting to the Euro*

Steps have been taken to improve the governance of the euro area in respect of fiscal policy. This is essential if the single currency is to be sustained and strengthened because it needs to move towards a fiscal union as well as a monetary union.

To increase the incentives for individual member countries to follow sustainable fiscal policies, the euro area must improve its surveillance of national economic policies, looking at all aspects of macroeconomic policy and performance. At present the concentration of the SGP on fiscal policy reduces its ability to identify wider macroeconomic imbalances.

Stronger sanctions are also required against member countries that do not follow sound fiscal policies. The SGP provided for fines on countries that breached fiscal guidelines. However, imposition of these fines remained to be decided by the member countries, and despite clear breaches of the guidelines in 2002 and 2003 the Council decided not to take this step.[11]

Finally, a framework for effective dialogue and decision-making for the overall fiscal stance at the euro area level must be developed. The ECB has strong analytical capacity to understand policy-making in the area of monetary policy. The euro area needs to build an equivalent capability for fiscal policy.

However, constructing what is in effect a federal structure for fiscal policy requires a clear understanding and agreement about the boundary between decisions at the euro area level and decisions that will remain purely national. It is also likely to highlight tensions over the fiscal adjustments required in different member states. This debate has already started as Greece struggles to reduce its fiscal deficit and debt. As part of the rebalancing of responsibilities for adjustment between surplus and deficit countries within the euro area, closer integration will make it impossible to ignore the politically difficult issue of fiscal transfers from the big surplus countries (in particular Germany) to the smaller countries running deficits, whether directly or through guarantees on deficit country debts. In the longer term, closer fiscal union is likely to require a permanent system of fiscal transfers.[12]

## 6.4 *The Euro as a Zone for Economic Growth*

While building a deeper currency union was intended to improve the growth prospects of all its members if they could adjust their domestic policy to the constraints of fixed exchange rates, there was a risk that it could also impart a bias against growth. Low growth makes it harder to run sound fiscal policies, and in extreme cases brings into play unsustainable debt dynamics.

The EU recognized many years ago the imperative of boosting growth. The Lisbon strategy was a response to this imperative.[13] However, if the aim

[11] The SGP was breached by Germany itself (together with France) in 2003, but neither country was fined. The previous year Portugal was reprimanded, but not fined, for having had a deficit of more than 3% of GDP.

[12] The EU as a whole does allow limited fiscal transfers through structural and cohesion funds. However, these are primarily intended to encourage convergence between the poorer and richer regions, not to compensate for the loss of monetary sovereignty.

[13] The Lisbon strategy was adopted in March 2000 when the Heads of States met in Lisbon to set out a new strategy to make Europe more dynamic and competitive. Given the moderate results in the initial years, the strategy narrowed its focus to growth and jobs and was relaunched in spring 2005.

was to close the growth gap between Europe and other parts of the world, it must be seen as a failure.

Growth policies remain the objective of every government, but there is little consensus on what constitutes an appropriate growth strategy for the euro area as a whole. It is likely to require primarily country- or region-specific measures, although there is also a role for European-wide policies to boost growth.

The experience of the last decade suggests that a good start would be to avoid European policies that are likely to damage growth. A new framework for euro area governance would be a desirable first step: avoiding a deflationary bias to fiscal policy at the aggregate level, allowing monetary policy to provide appropriate support for growth, and rebalancing the adjustment burden between deficit and surplus countries to allow periphery countries to maintain competitiveness within a single currency. Another way to support growth would be further steps to complete the single market. The "European banking union" has the potential to help here, since there are still significant restrictions on cross-border provision of financial services.

Crises, especially financial crises, tend to have a huge negative impact on growth.[14] Setting in place a system that makes the euro area more stable and sustainable, and hence makes crises less likely, will itself make a big contribution to allowing Europe to enjoy faster growth over the longer term.

## 7 Conclusion: The Alternative

Without these changes, both to deal with the current crisis and to address some of the underlying problems that prevent the euro area from effectively coordinating its policies, it is hard to see the euro surviving in its current form. The costs and benefits of membership of the single currency are spread unevenly between its members, and the economic and political strains placed on individual countries by living within the constraints of the single currency are substantial.

Nevertheless, the benefits of membership of the euro are significant. Members are able to trade with each other without facing currency risk, and the economic costs of currency conversion are eliminated. Many of the periphery countries have enjoyed substantially lower borrowing costs, as well as significant political benefits from membership.

Ultimately, if the cost-benefit balance tilts too far, it could force the break-up of the euro, either by forcing out some of its weaker members or by encouraging the stronger members to leave because they are not prepared to accept the consequences for themselves. However, this would be a last resort option, and would potentially reverse the trend towards greater integration at all levels within Europe. Nevertheless, unless further changes are made to the structure of the single currency to put it on a sustainable footing, it may still come to pass.

[14] On how financial crises impact on the real economy see Rogoff and Reinhart (2009).

## References

Buiter W (2011) What happens if the Euro collapses? Citi GPS: global perspectives & solutions, 8 Dec 2011, https://www.citivelocity.com/citigps/OpArticleDetail.action?recordId=1

McKinnon RI (2000) Mundell, the Euro, and optimum currency areas. Stanford Institute for Economic policy research working paper, May

Mundell RA (1961) A theory of optimum currency areas. Am Econ Rev 51:509–517

Mundell RA (1963) Capital mobility and stabilization policy under fixed and flexible exchange rates. Can J Econ Polit Sci 29:475–485

Mundell RA (1973a) Uncommon arguments for common currencies. In: Johnson HG, Swoboda AK (eds) The economics of common currencies. Allen and Unwin, London, pp 114–132

Mundell RA (1973b) A plan for a European currency. In: Johnson HG, Swoboda AK (eds) The economics of common currencies. Allen and Unwin, London, pp 143–172

Rogoff KS, Reinhart CM (2009) This time is different. Princeton University Press

Subacchi P (2011) Europe: from one crisis to the other. In: Savona P, Kirton JJ, Oldani C (eds) Global financial crisis: global impact and solutions. Ashgate global finance series, pp 65–78

# Comment Paper to Chapter "Europe's Unresolved Crisis"

**Kentaro Kawasaki**

The motivation of this chapter is to explore the source of the current European fiscal crisis after the Lehman Shocks and the challenge is to present the solutions as long-term crisis prevention rather than short-term crisis prescriptions.

Since the adoption of the single currency in 1999, euro exchange rates against other international currencies have been appreciating. Hence, the appreciation of the EUR had been regarded as a success of the European Monetary Union. When the U.S. sub-prime problem began to severely impact the European financial market, the currencies of those Eastern European countries that were expected to join the Eurozone, and then adopted the ERM II, sharply depreciated against the EUR while the exchange rates of the EUR vis-à-vis the USD and the JPY remained stable until the end of 2006. The relative calm of the Eurozone contrasted with the turmoil in the "emerging EU", possibly exaggerating the success of the monetary integration. As a result, it prevented each member state from focusing on the underlying and internal structural issues in the Eurozone, with the genesis of the European fiscal crisis stemming from the Greek fiscal debt crisis.

Therefore, the most prominent contribution of this paper is the claim that the "genesis" of the crisis originates from the early period of the euro or the pre-crisis period; that is, that our scope of analysis should begin from the Maastricht Treaty or the adoption of the single currency in 1999.

The paper states the following points: (1) the problems were concentrated in countries with fast but unsustainable growth in the pre-crisis years or with pre-existing critical fiscal positions, or both, as shown in Table 1; (2) such countries share a common problem of competitiveness in terms of labor costs and consumer prices, which are reflected as inefficiencies and distortions in the labor, goods and services markets, see Figs. 2, 3, and 4; and (3) as a result, large intra-EMU imbalances emerged, as shown in Fig. 5. Therefore, we should ask whether the Eurozone was the optimum currency area

K. Kawasaki (✉)
Faculty of Business Administration, Toyo University,
Tokyo, Japan
e-mail: kawasaki-k@toyonet.toyo.ac.jp

S. Kaji and E. Ogawa (eds.), *Who Will Provide the Next Financial Model?: Asia's Financial Muscle and Europe's Financial Maturity*,
DOI 10.1007/978-4-431-54282-7_22, © Springer Japan 2013

(OCA) in the sense of "Mundell" before the euro crisis. This view is essential to address the issue of the euro crisis and is helpful for the future of the euro.

As pointed out in this paper, periphery countries might have been problematic in terms of their economic structure or macro economies before the launching of the EMU. While Figs. 2 and 3 do show a rubric feature for Greece, these figures fail to show any common trends among these periphery countries after the EMU was introduced.

Figure 2 shows the nominal unit labor costs for Greece, Portugal, Spain, Italy, Ireland, France, and Germany. Although the graph line for Greece has several kinks, the lines for the other peripheries seem to move together and gradually increase after 1999. Although this graphical feature comes from the base year of the indicators, it is not easy to capture the similarities and differences among these countries. During the period before the Maastricht Treaty in 1994, there were no clear rules regarding the integration of their economies, and there was no convergence of economic indicators from 1991 to 1994. Hence, in 1991, economic structures and labor markets were quite different among countries.

Figure 3 shows the movement of consumer price indices for Greece, Portugal, Spain, Italy, Ireland, and Germany. As this paper mentioned, the rapid growth in Irish and Spanish inflation might reflect the boom in the housing sector via huge capital inflows into these two countries after 1999. However, since the indices in Fig. 3 are also based on 1991, the figure fails to capture the influence of the huge capital inflows on the two economies, which might be one of the beneficial aspects of the EMU. However, the paper pointed out that high inflation in Greece, Portugal, and Italy reflected inefficiencies and distortions in the labor and goods markets. Another important aspect of economic integration is to redress the imbalance among member states by arbitrage. If the power of arbitrage works well among cross-border markets, inefficiencies or distortions in the markets can be corrected, and then inflation would be converged among the countries. To capture this effect, the base year should be 1999 or, at the very least, the average of 1999–2002. Unfortunately, Fig. 3 reduces the impact of the analysis.

Figure 5 shows the current account balances for 11 European countries. Usually, a huge current account deficit is regarded as a signal of a currency crisis because it indicates a sharply decreasing foreign exchange reserve. Hence, it is important to take a closer look at the GDP share of the current account deficit. However, in the case of the euro, it is more important to investigate whether the current account deficit could be financed by other member states in the Eurozone or by outside countries like the U.S. or Japan. As long as the peripheries could finance the huge current account deficit by smooth capital inflows from other member states like Germany, Netherland, or Austria, a current account or capital account crisis like the Asian crisis in 1997–1998 would never happen. Unfortunately, Fig. 5 cannot tell us the details of the capital inflows; therefore, the question of whether the current account imbalance among member states matters or not, has not been answered.

Although there are some problems in the analytical section, the solutions suggested in this paper are clear and practical for the euro crisis. Even if each of the crisis-hit countries has to face severe fiscal constraint to recover within the Eurozone, there still exists room for rapid and substantial economic growth (better than that compared with a country outside the Eurozone) by deepening economic integration. As shown in Bouis and Duval (2011), the potential gains from a broad reform package for Eurozone countries are twice the size of that of other OECD countries. This means economic integration still offers significant beneficial synergy effects among countries. Hence, the conclusions offered in this paper will be helpful in the search for solutions.

## Reference

Bouis R, Duval R (2011) Raising the potential growth after the crisis: a quantitative assessment of the potential gains from various structural reforms in the OECD area and beyond. OECD economics department working papers, no. 835, Fig. 15, OECD Publishing, Paris

# The Exchange Rate Regime as a Tool to Advance Reform: Success or Failure?

**Sahoko Kaji**

**Abstract** The euro crisis should not be seen as a mere failure in monetary unification. Rather, it is an example of what happens when countries and supra-national institutions postpone the necessary reforms, including reforms in governance. In other words, it is a test of whether choosing the single currency as the exchange rate regime can help bring about changes needed to make prosperity sustainable. A single currency takes away monetary and fiscal policy autonomy, thereby removing the easy choice of expansionary policy. It also makes price and cost comparisons easy across national borders. For these reasons, the euro was expected to enhance much needed structural reform. This did not happen sufficiently, asymmetries in competitiveness remained, and the euro is in difficulty. But if the governance overhaul underway since the crisis finally hastens convergence towards higher productivity, that will be the silver lining. How to implement reforms that are unpopular to voters but good for sustainable well-being is a problem common to all democracies. In that sense, Europe leads the way, showing the rest of the world how or how not to tackle this problem. If Asian countries criticise the euro and choose not to move in the direction of monetary unification, they need to think of an alternative.

**Keywords** Democracy • Euro • Governance • Reform • Sustainability

---

The author would like to thank all who contributed to the EUSI conference in December 2011, including those who worked hard in preparing the conference. Ryuichiro Izumi, a 4th year undergraduate student at the faculty of economics at Keio University, provided excellent assistance in preparing the graphs for this paper. Information contained in this paper is correct as of June 2012.

S. Kaji (✉)
Keio University, 2-15-45 Mita, Minato-ku, Tokyo 108-8345, Japan

EUSI, Tokyo, Japan
e-mail: kaji@econ.keio.ac.jp

S. Kaji and E. Ogawa (eds.), *Who Will Provide the Next Financial Model?: Asia's Financial Muscle and Europe's Financial Maturity*,
DOI 10.1007/978-4-431-54282-7_23, © Springer Japan 2013

## 1 Introduction

Throughout history, Europe has been the birthplace of new ideas, instruments and institutions. However, not all of these have been durable. At the time of writing this paper, the world is asking "how durable is the euro?"

Introduced on paper in 1999 and in coin and note form in 2002, the euro is a single currency used by 17 member states of the European Union (EU). In the 10 years since its advent, the single currency has grown to become one of the major global currencies alongside the US dollar. The Europeans who planned and executed the Economic and Monetary Union (EMU), and thus introduced the euro, knew that Europe was not an "Optimum Currency Area".[1] They also knew that the euro area, as it came to be called, was to be an area with a single monetary authority without a single fiscal authority. These facts did not appear to cause concern until October 2009, when a new government led by Andrea Papandreou's Panhellenic Socialist Movement (PASOK) came into power in Greece. Before long, the world learnt that the ratio of Greece's government deficit to GDP was approximately 13%, much higher than the previous government had admitted.[2] The rest is on-going history. Despite the agreements regarding rescue packages and the initiation of reform, the situation turned for the worse.

Many criticize the heads of state and policy authorities for doing "too little, too late". Some argue that the euro should not have been introduced in the first place. This paper does not take these routes and attempts to explain the crisis by looking at the single currency as a potential tool to advance reform.

There were several reasons why the euro was introduced through the EMU. One of them was to further much needed structural reform by removing monetary and fiscal policy autonomy and by introducing price transparency[3]. If reform proceeded and economies converged to a productive and competitive state, the euro would have been considered a success. A single currency never works well if economies are divergent. In this sense, the euro had a potentially self-destructive structure—it was near impossible to continue unless one of its original goals was attained.

---

[1] The theory of the Optimum Currency Area (OCA) was developed by Robert Mundell, the winner of the 1999 Nobel Prize in Economics. Mundell (1968) stated that whether a particular region should introduce a single currency depended on whether factors of production (such as labour and capital) were mobile across borders within that region, and thus was an empirical question. As early as 1990, the European Commission carefully analysed the OCA theory and concluded it was not to be their guiding principle. See Box 2.3 of the European Commission (1990), page 46, which concludes, "summing up, the optimum currency area approach provides useful insights but cannot be considered a comprehensive framework in which the costs and benefits of EMU can be analysed".

[2] According to Barber (2010), this was not news to EU policymakers. As early as July 2009, the then Commissioner of Monetary Affairs Joaquin Almunia had circulated a memorandum to European finance ministers predicting that the Greek budget deficit would likely soar above 10% of GDP. However, nobody took any effective action. As Barber's article implies, this fact, along with the malfunctioning of the Stability and Growth Pact, revealed the need to improve governance.

[3] For an early discussion of the relationship between structural reform and EMU, see Kaji (1998).

In this paper, we argue that the current European crisis should be looked at in this light instead of as a simple failure of currency unification. Through EMU, Europe asked whether the exchange rate regime could serve as a device to advance politically unpalatable reforms. The answer was unfortunately no, at least not until the crisis. But the crisis seems to be changing this. Now Member States are undertaking painful, unpopular reforms, and governance in the EU is being overhauled at a rapid pace[4]. If the crisis succeeds in bringing about the necessary reforms to increase the competitiveness of all members, it will be the silver lining.

If competitiveness is improved, but only for some members, then Europe will have to be a "multi-speed" union. If the danger of "disorderly default" and contagion are too high, it would be difficult for any member to leave the euro. But once this is not the case, the euro may "disintegrate" to contain only a "core". EU members outside of this core must then choose their degree of integration with the core. An arrangement similar to the current Exchange Rate Mechanism II (ERM II) may be re-established. Eventually, some may choose to join the core again, by accepting the rigid conditions.

The reasons for European integration still remain: members are highly interdependent, and they profit from the weight they have together as an integrated entity. The question is whether Europe can now establish the kind of governance that makes integration sustainable.

Below, we first look back on the reasons for EMU. We point out that the present crisis roots in the euro's inability to effectively advance reform as originally hoped. In the second section, we review the governance overhaul underway in the EU. In the third section, we discuss three important aspects of policy under the reformed governance. In the final section, we ask whether the choice of exchange rate regimes can be an effective tool in advancing reform in democracies in Europe and Asia.

## 2 The Crisis and the Choice of the EMU

Many blame the euro for the current crisis, arguing that the euro should not have been introduced in the first place. However, if we look around the world, we can see that there is no one-to-one relationship between a particular exchange rate regime and an increase in sovereign risk.[5]

For instance, Japan's exchange rate regime is a "dirty" float. But its government debt to GDP ratio is the highest in the G20, and Japanese government bonds (JGBs) are not immune to downgrades by credit rating agencies (even if nearly 95% of JGBs are held domestically). The Lehmann shock and its aftermath have discredited the credit rating agencies. However, if their downgrades prompt a selling of JGBs, all traders, including those who are sceptical about the agencies' judgment, will follow to protect their asset value. Japan could experience a sovereign debt crisis if markets behave in this manner.

[4] For a comprehensive account see Begg (2010).

[5] Sovereign risk is the risk of a sovereign country changing the conditions of payment of the debt it owes. An extreme form of such a change is outright default. Others include demanding the lender to repurchase long-term bonds or rollovers.

In other parts of Asia, the Asian financial crisis of 1997–1998 occurred to countries that pegged their currencies to the US dollar. In Europe today, the countries facing a sovereign crises are members of the euro area. Their exchange rate regime is the ultimate form of fixed exchange rates. At the same time, countries like Latvia and Estonia, while pegging their currencies to the euro, have put themselves through harsh reforms and managed to contain their economic crises.[6]

Therefore, we can see that the choice of exchange rate regimes does not have a one-to-one relationship with whether a country avoids crises. Countries with and without a single currency have experienced a loss of market confidence. It is true that fixed exchange rates can induce capital flight, but capital flight can happen without fixed exchange rates. It is also true that stopping the adjustment of one variable (exchange rate) means shifting the burden of adjustment to another variable, for example, sovereign borrowing costs. If the adjustment is large, a sovereign crisis can occur instead of a currency crisis. This is what is happening within the euro area today. However, fixed exchange rates do not automatically mean crises. If a variable other than the exchange rate or the sovereign borrowing cost can adjust, a crisis is not inevitable.[7]

This leads us to the question of why a nation chooses to adopt a particular exchange rate regime. For those countries that joined the euro, one reason for that choice was that the single currency was the "logical consequence of the single market". The Single Market project was proposed by the European Commission in 1985 to remove non-tariff barriers within the European Economic Community (later the EU) by the end of 1992. But it then became apparent that the free movement of goods, services and capital were still hampered by non-tariff barriers. Europe dealt with this problem by introducing the Single Market (1992) project. However, wild swings in exchange rates remained an obstacle so Europe decided to do away with exchange rates with the EMU. The currency crises of 1992 and 1993, called "the end of the EMU", actually increased the determination of European leaders to permanently do away with exchange rates.[8]

Another reason for the euro was that Europe wished to have an international currency that rivalled the US dollar and differed from the Deutsche Mark. A further reason for the euro was to encourage structural reform. This is the most important reason in relation to the present crisis. A single currency facilitates price and cost comparisons. It also constrains monetary and fiscal policies. In the 1980s, economists explained the European Monetary System as a means to "hire a conservative central banker".[9] The Maastricht convergence criteria and later the Stability and Growth Pact (SGP) were supposed to provide a way to hire a conservative fiscal authority.

[6] Estonia joined the euro area in January 2012. President Toomas Ilves of Estonia, in an interview with the UK financial journal Money Week, stated, "after [Stalin's] mass deportations, [austerity] didn't seem that bad. I guess it's harder if you've been living the good life of bunga bunga parties" (Money Week 2011).

[7] The domestic price level and/or production costs could be such a variable. This is now called "internal devaluation" and actually happened in Germany, Latvia and Estonia among others.

[8] Looking at matters from this historical perspective, we can see that the governance overhaul currently underway is also a "logical consequence", exactly on the same trajectory as all the integration milestones.

[9] For instance, see Giavazzi and Pagano (1986) and Rogoff (1985).

The single currency was intended to make it easier for governments to implement unpopular reforms, by giving them no other choice. Through the structural reform induced by the euro, economies were expected to converge in a desirable direction of higher productivity and competitiveness. The project was called the EMU because economic convergence, not just monetary unification, was important to the participants. If economies did not converge, asymmetries would remain, making it difficult to maintain currency unification. The structure of the euro was such that trouble would befall if one of its own goals was not achieved.

The demise of the euro may appear sudden to some people. In fact, the euro was not always a "strong" currency. Towards the end of 2000 the euro depreciated against both the US dollar and the yen.[10] Furthermore, the euro was not made in a day, and those involved were always aware of the potential problems. One of these problems was asymmetry between the members Kaji (2012). Fixing the exchange rate is difficult when there is asymmetry because people buy one currency and sell another when something happens in one country but not in the other (which economists call asymmetry). A single currency is the ultimate form of fixing the exchange rate (Figs. 1 and 2). Therefore, from the beginning it was clear that unless member states converged in a desired direction, the euro would face difficulties.[11]

The euro is facing difficulty today because the question it was supposed to help answer was not answered. In that sense, there is nothing illogical occurring. The question asked was "how can we implement policies that are domestically unpopular but good for the economy as a whole?"[12]

It did not help that the introduction of the single money coincided with the end of the Cold War. Transfers to the former East Germany, together with social welfare reform, led to an increase in German fiscal deficits towards 2005. During the same period, French fiscal deficits also expanded and the SGP ended up being ineffective[13]. Around the same time, the euro began to gain respect from the markets, as the

---

[10] The depreciation was such that some even called the euro "the toilet currency".

[11] Removing asymmetry does not mean eliminating diversity. The theory of comparative advantage tells us that even if a country is less productive in everything it does, it still has a comparative advantage in some production process if the amount of A it can produce by giving up production of one unit of B is different from another country. All countries have a comparative advantage in some good and/or service, but some have current account deficits and others have surpluses. The important point is that convergence in competitiveness does NOT mean all countries becoming alike. It means all countries becoming competitive in producing the goods and services in which they have a comparative advantage, so that their current account deficits do not lead to dangerous levels of external debt, and their unemployment rates and government deficits remain at sustainable levels. So symmetry in productivity does not mean "no gains from trade". It is true, however, that removing asymmetry in industrial structures can mean certain types of trade disappear.

[12] Another way to pose this question is "how will voters willingly choose to pay the cost of obtaining a particular benefit?" A successful example of voters choosing to pay the cost and enjoying the benefit is Germany today. The country has the strongest economy in Europe and is resentful of demands for transfers to the weaker economies. However, it is also the member state that benefited most from the single currency. Germans chose to undergo the rigorous structural change called for by the euro and the weakness of other member states pulled down the external value of the euro, helping its export sector enjoy a boom.

[13] Kaji (2005) describes in detail how this happened (in Japanese).

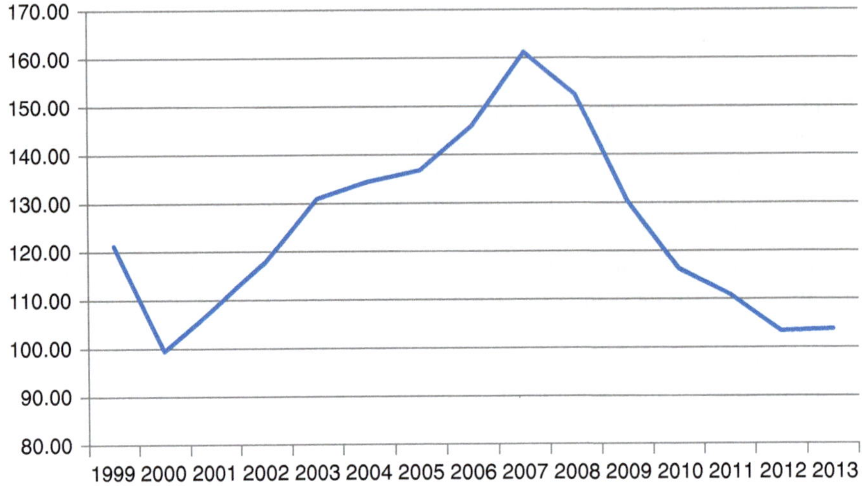


**Fig. 1** Annual exchange rate (Japanese yen per Euro). Source: Eurostat, http://appsso.eurostat.ec.europa.eu/nui/show.do?dataset=ert_bil_eur_a&lang=en

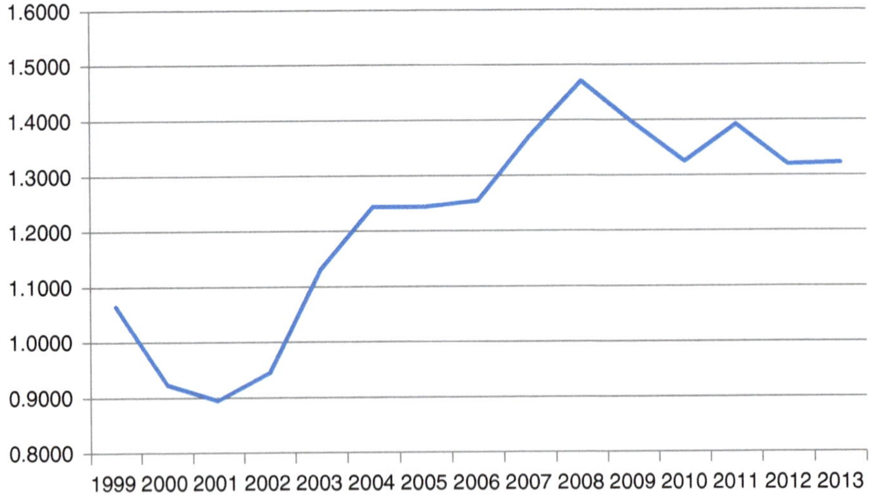


**Fig. 2** Annual exchange rate (US dollar per Euro). Source: Eurostat, http://appsso.eurostat.ec.europa.eu/nui/show.do?dataset=ert_bil_eur_a&lang=en

European Central Bank (ECB) gained credibility. Interest rates on all euro area government bonds began to converge towards German levels.

These events led to lax spending in many countries, not just in the public sector but also in the private sector.[14] Eventually the situation turned into a European crisis. Even as the crisis deepened, governance overhauls and institutional reform did not come easily. Only after borrowing costs for Italy rose above 7% and the downgrading of French government bonds became a serious possibility did governance overhaul begin in earnest. In fact, many have criticized different aspects of the reactions of euro area leaders. Some say that Greece should have been allowed to default, because this would have kept it a Greek crisis instead of a European crisis. Others say it was the "private sector involvement" (PSI) that pushed interest rates above 7%. While these comments may contain some truth, the fundamental fact remains that these leaders were democratically elected leaders who had to listen to their voters.

It is easy to say that the euro was a failure, that it should not have been introduced. But the original goal of convergence towards a reformed economy remains. If the euro should be abandoned or changed, we need to discuss alternative ways to arrive at this goal. Without establishing structures that make its members competitive and productive, the EU will not have sustainable prosperity, with or without the euro.

Even before the current crisis, Europe was attempting to press reforms forward. The Lisbon Strategy launched in 2000 was supposed to make Europe "the most dynamic and competitive knowledge-based economy in the world", which was "capable of sustainable economic growth with more and better jobs and greater social cohesion and respect for the environment". The reason why the goal was not achieved is because the strategy relied on the Open Method of Coordination.[15] There were no sanctions against missed goals, only peer pressure. The "re-launch" of the strategy in 2005 may have increased the sense of ownership on the part of Member States, but not on the part of the citizens.

As foreseen,[16] without the increased sense of ownership on the part of citizens, many democratically elected governments were unable to remove inefficiencies and structural rigidities on their own. Jean Clade Junker's famous words sum up the situation: "we all know what to do, but we don't know how to get re-elected once we have done it."

---

[14] Private sector debt exploded in countries outside Europe too. According to the McKinsey Institute (2012), US private-sector debt rose from 148% of GDP to 234% between 1990 and 2008. Private risk may be as serious as sovereign risk. At the same time, in 2010 there were 70 private US firms whose bond CDS spreads are lower than US government bonds. The fact that government bonds are no longer the "safest asset" fundamentally challenges economic models. Another interesting topic of analysis is whether crises can occur even if all current accounts balance. The 2011 IMF Economic Outlook as well as Taylor and Pradhan (2011) discuss the relationship between current account imbalances and crises.

[15] In 2010 the Lisbon Strategy became Europe 2020 to make Europe "a smart, sustainable and inclusive economy delivering high levels of employment, productivity and social cohesion". However, this also relies on the Open Method of Coordination. No major progress can be expected without successful governance overhaul.

[16] For instance, Kaji (2007) emphasized that "until EU citizens come to realize that they themselves have ... responsibilities in reaching the Lisbon goals, the ultimate goal of Lisbon is unlikely to be reached" and predicted that "in as much as citizens in some Member States accept such responsibilities more than in others, the relative success in the re-launch will vary across the Member States" (page 5).

The single currency was expected to provide constraints that made it easier for member states to move in the right direction. This did not happen.[17] However, if a single currency is not the answer, how should EU member nations achieve convergence towards a vibrant, productive economy? Europe is now trying to answer this question with stronger, more effective governance.

Europe needs this, because integration is the only way to peaceful prosperity in Europe. Even if the euro "disintegrated", after a while many countries would begin to adopt exchange rate policies to stabilise their exchange rate against (what remains of) the euro. It would simply make economic sense to do so. Exchange rate gyrations are a nuisance, especially for open democracies. Openness makes them highly interdependent with each other, and democracy makes it difficult for politicians to implement unpopular reforms[18]. The more open the economy, and the more difficult it is to implement unpopular policies, the larger the merit of fixing the exchange rate to a currency backed by a conservative policy authority. Tying one's hands through fixed exchange rates may even be the only way to push unpopular reforms forward in some European countries.

As long as there is the incentive to peg to a stable currency, the single currency that "disintegrated" will be rebuilt bit by bit. Whether this rebuilt single currency ends again in a similar crisis down the line depends on whether Europe succeeds in introducing the required institutional reforms.

## 3 The Crisis and Governance Overhaul

The urgent task is to contain the crisis; however, European leaders must also tackle the longer-term issue of reforming the EU's institutions so that integration can continue and a crisis does not occur again. Whether or not any country leaves the euro, all countries within and outside the euro area cannot enjoy sustainable prosperity without solid economic structures. To have such structures, reforms are necessary, and to have such reforms, governance must be conducive to such reforms. Europe is in need of a "governance overhaul".[19] EU leaders must produce a clear and convincing roadmap, for its citizens and for all EU institutions. Such a roadmap will also contribute to the short-term goal of market stability. Northern governments and the ECB are reluctant to become further involved in the resolution of the crisis unless a clear design is given regarding a long-term solution.

A governance overhaul is required at both EU and national levels. If governance at the national level is such that the politicians who manage to implement unpopular but beneficial policies can be voted into office, reforms can take place. Even if this is too difficult, Europe

[17] Kaji (2012) contains graphs showing this, comparing Member States' performances in terms of labour productivity, employment protection, product market regulation, housing prices and household debt among others.

[18] Kaji (2010) emphasises this aspect of the euro crisis.

[19] Shoji (2011b) provides a comprehensive account of the relationship between the crisis and the EU's institutional shortcomings.

has the choice to rely on supra-national commitments, a choice that still lacks in Asia. Such a commitment can actually encourage voters to support reform-minded politicians. For this to happen, the commitment must be credible. In other words, Member States must relinquish further sovereignty (allow intervention in domestic policymaking) for the sake of sustainable integration. Integration is the only choice for peaceful economic stability in Europe, but it is not sustainable unless member economies become more uniformly sustainable in terms of productivity, unemployment and budget deficits. The crisis made it clear that there is no longer any room for hesitation regarding further interference into domestic policymaking, for the sake of prosperous coexistence.

In May of 2010, a taskforce was formed, headed by the President of the European Council Herman Van Rompuy. On 21 October 2010, the taskforce issued its final report.[20] Its proposals had five main pillars:

(i) Fiscal discipline, notably through a stronger SGP;
(ii) Broader economic surveillance to encompass macro imbalances and competitiveness;
(iii) Deeper and broader coordination;
(iv) A robust framework for crisis management; and
(v) Stronger institutions and more effective and rule-based decision making.

In October 2010, European leaders were not yet convinced that it was time to further relinquish their sovereignty. At the Franco-German meeting on 18 October 2010, sanctions against breaking fiscal rules were to be "near-automatic" instead of "automatic". The then ECB president Trichet as well as members such as Finland were not happy, but France was not ready to acquiesce.

However, at a crucial meeting on 5 December 2011, Chancellor Merkel and President Sarkozy agreed a "fiscal compact" (discussed below) and the start of the European Stability Mechanism (ESM)[21] was brought forward to July 2012. Following the announcement by S&P (the ratings agency) that euro area countries were under a downgrade review, Paris and Bonn issued a joint statement confirming their "determination to take all the necessary measures, in liaison with their partners and the European institutions to ensure the stability of the euro area".[22]

[20] Van Rompuy Task Force (2010).

[21] Unlike the European Financial Stability Fund, the ESM is a permanent mechanism. Initially, Germany was against the idea of a permanent institution to fund crisis-hit countries, but later decided that ESM was necessary to build solid rules for financial support and to advance debt restructuring. For this, Germany argued for a re-negotiation of the EU treaties, partly because the constitutional court in Karlsruhe could denounce a "crisis resolution mechanism" as illegal if it threatened the stability of the euro. Many members were against the re-negotiation of the EU treaties. However, once France and Germany decided to proceed, an ESM was agreed by the euro area finance ministers on 28 November 2010; the re-negotiation took a minimalist form, making it possible for the ESM to come into being on 1 July 2013. Information on the treaty establishing the European Stability Mechanism is available at http://ec.europa.eu/economy_finance/articles/financial_operations/2011-07-11-esm-treaty_en.htm

[22] Carnegy and Milne (2011). http://www.reconproject.eu/main.php/RECON_wp_1028.pdf?fileitem=5456450

To the Germans, fiscal integration meant centralized fiscal discipline, not joint financing or Eurobonds (not until there was sufficient fiscal discipline). At this meeting on 5 December 2011, France accepted this idea, at least in part. Those waiting for a Eurobond would have been disappointed by the December 5 meeting, as the two leaders rejected the launch of such bonds. However, this was to change after the election of Francois Hollande as France's president in May 2012. Since then there has been more serious talk of Eurobonds, and increasing importance has been placed on growth.[23]

In the meantime, governance was being overhauled to enhance fiscal discipline by making the SGP more effective. First, the so-called "six-pack", a collection of five regulations and a single directive came into force on 13 December 2011.[24] Among other things, it introduced a debt rule in addition to the deficit rule.

Parallel to this, the Treaty on Stability, Coordination and Governance (TSCG) was decided. The TSCG contains a section on fiscal balances, called the "fiscal compact", and is even stronger than the six-pack. First, the TSCG sets a lower deficit limit of 0.5% of GDP for the "structural deficit" (excluding cyclical effects and one-off measures), and a limit of 1.0% of GDP for Member States with a debt ratio significantly below 60% of GDP. Second, budget rules must be written into national law, with "binding force and permanent character, preferably constitutional". Third, the European Court of Justice (CoJ) may impose a financial sanction of 0.1% of GDP if a country does not properly implement the new budget rules in national law, and fails to comply with a CoJ ruling that requires it to do so. Fourth, the decision on whether to impose sanctions will be made by Reverse Qualified Majority Voting among euro area Member States, making it less likely that a blocking majority will be formed to stop the sanctions from being implemented.[25]

Importantly, fiscal discipline is not the only focus. Member States are also moving towards giving up sovereignty on other aspects of the macro economy. Both the six-pack and TSCG include articles related to mutual surveillance of macroeconomic indicators. In the six-pack, there is surveillance based on the new Macroeconomic Imbalance Procedure.[26] This is strengthened in the TSCG by including the ex-ante coordination of debt issuance plans. The TSCG also introduces economic

---

[23] For discussions on the Eurobond, see for instance Bonnevay (2010), von Weizsäcker and Delpla (2010), Juncker J-C, Tremonti G (2010), De Le Dehesa (2011) and European Commission (2011a, b). Joaquin Almunia, vice president of the European Commission said in May 2012 that Eurobonds "are one of the possible solutions to Europe's debt crisis", but "many conditions would have to be met" before they are introduced.

[24] Explanation of the six pack and TSCG in this paper relies partly on http://ec.europa.eu/economy_finance/articles/governance/2012-03-14_six_pack_en.htm

[25] Shoji (2011b) points out that sanctions remain "near-automatic" instead of "automatic" because the Commission's "proposal" to impose sanctions was changed to "recommendation", and the Council can revise this by a Qualified Majority.

[26] The Euro Plus Pact also strengthens the Macroeconomic Imbalance Procedure. The pact (its official name is The Euro Plus Pact: Stronger Economic Policy Coordination for Competitiveness and Convergence) was adopted by the EU Council on 24 and 25 March 2011. The pact sets common goals in the four areas of strengthened competitiveness, increased employment, fiscal sustainability and financial stability, to be obtained via mutual surveillance.

partnership programmes for Member States in the Excessive Deficit Procedure, which "detail the structural reforms needed for an effective and durable correction of their excessive deficit". In addition, a Euro Summit must be held at least twice a year.

The TSCG will be signed by 25 EU Member States excluding the UK and Czech Republic, and is not EU law but an intergovernmental agreement. It will only be binding for euro area Member States, and will enter into force following ratification by at least 12 euro area Member States. This is expected to occur by the first day of 2013, and after that, it will run alongside the six-pack. The goal is to turn it into EU law within 5 years. As of March 2013, only countries that ratify this agreement have access to support from the ESM. After one year of coming into force, only countries implementing the fiscal rules of this agreement have that access.

These measures can be interpreted as the EU's opinion that they are no longer willing or able to stay on the same boat with members that do not or cannot reform their economies and stabilise their finances. There is perhaps also the hope that profligate and tardy members will finally speed up their reforms in light of the stricter conditions. The EU has long been aware of the "democratic deficit" and has been making efforts, ineffective as they may have been, to increase the sense of ownership on the part of its citizens. The EU is now asking the citizens to ask themselves—what is the EU worth? Even Germany, with sporadic rumours of credit downgrades and shaky regional finances, cannot be expected to provide funds indefinitely. Rather than to see a wholesale collapse, the EU is turning towards continuity and stability with members that are ready and able to come along—in other words, a "multi-speed Europe". After all, Denmark and the UK already have "opt-outs" from the euro, in which all Member States meeting the criteria must automatically join.[27] It is time for EU citizens to seriously reconsider what they are prepared to give up, to remain members of the EU and the euro area.

A poll published by Pew Research Centre on 29 May 2012 showed that in six of the eight countries surveyed, majorities believed that European integration had damaged their economies. The six include Spain (by a narrow majority), France, Italy and Britain (by large majorities). Only in Germany and Poland did the majorities answer that the EU had been good for prosperity. What the poll did not ask, however, was whether citizens are ready to give up all that integration has already provided and continues to provide them. Furthermore, for the EU to continue to exist, it must continue to change. Some voters find the changes objectionable. But just because majorities find certain changes objectionable does not mean they are ready to accept the consequence of not making the changes, i.e., losing the benefits they currently enjoy.

[27] Henkel (2011) argued that instead of fiscally troubled members leaving the euro, fiscally sound members such as Germany should leave and establish a stable single currency area. However, this does not seem to take into account the benefits enjoyed by Germany and others due to the external weakness of the euro, made possible by the weakness of some members.

When times are hard, extremists on both the right and the left enjoy an increase in support—that is the danger. France's new president won the election promising a "re-negotiation" of the fiscal pact. Fortunately, this is unlikely to mean the re-writing of the whole text, but rather the addition of a "growth pact". However, a Franco-German agreement at the level of heads of state is not the final word. The real test is whether citizens will choose to pay the price for enjoying the past and future fruits of integration.

## 4 Goals of the Governance Overhaul

As seen in the previous section, Europe is already taking steps towards concessions of sovereignty, in the direction of a major change in governance. Europe must avoid another crisis and create an environment in which prosperity is sustainable. If the current form of governance is getting in the way of achieving these goals, a new form of governance is called for. In particular, Europe needs governance that enables policymakers to focus on the following three important aspects.

One is the nature of government spending. Too much austerity can decrease economic activity, one consequence of which is lower tax revenues and worse fiscal balances. What Europe needs is not fiscal spending that perpetuates rigidity, but spending that leads to higher productivity and efficiency. If the EU is to survive as a union of prosperous states, further steps must be taken in the name of reform-oriented spending that leads to economic vitality.

Another important aspect is financial regulation. In Spain, the fiscal situation was even better than in Germany before the euro crisis. However, the burst of the real estate bubble and the banking sector crisis marked the beginning of their troubles. Reckless real estate lending was also a central feature of the crisis in Ireland as well. Since the Lehman crisis, the world has come to share the understanding that the financial industry is a dangerous industry. It can cause market turmoil, and even pull the entire world economy into the abyss. And yet, the industry has political power because of the sheer amount of money it makes, as well as its crucial importance to the economy. No economy can function without financial intermediation. And high-return investments are in high demand because the increasing number of retirees must find ways to sustain their standard of living without becoming too much of a burden on the working population. In addition, finance can move from one location to another with little cost, especially with advances in technology; if doing business in one country becomes too costly, a financial operation can move to another more easily than other operations. As a result, regulating the financial industry is difficult.

However, it is clear that changing nothing can invite another financial crisis. At the global level, BIS III is to be gradually introduced from the beginning of 2013. The shadow banking sector is also coming under the scrutiny of the world's regulatory authorities. In the meantime, Europe is making its own efforts. As early as 2 September 2010, European leaders agreed to establish new financial authorities.

Those for banking, insurance and securities were to be located in London, Frankfurt and Paris, respectively. The 2010 agreement left national supervision at national levels, strengthening EU-level authority only "in an emergency". However, events since then indicate that macro-prudential regulation must be effectively conducted in all member states, as uniformly as possible. Furthermore, the EU is to establish a "European Banking Union". This aims to integrate financial oversight and deposit insurance in the EU.

As would be expected, how best to do this is an important point of contention between the UK and the remaining members. Since the Lehman crisis, the UK has been taking major steps to reform their financial regulations. They do not wish to have to seek permission from the Commission at each step. With respect to the capital adequacy ratio for instance, the UK Treasury refused to accept that no member could enjoy a higher ratio than the rest of the EU without first consulting the Commission. The Conservative government sees the EU's approach to financial regulation as a threat to the City. If the UK opts out of EU financial regulation, then the City may be able to retain its position in the world, but this would mean that there will no longer be a "single market" in finance.[28]

The European Banking Union (EBU) is also controversial in Germany, if it means that German banks with solid balance sheets must help banks in other countries that are laden with bad debts. However, the Union's long-term goal is to avoid repeating the dangerous structure of "banks with shaky balance sheets and sovereigns with shaky balance sheets sustaining each other". Another important long-term goal is to make sure taxpayers do not have to rescue financial institutions (and their well-paid employees) by introducing some form of "bailing-in". This latter goal will be achieved only as of 2018, but is especially important for Germany.

If it does indeed become a norm that investors (and not taxpayers) pay for their own decision to invest in a borrower that eventually defaults, that would fundamentally change decision-making in financial investment. Of course, taxpayers will indirectly pay the cost, as more cautious investments by fund managers yield lower returns. However, this might be a cost that has to be shared for the sake of avoiding a global meltdown.

How the UK and other members narrow their differences over this issue has strong implications for the rest of the world. In the US, the financial sector has even stronger political clout than in the UK. According to the Essential Information Consumer Education Foundation,[29] between 1998 and 2008 "Wall Street investment firms, commercial banks, hedge funds, real estate companies and insurance conglomerates made \$1.725 billion in political contributions and spent another \$3.4 billion on lobbyists". Further, "nearly 3,000 officially registered federal lobbyists

[28] An additional but crucial question is what the UK plans to have as its major industry. Most of the Labour government's policies were made possible by economic expansion enhanced by prosperity in the City. Prime Minister Cameron said the Franco-German plans for a financial transaction tax were like Britain proposing the French "a tax on cheese". However, by choosing to keep finance as its main industry, the UK is left to sink or swim with an increasingly volatile industry.

[29] http://wallstreetwatch.org/reports/sold_out.pdf

worked for the industry in 2007 alone." In 2010, a US Supreme Court decision made it easier for money to speak loudly in the US policymaking process.[30] For these reasons, if effective change in financial regulation were to arise from somewhere, it would more likely be in Continental Europe than in the US.

For those of us in Asia, therefore, the hope is that the EU Member States agree a compromise and establish an effective EBU, effective in the sense that it can minimize the risk of another financial crisis and show us the way.

The third important aspect of policy under improved governance is improved productivity through structural reform. In Continental Europe, the hesitation to reform and liberalize is much stronger than in the UK and US. Europeans know very well that economic stagnation leads to higher unemployment, xenophobia and at worst, war. The goal of European integration was peaceful coexistence and prosperity. Although no longer widely appreciated, integration still contributes to these goals. Policies that are good for prosperity but domestically unpopular can be adopted in the name of integration. Bigger markets and competitiveness can reduce unemployment.

## 5 Choice of Exchange Rate Regimes and Sustainable Prosperity

The most effective way to advance necessary reform in a democracy is to convince the voters that it is in their best interest to do so. This does happen: the most recent examples are Latvia and Estonia, and the Herz reform in Germany is another. The reforms in Latvia and Estonia took place while their currencies were pegged to the euro; in Germany, it occurred after having joined the euro.

In contrast, Japan is an example of a country unable to convince its voters. Japan knows very well the relationship between (or lack of) structural reforms, inadequate financial regulation and bubbles. In advanced countries with well-established social welfare systems and employment protection, where most households are well-stocked with consumer goods, the growth rate tends to go down. Monetary expansion is the easy, painless way to stimulate the economy without deregulation or structural reform. Lowering the interest rate does not hurt most voters. Even those who depend on interest income have no reason to complain if a bubble develops to ensure strong capital gains. And a bubble will most likely develop, because the extra money can be spent in only so many ways when most products and services have

[30] The Supreme Court ruled that under certain conditions, no upper limit should be set to political contributions to Political Action Committees (PACs). The conditions are that the contributions cannot go directly to political parties or candidates, and expenditure from the donations must be done "independently" of elections. Thus "independent-expenditure only committees" or "Super-PACs" were created which can receive infinite amounts of money from corporations, unions and individuals. Spending that is independent of an election can still support candidates. Hence, the birth of Super-PACs has made it much easier for the power of money to influence policymaking in the US.

already been purchased. Unless deregulation occurs at the same time to enable growth in new industries, the money supplied will eventually head towards the real estate and financial markets.

Not all bubbles develop this way, but this is one way that they can. There is some evidence that this is what occurred in Spain and Ireland. Furthermore, when financial intermediaries ride the bubble and expand lending, the bubble expands further. Reckless borrowing occurs, not just by government but also private sector agents in some euro members. Private sector debt is just as dangerous as public sector debt, and in any case turns into the latter in a crisis. This is usually followed by "lender of last resort" actions by the central bank, and results in an improvement of banks' balance sheets, which then funds government spending to sustain the economy and the banks themselves. Banks with balance sheet problems and governments with balance sheet problems end up sustaining each other.

Even after 20 years of stagnation, Japan has not yet been able to implement all the necessary structural reforms to revitalize the economy; and the fiscal situation is worsening. The reverse wealth effect after the burst of the bubble, uncertainty created by government deficit and an ageing population have all contributed to a low response to interest rate changes, making monetary policy less effective. Fiscal policy is also less effective, as people keenly aware of the aging problem anticipate future tax and social security burdens. The US and Europe used to criticize Japan for its failure to revitalize its economy. However, now the risk is that some of them are "turning Japanese".

Since WWII, debt levels have been rising in the US as well as in Europe, reflecting the welfare state. G20 advanced nations' debt levels are the highest in peacetime history (Fig. 3).

Bond issuers with lax control on revenue and spending cannot reasonably be expected to maintain high ratings. When so-called "advanced" countries' government bonds were downgraded, people expressed surprise. But if a government cannot collect taxes or rein in expenditures, its bonds do not deserve a high rating.[31] The current crisis has shown that a democracy can fail as a bond-issuer. It has also shown that without proper governance, democracy can fail as medium of economic vitality.

If the present form of governance fails as a medium of economic vitality and stability, some other method must be found to remedy the failure. The choice of exchange rate regimes can be one such method. By choosing the right exchange rate regime, a country may be able to impose on itself constraints that induce its voters to "do the right thing", i.e., choose reform that leads to sustainable prosperity. If Japan had been under fixed exchange rates in 1985, it may or may not have chosen structural reforms. This depends partly on the global interest rate environment. But Japan under fixed exchange rates would definitely not have been able to choose *unilateral* monetary expansion that led to the bubble.

[31] For instance, in Greece, one of its main industries, shipping, is exempt from corporate tax. See Grammenos and Chong Ju Choi (1999).

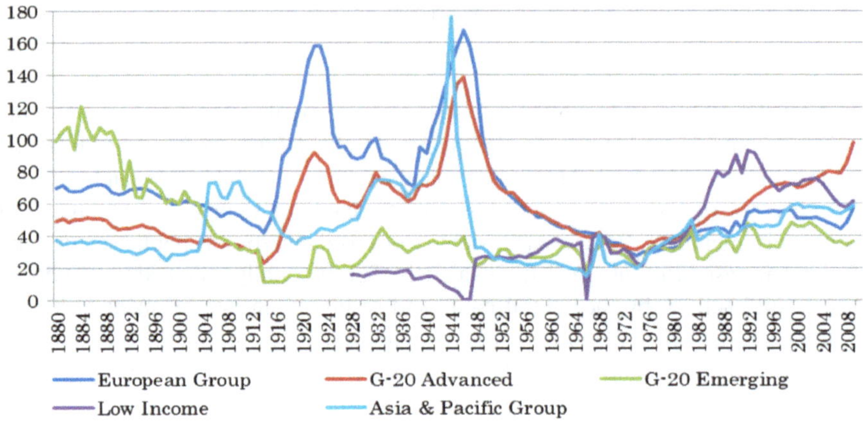


**Fig. 3** Debt (PPPGDP-weighted averages) as % of GDP. Source: http://www.imf.org/external/datamapper/index.php

The euro area Member States chose the euro, which was expected to work as a tool to advance politically unpopular structural reforms; so far, the record is mixed. Member States currently in crisis have not succeeded in recovering competitiveness. Unless they do, there is no long-term future for stability in Europe, whether or not a break-up of the euro is avoided in the short-term. Even if a break-up occurs, eventually those countries that leave the euro will want to stabilise their currencies against (what is left of) the euro. By and by, a similar system will be re-established. Whether this system lasts depends on whether the governance overhaul succeeds. This is why institutional reform is crucial to the future of the EU.

If exchange rate regimes are not the tool of choice, then countries will have to find another tool to push ahead unpopular reforms in a democracy. If others are too polite to ask a country to "get its house in order", markets will do the job, and not politely. Whether it is labour, capital or goods and services, if we try to sell something at a price that does not meet the quality, the result will be what economists call a "distortion". Often this distortion is sustained by the government. If the distortion becomes too big, it will be brought to the surface in the form of persistently high unemployment, deficits, inflation and/or currency depreciation. Eventually, the government will find it difficult to sustain, but democracy gets in the way of removing such a distortion.

Europe chose to maintain democracy and remove this distortion at the same time by European integration. Europe's institutional construction, economic policies and laws made this possible and the euro is an integral part of this. However, the existing governance and institutional arrangements are no longer sufficient to attain the original goals of integration. The current crisis is the markets' signal that the EU needs a reformed institutional arrangement if it wants to achieve its goal of peaceful prosperity.

If the crisis makes all Member States ask themselves what they are ready to give up for a successful integration, it may even be a blessing in disguise. Clearly, the EU could not have continued unchanged. Those who argue that the situation would not have been so dire if only political leaders had not made the situation worse are doing so on the presumption that the pre-crisis EU is where the EU should go back to. But going back to a pre-crisis EU without fundamental change only invites another crisis down the line[32].

Thus there are two aspects to the euro crisis, one is related to democracy and one is based on economic logic—neither is purely European.

Some say that there is a European factor; European voters no longer support integration in the way they used to, but voter sentiments are changing all over the world. Such change manifests itself in three ways: (1) voters' voices are louder and heard more often, to the extent it can be called a "hyper-democracy"; (2) development of technology enables and encourages global and local communication and organization of such voters; and (3) voters are divided into those who think they benefit from globalisation and those who do not.

Others may state that the fundamentally political nature of European integration is a uniquely European factor. However, this should not make us forget the economic reasons for integration. Certainly, those who joined the euro did not exactly "meet" the "convergence criteria", which were not "conditions" but only "criteria". Even so, not all the reasons for the euro were political. As noted several times already, the euro was expected to introduce constraints that would make it easier for voters to accept reform. Reform was necessary because government cannot forever prop up prices that do not correspond to quality. This is an important economic logic behind the euro. We should also not forget the inconsistent triangle: (1) autonomous monetary policy; (2) stable exchange rates; and (3) the free movement of capital cannot all be achieved at the same time.[33]

European integration will not stop even if the EU becomes a "multi-speed" union. As long as economic interdependence is high and the goal of stable prosperity remains the same, integration has to continue. Only its institutional design will keep evolving. In terms of the institutional changes that will result from the current crisis, members will need to be even more prepared to relinquish sovereignty.

As Shoji (2011a, b) explains, institutional changes can take two forms. One is federalist, with the democratic making of decisions at the European level—the European Commission, European Parliament and other EU institutions draw up the designs for institutional change. The other method is the "golden straightjacket" where the European Council takes the lead. According to Shoji (2011b), Europe is choosing the latter for the moment, and "compared to the case where regulations that apply to all members are written as EU law, setting regulations through intergovernmental agreements requiring national ratifications is more time consuming"(my translation). However, even if EU law can be established more quickly, the fundamental question of "whose voice should be reflected in that law" remains. This is a question that democracies will be forever grappling with.

[32] In fact, the fundamental nature of financial markets implies that crises can easily be triggered if markets lose confidence. See Kaji (2001).

[33] Dani Rodrick (2000) pointed out that democracy, globalisation and sovereign nations cannot be sustained simultaneously.

Democracy is a core value for the EU. Some democracies may choose to opt-out from more and more EU-level arrangements. Even if they do so, their economic ties to those who do not opt-out remain. As long as economies are closely integrated, closer integration of laws and regulations make economic sense, and the desirable exchange rate system will be one in which exchange rates do not fluctuate, or even disappear altogether.

As globalisation proceeds, all nations will, sooner or later, face the question that Europe is trying to answer: what degree of sovereignty are we prepared to give up to obtain the benefits of closer economic ties? The question's history is as long as the history of sovereignty itself, and under democracy, it is the voters who must find the answer.

The euro is asking voters for an answer. Criticizing the euro now is easy, but the critic must also provide a viable alternative. Euro area members showed the rest of the world what can happen when a single currency is introduced without sufficient convergence. We can conclude that if nations wanted to introduce a single currency, they need a strong, enforceable mechanism to minimize asymmetry.[34] This will not be easy, but there is reason for hope. Europe was brutally made aware of this conclusion and the leaders, at least for now, seem to have got the message. There are disagreements, but that shows there is movement.

The euro could not attain one of its important goals, and is therefore experiencing a crisis. In that sense, it is possible to say it failed. But giving up on the euro solves nothing. Member states are mutually highly interdependent, and exchange rate changes hinder economic activity. The only way for Europe to prosper peacefully is integration.

This has huge implications for Asia and the rest of the world. Europe is not the only area in the world where countries need to implement domestically unpopular reforms. Japan has the highest public debt to GDP ratio among the "rich" nations, but other governments' deficits and debts are climbing. And Japan's dire need for pension reform is shared by the United States, among other countries.

Non-Japan Asia still enjoys high growth rates, but there is already talk of a "middle-income-trap". When the growth rate drops, the need for structural reform will become more apparent in these countries. Thus the question of "how to implement reforms that constituents are not eager to vote for" is shared by East and West alike. By choosing and introducing the single currency as a possible answer, Europe is showing the way. Rather than criticize the euro and the policy reactions since the crisis, Asia needs to ask what method we will use to implement structural reforms and achieve sustainable prosperity.

[34] Exchange rates move because of asymmetry in exogenous changes, and asymmetry in the way economies respond to such changes (partial derivatives). This can be shown, as in Kaji (2006), by deriving a reduced form for the exchange rate in a simple, two-country-model.

## References


Barber T (2010) Tall ambition, flawed foundations, part two of a three-part FT investigation. Financial Times, Tuesday October 12th

Begg I (2010) Economic and social governance in the making: EU governance in flux. Eur Integration 32(1):1–16

Bonnevay F (2010) The argument for a Eurobond. A coordinated strategy for emerging from the crisis. Institut Montaigne, Paris, February

Carnegy H, Milne R (2011) France and Germany agree new rules. Financial Times, 5 Dec 2011

De Le Dehesa G (2011) Eurobonds: concepts and implications. European parliament, directorate general for internal policies, policy department A: economic and scientific polices, economic and monetary affaris, briefing note, IP/A/ECON/NT/2011-01, March

European Commission (1990) One market, one money. An evaluation of the potential benefits and costs of forming an economic and monetary union, study of the directorate-general for economic and financial affairs. http://ec.europa.eu/economy_finance/publications/publication_summary7520_en.htm

European Commission (2011a) Stakeholder consultation paper, commission staff working paper on the Europe 2020 Project bond initiative, 28 February. http://ec.europa.eu/economy_finance/consultation/pdf/bonds_consultation_en.pdf

European Commission (2011b) GREEN paper on the feasibility of introducing stability bonds, COM (2011) 818 final, Brussels, 23 Nov 2011. http://ec.europa.eu/economy_finance/consultation/stability_bonds/pdf/green-pepr-stability-bonds_en.pdf

Giavazzi F, Pagano M (1986) The advantages of tying one's hands: EMS discipline and central bank credibility. CEPR discussion papers 135

Grammenos CT, Choi CJ (1999) The Greek shipping industry: evolving organisational forms. Int Stud Manage Organ 29(1):34–52

Henkel H-O (2011) A sceptic's solution – a breakaway currency. Financial Times, Aug 29

Juncker J-C, Tremonti G (2010) E-bonds would end the crisis. Financial Times, 5 Dec 2010

Kaji S (1998) Successful structural reforms after EMU. J Jpn Int Econ 12:507–534

Kaji S (2001) What can countries do to avoid a financial crisis? World Econ 24(2):567–589

Kaji S (2005) Dai goji EU kakudai no keizaiteki sokumen—Anteiseichokyoutei no kongo (The economic aspects of the fifth EU enlargement the future of the stability and growth pact) in Japanese, Japan society for EU studies annual report, no.25, pp 174–196

Kaji S (2006) Lecture notes, open economy macroeconomics. http://koara-a.lib.keio.ac.jp/ocw/j/economics/02A-008_j/list.html

Kaji S (2007) The re-launch of Lisbon: a wake-up call to citizens. Asia Pac J EU Stud; EUSA Asia-Pacific 5(1):9–29

Kaji S (2010) What Greece teaches us about democracy. J Polit Sci Sociol 14:1–16

Kaji S (2012) Economic stability and choice of exchange rate regimes. Public Policy Rev 8(3):341–365

McKinsey Institute (2012) Debt and deleveraging: uneven progress on the path to growth, updated report, January. http://www.mckinsey.com /insights/mgi /research/financial_markets / uneven_progress_on_the_path_to_growth

Money Week (2011) Baltic states bounce back from austerity. 30 Sep 2011. http://www.moneyweek.com/news-and-charts/economics/europe/baltic-states-bounce-back-from-austerity-55706

Mundell RA (1968) A theory of optimum currency areas, adapted from the paper in the American Economic Review 51:509–517 (Nov 1961) and contained in Mudell (1968), pp 177–186, available at http://www.columbia.edu/~ram15/ie/ie-12.html

Rodrick D (2000) How far will international economic integration go? J Econ Perspect 14(1):177–186

Rogoff K (1985) The optimal degree of commitment to an intermediate monetary target. Q J Econ 100:1169–1190

Shoji K (2011a) EU ho no tenkai to kadai—EU togo no sankakukei model (The development and task of EU law—the triangular model of EU integration), in Japanese, Jurist (No.1418): 15–20

Shoji K (2011b) Euro kiki no houseidoteki kensho (Examination of the legal aspects of the Euro crisis), in Japanese, Mita Hyouron, November

Taylor A, Pradhan M (2011) The great rebalancing. Morgan Stanley global economic forum, Feb 18. http://relooney.info/0_New_9586.pdf

van Rompuy H (2010) Strengthening economic governance in the EU, final report of the task force to the European Council. http://www.consilium.europa.eu/uedocs/cms_data/docs/pressdata/en/ec/117236.pdf

von Weizsäcker J, Delpla J (2010) The blue bond proposal. Bruegelpolicybrief, Issue 2010/3, 6th May

# Comment Paper to Chapter "The Exchange Rate Regime as a Tool to Advance Reform: Success or Failure?"

**Junko Shimizu**

The main value of this paper is that it attempts to explain the euro as a potential tool to advance reform in Europe. As the euro was introduced to progress further necessary reform by removing monetary and fiscal policy autonomy and by introducing price transparency, it would have been successful if reform had progressed and economies converged. Unfortunately, only a few countries, Germany for example, have been successful. If the institutional reforms succeed in bringing about reforms to increase the competitiveness of all members, then the euro can fulfill its role. This will be the true economic test as to whether the euro will survive or not. Prof. Kaji predicts that many countries will, sooner or later, choose a similar arrangement, for example, pegging the euro or "a kind of euro", even if the euro failed this time. Why will they do so? Because, for better or worse, the European economy is closely integrated. In this decade, the world economy has moved to a "new global regionalism" in North America, East Asia, Latin America, the Gulf States, and Africa. The problems that face euro area countries issue a grave warning about the important role of exchange rate. We realize how strong governance affects the effectiveness of economic policies, and in this sense, this paper is worthwhile reading for all. Regarding this paper, I would like to clarify some points as follows.

- The choice of exchange rate regime

If the euro, or in other words the monetary union, turns out to be a bad choice, which other regimes should we adopt? Figure 1 shows the famous "Impossible trinity", where it is impossible to have a fixed exchange rate, monetary policy autonomy, and open capital markets at the same time. For example, Japan chose a monetary policy autonomy and

J. Shimizu (✉)
Faculty of Economics, Gakushuin University,
Tokyo, Japan
e-mail: junko.shimizu@gakushuin.ac.jp

S. Kaji and E. Ogawa (eds.), *Who Will Provide the Next Financial Model?: Asia's Financial Muscle and Europe's Financial Maturity*,
DOI 10.1007/978-4-431-54282-7_24, © Springer Japan 2013

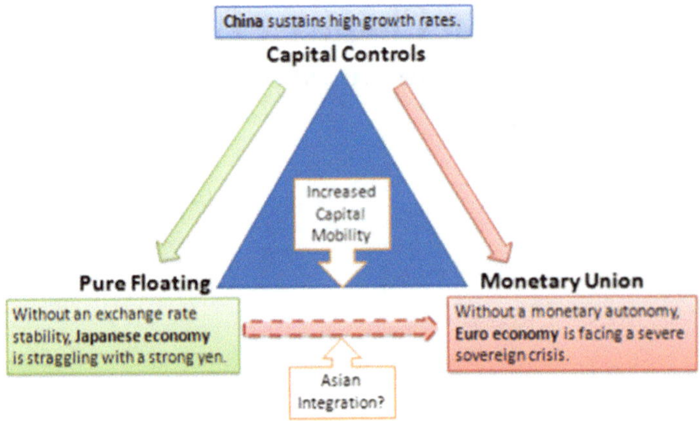


**Fig. 1** Impossible trinity

open capital markets, and now is straggling with a strong yen under a floating regime. On the other hand, Eurozone countries, which abandoned monetary autonomy for a monetary union with open capital markets, face a severe sovereign crisis. Currently only China, who adopted a stable exchange rate and monetary autonomy under strong capital controls, is maintaining high economic growth rates. However, even China cannot remain in its current position with increased capital mobility. Asian economies will move toward regional economic integration in the future. As globalization proceeds, all nations will face the same problems that Europe is facing now. In other words, as Prof. Kaji suggests, the choice of exchange rate regime can be an effective tool to advance reform in democracies in Europe and Asia.

- Disadvantages of a fixed exchange rate

Facing the recent European crisis, we wonder whether the euro convergence criteria were strong enough to compensate for the disadvantages of a fixed exchange rate. Two criteria of government finance were introduced (annual government deficit and government debt) without the existence of an autonomous monetary policy. As mentioned in the previous section, a monetary union can achieve exchange rate stability. However, another aspect of monetary union is that it has no ability to automatically adjust balance of payments. To address this disadvantage, additional criteria regarding balance of payments should be established.

After introducing the euro, the trade imbalance within the Eurozone countries widened under the fixed regime. As Fig. 2 shows, only Germany and the Netherlands increased their trade surplus—most crisis countries are deficit countries. Although the euro has depreciated since the global financial crisis started in 2008, such depreciation cannot restore the competitiveness of Greece, or Spain's exports with regard to EU partners such as France and Germany. Such a trade imbalance would have been corrected by currency depreciation relative to the mark, if each state had its own currency.

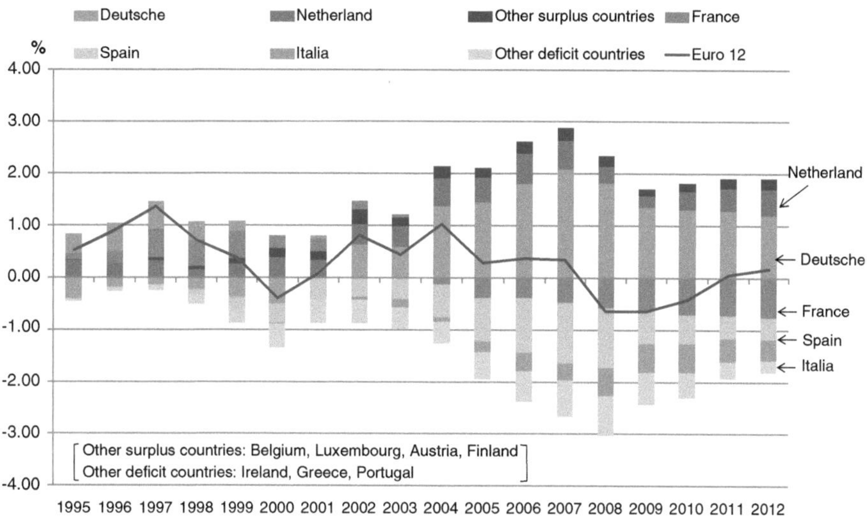


**Fig. 2** Eurozone countries' current accounts (as a percentage of GDP, %). Source: European Commission, AMECO

- The euro as a device to encourage structural reform

We are now concerned that structural reforms under the fixed regime may need more time than those under depreciation. Thus, the point is how long will Eurozone countries have to endure the burden of structural reform under the euro. With a fixed exchange rate, curing a trade deficit could involve a general deflationary policy in deficit countries. This would mean that Greece should make their economy more deflated than other Eurozone countries. If Eurozone-wide structural reforms were executed, for example German firms creating factories in Greece, the asymmetries between member countries would be resolved. However, it seems that leaving the euro might be far easier for Greek citizens than waiting for structural reform.

- Lessons for future integration in Asia

The Asian economy has been gradually integrated via supply chain management. At this moment in time, firm-level integration may be enough for Asian countries. In the future, however, if the Asian economy adopts a coordinated exchange rate policy, what kind of arrangement is needed to avoid crisis? The recent euro crisis has shown us the difficulty of the fixed regime. We have to discuss the importance of the so-called BBC rule, pegging to a common currency basket with a fluctuation and crawling band, which might be better for countries with economic asymmetries.

# Index



S. Kaji and E. Ogawa (eds.), *Who Will Provide the Next Financial Model?: Asia's Financial Muscle and Europe's Financial Maturity*,
DOI 10.1007/978-4-431-54282-7, 

MIX
Papier aus verantwortungsvollen Quellen
Paper from responsible sources
FSC® C105338

If you have any concerns about our products,
you can contact us on
**ProductSafety@springernature.com**

In case Publisher is established outside the EU,
the EU authorized representative is:
**Springer Nature Customer Service Center GmbH**
**Europaplatz 3, 69115 Heidelberg, Germany**

Printed by Libri Plureos GmbH
in Hamburg, Germany